FROM THE BOOKS OF
Ralph G Petersen

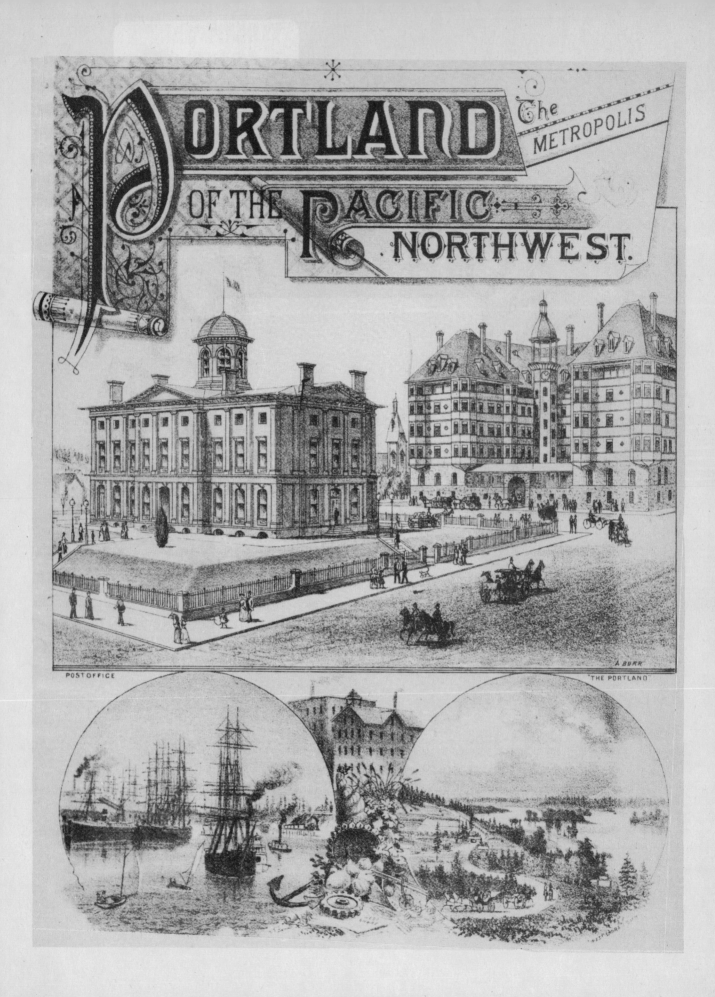

PORTLAND The METROPOLIS OF THE PACIFIC NORTHWEST.

POST OFFICE

A BURK

THE PORTLAND

ROUND THE ROSES

Portland
Past Perspectives

by
Karl Klooster

A Collection of Columns
Published in This Week Magazine
Between May 1983 and November 1987

First Edition
December 1987

Second Printing
November, 1990

Library of Congress Catalog Card No. 87-92154

ISBN 0-9619847-0-8

Printed in U.S.A.

Direct all correspondence to:

Karl T. Klooster
P.O. Box 15173
Portland, OR 97215

Frontispiece: *West Shore* Magazine, September 1883

Dedication

I would like to dedicate this book to the bright and prosperous future that the city it is about has the potential to achieve. However, since the time honored tradition of book dedications dictates that a person is the dedicatee of choice, there is only one choice.

To Christine Marie Olsen, without whose singular, unswerving support, encouragement and contributions, from the time some five years ago that the initial idea for *Round the Roses* was scratched out for her on a paper napkin at the Elephant and Castle, this book would not have been possible.

Acknowledgements

The publications, periodicals and articles on Pacific Northwest, Oregon and Portland history that would comprise the bibliography of this book are too numerous to enumerate here. A few of the most important ones do merit individual mention.

E. Kimbark MacColl's two excellent works (though he says they are incomplete and is working on a more definitive volume), *Shaping of A City* and *Growth of A City*, are the most dog-eared of any in my library. In fact, since they are paperbacks, I am well into my second set. For information on the early days, Eugene Snyder's *Early Portland: Stumptown Triumphant* has consistently proved to be a valuable source.

Members of the library and photo library staffs of the Oregon Historical Society come in for particular commendation. I would especially like to thank Elizabeth Winroth and Susan Seyl for their knowledgable assistance over these past four and one-half years.

In matters of historic preservation, Eric Eisemann and his staff at the Historic Preservation League of Oregon have been most helpful.

There would be no Round the Roses column were it not for the people at *This Week* magazine. Many staff members take part and their efforts are much appreciated by this writer. Specifically singled out should be Larry Miller, who bought the idea in the first place, Joe Bonney and his successor, George Dworin, Steve Sinovic and his successor, Don Campbell, all of whom kept me in line week after week to make the Roses bloom.

As to production of this book, I would like to express my special appreciation to Jane Olsen for her marathon proofreading, to the Daily Journal of Commerce for their always professional production and printing and, once again, to Christine Olsen for her exceptional efforts on everything. A blooming garden of long-stemmed *Round the Roses* to each and every one of you.

6

CONTENTS

8

Table of Contents (Cont'd.)

7. PORTLAND POTPOURRI

8. ON A BLOOMIN' SOAPBOX

9. DISASTER STRIKES

10. CITY OF ROSES: NOTES & ANECDOTES

Table of Contents (Cont'd.)

PREFACE

Welcome to the world of two and one-half minute history lessons. That's approximately how long it takes the average reader to complete a single story in this book. During that time, he or she has been exposed to between 450 and 600 words, two or three photographs with captions, a question and its answer, and an accompanying editorial cartoon.

I call it the adman's approach to history. Like a broadcast or print commercial message, each story contains visual and copy elements. Only one subject is treated at a time. And it is approached from more than one angle in an effort to be educational, entertaining and memorable.

Two decades as an advertising and marketing professional tell me that I should be more than satisfied if my message influences only a small percentage of those who look at it. But, this time the goal goes beyond mere product motivation. I honestly hope that you will gain newfound insight and derive considerable pleasure from the words you find within. After all, if you're reading this, you've already bought the book.

The columns reprinted here initially appeared in *This Week* Magazine between May 1983 and November 1987. This Week has the largest circulation of any publication in the Pacific Northwest. It is mailed each week to more than 450,000 homes in the three Oregon counties (Multnomah, Washington and Clackamas) that comprise the Greater Portland Metropolitan Area.

The creation and development of more than 230 weekly columns has taken me to fascinating places I'd probably never have seen and allowed me to get to know interesting people I'd not otherwise have met. The experience has greatly enriched my life. My knowledge of Portland and its history has increased many fold in the process, as much through osmosis as study.

A conscious attempt has been made to avoid the sort of pedantic style that pervades so many history pieces. It seems to me that, no matter how painstakingly researched and thoroughly detailed a work may be, if it drones on in a dull, plodding manner, nobody will want to read it.

Taking the opposite tack, of course, has its own pitfalls. By being light and casual, sometimes even flippant in subject treatment, one runs the risk of critical purgatory — to not be given serious consideration. In retort, I would say "the proof is in the pudding." An unread work is a waste. *Round the Roses* contains good, solid information and it has gained an audience. More adherents to the lessons of history, more advocates of historic preservation and more enthusiastic supporters for all efforts that keep vibrantly alive the legacy of the past.

(Cont'd.)

10

(Cont'd.)

With a weekly circulation that reaches over 90 percent of local residents, a columnist is bound to get a lot of feedback in four and a half years. The old adage that "if you're doing things right, you'll hear nothing, but make one mistake and find out what happens" has been only partially applicable.

It's true that scarcely a single error of any consequence has escaped notice or comment. On a few occasions, as you'll see in Chapter 10, a deluge of vehement complaints descended. Far from being hate mail, however, they were constructive criticisms meant to set the record straight. Often, detailed information and materials were enclosed.

If the negative responses weren't bad, the positive ones were wonderful. Filled with words of appreciation, encouragement and even praise, they prompted me to proceed with the promotion and production of this book. Readers were clipping and saving the column, writing in and asking for copies of ones they'd missed. It seemed reasonable to conclude that they might like to have them in a more comprehensive and durable form. But what of the format?

Presenting the columns in the order they originally appeared was an alternative. I quickly dismissed it as too prosaic. Subject groupings, arranged in order of historic chronology wherever possible, was the answer. As a result, you will see, for example, a story published in 1986 placed before one published in 1983 in the same chapter. The idea is to facilitate subject flow from earlier to later time periods.

These stories span more than 180 years from Lt. William Broughton's "official" discovery of the Columbia River in 1792 to the end of Terry Schrunk's fourth term as mayor of Portland in 1972. A few special ones deal with commentary on contemporary subjects and situations.

This book should not, however, be considered a comprehensive chronology of Portland history. Comprehensive, as I interpret it, would have required far greater length and interconnection than encompassed here. Perhaps, as *Round the Roses* continues, there will be enough articles for a companion book four or so years in the future to augment this work.

A representative cross-section of pivotal events, principal people, primary activities and important organizations is presented. Academic historians, I am sure, would not consider this to be a scholarly work. Admittedly, it contains only a smattering of first-hand research. But, any good journalist checks for authenticity and, in most instances, several sources were cross-referenced. To develop further perspective, many stories include information gathered from personal interviews. I believe these accounts to be accurate and, I hope, compelling.

If pressed to point out its greatest flaw as a history piece, I would have to say excessive weighting of one period over another. The culprit is my fascination with the Forties and Fifties. This weakness will, I trust, be understood. It's difficult not to be nostalgic about one's own formative years.

Not to say that the early decades of this century have been neglected. Nor have the latter ones of the last. In fact, more stories focus on this 40-year period than any other. It is the early years that are the weakest in this work — the pioneer era. Coincidentally, those years are the ones that have been most voluminously covered in the past.

Stories of the settlers and steamboats, trappers and native tribes, the taming of the frontier have been most often recounted elsewhere. Upcoming columns will contain some of this legend and lore. Personal recollections — oral histories — from an amazing group of local old-timers will also be told. That's a hint of what's in the offing for *Round the Roses*. But it's all future tense.

Here and now, in your hands, are the results of *Roses* that have already bloomed. May they bring you hours of enjoyment for years to come.

Karl Klooster
Portland, Oregon
November, 1987

1. WILLAMETTE CLASS

Trials, triumphs and trappings of the pioneer power elite

From its rugged, wilderness beginnings, Portland's destiny was determined by tough-minded Victorian businessmen. Its founders and first generation promoters focused first on enterprise and only later on quality-of-life considerations.

When they did turn their attentions to creature comforts and social amenities, River City's early elite spared no expense. Their approach was conservative, tasteful and low key. Flamboyance, opulence or showiness were not in the vocabulary of proper Portlanders.

This tradition carries forward to the present day. Long-established, private clubs are as exclusive as ever. Old families just as cliquish. Holders of private purse strings remain resistant to risk taking.

With few exceptions, the big money that makes things happen in town no longer comes from the still ample pocketbooks of Portland Heights or Dunthorpe dwellers. In many cases its from California and, sometimes, even Seattle. Millionaire "movers" in residence can almost be counted on one hand. Names such as Chiles, Gray, Merlo, Naito, Schnitzer and Winningstad come most quickly to mind.

With the impetus of that outside financing, downtown Portland saw a renaissance in the 1970s. The skyline sports a spiffy new appearance. Old Town has undergone its own rebirth. Society matrons set the style only among their own circles these days. The big, little city has grown and diversified. A gamut of groups contribute to the matrix that comprises this modern metropolis.

Yet, heirs of founding fortunes continue to wield considerable influence. If only they could be persuaded to spend more of their time and money in Portland rather than Paris, or Puerto Vallarta.

Oregon: How came thee by thy name?

September 23, 1987

From Remondini's Atlas, 1776, Aguilar's entrance to the River of the West shown leading to the Inland Sea (Puget Sound). How long before this was the river believed to exist? (Answer below cartoon.)

The mighty Columbia has long been heralded for the vital role it plays in the geography and enterprise of the Pacific Northwest. Today it is a well-known commodity — harnessed to serve the region. Once it was the stuff of legends — the source from which the elusive name "Oregon" sprang.

Before its boundaries had been charted, before its full course was traveled by a white man, before any sailing ship braved its perilous mouth, the river took on larger than life proportions. It was called many names by intrepid explorers who flew the standards of Europe's grand monarchies. Riviere St. Roc. River of Aguilar, Rio de los Estrecha, River Theyago, Ensenada de Heceta — they were all the Great River of the West.

It became an almost mythical waterway believed by many to have its headwaters deep in the body of the mid-American continent; from there flowing and growing westward until it poured tempestuously into the Pacific.

One American adventurer, Captain John Carver of Connecticut, never laid eyes on any portion of the Columbia. Yet he was the man responsible for dubbing it "the Oregon" or a permutation thereof, thus creating the name of the vast territory and eventually the state, itself.

Carver ostensibly spent two years during 1766-68 among the Indian tribes of the Upper Mississippi. The area is now part of Wisconsin and Iowa. Like certain glory seekers a century or more before him, Captain Carver was apparently prone to exaggeration and even fabrication in pursuit of self-aggrandizement.

The Captain's assertion that "the four most capital rivers on the continent of North America — the St. Lawrence, the Mississippi, the River Bourbon (the Red River of the North) and the Origan, or River of the West — have their sources in the same neighborhood" was patently preposterous. Yet, another 40 years would pass before Lewis and Clark definitively disproved the statement.

Despite Carver's cavalier disregard for hard facts, his use of the term "Origan" has proved to be his most enduring, though probably inadvertent, claim to fame. Where the word itself originated remains the subject of wide and perhaps never to be satisfactorily resolved, debate.

It appears that Carver borrowed the word from another American, Major Robert Rogers, who first mentioned "the River called by the Indians Ouragon" in a communication to the British government in 1765. Both Rogers and Carver credit Indians as the source.

One plausible theory is that it came from "Ouricon-sint," the French term of the time for "Wisconsin." The old French language had no "W." From Ouricon (considering the glottal "g" sound for "c"), to Ourigon, to Origan or Origon (at which point Carver may have picked it up) and finally Oregon. Far more improbable progressions have hatched full-bloom in fewer steps. Walamet to Willamette is an appropriate case in point.

The French connection is, however, not the only theory that has been bandied about. Another goes back to the swashbuckling Spaniards who made their way up the coast in the late 16th and early 17th centuries. Could the organum plant they found abundantly along Puget Sound shorelines have made its way into the vernacular and named the region?

Bishop Frances Norbert Blanchet, who first brought Catholicism to the Oregon Country, ventured a possibility in 1863. The unusually large and elongated ears of the area's natives, brought about by the custom of wearing heavy earrings, may have prompted those early Spanish sailors to refer to the Indians as "Orejons" or big ears.

A close similarity, but the possibility of that term traveling from the Clatsops and Klickitats to the far off Chippewas and Dakotas with whom Carver had contact is remote. More likely is the "Oragan" in the Sautee language, meaning a plate or place of bark.

What we are left with is speculation and uncertainty. There is no clear, easily agreed upon answer for the origin of the word "Oregon." No historic place or event has a direct association. But Oregon it became. And, remember, that's OR-e-gun.

Answer: More than two centuries prior. A German map of the new World from 1550 indicates such a river.

Fort Vancouver: The original outpost

March 18, 1987

Chief Factor's residence at Fort Vancouver, 1860. Who occupied it after McLoughlin left? (Answer below story.)

In late 1824, Dr. John McLoughlin, the Hudson's Bay Company's newly appointed chief factor for the Columbia Department, and Alexander Kennedy, McLoughlin's predecessor who was stationed at Fort George, struck out upriver in search of a replacement for the Astoria outpost which had become inadequate for company needs.

Their quest ended 100 miles inland, where they came upon an open stretch of land on the river's northern shore. Its three-mile downriver view and gently sloping lower plain leading to a bluff and elevated plain seemed ideal for the company's second Columbia settlement.

Under orders from his superior, Governor Sir George Simpson, McLoughlin commenced construction of a stockage on the wooded bluff a mile back from the river. The site was well-suited militarily but lacked a nearby water supply. Though four years of effort went into the "first" Fort Vancouver, it was finally abandoned in 1829.

By 1845, the year of McLoughlin's forced retirement, development almost surrounded the fort. The village, to the west and southwest, had as many as 40 buildings. A hospital, boat sheds, a distillery and storehouses spread along the wharf. On the bluff were a church, two schoolhouses and "Dundas Folly," a hilltop retreat inspired by a naval officer.

Altogether, Fort Vancouver must have appeared a most impressive place to the pioneers who began pouring into the region during the early 1840s. The fort's decline, already predetermined by the dwindling fur trade, was hastened by these new arrivals. With its importance diminished and territorial sovereignty decided in favor of the Americans, the Hudson's Bay Company moved its Columbia Department headquarters to Fort Victoria on Vancouver Island. Squatters encroached on the surrounding lands, the fort was reduced to a marginal mercantile trade, and, when its exclusive trading privileges expired on May 30, 1859, the company abandoned the operation within a year.

Fort Vancouver was strictly a stockade in 1833, (left). By 1845, (right) surrounding development had far outstripped that within the walls.

Initially, the Hudson's Bay men had concluded that the entire lower plain, called the "Jolie Prairie" by French trappers, would be subject to flood risk. But, several seasons of firsthand observation proved otherwise. In 1829, the second fort was erected 400 yards from the riverbank.

That 300-foot stockade saw enlargement and expansion over the next 15 years, eventually more than doubling in size to 735 feet by 320 feet. At its height, 36 buildings grouped in two courts filled the enclosure. Chief factor McLoughlin's residence was the fort's focal point.

Living quarters, storehouses, work shops, a bakery, a chapel, an Indian trade store, a granary and a powder magazine (the only brick structure) were all within its fir-log walls. The support system outside the stockade was even more prolific.

The Mill Plain, six miles upriver from the fort, boasted seven barns, a stable, a storehouse and a dwelling on 962 acres of fenced land. Along the river another mile east, was a sawmill operation with a dozen buildings. On the "Fort" and "Dairy" plains were enclosed acres with three barns, a stable, an ox byre and a piggery.

The U.S. Army, which had established its "Columbia Barracks" on the bluff in 1849, took possession of the 640-acre reserve. By the mid-1860s, no visible vestige of the old fort, or its satellites, remained.

Celebration of the fort's centennial in 1925 generated new interest in the site and saw the beginnings of a 30-year effort to ensure its preservation and eventual restoration.

Championing the effort was the Fort Vancouver Restoration and Historical Society in 1940. Six years later, when the army designated much of the Military Reserve as surplus, the movement gained full momentum. On July 19, 1948, congress authorized establishment (accomplished July 9, 1954) of the Fort Vancouver National Monument.

Extensive and painstaking excavation, which continues to the present day, rediscovered much of the complex and led to reconstruction of the fort walls and several buildings on the original sites in the early 1970s.

Answer: Chief Factor James Douglas (1845-49), Peter Skene Ogden (1849-51 & 1853-54), John Ballendin (1851-53), Dugald Mactavish (1854-58), Chief Trader James Grahame (1858-60).

Oregon pioneers: Wagon wheels a-rollin'

September 7, 1983

Fort Vancouver in 1845. Why was it so important to the Oregon Territory? (Answer below cartoon.)

Before the first great wagon train made its way to Oregon in 1843, fewer than a thousand civilized souls inhabited the entire territory. Dr. John McLoughlin, who had established Fort Vancouver in 1824, and his hardy fur trappers led the way followed by the missionaries under Jason Lee (1834) and Dr. Marcus Whitman (1836).

luxury of popping a frozen dinner in the microwave, plopping down on the sofa and switching on the 54-channel TV remote control.

With more new arrivals than established settlers, many had no place to stay during their first winter. That one fine dress, grandfather clock or precious heriloom was all too

Where the Oregon and California Trail s parted: from Paramount's 1923 silent classic, "The Wagon Train."

It was Whitman, accompanied by Portland founder, A.L. Lovejoy, who guided that "Great Migration of '43", which more than doubled Oregon's population. But the honors for the first wagon train to roll over the Blue Mountains to the Columbia go to Joe Meek and his fellow mountain men who came in 1840.

This now-famous trail saw another 1,400 new arrivals in 1844. The immigration of 1845 brought as many wagons as all those before it combined—over 3,000.

Word was out on Missouri Senator Linn's bill giving each settler a square mile of land and a quarter section for every child. This was strong motivation for drought-plagued, Midwest farm families to move to the more promising land in the West.

Not that pioneering was a bed of roses (pardon the analogy). The trek took its toll in loss of possessions, sickness and death. Upon arrival, the newcomers didn't have the

often bartered for food or temporary shelter. But they made it up the next year when their cabin was built and first crop was in as the next group of needy newcomers descended upon them.

In 1846, migrant flow to the territory was reduced by half due to concern over the unresolved question of American vs. British sovereignty. Averting war, the two governments abandoned their polarized positions (American—54°40' or Fight; British—Everything north of the Columbia) and agreed on the 49th parallel, today's boundary with Canada.

With stability, the floodgates were opened to a steady stream of American immigrants staved only temporarily by a massive male desertion to California's gold fields. The wagons rolled through the early '50s, and by 1855, when the land law expired, all the best land in the Willamette Valley—as well as the Umpqua and Rogue—was claimed. *(McLoughlin's Oregon City and "The Falls."—pg. 15)*

Answer: Under Dr. John McLoughlin, it was the center of all power, wealth, culture and stability for 20 years.

McLoughlin's Oregon City: The Falls were first

September 14, 1983

What brought about Dr. McLoughlin's retirement from the Hudson's Bay Company? (Answer below cartoon.)

The early days of our state, and in particular the Willamette Valley, were shaped by one man—Dr. John McLoughlin. Little wonder that our longest metropolitan boulevard was named in his honor.

Arriving in 1824 as Chief Factor of the Hudson's Bay Company's western fur-trading operations (who says they didn't have corporate conglomerates back in those days), he wasted no time in erecting Fort Vancouver and establish-

McLoughlin filed a claim on his Oregon City townsite and, with growing boat portage traffic as well as the grist mill, the place became increasingly important. By 1845, when the Chief Factor moved his family there, the town had become the center of the Willamette Valley commerce. Jesse Applegate, a leader of the 1843 immigrants, convinced the doctor to support their new provisional government with its territorial seat at Oregon City.

Oregon City looking south to the Falls in 1867.

ing the company's absolute supremacy over the territory.

If supreme, McLoughlin was also benevolent. The Oregon Trail went right past his doorstep and, although it would have been in his own interests to delay development, he never turned away travelers in need. From the missionaries to the mountain men and, later, the massive migrations, rather than suppressing settlement, he promoted it.

In 1829, recognizing the power potential of The Falls of the Willamette, McLoughlin sent a group of his men, headed by French Canadian Etienne Lucier, to blast out a millrace in its east side. Lucier also has the distinction of being Portland's first settler, having built a cabin near the river's east bank that year.

Retiring the following year, the Great White Eagle was forced to fight congress and Jason Lee for his ownership of The Falls during the last dozen years of his long life. He lost but his heirs benefited as the water rights were later restored to them.

Sale of those rights to various commercial interests in the 1860s touched off the development that led to such historic milestones as the original fish ladder (1887) — first in the nation — and the long distance electric transmission line to Portland (1889) — first in the world.

Once a resounding roar, The Falls have been reduced to a little more than a ripple. But this great natural resource and the man who first harnessed it are an original only-in-Oregon story.

Answer: McLoughlin wanted to keep his Oregon City holdings which became part of the U.S. in 1846. besides, he was 62 years old.

Pettygrove's Portland: A coin toss

May 25, 1983

Francis Pettygrove's "Large Copper" Penny. (actual size) Who called "heads" and who "tails"? (Answer below cartoon).

In early 1844 Asa Lawrence Lovejoy, a lawyer at Oregon's only town of any consequence at the time, Oregon City, acquired half ownership of an undeveloped townsite on the west bank of the lower Willamette River. For his services in filing the townsite claim and payment of the 25-cent filing fee, Lovejoy became co-owner, with William Overton, of the square mile destined to become the core of downtown Portland.

Oregon City referred to only as "The Clearing," deserved a more dignified designation.

Pettygrove insisted that it be named after the principal city of his home state, Maine. Lovejoy, faithful to his alma mater, Amherst College in his native Massachusetts, held steadfast for Boston. With the toss of a copper penny belonging to Pettygrove, now on display at the Oregon Historical Society, the choice was made.

Asa L. Loveyoy (1808-1882) and Francis W. Pettygrove (1812-1887). In background, Portland's first house.

Later that spring, Overton, lacking the funds to improve the claim, sold his half interest to Francis Pettygrove, an Oregon City merchant. He received $50 worth of clothing, food and equipment to provision him for a journey to hope-fully brighter horizons, some say in California, others, Texas. In either event, Mr. Overton was never heard from again.

Although it might be said that he lacked foresight, Overton was $50 to the good and it's pretty difficult to envision a city when you are broke and looking at a rough clearing surrounded by tall timber.

The new ownership team, possessed of both capital and enterprise, determined that their townsite, a stopping-off point approximately halfway between Fort Vancouver and

If there is any documentation as to who called what, I admit to a lack of diligence in discovering it. The result, however, needs no further elaboration. We have only to consider the thoughts of both men years later when reflect-ing upon their decisions to sell out so early on.

Lovejoy, having held his interest for less than two years, sold to Captain Benjamin Stark in November, 1845. The deal, totalling $1,215, included the townsite ownership and 115 cattle. The cattle represented about two-thirds of the total. Just three years later, Pettygrove, to whom singular credit must go for putting Portland on the map, bartered his half to Daniel Lownsdale, the local tanner, for $5,000 worth of leather.

Answer: I have been unable to find out. If you have the answer, please document and write me c/o *This Week*.
Note: This was a teaser/reader response question. Pettygrove won with "heads" called on two consecutive tosses.

Early Portland: The Willamette Wars

September 21, 1983

The St. John's Episcopal Church of Milwaukie, dedicated on Dec. 10, 1851, is the oldest surviving church building in Oregon. Where is it located today?

If *Oregonian* Editor Thomas Jefferson Dryer had published an annual edition in 1851, the headlines might have read, CITY INCORPORATED...*OREGONIAN* CELEBRATES 1st ANNIVERSARY...PORTLAND WINNING WILLAMETTE WARS!

The *Portland Oregonian* began operation in December, 1850, just in time to herald the state Legislature's approval of its namesake's city charter on January 14. First official act of the city council was to authorize construction of a public building—the jail. Its first occupant, a Mr. Travolet, was arrested for "riding at a furious rate through the streets of the City of Portland."

1851 marked a turning point in the often heated battle to become Oregon's premier city. The outcome of this river rivalry would, in sports page parlance, be Portland-7, Others-0. But only after a protracted competition, a war of words, wooing of ship owners and even dirty tricks such as Milwaukie's Lot Whitcomb delaying the *Oregonian's* printing press, coming upriver aboard one of his ships, from arriving until after he had published the first edition of his own paper.

The Clackamas Rapids, at its confluence with the Willamette, was Oregon City's eventual undoing and the Ross Island bar sealed Milwaukie's fate. St. Helens was just too far downriver and Linnton, St. John's, West Linn and the no-

An artist's depiction of Portland in 1858.

As the fledgling city, all 900 residents of it, opened a new chapter, its principal promoters and primary owners, Stephen Coffin, Daniel Lownsdale and William Chapman, were pushing the superiority of "Little Stumptown" (many tree stumps had not yet been removed from the streets) over other townsites along the lower Willamette.

The key to victory was "The Head of Navigation." Put simply, how far could ocean-going vessels sail upstream without risk of running aground no matter what time of year. Captain John Couch bolstered Portland's cause by declaring it to be that place.

longer-existing Milton were never serious contenders. Portland was "the head of navigation" and, with that realization, the ambitious settled in Little Stumptown.

H.C. Leonard and Henry D. Green, pioneers who later founded the predecessor of the Northwest Natural Gas Co., built the first landing dock that year and the ships came in ever-increasing numbers to fill their holds with the wonderful wealth of lumber, flour and foodstuffs to be sold in gold-rich California at a handsome profit.

Such freewheeling frontier enterprise was the driving force that would shape Portland's future for decades.

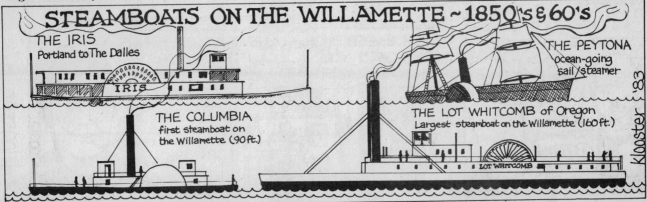

STEAMBOATS ON THE WILLAMETTE ~ 1850's & 60's

THE IRIS
Portland to The Dalles

IRIS

THE PEYTONA
ocean-going sail steamer

THE COLUMBIA
first steamboat on the Willamette (90 ft.)

THE LOT WHITCOMB of Oregon
Largest steamboat on the Willamette (160 ft.)

LOT WHITCOMB

Klooster '83

Answer: Now OAKS PIONEER MUSEUM, it was moved by river barge in 1961 to a river-view park site in Sellwood.

James B. Stephens: East Portland's founder

August 26, 1987

The Stark Street Ferry, ca. 1870. How long did it continue to operate? (Answer below cartoon.)

The subject of Portland's founding fathers evokes the names of Lovejoy and Pettygrove, Couch and Lownsdale. Separate but equal credit is accorded Ladd, Corbett and Failing for building the edifice on the foundation.

Immediately across the river, the pioneering of East Portland evolved quite differently. For 20 years, its principal founder, promoter and developer was one man — James B. Stephens. Like his west-side counterparts, Stephens was an entrepreneur. Unlike them, his quest to expand his enterprise was beset with misfortune.

The 38-year-old Virginia native arrived by wagon train from Missouri, along with his family, just in time to celebrate Christmas Eve of 1844 at Oregon City.

creditors seized the assets of the buyer including the timber. Goodbye to another $16,000.

Stephens returned home determined to confine his business to Oregon in the future. In 1850 he laid out the East Portland townsite and three years later was granted a charter from the territorial legislature for his Stark Street ferry operation. He used a skiff for passengers and a large flatboat for horses and wagons.

In a homegrown stroke of bad luck, he was remunerated in government scrip for transporting soldiers and supplies back and forth during the Indian uprising of 1855-56. The scrip was not redeemed until after the beginning of the Civil War and Stephen's loss due to depreciated value was approximately $15,000. In 1865 he sold the ferry business to Joseph Knott.

The Stephens' house stood prominently on the river's east bank directly across from central Portland, 1871.

The next year he bought the rights to a square-mile squatter's claim on the east side of the Willamette for $200 from the legendary Dr. John McLoughlin. As administrator of the estate of a Mr. Porier, a former Hudson's Bay employee, McLoughlin was overseeing land he had given by personal fiat. Nonetheless, at the time, he held the sovereignty of longevity. To hedge the bet, Stephens also filed a donation land claim with the provisional government.

Stephens became Oregon's first cooper, plying his trade for McLoughlin, and picked up a little extra ferrying horsemen across the Willamette on a small flatboat. In 1848, the lure of California gold drew him and most of the male population away.

It also precipitated the first of James' ill-founded investments — a bridge over the American River near Sacramento. It washed away in a flood the following winter, taking his estimated $20,000 interest with it.

Trying a new tack in the summer of 1849, Stephens shipped a load of square-hewn timbers to a guaranteed buyer in California. A squatter's riot occurred the day of the shipment's arrival and

Stephens began selling off his one enduring asset, the land, in the early 1860s and the town of East Portland started to take shape. With the gains from real estate, he entered into one final get-rich scheme, a bank, with his son-in-law, Dr. A.M. Loryea. Its ultimate failure almost cost his entire property holdings.

Through it all, Uncle Jimmy, as he came to be called, remained an optimistic and popular local figure. His wife, Elizabeth, died in 1887, two years before him. Both are buried beneath a gravestone bearing their likenesses at the far east end of their former property — now Lone Fir Cemetery.

The couple spent the last 25 years of their lives together in the home they had built just above the banks of the Willamette directly across from the center of Portland. That house, believed to be the oldest surviving residence in the city, was moved to Southeast 12th and Stephens (named for them) in about 1905.

There are the murmurings of a movement to move the house to the new OMSI site as a museum. It would be a fitting memorial to East Portland's founder and to the spirit he represents — persistence and progress despite adversity.

BASED ON OUR EXPERIENCE, WHAT ADVICE WOULD **YOU** GIVE TO FOLKS, ELIZABETH?

NEVER TRUST BANKS, CALIFORNIANS **OR** THE U.S. GOVERNMENT!

James B. Stephens (1806-1889)

Elizabeth Stephens (1807-1887)

Klooster '87

Answer: It was sold to the city in 1895 for $40,000 and discontinued.

Vancouver Barracks: General development

March 25, 1987

The main barracks of Vancouver Barracks. What innovative, new facility was made available to enlisted personnel in 1880? (Answer below cartoon.)

The infamous Whitman massacre in 1847 raised out-cry for resolution of the Oregon question to a fever pitch. It prompted mountain man Joe Meek's personal march on Washington to twist a few legislative arms. With territorial status achieved the following year, the Oregon Country was entitled to military protection and the strategic point was Fort Vancouver.

Arriving at the Hudson's Bay Company outpost in early 1849, a First Artillery detachment rented buildings on the bluff from Chief Factor James Douglas. These quarters, then called Columbia Barracks, were only the beginning of a base that would eventually earn its own honored place in history.

Spanish-American War Unit, 1889.

As the once-burgeoning British role diminished, the American presence grew to take its place. Over the years, some 70 officers who later rose to the rank of general served at the installation. Among them were Bonneville, Grant, McClellan, Sheridan, Picket, Ord, Harney, Miles, Howard and Martin.

Capt. Ulysses S. Grant, who is memorialized by the oldest house on Officers' Row, called his two-year stay as quartermaster at Columbia Barracks (1852-53) the most miserable in his career. Beset by financial woes, Grant almost drank himself into a discharge. He resigned his commission in 1854 only to take it up again in 1861 and ultimately replace McClellan as commander of the Union Army during the Civil War.

Indian uprisings posed the primary threat as a flood of homesteaders invaded the homelands of the native inhabitants. Discovery of gold in the Colville area of Washington Territory led to more bloody incidents. In 1855-56, frightened settlers sought safety on more than one occasion in the shadow of Fort Vancouver's walls.

Capt. George McClellan, a Mexican War veteran, led forays into northeastern Washington. Another general in the making, Lieutenant Phil Sheridan, joined him in skirmishes against the Yakimas and Klickitats. In 1858, Brig. Gen. William Harney dealt the final blows to the belligerent tribes at the Battles of Four Lakes and Spokane Plains.

When the Hudson's Bay Company relinquished its claim on the Columbia in 1860, the Army post spread over the old fort obliterating it within a few years. The old stockade was destroyed by fire. Barracks, storehouses and corrals were built on the lower plain. Nine residences lined up along the bluff creating the earliest elements of Officers' Row.

As the major military base in the Pacific Northwest, Vancouver Barracks took to training troops and sent out even more far-flung expeditions. Lt. C.E.S. Wood, who never wore stars on his shoulders, but later made his mark as a Portland attorney and avant-garde liberal, was posted at the Barracks from 1877 to 1881. He saw action in the last of the Indian wars against renegade Chief Joseph and the Bannock tribe in Eastern Oregon. Wood's fonder memories were of the festive occasions when officers and their wives were invited to hobnob with Portland society.

By the time Second Lt. Charles H. Martin came to Vancouver in 1887, 16 residential structures could be counted on Officers' Row. Among them was an elaborate Queen Anne completed the previous year as the post commander's residence.

Martin, destined to become a major general in World War One, commander of the Canal Zone, an Oregon congressman and 21st governor of Oregon in 1934, returned to the base in 1906 as a captain and construction quartermaster.

Under his direction, the last major structures were built including the post headquarters, new barracks, a recreation hall and two more Officers' Row houses, done in the neoclassical style, bringing the total on "The Row" to 21. Vancouver Barracks was at its height. But its vital service in two world wars was yet to come.

Answer: In Nov. 1880, Col. Henry Morrow opened the first post canteen in U.S. military history at Vancouver Barracks. A total success, it was eventually adopted throughout the armed services.

Holladay & Villard: Workin' on the railroad

October 26, 1983

Ben Holladay (1819-1887) What was Holladay's big slap in the face to Portland society? We know Holladay Park, Street and School. But where was Holladay House? (Answer below cartoon.)

In 1868 Portlanders knew they desperately needed a railroad. But who would build it? Two factions, the west- and east-siders, both calling themselves the Oregon Central Railroad Co., were locked in a bitter battle to secure the 3.8 million-acre land grant for the right-of-way.

Enter brash and bold Ben Holladay, owner of stage coaches and freight wagons, steam ships and river boats. Recognizing that railroading was transportation's future, but too late to cash in on California, he turned his attention to Oregon.

Placid Portlanders had never seen the likes of the flamboyant, 49-year-old, Kentucky-born entrepreneur whose

operation by Christmas 1869.

Depleting his own far-flung financial resources (Wash. D.C. N.Y., Calif.) in winning the race, Holladay sought outside capital by selling bonds to Eurpoean investors. Even with this $11 million infusion, down-state progress was slow and expensive.

Fall 1873 found the railroad at Roseburg. Holladay, again overextended and embroiled in costly litigation, defaulted on the interest payments to his principal creditors—a German group. Growing anxious about their investment, they dispatched fellow countryman Henry Villard to deal with Holladay.

Henry Villard (1835-1890) and the Albina shops of his O.R. & N. Co., circa 1890.

motto was "all's fair in love, war, business and politics."

Big (6'2") Ben cut a wide swath buying up property on both sides of the river, building two hotels, a huge sawmill with the finest wharf on the West Coast, founding several companies and earning the enmity of the Portland establishment.

Though Holladay wined and dined state legislators, finally securing the land grant for his "Eastsiders," Congress refused to approve it. They opted instead to award the grant to whichever group laid 20 miles of track and was in

Villard was a tough and talented negotiator but it took him almost two years to dislodge tenacious Big Ben, even with the enthusiastic assistance of prominent Portlanders.

Once in control, Villard proved to be the real visionary. With the backing of an Eastern syndicate, he bought out the stockholders in 1879, formed the Oregon Railway and Navigation Co., began planning with Puget Sound interests and built a $60 million empire within two years.

The first transcontinental train rolled into East Portland on September 11, 1883 — a century ago.

Answers: His affair with and eventual marriage to Esther Campbell, 30 years his junior. Seaside (Holladay) House gave the coastal town its name.

Early Portland: When 'Old Town' was new

May 23, 1984

East side of Front St. between Yamhill and Morrison in the 1860s. What happened to these early buildings? (Answer below cartoon.)

The little riverfront village emerged from its embryonic period filled with energy. Its founders weren't frontiersmen, they were entrepreneurs. And what they saw in Portland was opportunity.

So it's scarcely surprising that, as the fledgling metropolis began to burgeon, they were eager to outwardly express its, and their, success.

1880s Portland. Front Street south from Ash.

Portland's earliest buildings of substance were brick and mortar. Although more enduring than wood, they were still simple in style. Local business leaders wanted something more as a statement.

Lacking the skilled craftsmen and accomplished artisans locally to create elegant edifices in the 1860s, they turned to San Francisco foundries and embellished the facades of their buildings with ornate ironwork.

The trend became so popular that, by the 1860s, local demand had spawned four Portland iron foundries, eliminating the need for the San Francisco connection. Following the Fire of 1873 Corinthian pillars became even more prevalent, presenting a promenade along Front and First from Everett ("E") to Yamhill.

Throughout that decade putting on a fine front could be accomplished at relatively low cost with cast iron and in 1881 the first of the entirely ironclad facades was completed. The Ladd and Tilton Bank, at the southwest corner of First and Stark, brought total unity to the popular architectural form. Up until that time, iron and masonry had been combined to complete the decoration.

In 1888 the last grand tribute to iron, and one of the few left standing today, was completed. The Blagen Block, on the east side of Front between Couch and Burnside, has been beautifully restored and, along with the New Market Theatre, is among the finest surviving examples of cast iron architecture anywhere.

Gazing at these gems of yesteryear one could nostalgically picture two or three "Old Town" blocks lined with ironclad columns in perfect repair. But the shortsighted expediencies of the 1940s and 1950s dashed any such dreams.

First Street north from Morrison

We can only be thankful for what remains — remembering that San Francisco lost all of its cast iron buildings in the 1906 Earthquake. Although only 20 of the nearly 200 ironfronts built in Portland escaped the wrecking ball, we still have the second-largest collection in the country next to New York's Soho District.

Answer: They were destroyed in the Great Portland Fire of 1872.

Judge Matthew Deady: Justice for all

October 18, 1986

U.S. District Court Judge Matthew P. Deady. Of what non-professional accomplishments was he particularly proud? (Answer below cartoon).

Among all the stories of early settlers who came to Oregon with next to nothing and made good, the career of jurist Matthew P. Deady is one of the most commendable.

Born in Maryland in 1824, Deady excelled in school at an early age. But, continuing his education had to take a backseat to earning a living. He apprenticed as a blacksmith in Barnesville, Ohio, and eventually saved enough to begin attending the Barnesville Academy in 1843. Studying under the academy's principal and primary instructor, young Matthew earned the equivalent of a teaching certificate within two years.

Deady family at Yaquina Bay, 1886.

With credentials in hand, Deady "obtained a school" (became the tutor to a few students) in St. Clairsville, Ohio, at a salary of $22 per month. As a result, he was able to "read law" with a noted local judge, William Kennon. On October 26, 1847, the 23-year-old was admitted to the bar of the Supreme Court of Ohio and worked in the law offices of the judge's brother for the next year and a half.

In the spring of 1849, the young attorney caught the westward-bound bug choosing to cast his lot with Oregon over "gold crazy" California. When his prearranged transportation fell through, Deady worked his way to the little village on the banks of the "Wallamet." In his biography by Hubert Howe Bancroft, the judge recalled, "I breakfasted at the Guild's place two miles below (Portland) where I staid (sic) all night and slept in a house for the first time in five months."

From that time forward, Deady's rise within the ranks of territorial legal circles was meteoric. In 1850, he was chosen to represent Yamhill County in the territorial legislature. The next year, he was elected to the legislative council. in 1853, President Pierce appointed him to one of the three positions on the Oregon Territorial Supreme Court, which required a change of residence to Southern Oregon.

A special convention was convened in 1857 to frame the state constitution and Judge M.P. Deady was selected as the delegate from Douglas County. His fellow delegates elected him president of the convention. Considerable credit has been given to Deady for his contributions to the document's overall formulation.

It was adopted by popular vote on November 9, 1857, and the state still operates under it today. In June 1858, a provisional election was held prior to admission and Deady was elected district judge running unopposed. With statehood, however, official appointment was another matter.

General Joseph Lane, territorial governor in 1848-49 and Oregon's first U.S. Senator along with Delazon Smith, was pushing his son-in-law, Col. L.F. Mosher, for the post. Mosher, an attorney in Douglas County, would have been a shoe-in with the support of the powerful senator. But he balked at the possible stigma of nepotism and recommended his respected colleague Deady.

Lane's influence in Washington, D.C., clinched the position for the interim judge over other aspirants including Thomas A. Hendricks who later became Vice President of the United States during Grover Clevland's first administration. Moving to Portland, Matthew Deady served the U.S. District Court with great distinction for 33 years until his death in 1893. Hundreds of crucial cases came before him during his long career. His decisions on important issues, both fundamental and statutory, have had more impact on the shaping of legal precedent in Oregon than any other jurist.

Answer: Episcopal lay church leader, Portland Library Association organizer and 20-year president, University of Oregon regent.

C.E.S. Wood: Renaissance radical

September 24, 1986

C.E.S. Wood at Mt. Hood Camp What special favor did he once do for his friend Mark Twain? (Answer below cartoon.)

Scholar, soldier, poet, painter, author, attorney, humorist and humanitarian. A life's work could be devoted to any one of these pursuits. Colonel Charles Erskine Scott Wood mastered them all, putting his own unique stamp on each endeavor.

Equally at home in the salons of San Francisco or the wilds of the Cascade Range, the boardrooms of mighty corporations or the meeting halls of the I.W.W., Wood moved in a dizzying diversity of worlds during a career that spanned six decades.

C.E.S. Wood was born on February 20, 1852, at a U.S. Naval base on Lake Erie, Penn. His father, Dr. William Maxwell Wood, was a military surgeon who rose to become the first surgeon

C.E.S. — the young soldier and the old sage.

general of the Navy. Dr. Wood achieved acclaim as the man who forewarned our military of the imminent outbreak of the Mexican War in 1846. This information prompted the Pacific naval commander to occupy California on behalf of the United States beating out the British fleet which was laying offshore awaiting the same opportunity.

President Ulysses S. Grant, a personal friend of Dr. Wood, secured an appointment to West Point for C.E.S. and to Annapolis for his older brother, William. Graduating in the class of 1874,

Second Lieutenant Wood soon found himself on active duty at Fort Bidwell, Calif. Shortly thereafter he was transferred to Vancouver Barracks, Washington Territory, and promoted to first lieutenant. He took part in the campaign against the Nez Perce led by Chief Joseph.

The Nez Perce experience and subsequent action in Eastern Oregon to subdue the Bannock tribe ultimately led Wood to reject a military career and later support the cause of Northwest Indians. Leaving the Army in 1883, after an assignment at the Academy, C.E.S. and his wife of four years, the former Nanny Moale Smith, decided to make their home in Portland.

While stationed at Vancouver Barracks, the outgoing young couple had made many friends among Stumptown's social elite. Having just completed his law studies in New York, Wood felt confident he could build a practice in the rapidly growing river city. As the family's fortunes began to flourish, Mrs. Wood, a former Washington, D.C., debutante, readily took on the role as one of Portland's leading hostesses.

The regard in which local leaders held Wood was reflected by the fact that, within three years of his arrival, he was given the responsibility of finding the sculptor for the Skidmore Fountain. C.E.S. selected New Yorker Olin Warner who was among his wide circle of art-world acquaintances.

By the turn of the century, the firm of Williams, Wood and Linthicum was one of Portland's most prominent. It represented blue-chip clients up and down the Pacific Coast. Both George H. Williams, a former U.S. Senator, and S.B. Linthicum were ultra-conservative republicans. The fact that Wood held diametrically opposed political views did not deter their mutual success.

Wood's uncanny ability to balance his position in Portland society with his own liberal convictions attests to brilliance of mind, candor, charm and wit. He defended the freedom of speech rights of birth-control advocate Margaret Sanger and anarchist Emma Goldman. He questioned the right of inheritance and long-term land speculation. In his later years, he had an open affair with Sara Bard Field whom he married after Nanny Wood's death.

The Colonel (a militia title) retired to the Bay Area in 1920 to write and be with his paramour. At first living in San Francisco, where he was a celebrity of sorts, and then building a handsome, hillside home, "The Cats," in Los Gatos, he could reflect on a life extraordinary by any terms — and long. There, Charles Erskine Scott Wood died in 1944 at 92.

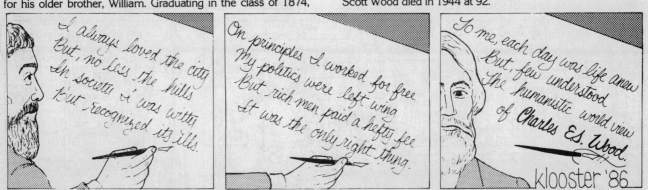

I always loved the city
But, no less the hills
In society I was witty
But recognized its ills.

On principles I worked for free
My politics were left wing
But rich men paid a hefty fee
It was the only right thing.

To me, each day was life anew
But, few understood
The humanistic world view
of Charles Es. Wood.

klooster '86

Answer: Wood had printed, on the West Point press, a small, controversial book entitled "1601" by Twain. It is now an extremely rare collector's item.

The Woods: A Portland family

October 8, 1986

New York sculptor Olin Warner's bronze plaque of the Wood children. What other famous American artist's work did C.E.S. own or sell? (Answer below cartoon.)

"As my father was extreme in his love for and indulgence of us, his children," Erskine Wood said of his father in the insightful, limited biography "Life of Charles Erskine Scott Wood" published in 1978.

C.E.S. sent his five children to the best schools and surrounded them with an intellectually stimulating environment. Few Victorian-era families in Portland or elsewhere were allowed such latitude. But, few had a father like C.E.S. Wood or a mother with the character of the former Nancy Moale Smith who commanded a position of great respect among Portland matrons.

According to Barbara Bartlett Hartwell, a friend and playmate of the Wood children, their home was one of seven households from her girlhood experiences that "possessed individual atmosphere. The H.W. Corbetts', the Ladds', the Henry Failings', the Lewis', the Tuckers, the Ayers', and lastly the Woods', where the Portland Heights car whined its way over the quivering wooden inadequacy called the Ford Bridge.

Erskine Wood and Tribal chiefs at McNary Dam

"The other six houses expressed hospitality, dignity, sumptuousness, wealth; the Wood's was of a different world. It was Bohemian without shabbiness, it was unconventional, but shot through with conventionality like changeable silk . . . the world of art, music, literature and also the world of 'who's who' and 'Society Bluebooks' and the I.W.W."

When the Woods moved to Portland in 1883, their eldest child Erskine, was just 4 years old. He was born in 1879 at Vancouver Barracks when his father, then an Army first lieutenant, was engaged in the Nez Perce campaign. Nanny,

their second child, was only 2 having been born in 1881 while C.E.S. was stationed at his alma mater, West Point, as adjutant and aide to the superintendent, his old commander, General Howard. The three younger children were all Portland born. Maxwell, in 1883, Lisa in 1886 and Berwick, in 1887.

On two separate occasions, spanning nine months during 1892 and 1893, C.E.S. sent Erskine to live with Chief Joseph in Eastern Washington. He went on to Harvard College and earned his law degree at the University of Oregon later joining the firm his father founded.

Nan, who married local hardware mogul, David Honeyman, had a distinguished career in public service. After serving as president of the Oregon League of Women Voters and chairing the Women's Organization for Prohibition Reform, she was elected to the State Senate in 1934, then won a term as Oregon's first-ever woman U.S. Representative.

After graduating from Cornell University in electrical engineering, Max entered into a promising career with Pacific Power & Light Co., which was cut short by his death in 1921 from blood poisoning. As Erskine recalled, "He would have been saved with penicillin, but we did not have it then. He was ill only about a week."

Lisa married successful businessman, George Kirkham Smith and lived much of her life in Northern California. Berwick was an All-American quarterback at Cornell before becoming an investment banker and, later an OLCC official. He and his brother, Erskine, were reputed raconteurs.

Ironically, Erskine outlived all his siblings. The eldest Wood offspring specialized in Admiralty law for 67 years and Wood, Tatum, Mosser, Brook and Holden continues as one of Portland's leading law firms to this day. The closeknit and widely accomplished Wood clan helped Erskine celebrate his 100th birthday in 1979. He died not quite four years later.

Ford Street has been renamed Vista Avenue and the Portland Garden Club now occupies the site where the Wood's handsome home once stood — a lovely and enduring memorial to a unique Northwest family.

Answer: Albert Ryder's "Jonah and the Whale" which C.E.S. sold for $20,000 giving $4,000 to each of his five children.

Early Portland Society: No gossip mill

March 11, 1987

William S. Ladd (1826-1893). What were his greatest contributions to Portland? (Answers below cartoon.)

Greek-born, jet-set gossip columnist Taki Theodoracopulos has said, "Give me a good, gossipy history book and I forget women and wine." The writings to which Taki refers chronicle the philanderings of world famous figures; not conservative, closemouthed, pioneer Portlanders.

Unlike the duc de Saint-Simon, who put a lifetime of listening at Versailles keyholes on paper, or Voltaire, who observed Frederick the Great's illicit affairs unfold first hand, there were no 19th-century gossip columnists regaling readers with juicy tidbits from private moments in the lives of River City's high and mighty.

Not to say that local notables didn't have their immoral moments. But, goings on behind closed doors were kept under wraps. That was the Victorian way. In any event, larceny, rather than hanky-panky, was the primary impropriety of Portland's powerful. With one infamous exception. The outrageous activities of former stagecoach king Ben Holladay.

During his seven-year Stumptown stint, Big Ben managed to alienate the entire local establishment. Having just sold his stage line to Wells Fargo, Holladay arrived in 1868, with $1.5 million in his pocket, intent on grabbing the transcontinental rail franchise. Unfortunately, his entrepreneurial ambitions were undone by his libido.

Launching a ludicrous lifestyle along with numerous new businesses, Holladay set up a personal harem in his Third Street mansion and proceeded to gain political favors through ladies and liquor. He then committed the ultimate social affront by marrying and humiliating young Esther Campbell, the daughter of a prominent Portland family.

Had Ben played his newfound position properly, he might have pulled off his plans. Eventually however, over-extended and unsupported, the unwelcome interloper failed, leaving town in disgrace.

Ben Holladay had a fatal flaw, but other ambitious men took full advantage of Portland's pioneer opportunities. William S. Ladd did it better than any other entrepreneur amassing a $10 million estate during a 40-year career.

Passed down in club-room conversation, a licentious story could have smeared Ladd's good name. Only the long-crippled, civic leader's physical affliction saved him from scandal.

Ladd's incapacity was not widely known. Riding to the Ladd and Tilton Bank in his carriage, the top executive would enter his office through a side door and seat himself behind a massive oak desk from which he conducted the day's business.

There, an attractive, well-dressed woman found him one afternoon in the early 1880s. Upon being ushered in, she saw a seemingly robust, elegantly attired older gentleman positioned at his place of authority. As the story goes, the woman spent 20 minutes or so in small talk under the pretense of obtaining a loan. Until, feeling that enough time had passed alone with Ladd, she revealed her true intentions.

"Mr. Ladd," she declared, "If you do not give me $25,000 on the spot, I shall tear my clothes, muss my hair, cry out hysterically and claim that you tried to force yourself upon me." The bemused banker leaned back in his chair and roared with laughter. "Young lady, if you can convince anyone in this town (meaning those who counted and were aware of his condition) that I've had (Censored) in the last 20 years, I'll give you $50,000."

Other tales are too tepid to bother telling. Shoddy saloon keepers, bawdy brothel owners, corrupt politicians and hanging judges make much more compelling copy. Even, the clearly unconventional Col. C.E.S. Wood eventually married his mistress and radical Jack Reed found proper Portland so stodgy he left home taking Louise Bryant with him.

As for the Rose City's current social set, dalliances of the day don't surface via Jonathan Nicholas. The Welsh wordsmith is decidely low-key when it comes to National Enquirerism. Is it because these modern makers and shakers have decided to follow the lead of their antecedents and keep mum? Or, could it be that their indiscretions aren't all that interesting?

HAS THAT **DESPICABLE** BEN HOLLADAY NO SHAME? MARRIED TO SWEET, LITTLE ESTHER CAMPBELL..

SHE'S **THIRTY** YEARS HIS JUNIOR, YOU KNOW!

..AND, STILL, HE **FLAUNTS** HIS FLOOSIES ALL OVER TOWN!

Klooster '87

Answer: Three large parcels of land which were later developed by his son, William M. Ladd — Ladd's Addition, Laurelhurst and Eastmoreland.

The stalwart Scotts: Abigail and Harvey — Part I

March 11, 1987

Abigail's life story has been recounted in numerous books. Has her brother, Harvey, been so eulogized? (Answer below cartoon.)

America has had its share of famous family combinations — fathers and sons, brothers and sisters, even cousins. But none are more noteworthy than brother and sister, Harvey Whitefield Scott and Abigail Scott Duniway of Oregon.

Members of a pioneer family of 1852, Abigail was 17 and Harvey was 14 when they arrived in Oregon City after an arduous trek from a farm near Peoria, Illinois. They lost their mother during the journey across the plains, learning early on that the Oregon Country could be as tough a taskmaster as any they'd left behind.

Harvey W. Scott (1838-1910) in Washington, D.C.

The widowed John Tucker Scott began farming and started up a sawmill on Gale's Creek near Forest Grove. His son, Harvey, pitched in and sister Abigail contributed by leaving the nest to establish her own.

Marrying Ben Duniway at 18, she exhibited the independent spirit that prevailed throughout her life by eliminating the word "obey" from her wedding vows. The young couple lost no time in taking advantage of the Donation Land Act of 1850 which gave 640 acres to a man and wife who staked a claim and settled on it.

Abigail spent the next dozen years in "hard scrabble," farming and child bearing. A slave to the land and her family, she seemed destined to that dismal role until her husband lost the farm, having put it up as security on a loan for a friend.

It was all part of a hard lesson that Abigail had come to resent. She had no control over her spouse's irresponsible action yet was subject to its consequences as much as he was. The Duniway family, now augmented by six, was forced to move into town and there Abigail found new opportunities never before available to her.

Young Harvey, meantime, was applying his talents as a scholar. Pacific University at Forest Grove had been operating for 10 years when, in 1859, he enrolled. Four years later, Harvey Scott became its first graduate.

The Civil War was raging in the East and Harvey requested that the Union pay his passage so he could join the fray. But the boys in blue apparently didn't feel they needed another body that badly so, unable to afford the fare, he went instead to try his luck in Idaho's mines.

But within a year he was back in Portland to study law under his former teacher, Judge Erasmus Shattuck. Scott was appointed as the first Portland librarian in 1864 and also began working for the then-weekly *Oregonian* newspaper. he took over as editor in May 1865 and was admitted to the Oregon bar that September.

Abigail, her husband now semi-invalid, supported the family by teaching school. Putting aside a few dollars, she went to Portland and persuaded merchant Aaron Meier to give her goods on credit to open a millinery shop in Albany. Soon her burgeoning business was catering to a wide spectrum of women who openly discussed their plight on the frontier.

As the 1870s began, both Scotts were poised to take even bolder steps along the banks of the Willamette and beyond.

Answer: Harvey Scott, often mentioned in local histories, has one scholarly biographer, Lee M. Nash, 1961, *Refining the Frontier.*

The stalwart Scotts: Abigail and Harvey — Part II

December 5, 1987

The first edition of *The New Northwest.* What was its position on temperance? In which Portland park is a statue of Harvey Scott? (Answers below cartoon.)

By 1871 Abigail Scott Duniway had gone from farmbound wife and mother to owner of a millinery shop in Albany and outspoken advocate of women's rights. That year she moved her family to Portland where her brother, Harvey, had held sway as editor of the *Oregonian* newspaper since 1865.

Inspired by the formation of the National Women's Suffrage Association in 1869, Abigail founded the Oregon State Equal Suffrage Society. Correctly assuming that her younger sibling's paper wouldn't be a champion of the women's cause, she published the first issue of her own newspaper, *The New Northwest*, on May 5, 1871.

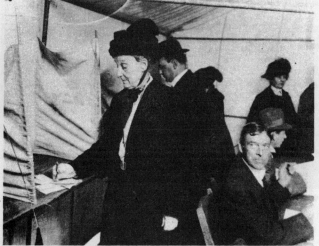

Abigail voting in Portland, 1914

Its masthead declared, "Free Speech, Free Press, Free People" and that meant people of both sexes. Operating from the second floor of their living quarters at Third and Washington, the entire Duniway family assisted in producing the paper.

Spurred on by the granting of equal suffrage in Wyoming and Utah, Abigail soon took to the highways of the Northwest in her quest to gain the vote for women. Traveling alone she was subject to ridicule and false rumor regarding her morality.

Harvey was concurrently conducting his own crusade. He considered the entire Oregon Country to be his community and set out to elevate its level of education. The young classical scholar never missed an opportunity to demonstrate his facility for erudite English liberally sprinkled in the midst of dissertations on Christian theology.

Abigail's pursuit of her goal was relentless. Selling her newspaper in 1887, she moved to Idaho and helped get a constitutional amendment passed. But Oregon was still unconquered. After her invalid husband, Ben, died in 1896, she spent even more time traveling throughout Oregon, talking anywhere and to anyone who would listen.

At the height of the Victorian era, Harvey Scott was the epitomy of the learned journalist. Highly regarded and widely respected, there is little doubt that he helped Oregon grow up. But as much power as there was in the pen, Harvey never forgot where the real power lay.

In a corrupt city, he could have waged a clean-up campaign. In a narrow, prejudiced world, he might have put his persuasive words to the task of advocating equality. But, in the late 19th Century, that would have spelled disaster for the commercial entity that carried those words.

Despite his protestations against the sadly inferior state of society in general and Portland in particular, in the end result, Harvey Scott proved to be just one of the boys. The one left-handed concession he made to supporting his sister's lifelong efforts was the insertion of occasional stories about injustices to women.

Following close but unsuccessful votes in 1900, 1906, 1908 and 1910, victory finally came in 1912. At 78, Abigail Scott Duniway lived to see the fruits of her labors spanning some 50 years. Brother Harvey never knew, having died suddenly two years before.

Answers: Abigail ignored it, feeling the over zealousness hurt the cause of women's suffrage. Mt. Tabor Park.

Simon Benson: A fountain of public spirit

November 7, 1984

Lumberman, hotelier, philanthropist, Simon Benson by one of his drinking fountains. What motivated him to donate them to Portland? (Answer below cartoon.)

In a city conspicuously short on philanthropy during its earlier days, Norwegian immigrant Simon Benson stands out as a notable exception.

He was among the second generation of Oregon entrepreneurs who, starting with almost nothing except energy and innate ability, amassed a fortune. But, unlike most of his contemporaries, Benson wanted to give something back to his adopted home.

Born to a Norwegian farming family in 1852, Simon Bergerson came with them to the United States at the age of 16. They settled in Wisconsin, where the eldest of seven children had earlier established himself and anglicized the family name to Benson.

included the first successful use of donkey engines and creation of the first log rafts, up to 850 feet long, which he had towed as far away as San Diego.

When Benson sold his logging operations and 25,000 acres of prime Northwestern Oregon timber lands in 1910, the deal totaled $4.5 million. Moving to Portland, the 58-year-old entrepreneur decided to embark on an entirely new venture.

What today remains as the Rose City's most enduring[1] and prestigious hotel, The Benson was completed in 1913. A replica of the Blackstone in Chicago, it occupies a prime downtown property originally leased from Benson's lumber baron buddy, John Yeon.

Yeon shared Benson's public mindedness and together

Presentation honoring the fountain gift, Sept. 30, 1916. Benson, in white; Henry Pittock on his left; Julius Meier standing fourth from left; John Yeon, fifth.

Young Simon quickly discovered that even farm labor paid three times what it did in Norway and he set about making the most of it. By 1875 he had married and opened a general store. This might have been where the story ended but fire took the store and all its assets four years later.

That year, Simon uprooted his family and departed for Oregon, where he decided to turn his hand to the timber trade. And here he found his pot of gold—at the end of an axe handle. More accurately, Benson's innovative techniques in the harvesting and marketing of timber

they were the driving force behind the Columbia River Highway. Benson bailed out the enterprise more than once with contributions totaling $85,000 while Yeon efficiently oversaw construction on behalf of the State Highway Commission.

Benson's generosity also included a $100,000 donation to the city which made Benson Polytechnic possible and, of course, his gift of 20 bronze drinking fountains strategically placed near downtown saloons. Apparently satisfied with his good works in Portland, he retired to Beverly Hills in 1921.

Answer: Benson, a teetotaler, hoped that the fountains would reduce drinking in downtown and, suprisingly, they did.

Julius Meier:
A gift
for governing
January 14, 1987

Meier's Columbia Gorge manse, Menucha. Who were some of America's other great Jewish merchant princes? (Answers below cartoon.)

The youngest son of the founder of Oregon's largest department store never intended to enter the family business. Nor did he plan to run for the governorship of his native state. But Julius Meier's talent, ability and character eventually led him to do both with distinction.

When Julius was born, on the last day of 1874, his parents were already respected members of Portland's business establishment and leaders of the local Jewish community. He earned his law degree from the University of Oregon in 1895 and set up a Portland practice in partnership with his close friend George Joseph. His father, Aaron, had died six years previously, leaving management of the Meier & Frank Company to Julius' uncle, Sigmund Frank, and his older brother, Abraham Meier.

large ones on shaky ground, Meier's American National Bank barely escaped the fate of many of its fellows.

Overextended due to his unprofitable hotel holdings and the bank's flagging fortunes, Julius borrowed from his nephew, Aaron Frank, to keep the financial institution afloat. Sale of the bank to the First National was negotiated the following year. Many observers credit Frank, who admired his uncle despite obvious disagreements, with personally preventing the bank's failure and preserving Meier's reputation. All the more crucial since Julius was governor of Oregon at the time.

Julius Meier's rise to the state's highest office was short and swift. His lifelong friend, George Joseph, had died in May 1930 just two months after securing the Republican nomination for the post.

(left) Meier, Aaron Frank, contractors L.H. Hoffman and W.S. Dinwiddie, 1930, (right) Gov. Meier and secretary.

It would be a good guess that Jeanette, the shrewd and strong-minded matriarch of the Meier family, played a pivotal role in persuading her son to leave the law profession for a position with the store. Abe, although an amiable front man, lacked administrative skills. When Uncle Sigmund passed away in 1910, Abe took the title of president but spent his time helping customers. Julius, as vice president and general manager, ran the operation.

Under his leadership, the store's success brought great wealth to both families, ranking them among America's most notable retail merchants. It also allowed Julius to pursue outside interests. In 1912 he became involved in the first of many civic activities helping to promote completion of the Columbia River Scenic Highway.

Meier's investments in a new banking venture and several hotels were a different story. At the urging of his former law partner, George Joseph, Julius used his controlling interest in the department store to finance purchase of the Pacific Bancorporation. September 1929 was a less than ideal time to enter the banking business. By 1932, with small local banks collapsing and even the

Julius shortly found himself taking to the hustings as an independent candidate under the banner of Joseph's power platform. Swept into office that November by a wide margin — 134,396 votes versus a combined 108,918 for his two opponents — Meier proved to be an able governor.

Though he lost control of Meier & Frank to his nephew, Aaron, during the bank debacle, Julius had a fruitful four years in the statehouse. He formed a state police force, instituted old-age pensions, a non-partisan judiciary and statewide conservation programs for parks and beaches, cut spending by 10 percent and reduced property taxes by 15 percent. Hear that, Governor Goldschmidt?

Deciding not to seek a second term or to run for the U.S. Senate, Meier retired in 1935. He spent considerable time relaxing and entertaining at his lavish summer retreat, Menucha, overlooking the Columbia at Corbett. "I was born on New Year's Eve and married on Christmas Eve. I never miss an opportunity to celebrate," the gregarious ex-governor said. he died on Bastille Day, 1937.

From *Meier & Frank* managing to OREGON politicking... the results were rewarding.

Klooster '87

STATE CAPITOL BLDG. (1876-1935)

Answers: The Gimbels, and Strauses of New York, Pittsburg's Kaufmanns, Atlanta's Riches, Neiman and Marcus of Dallas and Federated's Lazarus clan.

Frank Branch Riley: Oregon's Ambassador

September 17, 1986

Frank Branch Riley at the height of his career. What did leading newspapers say about his travel lectures? (Answers below cartoon.)

The straightforward style of mainstream Portland society was set early by its founding fathers. Strong-minded individuals they may have been, but personally they were low profile and proper — Victorians with a pioneer spirit. If an outgoing character appeared among them, his flamboyance had better be coupled with accomplishment . Such a man was Frank Branch Riley.

Riley was 16 when his family moved to Portland from Osceola, Iowa, in 1891. His father, Edward Francis Riley, had already achieved considerable success as a lawyer, banker and civic leader during a career spanning 30 years in Iowa. Having answered the call to new horizons, the elder Riley continued his winning ways. He established a law practice in Portland and founded the Clackamas Title Company.

applied his oratorical abilities to the local stage. In addition to leading Little Theater roles, he became a leader in the promotion of the performing arts. Trustee of the Portland Junior Symphony and a founder of the Drama League were but two of his offstage activities.

In the early 1920s, Riley created the role for which he would earn his greatest acclaim. It was a one-man show involving hundreds of public performances over a run of more than 40 years. Frank Branch Riley, Pacific Northwest travel lecturer. Oregon's ambassador to the world.

Putting together a superb, stereopticon slide presentation on the region's sights and delights, augmented by his personal persuasiveness, Riley took to the road time and time again. in cities across the country, he captivated audiences with this one-of-a-kind travelogue entitled "Lure

(left) Riley as Napoleon, ca. 1915 (center) taking United inaugural flight, 1960 (right) Mazamas president, 1920s.

Frank continued his education at Portland (Lincoln) High School and Portland Academy and then went on to Stanford University where he graduated in 1900. The following year, he studied at Harvard Law School and topped off his East Coast experience with an extended European tour.

Upon returning to Portland, the younger lawyer joined his father in the renamed firm of Riley and Riley. He also took on the duties of secretary and general counsel to the Clackamas Title Company. Successfully performing these responsibilities apparently came as a matter of course for Frank because he soon sought additional challenging roles.

Taking advantage of a talent for public speaking, Riley

of the Great Northwest."

Troubadour of tourism, unabashed booster, promoter without peer, author and orator who did not relinquish the podium until he was in his early 90s.

Near the end of his life, the grand old man's accomplishments were given wide public recognition. Portland mayor Terry Schrunk proclaimed "Frank Branch Riley Day" in his honor on June 1, 1971. Two years later, on November 15, 1973, he was the first motorist to cross the newly dedicated Fremont Bridge. The commemorative plaque presented to him read "for his tireless efforts toward the betterment of Oregon road building." Riley died in February 1975, six months short of his 100th birthday.

WHEN I PLAYED NAPOLEON, I WAS ONLY **ACTING**!

WATERLOO

AS AN ADVOCATE OF GOOD ROADS, I **ACTED**!

INTERSTATE BRIDGE OPENING

AND, MY ROLE AS THE PIED PIPER OF PORTLAND REALLY GOT **ACTION**!

THE NORTHWEST IS BEST!

RILEY GOT US GOING!

OREGON LOOKS GREAT!

Klooster '86

Asnwers: "Mr. Riley's descriptions, now bold, now poetic, were in perfect complement with his screen pictures" — *Boston Globe.* "The audience gasped in admiration and wonder" — *Philadelphia Record.* "Dynamic eloquence and irresistible humor" — *Indianapolis Star.*

Portland plans: Olmsted and Bennett

February 19, 1986

Proposed Park Block development looking toward a new bridge and train station. Where are the original Bennett Plan drawings? (Answer below cartoon.)

At the turn of the century, Portland's city fathers started to take a serious look at what the philosophy of unfettered free enterprise had wrought upon the surrounding landscape.

It had created a city center strangled by 60-foot-wide streets and 200-foot-square blocks. It provided far too few open spaces. Planners pointed out that Portland had the least amount of land devoted to parks of any city on the Pacific Coast.

When the administration of Mayor George H. Williams decided to do something about the situation in 1903, it must be said that they hired the best. Olmsted Bros. Landscape Architects of Brookline, Massachusetts, were planning consultants to major cities across the country.

infinite wisdom, chose "Washington."

A far more extensive, even grandiose plan was prepared in 1912. By this time, the future impact of the automobile was being considered and projections for the city's growth were phenomenal. As a result of the Lewis & Clark Fair's success, Portland's population increased more than 50 percent between 1905 and 1910. Based on those statistics, zealous promoters were predicting a metropolis of three million by 1980.

As a result, the newly formed Greater Portland Plan Association retained Chicago planner Edward Bennett in 1911. Contributions to the association and the "City Beautiful" fund, which had been launched by former Mayor

Bennett's Civic Center proposal looking south from S.W. Main and Third streets.

Though the Olmsteds submitted a sweeping plan the following year providing for a system of parkways and boulevards connecting playgrounds, parks and city squares, precious little was actually implemented. The only aspect of the ambitious scheme that eventually made it past the drawing board was the Hillside Parkway (Terwilliger Boulevard).

However, several municipal parks recommended for development, improvement or preservation did benefit from the plan. Mount Tabor and Rocky Butte are prominent among them as well as Forest Park. The Olmsted plan also proposed that the generic "City" Park name be changed to something unique to the area such as Settler's, Explorer's or Lewis and Clark Park. Portland decision makers, in their

Joe Simon in 1909, financed Bennett's work on a comprehensive, city-wide design scheme.

The plan, submitted in October 1912, employed broad, tree-lined boulevards radiating from obelisk-adorned traffic circles and classic public buildings emanating along a central mall. The waterfront was to be reclaimed for public use with parkway access. It would have transformed Portland into a blend of Paris and Budapest.

The public approved Bennett's proposal by a two-to-one margin at the polls. But the boys who controlled the bucks, thought the plan pretentious and, even more critical, prohibitively expensive. Hindsight suggests that it was out of proportion for Portland, but today we'd all welcome another ample, arbored avenue or two.

Answer: Last exhibited in 1957, the Bennett drawings, according to Jean LeJeune of the Oregon School of Design, have disappeared.

Portland plans: Lloyd, Moses and more

February 26, 1986

Proposed Sandy Blvd, entrance to Portland, 1932. What was Sandy's short-lived nickname and what was the colorful idea behind it? (Answers below cartoon)

In 1904 the Olmsted Plan for a citywide system of parks and parkways produced only the Multnomah Parkway now called Terwilliger Boulevard. Six years later, the patriarchs who held the purse strings found Edward Bennett's Paris-cum-Budapest plan too princely for their pocketbooks.

Undaunted by the fact that these previous plans had gone nearly for naught, city fathers once again commissioned studies for a series of civic design schemes in the 1920s, 30s and 40s.

The most significant difference between the former and latter strategies was the impending importance of the automobile. The Olmsted Bros. had considered it in the same context as carriages. Bennett's broad boulevards would have relegated it to traffic circle melees reminiscent of Gay Paree's raucous Arc de Triomphe roundabout.

Ralph B. Lloyd and his eastside civic center proposal, 1931.

Protection of private property rights continued to prevail when the public interest should have taken precedence. Portland did not establish a planning commission until 1918 and, even then, its members were criticized for their impractical idealism. A zoning ordinance, initially defeated in 1919, finally passed, in modified form, four years later.

The "feeble" code, though better than none, gave real estate interests the leeway to run rampant over the landscape. But one developer had loftier goals than mere exploitation for quick profit. California oil magnate, Ralph B. Lloyd envisioned a showpiece center of civic and commercial activity. What Lloyd did not anticipate was the westside resistance to an out-of-state interloper and, even worse, extensive eastside development.

Over the decade 1923 to 1933, Lloyd acquired most of the original tract assembled by 19th century railroad tycoon Ben Holladay. Despite his commitment to $25 million and actual investment of more than $4 million in property and improvements, including a golf course and club house (now Sweet Tibbie Dunbar's), Lloyd's civic center proposal was ultimately thwarted by Portland's establishment aided by the Great Depression.

The property remained vacant until 1960 when the then largest shopping center in the world, Lloyd Center, was completed. It was the centerpiece of a complex that included a Sheraton Hotel, the headquarters of the Bonneville Power Administration and, a decade later, the loftiest office buildings on the eastside.

Lloyd's ambitious proposal was unsolicited but the "bought and paid for" plan submitted by Harland Bartholomew and Associates of St. Louis met with no results. Bartholomew recommended a revitalization of the original waterfront (Old Town) area, widening of Front Street and the Morrison and Hawthorne Bridges and construction of the Fremont Bridge. This was in 1932.

City engineer Olaf Laurgaard could take pride in the fact that his home-grown 1923 proposal had borne fruit where nationally known planners had failed. A new Burnside Bridge was completed in 1926, the seawall in 1928.

Fifteen years later New York City Park Commissioner Robert Moses, "America's #1 public works planner" came to town for a week. Moses immediately saw that the downtown area was ill equipped to handle the hordes of horseless carriages descending upon it daily in 1943. What he did not recognize was that the broad brush solutions resulting from his "seven day" study could never be implemented in the self-serving environment that prevailed.

In subsequent years arterials, tunnels and freeways have been underbuilt—inadequate before they opened. We still struggle with the problem to this day.

I WAS SURE PORTLAND WOULD **WANT** A BEAUTIFUL NEW EASTSIDE CIVIC CENTER!

WELL, MR. LLOYD, THE WESTSIDE BOYS **MIGHT** HAVE BOUGHT IT..

IF YOUR PROPOSED HOTEL HADN'T BEEN THE **TALLEST** BUILDING ON THE WEST COAST!

Klooster '86

Answers: Sandy Blvd. was called "The Roseway" in the 1930s because of a plan to plant roses along it.

Portland power elite: Arlington Club

July 30, 1986

Original Arlington Club interior, ca 1912. How many members does the club currently have and how much does it cost? (Answers below cartoon.)

By the mid-19th century, exclusivity in Western cultures had been honed to a fine art. The socially conscious British structured their cliquishness around the private men's club. Men of position and accomplishment could gather together to plot the destiny of empire and personal future. Close acquaintanceship, fostered in an informal social atmosphere, served to enhance those interests. And it could, not incidentally, be quite enjoyable. The upper crust's culmination of the boys' night out.

The benefits of such associations did not escape the attention of Victorian America. Boston's Somerset Club was founded in 1842. Honolulu's Pacific Club dates from 1851, and the Pacific Union Club in San Francisco was formed the following year. Many others — San Francisco's Olympic Club, the Philadelphia and New York Union Clubs and the Rochester Club among them — came into existence during the Civil War.

"nowhere else on earth can the fellowship generated in this club be surpassed."

Arlington Club's influence on its city, state and region in the early 20th century cannot be understated. During the two decades when Portland's growth was at its greatest, the decisions made within those walls determined much of the Northwest's economic and political direction.

By 1910 the needs of an increased membership demanded larger facilities. A new clubhouse on Southwest Salmon Street facing the South Park Blocks was designed by Portland architects Whidden and Lewis and completed in June of that year. Through the prosperity of the 1920s club members steered a conservative course for the city. Owing to the now much-maligned philosophy, the Great Depression had less impact in Portland than elsewhere. Although its membership dwindled to fewer than 125, Arlington

(left) Arlington's first home, 3rd & Pine, 1881-92 (center) Second home, Park & Alder, 1892-1910 (right) Current , Salmon and Park.

In Portland, the first men's club, and by most accounts still the most exclusive, was established in 1867. Names such as Capt. John C. Ainsworth, Henry Failing, William S. Ladd and Donald Macleay were among the 35 members of the pioneer power elite who pledged to contribute up to $100 each to form "a club" and to furnish "suitable rooms."

For its first 14 years, the club met at various downtown locations until 1881 when they leased Capt. Ainsworth's former home at Southwest Third Avenue and Pine Street and took the name Arlington. The club was incorporated in 1890, with Portland Gas Company founder John Green as its first president.

Two years later, a handsome building was erected at the Northwest corner of Park Avenue and Alder Street, which the club occupied until 1910. Arlington could count among its membership many of Oregon's most prominent men and proudly stated

Club's core group carried it through the country's most devastating decade.

As the size and scope of the city changed, direct participation of Arlington clubbers in politics diminished. Their leadership roles in the less conspicuous, though equally influential, positions on civic commissions, boards and committees continue to this day. From Arlington's ranks come many of the men who hold together Portland's economic and cultural fabric.

Often criticized for anachronistic attitudes — exclusion of women being the most often mentioned — Arlington Club no longer denies admission to Jews or Orientals. Power imperfect though it may be, this organization and ones like it across the country, reflect prevailing values and a station in life to which many still aspire.

Answers: 525 resident members and 130 non-resident. $3,000 initiation fee plus $90 per month dues.

Portland prestige: The university club

August 6, 1986

The backbar of the Men's Grill has a niche for each member's dice cup. What makes this one room unique? Who is the bartender? (Answers below cartoon.)

Prior to the formation of Portland's first private men's club — the predecessor of Arlington Club — in 1867, volunteer fire companies served the comraderie of a select few. With the advent of Arlington, a place was provided where Stumptown's business, political and social elite could fraternize informally.

Architect's rendering of the University Club completed 1913.

Excluded from this ostensible ultimate in social status, local Jewish men, many of whom were playing prominent roles in the city's development, founded their own club —the Concordia — in 1878. Like their Arlington counterparts, Concordia clubbers fromed alliances, planned futures and fortunes or simply had fun swapping stories, playing cards and bending elbows.

By 1898, when Portland's third private men's club appeared on the scene, the little river city which had only 6,717 inhabitants in 1867 was now a major commercial center boasting 81,637 citizens.

A gathering of college men at the Portland Hotel on December 7, 1897 precipitated the organization of the city's own University Club on May 2, 1898. Fifty-six graduates of 26 American (and one Canadian) schools met that day at the offices of architects Whidden and Lewis to formalize the group in the fashion set by major Eastern cities.

William Whidden, a graduate of Massachusetts Institute of Technology, and his partner, L. Allen Lewis, a Princeton alumnus, were elected the club's first president and vice president, respectively. Of the founding members only six were from Western colleges and universities — two from the University of California (Berkeley) and one each from Oregon, Pacific, Utah and Stanford.

Although the charter members were all men of means as well as formal learning, the club had modest beginnings. In April 1900 it occupied an unfurnished room at Sixth Avenue and Alder Street, with meals provided by Richard's, a well-known restaurant next door. The following year an entire floor was leased at Third Avenue and Washington Street from which, as long-time member Frank Branch Riley stated, "the convivial sounds of singing and merriment emitted."

The most significant departure in style, if not substance, between the University and Arlington clubs occurred in October 1903 when the former allowed admittance of wives "for Wednesday night dinners and other functions." From that beginning women were eventually granted full membership status.

In 1905 the club purchased the Pfunder House on Washington Street and moved it to a lot at West Park and Stark streets. Within a half dozen years membership outgrew those quarters and plans were laid for construction of the present palatial home.

Noted local architects Whitehouse and Fouilhoux created the classic, four-story Jacobean Revival structure which graces the northwest corner of Southwest Sixth Avenue and Jefferson Street. When completed in 1913, at a cost of $130,000, the new University Club was in the heart of a residential area. Directly south stood the Ladd estate, which occupied the entire block where the *Oregonian* building is now located.

Current membership is limited to 1,000, including 120 non-residents and 25 women who, up until 1979, entered the club only on the Jefferson side. Annual events include a golf tournament held at Waverley Country Club, pitch and domino competitions, Oktoberfest and a New Year's Eve party celebrated at 9 p.m. — Times Square time.

Answers: It is the only room in the club where women are not allowed. 41-year employee Leo Balancia is the master mixologist.

Willamette Greens: Waverley Country Club

August 13, 1986

The Junor brothers, long time Waverly groundskeepers, with early gas mower, ca 1920. Why couldn't the 17th and 18th fairways be cut in June 1964? Who is Waverly's most famous golfer currently? (Answers below cartoon.)

The venerable and vexing athletic activity of putting the little white ball in the seemingly smaller round hole can be traced to 15th-century Scotland. When, three centuries later, it was institutionalized on those same shores, the ball really got rolling. Or that is hooking, slicing, chipping and, for many of us, duffing.

1754 was the year of enshrinement at the world's first golf links. The Royal and Ancient Golf Club of St. Andrews. The sport's earliest establishment in the Americas was more than a century later in coming. Canada's Royal Montreal Club was founded in 1873 and it was 15 more years before the United States had a course it could call its own.

First course near Cleveland H.S. site, ca. 1896.

The St. Andrews Golf Club of Yonkers, N.Y., predated Portland's first club by only eight years. In 1896 the then Portland Golf Club had its "rough" beginnings on the present site of Cleveland High School. Those initial links, which everyone referred to as Waverly without the "e," lasted just two years. In 1897, Scotsman and local grain mogul Peter Kerr won the monthly handicap with a 142.

In 1898, the Waverly Association was formed and the new course, a 9-holer running east and west, was laid out in the Garthwick district. Sheep were the groundskeepers in those days and the game was not played in mid-summer because the four-legged mowers couldn't keep up with the growth. Waverly clubber

P.B. Gifford shot a 106 in 1900 to win the Pacific Northwest Championship.

By 1906 groundskeeping had taken a significant step forward. Horses with pads on their hooves pulled mowers over the course. And the level of play was improving with another Scotsman and prominent Portlander Donald MacLeay shooting in the low 80s. (Part of this improvement was undoubtedly due to the introduction of the dimpled, gutta-percha covered golf ball which could be driven at least a third farther than the old leather-covered ball.)

Waverly's first small clubhouse was built just south of Ochoco Street when the club relocated. It was expanded over the years and finally torn down in 1927. The handsome white building that now houses the club was the work of local architects Whitehouse and Fouilhoux, who also designed the University Club. Completed in 1913, the new clubhouse graced the south end of a completely redesigned, 18-hole course that remains essentially the same today. In 1914 a gas-powered mower took over the job of grooming the fairways and greens.

The same year it got its new facilities, Waverley Country Club took on its official name with the "e." Local legend has it that the spelling change was inadvertent. When new stationery was delivered, the printer had inserted the additional "e" in error and the usage stuck.

Membership escalated to 250 in the '20s and the club produced a number of national-class players. Local dentist Oscar Willing was on three Walker Cup teams and reached the 1929 Pebble Beach Amateur finals. Social activities have always been a part of Waverley's world. From its earliest days, luncheons, dinner dances and holiday parties were on the agenda.

World-class names and national championships have highlighted the club's recent history. The Women's National Amateur was held at Waverley in 1962 and the U.S. Men's Senior Tourney, won by member Ed Murphy, took place two years later. In 1970 Lanny Wadkins beat Tom Kite to take the National Men's Amateur. The club hosted that event again in 1982.

Today, the Portland area boasts nine private and 22 public golf courses to satisfy an apparently considerable craving to the little white ball. The 475 Waverley clubbers and their families do it over the course with the longest tradition and at the highest cost of any local links.

(left) first course near Cleveland H.S. site, ca. 1896. (right) Waverly Links clubhouse near Ochoco St., ca. 1910.

THE WAVERLEY CLUB ARCHITECTS CERTAINLY HAD **FORE**SIGHT!

HOW'S THAT?

SMALL WINDOW PANES!

CRASH!

Klooster '86

Answers: The 17th and 18th fairways were underwater due to the major flood that year. Touring pro Peter Jacobsen.

Heights society:
The Racquet Club

September 10, 1986

Tree trellising conceals the Racquet Clubs outdoor courts. Can you name some of its prominent presidents? (Answers below.)

Among the last of the prestige West Hills residential developments was "The Highlands," conceived and promoted by prominent local lumberman L.B. Menefee. From 1929 through World War II, these lovely, wooded lots located above Canyon Road west of the present day OMSI site, slowly sold and an attractive, upper-middle class area emerged.

The English country-style clubhouse.

To sell upscale homesites during the Depression, Menefee offered an innovative extra—a handsome, English country style clubhouse with two tennis courts and a swimming pool. This additional inducement obviously worked well. The quasi-public club, with its stunning centerpiece, attracted an extended membership including Highlands residents and a select group of friends. By the late 1930s, the Racquet Club had become a very popular, but still unofficial, entity.

At the end of the war, Menefee called together 10 of the club's most avid supporters, a few just out of uniform, and posed to them an interesting proposition. The Highlands was virtually sold out and the community recreation facility no longer qualified for its tax-exempt status. Would they consider buying him out and formalizing what, in fact, was already a private tennis and social club?

The nucleus of devotees decided to accept the offer. One hundred individuals and families were invited to become members of the Racquet Club for a $300 initiation fee. Previously, they had paid a few dollars a month for the club's upkeep. There was no problem in getting takers. For many of them, the place was an institution—an integral part of their lives.

With its $30,000 nest egg, the old/new club bought the property and facilities for a nominal $10,000 and used the remaining $20,000 for improvements, including an additional court. The Racquet Club had finally come of age.

From 1946 forward, its has been a reflection of Portland society—exclusive and low key. Its first president, owner of Jones Stevedoring, Jack Hering, and his successors reflect a cross-section of local business and professional leaders. Over 20 years, memberships gradually increased — first to 150, then 200 and, finally, to the present level of 250 families.

Driving by the club on S.W. Highland Road, the unaware passerby might easily mistake it for a palatial private residence. The immaculately maintained grounds are a showplace in themselves. Directly across the road are three outdoor tennis courts embellished by a series of immaculately trellised trees lining the length of the south fence. To appease the pressure for year-round play, two indoor courts were built on nearby property in 1976.

Until 1982, the only organized competition at the Racquet Club had been its own annual members' tournament. That year, Portland tennis legends Sam Lee and Emery Neale convinced the club to host the most prestigious Seniors' Tournament in North America.

The Gordon Trophy matches have pitted the top U.S. Seniors against their Canadian counterparts annually since 1949. Played alternately in the two countries, the 38th consecutive edition was just contested at the Racquet Club on August 2-3, 1986. This was the third straight meeting in Portland, attesting to the quality and hospitality of the quiet West Hills tennis club with more than a touch of class.

THIS HAS GOT TO BE THE **MOST** PRIVATE CLUB IN PORTLAND HISTORY!

IT WAS A GOING CONCERN FOR FIFTEEN YEARS **BEFORE** IT CAME INTO EXISTENCE!

RACQUET CLUB

Klooster '86

Answers: Racquet Club presidents have included: Russ Caldwell, Curt & Peter Koehler, Sir James McDonald, Henry Labbe, Pierre Kolisch, Walker Treece, Peter Pope, Kim MacColl, Brian Booth and Richard Estey.

Heights Society: The Town Club

September 3, 1986

The immaculately maintained Town Club's main lounge. What is its current membership. What is the club's policy toward males? (Answers below cartoon.)

Times were good in America during the mid-1920s. For Portland's upper crust they were better. Those symbols of local social status — the Arlington, University, Multnomah Athletic and Waverley Country clubs — were well established with the wealthiest families well represented in all of them. For the female side of the fortune, however, something was missing. They had no club to call their own.

At the outset of 1928, nine of those leading local ladies decided to change the situation. On January 31, the Mesdames Henry F. Chaney, C.H. Davis Jr., David T. Honeyman, Daniel D. Madden, Ray W. Matson, Joseph A. Minott, J.V.G. Posey, Donald J. Sterling and Irving L. Webster signed the articles of incorporation establishing the Town Club.

The Town Club's dining patio and garden

The club found immediate acceptance among the town's top matrons with 235 of them becoming charter members. One of Portland's wealthiest widows, Mrs. Theodore B. Wilcox, was elected its first president. Her husband, protege of William S. Ladd, enjoyed a long and very successful career rising to become president of Portland Flouring Mills. Upon his death in 1918, he left a $10 million estate.

Mrs. Wilcox became the Town Club's most important benefactor when she donated the property for its new clubhouse and grounds in 1929. That property consisted of the gardens descending the hillside in front of her stately King's Hill home. Today, the former Wilcox mansion at the corner of S.W. King and Park streets houses the offices and studios of KWJJ Radio. In Mrs. Wilcox's day, King Street was part of her front yard, leading to the gardens and carriage house below.

During its first three and one-half years, the club, occupied the white Victorian Jarvis House at S.W. Salmon Street and Park Avenue across from the Wilcox property where plans were underway for the new facility. They would not be deterred by the onset of the Depression. Though the stock-market crash took its toll on the finances of the local elite, for the old families, substance was not merely a state of mind.

In recognition of her contributions, Mrs. Wilcox continued as honorary president for 10 years following her term of office. The Town Club's second president, Mrs. Thomas (Mabel Macleay) Kerr, continued the grain connection. Her husband and his brother, Peter, were then the principal grain merchants on the Pacific Coast.

On July 1, 1931, the club's fourth president, Mrs. Thomas B. Honeyman, dedicated a magnificent new, Mediterranean-style clubhouse at 2115 Salmon St. for its 250 members. Architect Folger Johnson's multi-level design with its lovely terrace and garden receives praise to this day. over the years many members have contributed rugs, furnishings and decor pieces to enhance the interior of their home away from home. Many of these fine antiques are used in the main lounge — a 50-foot-long reception room that, in this writer's view, is the class of the city.

If there are any scintillating stories about this very private club, nobody's telling them. What you see is what you get. A proud tradition of quiet quality. A place to entertain and socialize. Mother-daughter-granddaughter legacies carried forward. In the dining room, what you get is even more. The award-winning cuisine originating in the Town Club's kitchen has made more than one gourmet try to wangle an invitation to the top of Southwest Salmon Street.

MY FATHER, MY HUSBAND, MY BROTHER AND MY SON ALL LOVE TO HAVE **LUNCH** AT THE CLUB!

MINE, TOO. THEY **REALLY** ENJOY THE FOOD!

I THINK THERE'S **ONE** THING THEY LIKE EVEN MORE!

WHAT'S THAT?

KNOWING THAT IT'S **OUR** TREAT!

Klooster '86

Answers: 400 members by invitation only. Currently full. Men are not excluded from membership.

MAC: The club and its stadium Part I

August 8, 1984

Fully equipped 1912 MAC gymnasium. In which sports did members excel? What MAC facility operated only 10 years? (Answers below cartoon.)

Multnomah Amateur Athletic Club (that's still MAC's official name) was founded in 1891 by 26 local sports enthusiasts with $10 apiece, who joined together in the spirit of sportsmanly competition.

The new MAC quickly became an "in" organization among the active set of the Rose City. The club's first facility, for 200 charter members, was at 2nd between Yamhill and Morrison. There were lockers, showers, a gymnasium, billiard room and reading room.

In its early decades, the club fielded football, baseball and

Integration came early to MAC. So popular were club activities with the fair sex that a ladies annex, with 42 members, was formed in April 1894. Juniors were also admitted early on at reduced dues.

The club's first home on their own property became a reality in 1900. Located on the Chapman (18th) Street side of Multnomah Field, it opened to the 1,479 members in July and featured a swimming pool, elaborate gymnasium, bowling alleys, Turkish bath, handball courts and social rooms.

The 3,300-seat Multnomah Field grandstand overflowed for this Oregon-Idaho game, Oct. 15, 1921. It was a tie, 7-7.

track teams that fared very well against Northwest colleges and other athletic clubs on the West Coast. MAC's footballers competed until 1926. Their record was 138 won, 22 tied and 58 lost.

Teams needed a place to practice and compete. A large flat field at the head of Morrison Street filled the bill ideally and the club rented the five acres in 1892. As with all MAC's athletic competitions, professionals were barred from participation.

Prominent banker and investor William S. Ladd was so taken with the admirable aims of the MAC men that he built a clubhouse at 10th and Yamhill (now the Public Library site) and leased it to the club for $3,000 a year, starting in 1893.

The 18th Street clubhouse and adjacent grandstand burned to the ground in 1910. The board met immediately and approved plans to build a new much more elaborate facility on Salmon Street, overlooking the field from the south.

Completed in 1912, with membership standing at 2,960, MAC's fourth home was a landmark for 62 years. Following suit, Multnomah Field rapidly evolved to stadium status. its 3,000 capacity was expanded to 15,000 in the early 20's. Still inadequate, in 1926 the club made a half-million dollar commitment to build a new semi-circular stadium seating 36,000. (Part II — Pg. 39)

IT'S ONE THING FOR A PRIVATE CLUB TO OWN THE **BIGGEST** STADIUM IN TOWN!

BIG GAME TODAY OSC vs. U of O

BUT IT'S QUITE ANOTHER NOT TO HAVE ANY CONTROL OVER THE **GUEST** LIST!

BEAVERS

DUCKS

Klooster '84

Answers: All major and minor sports of the time. The Multnomah Golf Course, between Canyon and Bertha — Beaverton, 1925-35.

MAC: The club and its stadium Part II

August 15, 1984

Packed grandstands for 1949 Rose Festival. What is the current capacity of Multnomah Civic Stadium? What is the record attendance? (Answers below cartoon.)

A club that boasts more than 17,500 members could hardly be called "exclusive." Yet, so many people want to join, the wait is up to five years.

Portland's own Multnomah Amateur Athletic Club, called MAC by members and nonmembers alike, is one of only a handful of such organizations in North America — prestigious, social, family oriented and dedicated to sports and physical fitness.

Since its rapidly burgeoning beginnings in 1891, MAC members have participated in almost every sport known and fielded teams in many. Regional and national champions, even Olympians, have risen from the ranks of this club founded on the amateur ideal.

Main entrance to 1913 clubhouse. In 1940's, front portico, too narrow for "modern" cars, was removed. Opulently paneled entry hall (right).

So strong, in fact, was this non-professional principal that, for many years, MAC did not let pro teams even practice on Multnomah Field.

The stadium underwent four stages of development under MAC ownership. After a small grandstand burned, along with the clubhouse, in 1910, a new 3,300-seat structure was built. By 1926 increased demands prompted a bond drive to build a bigger facility. Dedication of the new "Winged M Bowl" took place on October 8, 1926, with 24,338 in attendance — the largest gathering ever in the state.

Bonded indebtedness was retired in 1948 and for the first time in its history, MAC property was debt free. The Rose Festival was hosted annually, greyhound racing was an ongoing activity and when the big names came to town they played the stadium.

In 1956 Beaver baseball made Multnomah its new home and the addition of bleachers brought capacity to 33,000. But the 1960s saw a change of fortune.

With completion of Memorial Coliseum in 1961, Rosaria and the road shows went under cover. Corvallis and Eugene were planning their own stadium enlargements, the Beavers were lackluster and MAC took a hard look at their investment.

Having completed a much-needed new building in 1965, the club had depleted its building fund. By membership vote the seven-acre property was put up for sale and Portland voters approved its purchase. The city got a "Civic" stadium and MAC, 75 years old and 10,900 strong, put $2.1 million in the bank.

In 1971 they built a new club facility, regrettably razing the classic 1912 clubhouse in the process. With addition of a parking lot and sports courts across Salmon in 1974, the fabulous, modern complex will serve up to 20,000 members.

Answers: 25,680 permanent seating, 36,000-plus with portable bleachers. 36,885 at OSU vs. USC game in 1957.

The Irvington Club: Still serving well

August 22, 1986

The Irvington Club, 1941. Who are the most famous modern stars to play at the club? What important tournament is still held here? (Answers below cartoon.)

The 640-acre donation land claim filed by sea Captain William Irving and his wife, Elizabeth, in 1851, was a long way from the action at the time. But, 36 years later, time had caught up with the area. In 1887, the widowed Mrs. Irving went in with three partners, John Brazee, David Thompson and Ellis Hughes, to plan and develop the Irvington District.

Irvington experienced its greatest growth after the turn of the century, but one significant addition came two years before. The Irvington Tennis Club was established in 1898 with a small clubhouse and one court built on property owned by C.H. Prescott at N.E. 21st Ave. and Tillamook Street — a block from the present club.

The Irvington Club, 1904.

Portland's first court, built by gas company founder Henry D. Green in 1880, soon prompted the construction of several other private courts around which lively local social events centered.

But the impetus for Irvington, Portland's first tennis-only club, was provided by a contingent of top-caliber Eastern players on a West Coast tour to promote the game as a nationwide competitive sport.

Within one year, the Irvington Club sponsored the first Oregon State Tennis Championships. Since the club had only two courts, the tournament was held at the Multnomah Athletic Club.

The growing popularity of the game and enthusiasm for the annual state tourney gave Irvington members the confidence to make a major move in 1905. Raising $10,000 via donations and life memberships, the newly formed Irvington Improvement Association purchased a full city block between 21st and 22nd avenues, Thompson and Brazee streets.

The streets were graded and sidewalks were still several years away. But that didn't deter the club from putting together a first-class facility. The original, one-story clubhouse featured a tea garden on the roof which was "a most advantageous position to watch the play." With six clay courts, Irvington was able to host the Oregon Championships, alternating for a decade thereafter with MAC.

During the '20s, taxes and street assessments caused a financial crunch for the club. Five hundred families, paying annual dues of $10, saw it through. Membership dwindled to 30 at the height of the Depression, spelling near disaster that was only averted by regrettably selling off the north end of the club's property.

Fiscal difficulties didn't prevent the club from producing outstanding stars. Following in the footsteps of Walter Goss, three-time Oregon singles champ in the Teens, and Phil Neer, 1922-23 National Intercollegiate titlist, Wayne Sabin and Elwood Cooke were ranked in the U.S. top 10 during the 30's. Cooke lost to Bobby Riggs in the 1939 Wimbledon singles final.

Sam Lee, who won the state title in 1937, and Emery Neale, who took it six times between 1941 and '51, have been the city's tennis stalwarts for nearly five decades. Between them, Neale, 65, and Lee, 72, have won more seniors' tournaments than they can recall. In 1967 and '68 they teamed up to reach the doubles quarter finals at Wimbledon.

Overcoming low periods through the 1940s and early '50s, the club built a swimming pool in 1957 to attract new members and was the first local tennis club to enclose its courts in 1965. Today, with a full membership of 300 families, the remodeled Irvington Club is thriving as one of the country's oldest and most well-known private tennis facilities.

IRVINGTON **ALMOST** LOST ALL OF ITS COURTS!

IT MIGHT HAVE BECOME THE IRVINGTON **SWIM** CLUB!

BUT THEN, THEY'D PROBABLY HAVE EXERCISED THE **ROOFTOP** OPTION!

Answers: Jimmy Connors and John McEnroe. The Oregon State Championships.

2. ROUND THE ROSE FESTIVAL

The city's annual self celebration

Yearly theme events are an important aspect of civic promotion in countless American cities and towns. A queen and her court, coupled with a parade, are often the focal points. In the West, these royal entourages are sometimes astride saddles. In the East, hansom cabs might be the conveyance. In the Midwest, a haywagon.

For the local citizenry, such extravaganzas are a matter of particular, provincial pride. These things Portland's Rose Festival shares with its counterparts elsewhere. But, there the comparison ends. Because the Rose City's annual tribute to its namesake is one of the country's oldest, most elaborate and widely acclaimed civic celebrations.

The Portland Rose Festival has blossomed over the course of eight decades from a modest, weekend "Rose Fiesta" in 1907 to a year round undertaking of encyclopedic complexity and massive proportions. Today, it is big business requiring a full-time staff of nine with an annual budget exceeding $3 million. Princess selection and other pre-festival activities begin almost two months before the official Festival Week which, with race events, actually stretches into two full weeks of city-wide celebration.

Planning for the next year's festival gets underway almost as soon as the current one ends. In a concession to increasing costs, the parade will have a corporate sponsor for the first time in 1988 — Lloyd Center. Floats have served as self-promotion tools for some time. This columnist's benefactor, This Week Magazine, as an example, sponsored the Junior Court's float in the 1987 Grand Floral Parade.

The Rose Festival Association has had a new executive manager since July 1987. Gene Leo, who replaced long-time manager Clayton Hanlon, comes from a successful stint as director of the Washington Park Zoo. He oversaw completion of the spectacular new polar bear exhibit during his tenure.

With strong leadership and solid community support, including hundreds of volunteers and the incomparable Royal Rosarians, the Portland Rose Festival continues as the Rose City's showcase event. The following stories trace some of its illustrious history.

City of Roses: A nickname takes root

June 22, 1983

What is the name of Portland's official rose? How many different varieties of modern roses are there? How many are in the International Rose Test Garden? (Answers below cartoon.)

In parks and public gardens, backyards, frontyards and sideyards, fence rows and parking strips, our symbol of beauty blooms. In a million places throughout the city it lends loveliness, making a synergism of the whole, helping Portland approach the grandeur it deserves.

It is the rose. And I don't mean Bette Midler, although they ought to name one after her.

Through the selfless efforts of dedicated individuals, this regal flower has achieved a place of singular significance for our city. Efforts that date back almost 100 years.

separate and equal recognition for his contributions to the promotion of the rose. It is due to Curry's tireless energies that our now-world-renowned International Rose Test Garden was established in 1917 at City (Washington) Park.

Not one to rest on his laurels, or rose bushes, Curry, with the enthusiastic support of other civic-minded Portlanders, formed a group called the "Kickers." Their primary goal was to "kick" the establishment out of its lethargy and first on the list was to firmly establish Portland's nickname — "The City of Roses."

The International rose Test Garden in Washington Park.

If one person could be called the Father of Portland's Roses, it would be Frederick V. Holman. Attorney Holman was the driving force and founder of the Portland Rose Society in 1888. Not coincidentally, he was also a prime mover behind the first official Rose Festival in 1907 and a founding member of the Royal Rosarians.

Fellow "first 100" Rosarian Jesse Curry deserves

Jefferson High teacher Bertha Slater Smith had kicked in with "For you a rose in Portland grows" in 1916. The city and the rose have been inseparable since.

This bond is celebrated each year with the Rose Festival in June — National Rose Month. None of this is news, I am sure, to the principal of 1983 Queen Kira's high school, Myra Rose.

Answers: Portland has no official rose. More than 13,000. Over 400 named and 100 unnamed varieties.

Rose Festival: Diamond anniversary plus
June 1, 1983

Rose Festival wouldn't be the same without this group of prominent business and professional men. Who are they and when did they come into existence? (Answers below cartoon.)

One could convincingly debate that 1983 is actually the 79th anniversary of the Rose Festival. On June 10, 1904, the Portland Rose Society held its first Floral parade and "the carbon arc lights flickered unfalteringly as the decorative procession, including 20 automobiles, paraded down 3rd Street." But this was an embryonic event.

On October 14, 1905, Mayor Harry Lane proposed that a "Rose Festival be held each year sometime between June and October." This declaration followed immediately on the heels of the tremendously successful Lewis and Clark Exposition.

very precise — Rex Oregonus, supreme monarch of the Kingdom of the Rose, emerged magically from the vital waters of the Willamette (remember that the river was Portland's lifeblood of commerce) and set foot on the Stark Street Wharf. Thus was proclaimed the commencement of festivities. The event was heralded by the clanging of Portland's great fire bell joined by the blowing of every factory whistle and the clamor of other steeple bells in town.

Miss Carrie Lee Chamberlain, daughter of Governor George Chamberlain, was proclaimed Queen Flora, obviously a political appointment. In addition to lavishly

1908 Rose Festival Parade.

The Oregon Historical Society, itself, bears blatant proof at this moment that we have already reached the 76th anniversary. Displayed in the window of their bookstore is a poster replica from the 1910 Rose Festival stating that it is "The 4th Annual."

So what's the bloomin' story?

Well, in 1907 Mayor Lane's challenge was taken up by local leaders and a Carnival and Fiesta were held on June 20-21. Then came 1908.

On June 1st, promptly at noon — the Victorians were

decorated horsedrawn floats, the parade boasted some 200 appropriately adorned automobiles — quite a collection considering they were still a novelty in 1908 —and was viewed by an estimated 90,000 persons.

Portland was a wealthy town and the promoters outdid themselves the next year. The floats gained national attention — Queen of the Nile, Fountain of Youth, Father Time, the Palace of Perfume and, of course, Queen of the Flowers. The crowd had grown to 150,000. The Portland Rose Festival had come of age.

Answer: Portland's Royal Rosarians, formed in 1912, marched on their first Rose Festival the next year.

Rose Festival: Rosaria's Royal Guard

June 12, 1984

Rosarian Prime Minister crowns Queen Dorothy Cole, 1950. Who is the 1985 Prime Minister? What international trips have Rosarians made recently? (Answers below cartoon.)

Rose Festival is upon us again. That time of year when Portland displays the epitomy of its "City of Roses" nickname. A time when our riverside metropolis undergoes an annual metamorphosis.

Exchanging its workaday garb for royal robes, the entire city becomes the realm of Rosaria ruled over by a court of regal young women. And everywhere that court convenes, it is accompanied by a royal guard of meticulous men in white whose history is almost as old as the festival itself.

Rosarian honor guard stands by while Sir Knight F.O. McCurdy escorts Princess Pat of Wilson during 1957 festival.

In fact, the organization we know so well, the Royal Rosarians, grew out of the event. During the 1911 festival, a delegation from Seattle invited Portland to be represented at their annual Golden Potlatch celebration that year.

The Portland Commercial Club, which later merged with the Chamber of Commerce, appointed a committee to represent the city. William J. Hoffman led a contingent which took a special train to Seattle, where they were entertained royally at the Potlatch.

With a promise to return in greater force the following year, on their trip home the Portlanders discussed the need for a hospitality group to represent the city. Over the next few weeks this embryonic idea grew into a full-blown plan to organize a uniformed marching organization of 100 business and professional men whose efforts would center around, but not be limited to, Rose Festival Week.

The first roster of members, published in 1913, was comprised of Portland's most civic-minded private citizens. It includes such names as premiere fashion merchant Charles F. Berg, publisher Henry Pittock, Rose Festival Association President George Hutchin, future governor Julius Meier, theater owner and future mayor George Baker and billboard baron George Kleiser.

The name "Royal Rosarians" was selected from the outset and white uniforms, allowing for minor updates over the decades, have always been the official attire. A band, fully outfitted in Rosarian garb, joined the members for their initial appearance in the 1913 parade.

In earlier years the festival might well have failed without the unflagging support of the Rosarians. They were integrally involved with organization as well as fund raising through the 1930s.

In 1917, when one of the original members, George L. Baker, began the first of his four terms as mayor, he made certain that the Rosarian-sponsored International Rose Test Garden became a reality, thus ensuring Portland's pre-eminent position as *the* City of Roses.

Over the years the core of Rosarian leaders has continued to come from prominent citizens who volunteer countless hours and travel to other cities at their own expense in the cause of Portland promotion.

But the focus of their efforts is on the city's premier event. Every year the flower-filled fantasy that transforms Portland into Rosaria is made more festive, more complete, more regal by the presence of the palace guard — the Royal Rosarians.

JACK, AS A NEW **ROSARIAN**, YOU ALREADY KNOW THAT YOU'LL BE A ROSE FESTIVAL ESCORT AND TRAVEL TO OTHER NORTHWEST CITIES.

I'M SURE YOU'RE ALSO AWARE THIS IS AT YOUR OWN EXPENSE. BUT ONE THING **MAY** NOT HAVE BEEN MENTIONED TO YOU.

THE **CLEANING** BILLS!

Klooster '85

Answers: Gary Ferlisi is the 1984-85 Rosarian Prime Minister. Rosarian delegations have gone to their sister cities Guadalajara and Sapporo.

Rose Festival: The Laurelhurst years

June 4, 1986

1924 Victoria, B.C., automobile float at Laurelhurst Park. What earlier sites hosted the coronation cermonies? (Answer below cartoon.)

For southeast residents, Laurelhurst Park can best be summed up in a Sunday stroll. Meandering down a peaceful pathway along grassy, tree-lined slopes beside a placid lake brings instant appreciation of this pastoral retreat in the midst of a hectic urban environment.

Even when that quiet weekend walk is interrupted by an occasional electronic intruder, the mind is in a more forgiving mood than on the transit mall. Laurelhurst Park is capable of creating that sort of scenario. That's probably why Rose Festival organizers first chose it as the Queen's coronation site in 1921.

1921 Rose Festival coronation at Laurelhurst Park.

' The park, laid out by the Ladd Estate Company in 1909 to complement their Laurelhurst residential development, offered a superb setting for Portland's most prominent public event in those early days — as long as it didn't rain. The Royal Rosarians proclaimed Miss Dorothy Metschan Queen of Rosaria that year under clear skies.

Queen Dorothy was presented with a golden key to the city and school children performed a Maypole dance. The 14th festival (there was none in 1918) was the first to have a knighting ceremony. It also saw the Rosarians establish their now famous Prime Ministers' Garden at City (now Washington) Park.

The 1922 festival was particularly distinguished by the efforts of Portland's Business and Professional Women's Club. The organization raised $1,200 through the sale of paper rosebuds at 25 cents apiece, which paid for a crown "worthy of Rosaria's Queen." An all-Oregon creation of 14-carat gold inlaid with 650 white sapphires and eight blood-red rubies, the crown is still used today.

For the second year Laurelhurst Park again was the setting as this dazzling, new headdress adorned its first queen — Miss Harriet Griffith (Mrs. Zina F. Wise).

Laurelhurst really earned its laurels in 1923, despite bad weather, as Queen Lucy Lee of Roosevelt High presided over a royal party that crossed the lake in gondolas. The queen and her court were honored with a 20-gun salute (only the U.S. president gets 21), and viewed a performance of "Taming of the Shrew" along with a crowd of 20,000.

The grandest and most unusual coronation pageant to grace the park came the following year. To honor the Business and Professional Women's Club for their crowning gift, the association chose one of their members from a photograph. Surrounded by secrecy, 28-year-old Edith Dailey, who managed the Portland Chamber of Commerce Building, was selected as the 1924 Rose Queen.

The dance performance by fairyland maidens.

Led down a rose-strewn path from the Laurelhurst Club, the queen-designate was unmasked before 35,000 subjects as she boarded her royal barge to cross the lake for the coronation ceremony. Elaborate entertainment ensued and later, Queen Edith was treated to an open-cockpit flight with Mr. Oakley Kelley, who had made the first non-stop, cross-country flight the previous year.

1931 marked the final festival coronation for Laurelhurst. The pageant had grown to unprecedented proportions and Multnomah (Civic) Stadium was selected as the park's successor, ending an elegant, 11-year era.

THIS MUST BE WHAT THEY **REALLY** MEAN BY A ROSE FESTIVAL FLOAT!

klooster '86

Answer: Stark Street Wharf (1914), Ladd's School (1915). South Park Blocks (1919, 1920) and Multnomah Field (1917).

Rose Festival: Students have a say

June 8, 1983

For more than 20 years, Rex Oregonus, "The King of Oregon," reigned over the Portland Rose Festival. He was, in fact, sole ruler until 1914, when the queen was elevated to regent status. From then until his last year of participation in the Festival, Rex was only a pretender, but he added a colorful presence, particularly in the person of gregarious florist Tommy Luke, who was the last to play the role from 1927 to 1929.

Deco splendor highlights the 1934 coronation in Multnomah (Civic) Stadium.

The queen had always been chosen in an arbitrary manner. Whether by whim or favor, there was no consistency to the selection process. As the event grew in prestige, one can imagine the escalation in political pressure tactics to achieve the appointment.

A stroke of diplomatic genius was accomplished in 1930 when the process was changed. It was decided to let the student body of each city high school elect a princess from among its own senior class. From this "court" a queen

would then be selected by a panel of judges.

And so it has worked ever since. The maneuverings among teen-age rivals have, no doubt, often been as intense as they were with the adults.

High schools have come, gone and changed names over the years. There are now ten. Next year, with the probable addition of Central Catholic, there will be 11. As few as eight and as many as 14 have taken part. Winner of the "Most Queens" Award through 1982 is Lincoln High with nine.

During my four years as a Grantonian we had two: Sharon Frey (1956) and Ruth Parrett (1958 — the 50th Anniversary). These were bright, attractive young women and, need I say, "popular."

Nothing has changed in 25 years. The Rose Festival Queen selection is like a mini-Miss America Pageant. In Portland it's certainly as important. To the winner and her school — much more meaningful.

Answers: 1922. Mr. Pennell's services were free. Displayed in U.S. National Bank Main Branch vault.

The Juniors: Rose Festival favorites

June 6, 1984

The Prime Minister bows to his Queen. How has the Junior Coronation changed over the years? What is each princess's commemorative? (Answers below cartoon.)

In 1918, one of only two years (the other being 1926) that the Rose Festival was not celebrated, the first Junior event — a parade with a couple dozen participants — was held in the Hollywood District.

From this modest beginning, Junior involvement became a growing part of each year's festival until, in 1936, elementary students made their first official debut as a court of 10 couples.

Each grade school chose a girl and boy to represent them in the 10 district competitions held at the magnificent movie houses of the day, like the Hollywood and the

One of the early still "unofficial" courts in 1933.

Bagdad. Unlike the Senior Court, where students had a say since 1930, at the elementary level teachers made the selections.

Boys were a part of Junior courts through 1966. That year the Rose Festival Association made the difficult decision to drop a 30-year tradition. With the rapidly changing attitudes of the late '60s, prepubescent males rebelled against proper behavior, dressing up and most certainly lipstick, all of which led to the demise of the princes.

In earlier times the demands on the little royal representatives were less overwhelming than today. Not only was their

wardrobe much simpler — the girls wore formals and the boys Rosarian outfits — but activities were fewer. Today, not including fittings and rehearsals, the Junior Court attends 48 events between April 29 and June 9.

These nine- and 10-year-olds are thrust into roles that require them to shake more hands, take more bows and say more "thank yous" than many people do in a lifetime. And her diminutive Highness, the Queen, must memorize a speech for every occasion.

First "get together" portrait of the 1957 court.

In past years one chaperone, assisted by Royal Rosarian escorts, was charged with the care of 20 princes and princesses. Today the official chaperone has the help of the Junior director and driver escorts, as well as the ever-present Rosarians, to look after the eight-girl court.

The Junior Parade is the largest children's event of its kind in America. No motorized floats are allowed and the Junior Court doesn't share the spotlight with the Seniors.

Their royal "big sisters" may get more press but that doesn't dim the ardor or enthusiasm of these delightful little ladies who, in an enduring and endearing tradition, proudly represent Rosaria.

Answers: Held at Civic Auditorium, it was larger and more elaborate. A rose bearing her name in Peninsula Park.

Rose Festival: The fleet makes it complete

May 30, 1984

Officers of the cruiser Helena welcome the 1955 Rose Festival court. What was the ship's big "clearance" problem? (Answer below cartoon)

Since the first Rose Festival in 1907, the river has played a part in our citywide celebration.

In 1913, a river parade highlighted the festival and the following year there was a water carnival. A river race was "viewed by thousands" in 1925 and regattas were held throughout the '20s and '30s.

"Destroyers here for the Rose Fiesta" in 1928 was the first major media mention of military vessels. Our own Battleship Oregon probably took part on numerous occasions prior to that year but naval records aren't available.

tours of vessels at the following year's festival.

Captain Webb spins several true tales about instances involving naval participation over the ensuing years. Here is one of the best:

Mayor Terry Schrunk was attending a reception in 1968 where he met a high-ranking Japanese officer. The mayor offhandedly remarked that Portland would welcome ships from the Nippon Navy at the upcoming Rose Festival.

Returning home, Schrunk neglected to mention his offer to Rose Festival officials. It wasn't until Pearl Harbor advised Portland that seven Japanese destroyers were enroute that

Battleship Oregon, 1925 (left); Cruiser Helena (center); and destroyer escorts next to Journal Building, 1955 (right)

During World War II the festival itself was limited and there was, understandably, no naval participation. After the war, ships unofficially attended the event on a fairly regular basis.

According to Retired Navy Captain Bob Webb, the 13th Naval District Commandant's representative to the festival for many years, the fleet visits were scheduled annually only after the USS Nautilus came to Portland.

In 1957, on its triumphant return from the first-ever voyage under the polar cap, the nuclear submarine created so much community interest and positive P.R. for the Navy that local officials struck upon the idea to plan organized

everyone realized the mayor's invitation had been taken seriously. A last minute scramble to reassign berths and arrange protocol would have made the State Department sit up and take notice.

In recent years the Canadians have become festival regulars. On occasion we've also hosted Australians, New Zealanders and Koreans as well as the Japanese.

Twenty-eight vessels in 1981 has been the largest contingent to date. Rose City hospitality, from darts at the Elephant and Castle to dinners at private homes, has made Portland a very popular port of call each June.

Answer: The radar mast was removed and Columbia dams were closed to lower the Willamette. It cleared the Steel Bridge by eight inches.

Queen Jan I: Royal reflections of 1954

June 10, 1987

Jan Markstaller Donnelly in 1985. She can quickly recite the names of her court members and their schools. What are they? (Answers below story?)

To be the ruler of a magical realm is the stuff of childhood fantasies. But each year in the Rose City that storybook world comes true for one special young lady. For Washington High School senior Jan Markstaller, that year was 1954.

Suddenly transformed into Queen Jan I, ruler of Rosaria, she and her court became the symbols of a special time in Portland. A time when the city is caught up in the spirit of self-celebration. That spirit was embodied in their charm and poise, their smiles and waves. It was the time of their lives.

"Our coronation was held in Multnomah (Civic) Stadium," Jan relates. "More than 20,000 people attended. The princesses arrived in 1954 Mercury convertibles preceeded by their school marching bands. Students had assembled in cheering sections and tried to outdo one another as each princess was escorted to the stage by her school's student body president."

Queen Jan I gets a hug from singer Johnny Ray at Fox Theater opening. August 1954.

At that time, the queen was told of her selection just before the official announcement. She was then put into a "one-size-fits-all" gown, draped with the royal robe, seated on a throne and slowly raised up through a hole in the stage floor by means of a hydraulic platform. The lights remained off until everyone was in place and then switched on accompanied by an immense roar of recognition.

"I was the first queen to wear the robe that is still used today," Jan recalls. "The old one was ruined by rain. I was also the first to have short hair. That caused some controversy. My teachers encouraged me to grow it out. Our principal really wanted me to win. He was a Royal Rosarian.

But I said to myself that this was the way I like to look and if they wanted me, they'd have to take me the way I was."

One of her most cherished memories came during the Grand Floral Parade. "I had worked as a fashion model at Charles F. Berg since my freshman year. When the queen's float reached the store on Broadway, there was a huge banner of congratulations and everyone was waving from the windows."

Other highlights included meeting the parade's grand marshall, Roy Rogers, who rode the route on Trigger; Gordon MacRae, who entertained at the stadium; composer David Rose and television personality Ed Sullivan.

A queen's duties don't end with the close of Rose Festival. "I went more places and met more important people after the festival than during it," she says. "After I started school at Oregon State, I can't count the number of times I received urgent requests to return to Portland and greet some movie star, politician or other bigwig." When Emperor Haile Selassie of Ethiopia came to town, he presented her with a gold coin bearing his profile.

Jan's farthest flung adventure took her to Fairbanks, AK for the North American Dog Sled Races that winter. "I was given a marvelous fur parka which I still have. And I needed it. It was c-c-cold." She stutters for emphasis. That kind of expressive aside reveals the warm, outgoing nature of this former queen.

After graduation from Brigham Young University, where she had transferred to major in fashion merchandising, Jan spent three years in Southern California as assistant fashion coordinator for the May Company. She then returned home to marry her college sweetheart Bob Donnelly, now a lumber industry executive.

The couple have lived in the same Glendoveer district home for 20 years. Assisted by Jan's mother, they have made an annual neighborhood tradition out of watching the Grand Floral Parade from the same spot. "I've never missed seeing a parade except for the one I was in," she says proudly.

She and her court have also created a tradition unprecedented in the history of the Festival. "We all live in the Portland area and get together at least once a year." Adding to her continued Rose Festival connection, Jan served as official chaperone to the Junior Court in 1985 and 1986.

Those two courts have become like an extension of the Donnelly family with Jan hosting two holiday gatherings for them last year and a pool party on tap during this Festival. Her own three children, three dogs, and one husband don't seem to mind. After all, it's in the cause of perpetuating the Royal Realm of Rosaria.

Answer: Princesses Donna of Cleveland, Elaine of Franklin, Joanne of Girls Poly, Thelma of Grant, Barbara of Jefferson, Maureen of Lincoln and Marilyn of Roosevelt.

Rose Festival: Racing for the roses

June 11, 1986

Monte Shelton in his '59 TR-3. How many times did he win the Rose Cup? Which company is the race's most stalwart sponsor? (Answers below cartoon.)

From the Rose Festival's earliest days, automobiles have been a part of it. In 1904, the Rose Fiesta, the festival's immediate predecessor, boasted four horseless carriages. More than 200 participated in the 1908 event.

An exciting first, the 1909 Portland Automobile Races highlighted the festival's third year. This four-part event, a series of auto races plus a motorcycle matchup over a 14.6 mile circuit in east Multnomah county, was held on the last day of the festival. There were 18 "A" entrants for the 102.2 mile, seven-lap test, including Auburn, Buick, Cadillac, Franklin, Locomobile, Stoddart-Dayton, Studebaker, and White.

Delta Park Raceway in the early 1960s The primitive pits.

A 10,000 seat grandstand set up at the start/finish line on Baseline Road (Stark Street) near 186th Avenue, was filled to capacity for this first-ever American Automobile Association sanctioned road race. The crowd viewed top professional driver Bert Dingley wheel his Chalmers-Detroit "40" around the course in one hour, 44 minutes and 18 seconds, winning with an average speed of 58 mph.

The success of the Portland race should have augered well for its continuance. Yet, auto racing did not again appear on the Rose Festival scene until 52 years later. Why? AAA priorities had shifted to all those ordinary citizens who were taking to the public roads. And racing interest was focusing on the oval track, where all the action could be seen. It wasn't until 1961 that Rose Festival racing was back on track—the West Delta Park track. Roads that once served the Vanport federal housing project were converted into a 2.4 mile sports car course. For 10 seasons the Rose Cup Races were run over slightly modified city strets. The Association officially assumed sponsorship in 1966 and introduced drag racing in 1969.

The following year, Sports Car Clubs of America (SCCA) sanctioned the Rose Cup for the first time and the Rose Festival underwrote $100,000 for track improvements. Continued public support allowed more renovations and additions to the facility. In 1975 an SCCA Trans-Am series was added to festival race events.

With construction of press and hospitality headquarters and paving of the paddock in 1977, the track was renamed Portland International Raceway. Rose City racing's greatest coup came seven years later when Championship Auto Racing Teams (CART) brought their Indy car series to P.I.R. Such a significant step could not have taken place without support from many people. But the efforts of two Portlanders were pivotal.

Bob Ames, president of First Interstate Bank, has been associated with local auto racing for 27 years, and was Rose Festival Association Rose Cup Chairman from 1969 to 1978. His successor as chairman, Bill Hildick, a 22-year racing enthusiast, is a Northwest account manager for Norton Company. Ames enlisted the support of business and political leaders and lined up $800,000 to bring P.I.R. up to international standards, while Hildick wooed CART officials.

The results of their labors will be roaring down the track at up to 200 mph this weekend for the third year in The Budweiser/G.I. Joe's 200—the Northwest's biggest sports event. The only thing that could best it would be a Super Bowl at the Kingdome.

THE STODDARD-DAYTON IS OVERTAKING THE POPE-HARTFORD. I KNEW THAT EXTRA HORSEPOWER WOULD PAY OFF!

HOW MUCH EXTRA?

TWO AND A HALF!

Klooster '86

Answers: Shelton won in 1972, '74 and '76. G.I. Joe's has been a primary Rose Cup sponsor since 1971.

Rose Festival: The 75th was a gem

June 15, 1983

Queen's Walk at the International Rose Test Garden features brass plaques with each Rose Festival queen's signature.

Why are 1908 through 1913 missing? (Answer below cartoon.)

A diamond anniversary occurs only once and deserves something special for its celebration. But what? Every year the Portland Rose Festival Association and scores of dedicated volunteers, without whom it couldn't happen, work 'round the clock to make each festival the best ever.

They knocked themselves out for the 75th. A non-stop schedule of blockbuster events—15 major and three times that many minor ones. Parades, races, amusements, tournaments, shows, concerts, contests, displays, open houses and ship tours. Even an Indian pow wow. And for the royal courts: breakfasts, luncheons, dinners, tours, ceremonies, appearances and photo sessions. What more could be packed into this ten-day period?

mond, imparting its incomparable sparkle to the occasion.

Kira Rembold, blond, bright and self-assured, set a new record by becoming Lincoln's "perfect 10th" Rose Festival queen. She and her talented, 3.5-GPA princesses are a classic court. The Junior Court was incurably cute, as usual. Queen Tricia Veit appears to have been born for the role. The Royal Rosarians looked particularly sharp and well-tailored, the floats especially spectacular and the Budweiser Clydesdales were an equine event all their own.

Even the "unofficial" events added luster. While a record 200,000 watched the 8th Annual Starlight Parade and Fun Run, Oregon's winegrowers were holding their most successful gala to date, the 3rd Annual Summerfest at the

Lincoln's Kira Rembold (3rd from rt.) exudes queenly radiance even before her selection at Civic Auditorium.

Yet, something more did happen. Something special. It was an attitude, a perception, a "one-time" state of mind that made this festival unique. There was Columbia Crossing. Occuring in the midst of princess announcements and pre-festival publicity, the one-time only, Oregon-Washington, over-the-bridge, road race struck an early spark to Portland's celebration spirit.

There were the striking "one-time", white-on-red banners emblazoning downtown with their special 75th Anniversary message. There was the anniversary symbol itself, the dia-

Marriott. On the last day of Rose Festival, the Elephant & Castle welcomed Canadian Naval Officers and Men to its 3rd Annual "Compete Against The Fleet" Dart Tournament.

As to the last crucial element, the elements, Old Man Sol shone bountifully the first six days of Rose Festival. Clouds and a bit of that famous Oregon liquid sunshine created a classic ending to the Diamond Jubilee of Portland's fantasy kingdom (or should that be queendom?), Rosaria, seventy-five years young.

Answer: Rex Oregonus, the self-decreed "King" of Rosaria, ruled over the festivals in those years.

The Rosarians: In full bloom at 75

June 3, 1987

The Royal Rosarian Band, 1913. How large was the organization originally? Who are the top three officers? (Answers below cartoon.)

Can you imagine the Rose City without a Rose Festival? Were it not for the efforts of the Royal Rosarians, Portland might not have its premier annual event today. Over the past 75 years, the splendid gentlemen in white have helped make the Festival go and grow.

In earlier years, Rosarians ran the entire show. During the Depression, they became the prime movers behind fund-raising spurred by introduction of lapel button drives in 1930. Even in years when no festivals were held (1918 and 1926) and the war years (1943 and '44) when activities were limited, the organization kept the momentum going and carried on their other role as the city's ambassadors of goodwill.

World's Fair. The Rosarians were there in full force for "Oregon Day" and other events.

The 220 Sir Knights, who comprise the general membership, plus 82 life members (25 years of service or more) including 28 Dukes of the Realm (past Prime Ministers) give countless hours, buy their own uniforms (consider the cleaning bills for all-white outfits) and pay their own way (often including wives) for the honor of representing Portland at events up and down the West Coast.

There are 37 standing committees and most members lend their talents to several at once. Advance planning and personal time management are musts. Not to mention the active cooperation of spouses. During Rose Festival Week,

First California visitation by Rosarians, Pasadena Tournament of Roses, Jan. 1, 1913.

It is evident that members have gone all out every year to create the Realm of Rosaria anew. Additional events they have instigated and orchestrated are too numerous to mention. But, highlights from their 25th and 50th anniversary years give an inkling of the breadth and depth of these contributions.

In 1937, the first Rose Sunday Service was held at Washington Park. It has become the "blessing of the Festival." The Rosarians were also in charge of the Grand Parade and the Queen's Dinner at the Benson Hotel. In addition to visitations throughout the Northwest, a contingent of the Royal Guard accompanied Queen Dorothy III to the opening of the Golden Gate Bridge.

Their 50th anniversary in 1962 was truly golden. It featured lighting of a golden rose, a golden marching banner and golden emblems worn by all members and distinguished visitors. The Rosarians working committee system was expanded to maximize participation by all Sir Knights. It was also the year of Seattle's highly successful "Century 21"

the Prime Minister attends some 49 individual events. Over the course of his year in office, he makes 16 out-of-city visitations and participates in 22 parades.

The Grand Floral Parade is the Rosarians's single most important involvement. Two members marshal each float. Another group coordinates pre-parade formation. The remainder march as a body in the parade, itself. For their Diamond Anniversary, the organization is entering its first-ever float—a giant, straw hat—34 feet long.

If you know a Rosarian personally, you are already aware of the pride he takes in being a part of this one-of-a-kind community service group. If you don't, talk to one during Rose Festival. You'll see the enthusiasm he exuded and the enjoyment he obviously gets from what he's doing. You'll also understand why, as former Prime Minister Jim Nielson puts it, "so long as there's a Rose Festival in Portland, there will be Rosarians." That statement may be even more valid the other way around.

Answers: 100 members. All had titles. Prime Minister, Lord High Chancelor and Secretary of State, elected each year. Eight other offices appointed.

Civil servants and civic services

Portland's current mayor, John Elwood "Bud" Clark, is the 49th occupant of the second floor office at 1220 S.W. Fifth Avenue. This grass-roots politician, neighborhood activist, publisher and highly successful saloon keeper has created more controversy than any mayor since Doc Harry Lane (1905-09).

Like Lane, Bud is a people's mayor. But the popular physician-turned-politician didn't come close to Clark in colorfulness. We must reach back to George L. Baker (1917-33), one of only two, four-term mayors (Terry Schrunk was the other), for a showman and headline grabber of equivalent cachet.

Doctors and lawyers, merchants and bankers, even a carpenter and a plumber have held the city's highest elective post. Many of them sat on the City Council for a spell to cut their political teeth. Without that prior experience, civic skeletons have had a habit of haunting the unwary. The Police Department has proved to be the biggest single source of City Hall headaches over the years.

Then, as now, the average citizen has never been that aware of internal police problems unless something scandalous surfaced. Protection of the general public has always held top priority. Rife with corruption and kickbacks during the 19th and early 20th Centuries, it has been a far better bureau in all respects since World War II.

The evolution of Portland's principal public services — police, fire, water and transportation — is chronicled in this chapter. The airports (yes, more than one), the freeway system and local mail service, are thrown in for good measure.

In the few years since these articles appeared, a myriad of changes have already taken place on the civic scene. The man who gave us MAX and squelched the Mount Hood Freeway, Neil Goldschmidt, is our governor. Fred "Pete" Peterson, our 43rd mayor who I interviewed in 1984, has passed away. Due to recent annexations, city population has broken 400,000 for the first time in 30 years. We had the driest fall on record in 1987 and should give thanks for the Water Bureau's foresight in building their back-up aquifers. Without them, we'd have been singing the Seattle Blues.

City Hall:
The 12-month mayors

February 8, 1984

Portland April 15, 1851
To the City Council of Portland.
Gentlemen
your Committee
appointed to draft by-laws for the governance
of the City Council respectfully beg leave to report the
following:

During Portland's early years, official documents were handwritten with one exception. What was it? When did the typewriter first come into use? (Answers below cartoon.)

With the granting of Portland's city charter on January 14, 1851, the attention of the town's voting populace turned to city government and the first mayoralty race.

Two hundred twenty-two voters turned out on April 5 to elect Hugh D. O'Bryant, a carpenter. The position of mayor, along with those of the city councilmen, was unpaid and the term of office was one year until 1869.

When the city was incorporated, it was in Washington County. Local powers quickly rectified that problem by creating Multnomah County in 1854 with its seat in Portland.

In addition to Ladd and the Failings, local businessmen who held the office included George Vaughn (1855) and J.M. Breck (1861). Law and politics being inextricably tied, attorneys W.H. Farrar (1862) and David Logan (1863) helped guide the city's early course.

Prominent jurist Aaron E. Wait, at one time Oregon's Chief Justice, was appointed in 1867 but declined six days later. As a result he is often omitted from the mayoral list. His term was filled by local physician J.A. Chapman, who served again from 1875 to 1877.

Left to right: Hugh D. O'Bryant (1st mayor), Josiah Failing (4th), William S. Ladd (5th & 9th), Henry Failing (16th, 17th & 25th), Dr. J.A. Chapman (21st & 30th)

That year the mayor was 28-year-old William S. Ladd, destined to become one of (if not the) wealthiest men the city has ever produced. He was elected again in 1857. Henry Failing, who also amassed a substantial fortune, held the office three times, in 1864, at the age of 30, again the following year and then for a two-year term from 1873 to 1875.

Henry's father, merchant Josiah Failing, was the city's fourth mayor (1853). By that year, local governmental activities had grown to the point where it was necessary to rent rooms on First Ave. between Alder and Morrison for 10 dollars per month—our first City Hall of sorts.

By 1869, when the one-year terms ended, Portland's population had increased tenfold from just under 900 to nearly 9,000. And its worth, both in terms of trade and property values, had multiplied much more.

Most notable in the arena of public progress were the city-franchised gas works in 1859, the establishment in 1864 of a public reading room (the predecessor of the library) and the opening of the first public high school in 1869.

On December 1st of that year the City Council initiated a building fund to erect a City Hall.

Answers: Tax notices were on printed forms. The first commercial typewriter was introduced by Remington in 1874.

City Hall: The political Victorians

Ex-mayor David P. Thompson gave his handsome Elk Fountain to the city in 1900. What is its next-door neighbor and when was it erected? (Answer below cartoon)

February 29, 1984

The City of Roses entered its elegant Victorian era later than the East Coast but with no less style. Portland's version of "doing all the best things so conservatively" included Italianate mansions, butlers, bustles and buggies prancing along the Park blocks.

By 1869 the demands of operating a growing, and certainly civilized, city called for a greater commitment on the part of its mayor. Two-year terms were adopted that year and hardware wholesaler Bernard Goldsmith was the first to hold office under a system that was to last 44 years.

and primarily served those interests for the next three years—1888 to 1891.

The first mayor to occupy our present City Hall was local groceryman William S. Mason. In marked contrast to most of his predecessors, Mason was a servant of the people who steadfastly separated public from private life. As a result, four years after completing his first term (1891-94), he was elected again and did an "official" housecleaning.

Mason's terms wrapped around those of businessman George Frank (no relation to M&F) and 65-year-old former

D.P. Thompson (1879-82), V.B. De Lashmutt (1888-91), W.S. Mason (1891-94 and 1898-99 died) and Sylvester Pennoyer (1896-98).

That pillar of Portland's establishment, philanthropic Henry Failing, took the top spot again from 1873 to 1875 and was followed by businessman/investor W.S. Newbury. We owe the Main Street Elk to Newbury's successor, prominent financier David P. Thompson.

In 1882 Dr. J.A. Chapman took the reins once again for his third term, having been mayor in 1867 and 1875-77. His successor, John Gates, died in office. He was a Portland pioneer of 1850 who revolutionized Oregon riverboating.

Banker Van Buren DeLashmutt was appointed to fill Gates' term. Van was the establishment's chief executive

governor Sylvester Pennoyer, who Judge Matthew Deady disparagingly called "Sylpester Annoyer."

Entering the Twentieth Century, the tightly controlled party system installed banker and railroad executive Henry S. Rowe in the office. But the traditional political heirarchy was on the wane.

Portland had grown from a frontier town into the third wealthiest city per capita in the world, boasting two dozen millionaires. In 1870 it had one-tenth of the state's population—8,293 vs. 90,923. By 1900 it had burgeoned to nearly one-fourth—90,426 vs. 413,536.

Answer: A monument placed in 1904, in honor of the Oregon Volunteers who died in the Spanish-American War.

City Hall: The municipal mansion

March 7, 1984

The Northwest corner of S.W. 2nd and Ash. What role did this building play in city government? (Answer below cartoon.)

Since 1854 the city had rented offices and meeting rooms. The longest duration in one location appears to be the "Council Building" at the N.E. corner of 3rd and Washington, where the City Directory lists "City Offices" in its 1885 through 1891 editions.

In 1890, Portland's Common Council approved a $175,000 bond issue to purchase the downtown block bounded by Madison, Jefferson, 4th and 5th, then occupied by St. Helen's Hall, for their first permanent home. They hired local architect Henry Hefty to design the new City Hall.

Hefty immodestly proclaimed that his edifice would be "of modern American style — substantial, towering, majestic and spacious" — all for just $500,000. What he

The financial burdens incurred to aid the city's new Eastside additions caused construction to be halted.

As with the Portland Hotel a few years prior, City Hall's foundation lay fallow, drawing public scorn. As with the hotel, city stalwarts, led by Ladd and Corbett, got things going again by backing a $500,000 bond issue.

Two young architects, William Whidden and Ion Lewis, who had directed completion of the Portland Hotel, were asked to propose a new City Hall design. The Italian Renaissance revival building they created was a very early example of steel-frame construction — the latest in engineering innovation — where the walls carry no floor or roof loads.

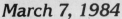

Henry Hefty's "Kremlin" City Hall design and the Whidden & Lewis proposal, with tower, flank the city seal.

came up with was a magnificent mess encompasssing five stories, five towers, gables, cornices, balconies, vestibules, domes, pillasters and elliptical arches.

Portland politicos went for this ponderous palace and work began on the foundation in 1891. The consolidation with East Portland and Albina in that year brought the project into perspective — price.

Already underway, the immensity of Hefty's scheme was estimated to end up costing double his initial indications.

Whidden and Lewis' City Hall was strictly for city administrative offices and council chambers, with fire and police facilities located elsewhere. When completed, detractors said it was too big and expensive. Just 30 years later they complained that it was too small and outdated.

Omitting the proposed 200-foot clock tower, this building is elegantly understated. Along with the Pioneer Courthouse, it is one of downtown's early architectural gems.

Answer: The City Offices were located on the second floor in 1892-93 just prior to completion of City Hall.

Early Portland: Law and order

October 3, 1984

S.W. 2nd and Oak.
When was it built?
When was it replaced?
(Answers below cartoon.)

Throughout the 19th Century, Portland's law enforcement was a direct reflection of its government — a pawn of private interests.

With incorporation of the city in 1851 came Ordinance #1 from the Common Council providing for "the appointment of a competent and discreet person to act as marshal." But no provision was made to pay him.

Instead the marshal's office was set up on a self-sustaining basis with income derived from fines and fees for services performed. By 1866 it had proved to be a very

was reappointed, his fortunes flowing with the political tide.

Although a questionable character, Lappeus was obviously politically connected. He and his entire 12-man force in 1872 were loyal Democrats. Appointed again in 1875, he was removed two years later for misconduct.

On June 18, 1874, Charles F. Schoppe became the first officer killed in the line of duty. Apparently stepping into a saloon squabble, Schoppe was unarmed. In fact, it was not until the early 1890s that the Police Commissioner made it mandatory for all uniformed officers to carry firearms.

The Portland Metropolitan Police Force was out in force for this 1882 group portrait.

profitable post. In addition to his peacekeeping duties, as city collector and public health officer, Marshal Henry Hoyt took home $4,421.

Deputies were appointed on a temporary basis without salaries. They too derived their incomes from "special" duties. The jail was the first public building erected. its deplorable condition was continually derided during the early decades. But very little was done to improve things since the city was usually short of funds.

In 1868, Marshal James Lappeus got two full-time salaried ($90 per month) deputies. A special ordinance of 1870 established the Metropolitan Police Force with Marshal Philip Sanders as its first chief. Two years later Lappeus

Gambling and liquor interests dominated enforcement policies through the 1880s and '90s. The police force was so politically partisan that the chief changed with every new mayor — 12 during those two decades.

In 1891, the merger of East Portland, Albina and Sellwood with Portland brought about a combined police force, boasting 84 officers by 1898. Despite the continued corruption, hunting down desperados, keeping the peace and protecting property, were effectively carried out (except in Chinatown). The selective maintenance of "law and order" benefited the power structure as well as the people. (Continued on page 64)

Answers: Completed in 1872. Torn down in 1912 to be replaced by the now unoccupied Police Bureau building completed in 1913.

Portland's Fire Department: The Volunteer Era

February 20, 1985

Multnomah Engine Co. No. 2 in 1866. What was the pole's purpose? Where was Portland's first firehouse? (Answers below cartoon)

In its earliest days, Portland's fire department consisted of the town's entire population. If a fire broke out, every man, woman and child capable of helping formed a bucket brigade. This informal system held sway until late 1850 when T.J. Dryer, owner of the *Weekly Oregonian* and unabashed Portland promoter, clamored for a change.

Dryer had been advocating an organized group of firefighters since he started the village's first paper the year before. When the founding fathers were slow in responding, he got 37 volunteers together and formed Pioneer Fire Company No. 1. Donations put a hand pump at their disposal and the two elements made for the most effective fire extinguishing the town had seen to date.

Knowing that Territorial Governor George Abernethy would be traveling to New York in November 1855, the council requested that he act as their representative in obtaining the engine. The governor effectively executed his obligation and a spiffy, Smith's piano-box steam engine arrived in San Francisco the following July, having come 'round the Horn.

A reorganized department of two companies, Vigilance Hook & Ladder No. 1 and Willamette Engine Co. No. 1, pressed the new engine and the old hand pumper into service. Cisterns built under the street intersections, initially made of pitched timber and then of brick, ensured an ample supply of water. Many of them are still in existence today.

The "redshirts" of Multnomah No. 2, July 9, 1858 (left). Protection Engine Co. No. 4, 1868 (right).

For the men of Portland's first volunteer fire company, this was only the beginning. Their riverside hamlet was growing and a better way to protect its predominantly wooden buildings was needed. That way was with a steam fire engine. But such state-of-the-art machines were beyond the capabilities of contributions from the citizenry. So Pioneer 1 went public.

First, they became an arm of the newly incorporated city by offering their services which the Common Council eagerly accepted on May 6, 1851. Later that month the council voted in favor of a tax levy to purchase a steam engine for its department. At the rate of one-half of one percent on all taxable property, it took three years to raise the money.

Through the 1860s new equipment was added along with more volunteer companies. Belonging to them became a matter of civic pride and prestige and they did their job well. In honor of the department's 20th anniversary in 1871, a celebration was held at public expense. Not one major fire had occurred over that period.

Finally, tragedy struck. On December 22, 1872, a blaze swept through three important city blocks, destroying almost a half-million dollars in property. The council took up discussion of increasing fire protection at every meeting for the next six months. But, due to a depressed economy, nothing was done. Then came August 2, 1873.
(See Chapter 9: The Fire of '73.)

THERE'S GOTTA BE A BETTER WAY!

Klooster '85

Answers: It was a 155-foot-high fire signal pole. Willamette No. 1's engine house on Yamhill was completed in 1853 with materials and property all donated.

Portland Trolleys: The horse, of course

July 10, 1985

Willamette Bridge railway horsecars at the intersection of 5th and N streets in East Portland. What are these streets called today? (Answer below cartoon.)

By 1871, Portland was rapidly outgrowing its frontier fetters. With a population of 9,800, the town still relied almost entirely upon the river for trade, travel and communication. The greatest growth was on or near the waterfront.

Horsecars of the Willamette Bridge Railway CO. on N. St. in East Portland, circa 1888.

Stretching some two miles along the shoreline, stores and services, offices and hotels, wet-your-whistle stops and warehouses were accessible only by narrow, primarily dirt streets. Much of the year those streets were a mass of mud. Negotiating the wooden sidewalks was tedious and the only other means of mobility, the horse, was impractical for the average person to maintain.

The solution came in the form of the horsecar trolley line. The first of several such systems, the Portland Street Railway Company, was granted a 25-year franchise in September 1871 to operate a line on First Street.

Opposition to the line was encountered because it was backed by Ben Holladay, who had already won the enmity of Portland's establishment with his high-handed tactics and high-rolling lifestyle. But the need for public transportation prevailed and planning began.

It was a year before construction commenced on the two-mile-long, single-line track. Once underway, completion was rapid and, on December 7, 1872, the first car was drawn over the line.

Holladay's horsecar line remained the city's only streetcar system until 1883. By then the downtown area had expanded to the west, and Third Street was on the ascendancy. Two new horsecar companies were formed to serve the changing needs of a city now boasting more than 22,000 citizens.

The Transcontinental Street Railway Company began operation at the end of 1883 and expanded over the next several years to become the most extensive of the horsecar lines with 30 cars and 110 horses operating over 14 miles of track.

The system stretched from N.W. 23rd and Savier to S.W. 1st and Whitaker. The competition for Third Street rights was keen but with its influential backers, including Ladd and Corbett, Transcontinental got the exclusive.

Although the Multnomah Street Railway Company lost out in their bid for Third Street, they proceeded with development of a system extending along Washington and , First, Thirteenth and N.W. 16th to Savier. Ridership had been high for the horsecars from the first and, as the city grew, so did the demand for public transportation.

Completing the horsecar roster was the Willamette Bridge Railway Company, a subsidiary of the Pacific Bridge Company, which completed the first bridge across the Willamette in 1887. As East Portland's only transit system, it ran along Grand from Holladay to Division with an arm that reached to the west end of the new (Morrison) bridge.

The stage was set for the next steps in the development of the city's trolley system — steam, cable and consolidation. (Continued on page 60)

Answer: Fifth is Grand Avenue and N is S.E. Morrison. The Intersection's southwest corner is pictured.

Portland trolleys: Full steam ahead

July 17, 1985

A locomotive at Portsmouth Station. Where was this stopover point? Which company served it? (Answers below cartoon.)

The usefulness of Portland's original public transit system, the horsecars, was limited to the city's central core. With the extension of routes into the hilly areas and the need for suburban service, other motive power became mandatory.

In 1888 steam was selected for the Willamette Bridge Railway Company's new line which was built to serve the Sunnyside district out of S.E. Belmont and extended over Mt. Tabor two years later.

To overcome objections about steam locomotives chugging over city streets, the so-called "dummy" was devised. It was a shelf that made the motor look like a

Steam was never a factor in westside systems with the single exception of the short-lived City & West Portland Park Line (1890-99) built by promoters of real estate development in Hillsdale and Multnomah. But what was lacking in huff and puff was made up in pull — cable style.

In July 1887, a group of Portlanders traveled to the California "City by the Golden Gate" to negotiate a deal with the Pacific Cable Railway Company for exclusive rights to the cable concept in Multnomah County. The resulting Portland Cable Railway Company was no rival to San Francisco's elaborate cable car system but it did have one unforgettable feature.

The Portland Mt. Tabor & Eastern Rwys. Number One (and only) motor (left).   Cable car tramway up Chapman (18th) St.

passenger coach and muffled the noise.

While the westside systems went directly from horses to electricity, the eastside systems initially opted for steam. The Portland, Chicago and Mt. Scott R.R. combined with the Mount Tabor Street Railway to create a line that stretched to Lents. The Mt. Tabor Co. was responsible for the first Madison Street (Hawthorne) Bridge, completed in January 1891. This system and the Portland & Vancouver Railway Co. started out with steam.

By the mid-1890s both lines were electrified. But Willamette's St. Johns run, completed in 1890, didn't go electric until 1903 and the suburban systems to Gresham, Troutdale and Estacada chugged into the Twentieth Century awaiting eventual electrification as power became available.

A spectacular 1,040-foot-long wooden trestle rose more than 200 feet above Chapman Street (now 18th) to make the Portland Heights connection at S.W. 18th and Spring, Although completed in just two months, on December 4, 1887, it stood idle for more than two years due to financing problems and construction delays.

Finally, in February 1890, the cable began operation. But accidents plagued the line and, beset by financial woes, the owners sold to a San Francisco group in September 1894.

Portland was not destined to have little cable cars for the decision to convert the line to electric power was expedited within two years, heralding the inevitable for the city's entire trolley system. Unification of a jumble of independent street railway companies would provide the catalyst. (Continued on page 66)

Answers: Lombard and Portsmouth on the Willamette Bridge Railway Company's St. Johns steam (1890-1903) line.

Portland water: Bull Run's Beginning

January 28, 1987

The Palatine Hill Pumping Station, 1884. What is all that remains of it today? (Answer below cartoon.)

Whenever and wherever a site is selected for a permanent settlement, water is a primary consideration. Portland's founders hardly gave it a second thought. The availability of water in profuse abundance appeared to go with the territory. But, pure, unpolluted drinking water became a concern more quickly than anyone had imagined.

During its early years, the little riverside village was able to ob;tain good water from wells. As the town expanded, however, groundwater became contaminated and a better source of the essential liquid had to be sought. No provisions were made in the city's 1851 charter for supplying water to its citizens. It was left to the private sector to fill this need.

1919 view of Portland Water Company reservoir, S.W. Broadway and Lincoln. Built 1871, abandoned 1895.

Early townsite promoter Stephen Coffin joined with Finice Caruthers, who owned the adjacent land claim on the south, to form the Pioneer Water Works. Securing approval from the Common Council in 1856, they laid a pipeline of fir logs from Caruthers Creek to Portland's central district. The logs were drilled through the center with holes two and one-half inces in diameter and connected by metal sleeves.

Three years later Coffin and Caruthers sold the company to Robert Pentland who installed a steam pump at the foot of Mill Street to supplement the system with Willamette River water. In 1862, financial reverses forced Pentland to sell out. new owners H.C. Leonard and Henry Green had established thw town's first utility, the Portland Gas Light Company, in 1859.

Leonard and Green undertook an extensive improvement and expansion program for their renamed Portland Water Company. They replaced the station at the foot of Market and constructed a storage reservoir at Fourth and Market, which Portland had originally planned. To serve the previously excluded areas above Fourth Street, they tapped Balch Creek near what is now Macleay Park and built another reservoir at Alder and Pacific (Southwest 15th Avenue).

Although these efforts did make a difference, demand continued to outstrip supply. Even the expansion of existing facilities, the addition of another pumping station at the foot of Lincoln and a new reservoir at Seventh (Broadway) and Lincoln were not enough. As early as 1871, the city's Fire and Water Committee studied the feasibility of funding a municipal water works.

In the 19th century, approval of the State Legislature was required before any oregon city could incur bonded indebtedness. Despite vigorous lobbying by Portland interests, it was not forthcoming. In 1883, the privately owned water company embarked on the last and most monumental project in its 25-year struggle to play catch up.

An imposing, two-story, brick structure, delivering 10 gallons a day, began operation in 1884 on the Willamette's west shore, four miles upstream from Portland. Unfortunately, the Palatine Hill Pumping Station was no panacea. Dissatisfaction with river water quality came almost immediately following the plant's completion. Pressure in Salem intensified and, at last, the legislators relented. In November 1885, Portland's newly created Water Committe, comprised of 15 prominent citizens, was empowered to act on a publicly owned water system.

Paramount on the blue-ribbon committee's agenda was supply — a copious and continuous source of pure water that could be relied upon to serve the great metropolis these local leaders were in the process of building. Their attention swiftly turned to the snow-laden peak on the eastern horizon and a deep, blue lake — Bull Run. (Continued on page 67)

Answer: Directly across the Willamette from the Waverley Country Club is a fragment of the station's once grand façade.

City Hall: Lane vs. the old-timers

March 14, 1984

George H. Williams was Oregon's most well-known citizen nationally at the turn of the century. What was his "Watergate"? (Answer below cartoon)

The election of 79-year-old George Williams as Portland's mayor in 1902 was a crippling blow to the political machine Joseph Simon had built up in Oregon over the previous 20 years.

Simon was the state's senior U.S. Senator. Williams had been a senator from 1865 to 1871 and attorney general in

guard Republican establishment.

The people bought honest Doc Lane, who fought for the public interest as no mayor had ever done before. Despite his unceasing efforts, the city's first "Eastside" mayor was often thwarted by an antagonistic City Council and a corrupt police department. It seems everyone was getting a rakeoff

Dr. Harry Lane enroute to the ballgame in Julius Meier's 1907 Thomas Flyer. Joseph Simon in his law office.

President Grant's Cabinet. Both men were prominent Portland attorneys. Although Williams and Simon were bitter political opponents, their values were identical — personal power. Against this setting of self-interest an entirely new contender came on the scene.

In the spring of 1905 the divided Republicans put up the 82-year-old Williams for reelection. To oppose him the Democrats nominated Dr. Harry Lane, a 50-year-old Portland physician and grandson of General Joseph Lane, first territorial governor of Oregon.

Williams had paid lipservice to keeping Portland's undesirable elements under control. Lane stated in no uncertain terms that, if elected, he intended to "close this wide-open city." The *Oregon Daily Journal*, established just three years earlier by Charles S. Jackson, supported Lane. The *Oregonian* stood behind Williams and the old-

from gambling and prostitution in one way or another.

Upon leaving office in 1909, Harry Lane could count few clear victories but he had changed the face of city government. The last gasp of the old guard came on the heels of Harry's departure as elder statesman Joe Simon brought a final two years of Westside establishment rule to city hall.

Simon's successor, councilman and plumbing contractor A.G. Rushlight, was the last two-year mayor under the old 15-member council/ward system. During his administration, the strongest anti-vice campaign in the city's history was carried out.

In 1912, Dr. Lane was elected to the U.S. Senate and served with independent distinction until death cut short his term in 1917.

WHAT THE DEVIL IS THE MAYOR UP TO?

HE REALLY **WANTS** TO CLOSE THE BROTHELS AND GAMBLING HALLS!

BUT DOESN'T HE KNOW WE **OWN** THE BUILDINGS THEY'RE IN?

OBVIOUSLY DOC LANE HAS NO SYMPATHY FOR THE LANDLORD'S **BLIGHT**.. I MEAN... PLIGHT!

Klooster '84

Answer: Because of his questionable record as attorney general, he had to decline the nomination for chief justice.

City Hall: The commission system

May 2, 1984

H.R. (Harry Russell) Albee, Portland's first four-year mayor (1913-1917), was Commissioner of Public Safety. What is the so-called "weak mayor's" greatest single power? (Answer below cartoon.)

Round the Roses readers learned in *Lane vs. the old liners* (Mary. 14) that Dr. Harry Lane laid the groundwork for better city government as mayor (1905-09). He was followed by Joe Simon, head of the Republican machine for 30 years, whose two-year term gave the old guard its last gasp of local glory.

Simon's successor, A.G. Rushlight, joined with Governor Oswald West to wage war on sin in the Rose City. During Rushlight's administration, a reform movement gained momentum. At its heart was a fundamental change in city government.

underside was as clearly unnerved by this threat to their very existence and expressed it with all the strength they could muster.

In support of the mayor and the system, numerous editorials appeared. An excerpt from *The Oregon Journal*, Jan. 14, 1914, read, "When an ordinance is passed now everybody knows what's what. Nobody surmises wrongdoing among the higher-ups. Nobody has misgivings about graft." Albee survived the challenge with a resounding vote of confidence — 33,687 to 15,455.

In 1913 city departments and bureaus were actually called "commissions."

The ward system fostered self-interest and corrupted the City Council. Local groups put strong support behind the new commission form, introduced in Galveston, Texas and praised across the country for its honesty and efficiency.

On June 2, 1913, the male electorate voted in the commission system, H.R. Albee as mayor, four commissioners and a city auditor. The 46-year-old Albee was an experienced public servant having served three years on the City Council and four as state senator.

Within six months of adoption, the new system was under fire and Albee faced a recall movement. The community's

After 71 years the council/commission/committee of five elected administrators still survives. but is the answer to early 20th-Century problems responsive to late-20-Century needs?

If Portland had a strong mayor with veto powers and direct jurisdiction over all the city's departments, would there be more competition for the post? If council members were elected at large, would they be more closely in touch with a broad cross-section of public needs?

These are important questions to ponder as Portland prepares to meet the challenges of the difficult decades ahead.

Answer: The mayor is empowered to make and change bureau assignments among the commissioners.

Portland Police: The force wasn't with us

October 10, 1984

Portland's first mounted patrol was formed in 1891 and disbanded in the early 1940s. When was it reinstated? How many members comprise the current patrol? (Answers below).

Until the ealy 20th Century, the status of Portland's police department could be summed up in one word — corrupt.

Not that murderers and thieves were allowed to run rampant. Quite the contrary. Some very effective law enforcement efforts were carried out. However, the kickback crimes — liquor, gambling and prostitution — somehow slipped into low priority.

Between 1905 and 1910 the city's population doubled but the City Council did not see the necessity to increase the Metropolitan Police Force accordingly.

Ford police car on S.E. Belmont (left) St. Johns station complement in 1915 (right).

The first stirrings of change in the status quo came during Mayor A.G. Rushlight's administration. Defeating the reelection bid of grandiose old-guard politician Joseph Simon, Rushlight took office in 1911. As a city councilman, the eastside plumbing contractor had come to know all too well that some of Portland's most powerful men had a hand in local vice.

Not until Governor Oswald West declared that he was determined to clean up Portland did Rushlight back the effort, ordering police raids on downtown and north-end establishments. Prior to this only those places that refused to pay protection were closed down.

With the advent of the new commission system in 1913, a study of conditions in city departments was undertaken. A New York Bureau of Municipal Research report found that Portland's police department was "poorly organized and inefficient. Records were faulty and information nonexistent."

The force was renamed that year, becoming the Bureau of Police under the department of Public Safety. And it moved into a brand-new four-story headquarters building and jail which replaced the old three-story structure at SW 2nd and Oak.

Flamboyant theater owner George L. Baker began the first of his four terms as mayor in 1917. Two years later he appointed Leon Jenkins as chief of police. Jenkins proved to be the most durable leader in the bureau's history, serving until 1933 and then again from 1946 to 1948.

Jenkins and Baker saw the city through the Prohibition era together. The undermanned force, averaging 375 through the 1920s, chalked up an admirable arrest record enforcing prohibition, then bootlegged the booze from the bureau's basement.

Neither the mayor nor the chief were ever directly implicated in these illicit activities. But their passive posture was testimony to the pervasive corruption that continued to plague Portland's police. (Concluded on Pg. 71.)

Answer: Reinstated in 1973, the mounted patrol presently has 14 members with expansion planned.

Portland's Fire Dept.: Paid protection

March 13, 1984

The Union Oil Company fire of June 26, 1911. Who was killed in this explosion-filled oil-tank inferno? (Answer below cartoon.)

The shock of 1873's disastrous fire forced Portland to take a hard look at its fire-fighting capabilities. The volunteer companies had served the city well for more than 20 years, but continued growth necessitated change.

A centrally located bell rallied the volunteers but a bigger town needed a bigger bell. In October 1873, the Common Council authorized the Committee on Fire and Water to purchase a new alarm bell "not less than 4,000 nor more than 4,500 pounds weight."

The equine addition to the department harkened its most nostalgic era. Tales of heroic horseflesh filled the station houses. The faithful service of Mack, Eagle, Prince and Bismarck, the devotion of Roachy and Blind Dick, the speed and intelligence of Colonel, who apparently understood the alarms, all were a part of local lore.

In 1909, the first department automobile, a ponderous, impressive Pierce-Arrow, was purchased for Fire Chief Campbell. With each alarm he sped to the scene to size up

Team surges from station house circa 1900 (left). Earliest motorized apparatus, 1912 (right).

Almost as soon as the city had forked over the funds—$2,200—for the gargantuan gonger, it was out of date. The latest in alarm systems, an electric telegraph, was on the market. Its superiority was so obvious that the council contracted for installation in February 1875 at a cost of $7,500.

By 1880, a dozen signal boxes, strategically situated around town, were connected to four engine houses. Paradoxically, the department was electrified before it was horsedrawn and, as Portland's population hit 21,500, still all volunteer.

Finally, in 1882, the council concluded that it was no longer realistic for firemen to serve without pay. The following year salaries were approved by a vote of the people, along with horses to pull the apparatus so the new city employees wouldn't be exhausted when they got to the fire.

the situation. It wasn't long before the efficiency of motorization became self-evident. By 1911, the last horse, gallant Jerry, with 21 years service, was retired.

Like the police, Portland's fire department did not escape the political machine's maneuverings of the late 19th and early 20th centuries. But inept blaze battlers were less tolerated by the public than corrupt cops. Low paid part-timers were eliminated in 1904. A fireboat, the George H. Williams, was put into service that same year.

With hiring and firing no longer at the whim of party bosses, the department entered a progressive new period. In 1905 the city spent $182,120 for its fire protection, almost double that of just two years prior. It was the year of the Lewis & Clark Expoosition and Portland would soon experience unprecedented growth, stretching the department to its limits.

Answer: Chief Engineer (Fire Chief) David Campbell, a reform advocate and 29-year veteran called "Our Dave," was trapped inside.

Portland Trolleys: a consolidated system

July 24, 1985

Last of the red & cream streetcar fleet at W. Burnside and 19th, late 1940s. When will trolleys once again run in Portland? (Answers below cartoon).

For the long-range development of Portland public transit, electricity was the ultimate goal. Horsecars and steam engines were merely interim measures. Mind you, these were the 1890s, not the 1980s. So, how much have we progressed in those 90-odd years?

The Willamette Bridge Railway Company led the way in electrification *and* consolidation. By 1891 it had put together the largest all-electric system in the West with 17 cars and 12 miles of track.

The earliest electrics of the Transcontinental Street Railway Co. at S.W. Third and Morrison, 1898.

That September the company and its affiliates, the Transcontinental Street Railway, which was the westside's largest line, and the Waverly-Woodstock Motor Line serving southeast Portland, merged to form a new local leviathan, the City & Suburban Railway Company.

This consolidated system lost little time in expanding. The greatest obstacle was availability of rolling stock. With transit mania sweeping the country, out-of-state sources were less reliable than local ones. Cars manufactured in Portland comprised a substanital portion of the fleet and splicing old horsecars was standard practice.

Most prominent among other operations was the Portland Consolidiated Street Railway Company created by eastern entrepreneur George B. Markle, Jr. In May 1892, he maneuvered a million-dollar merger among the Multnomah Street Railway Co.,

the Metropolitan Railway Co. and the Portland & Vancouver R.R. On this new system one could ride from Riverview Cemetery to North Vancouver.

But Markle was faced with standardizing three different gauge tracks at no small expense. These demands contributed to the demise of his overextended local empire and spawned a streetcar survivor. The Portland Railway Company, comprised of Eastern investors, revitalized the line over the next several years, making it the finest on the coast, In 1900, the then profitable venture was sold to a California group.

Despite the occasional collision and even a couple of fatal mishaps, the two systems continued their expansion and modernization programs. Finally, after several months of negotioation, a merger was effected on September 1, 1904, creating a unified all-city system, the Portland & Suburban Railway Co., considered to be one of the best in the country.

A public transportation monopoly was a valuable commodity and essential to that commodity was electric power. Small wonder then that, after considerable corporate conniving during the first years of the century, ownership ultimately went in 1906 to a new organization called the Portland Railway Light & Power Company.

A gaggle of suburban and rural railways operated with varying degrees of success into the early 1900s. Most noteworthy was the East Side Railway Co. which eventually became the Oregon Water Power & Railway Company. It had expanded its routes to Oregon City, Cazadero and Troutdale by 1908 when it became a part of the jointly owned Portland Railway Company. This merger was the final step in the consolidation of all Portland area lines.

The stellar status of Portland's streetcar system was at its zenith in 1912. Ascendancy of the automobile was already apparent and its effects steadily eroded ridership over the next decade. In 1924 a reorganized Portland Electric Power Company (PEPCO) set out to stem the tide of defection.

Rolling stock was completely updated in the early 1930s and a fleet of trolley buses was added in 1936. But these efforts proved unsuccessful in reversing the trend. The interurban freight operation was the entire system's only profitable entity.

Over a period of several years, PEPCO petitioned to drop passenger service. Though the object of tremendous public oppostion, westside trolleys ceased operation on February 20, 1950. And, even with their consistent ridership, the interurbans discontinued eastside passenger routes on January 25, 1958. The era of privately owned, public mass transportation was at an end.

Answer: When the Light Rail opens, Brill cars purchased in Portugal by Bill Naito will run between Old Town and Lloyd Center.

Portland water: Building Bull Run

February 4, 1987

Reservoir No. 3 in City (Washington) Park, completed 1895. What makes it different from the other three Bull Run reservoirs? (Answers below cartoon).

Ten years, one month and seven days after the newly formed Portland Water Committee first met, Bull Run's bounty began to flow. During that decade, the rapidly growing city endured an inadequate and often tainted supply of the irreplacable liquid.

Prominent banker and civic leader Henry Failing put down the gavel for that inital committee session on Nov. 25, 1885. As chairman of the 15-man group, Failing joined with other local luminaries such as Henry W. Corbett, Frank Dekum, William S. Ladd, C.H. Lewis and Simeon Reed to address the complex logistics of this monumental project.

Installation of pipe brought by horse and wagon, 1893.

Heading the list was acquistion of the existing water works. It took a year of negotiations and an Oregon Supreme Court decision as to the committee's constitutional legitimacy; but, in the end, eminent domain and the public interest prevailed. Portland Water Company owners H.C. Leaonard and John Green sold out for $450,000 and the committee concentrated on its next critical hurdle — the source.

Pivotal in that process was Col. Isaac W. Smith. A Virginia native, Smith was a civil engineer and surveyor who had come to the Northwest after serving on the losing side in the Civil War. His record of accomplishments as a builder of railroad lines and the locks around Willamette Falls at Oregon City won the confidence of Water Committee members.

Col. Smith needed little time to determine that Bull Run Lake was far and away the most desirable of the several sources under consideration. Its water purity was unsurpassed and it could be brought to the city by gravity alone. Gaining access, both legal and physical, were the major obstacles remaining.

Securing the right-of-way and riparian (waterway) rights meant going from landowner to landowner along the route Smith had laid out as the result of a trek on foot through thick forest and tangled underbrush. Almost without exception, owners agreed for a few dollars each. The single stumbling block came from Charles Talbot and A.G. Cunningham, two railroad executives who had bought a large portion of the right-of-way in 1883 in anticipation of Bull Run's potential.

Legal maneuvers of the capitalistic kind finally led to a settlement in mid-1887 and the committee moved on to a confrontation with Governor Sylvester Pennoyer. Dubbed "Sylpester Annoyer" by *Oregonian* editor Harvey Scott, the governor objected to the Bull Run project primarily on the basis of partisan politics. Pennoyer was a Democrat in a Republican-dominated state. But he used the ruse of opposing tax-free bonds for construction.

Forging ahead, Failing and his fellow committee members decided to seek a much increased ($2.5 million) taxable bond issue. Pennoyer's objection was overcome and the 1891 Legislature approved issuance. Chief engineer Smith proceeded with his plans for the pipeline and Chairman Failing carried an equally important element all the way to Washington, D.C. Owing to ardent persuasion from Oregon's congressional delegation, on June 17, 1892, President Benjamin Harrison proclaimed the Bull Run watershed a national forest preserve.

In 1893, with access roads and headworks already in place, the arduous task of pipeline construction began. Despite seasonal stoppages, within two years the 35-mile system was complete. Four storage reservoirs, No. 1 and No. 2 at Mt. Tabor and No. 3 and No. 4 at City (Washington) Park, boasted a combined capacity of 66 million gallons.

On Jan. 2, 1895, Governor Pennoyer took the first ceremonial drink declaring derisively, "No body." But the governor's sour grapes could not dampen the spirit of the day. Bull Run was its own testimonial to a triumph of late-19th century technology.

(Cont. on Pg. 73.)

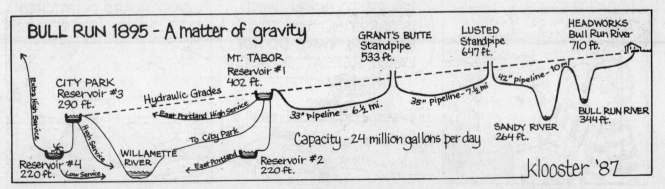

BULL RUN 1895 - A matter of gravity

HEADWORKS
Bull Run River
710 ft.

LUSTED
Standpipe
647 ft.

GRANT'S BUTTE
Standpipe
533 ft.

MT. TABOR
Reservoir #1
402 ft.

CITY PARK
Reservoir #3
290 ft.

Hydraulic Grades

East Portland High Service

Extra High Service

High Service

To City Park

Low Service

Reservoir #4
220 ft.

WILLAMETTE RIVER

East Portland

Reservoir #2
220 ft.

33" pipeline - 6½ mi.

35" pipeline - 7½ mi.

42" pipeline - 10 mi.

SANDY RIVER
264 ft.

BULL RUN RIVER
344 ft.

Capacity - 24 million gallons per day

klooster '87

Answer: Its water drove two hydraulic pumps (one of which still operates) delivering service to homes at higher elevations.

Portland airports: First were the fairways

March 21, 1983

The DC-3 spelled doom for Swan Island Airport. What severe problem did it encounter there? (Answer below cartoon).

Everyone knows that Portland has an airport. But how many of you know that we have had *two* airports? Glad to see so many long-time Portlanders who recall the Portland Columbia "Super" Airport in 1940 at N.E. 47th and Marine Drive.

Now, who knows that we've had *three* airports? Ah, a few waves of recollection for the old Swan Island Airport which operated between 1927 and the end of the 1930s. And, has anyone heard of Broomfield, a privately owned and operated sod strip which occupied the present day Westmoreland park property in the early 1920s?

Finally, what did Portland do to accommodate those magnificent flying machines before we had *any* airport? They used the golf courses. Fairways being better suited to tee shots than takeoffs, however, by the mid-'20s a bonafide public aerodrome was badly needed.

1927. "Lucky Lindy," in the full flush of his nonstop New York to Paris triumph, addressed a cheering crowd of 30,000 at Multnomah Stadium that afternoon. (See story pg. 196).

When the airport's striking deco terminal was completed in May, 1930, it was envisioned that this modern, conveniently located facility would serve Portland's needs for decades. Improvements totaling $1.3 million included filling, grading, runways and taxiways, landscaping, lights and equipment.

By 1931, four airlines, — West Coast, Pacific, Bennett Air Transport and Varney — were providing daily passenger, express and mail service out of Portland. Varney Airlines was the largest with 14 Boeing planes logging nearly 25,000 miles each week to Tacoma, Pasco, Spokane, Boise and Salt Lake City.

Although Swan Island was adequate for the early com-

Swan Island's deco air terminal dominated the field in the '30s.

In 1926 an empty spit of land skirting the Wilamette's eastern shore just north of downtown was selected. When the new Swan Island strip opened the next year, it had an incomparable introduction to the aviation age.

Colonel Charles Lindbergh, America's premier aviator and leading spokesman for the fledgling industry, flew his "Spirit of St. Louis" into the new airfield on September 14,

mercial craft, it could barely accommodate the "powerful" new twin-engine DC-3s introduced in the mid-1930s. Reluctantly, city fathers were forced to seek a new site.

Recently filled land behind the Columbia River levee was chosen and Swan Island abandoned. In 1942 it sprang to life once again, serving the war effort as a Kaiser shipyard. (Cont. on Pg. 74).

Answer: Crosswinds from the adjacent bluffs affected the "Gooney Bird" on land approach.

City Hall: 'Big George' Baker

May 16, 1983

Cordray's Theatre, where young George Baker got his show-biz start. Where was it located? (Answer below cartoon.)

For 16 eventful years, from America's entry into World War I in 1917 through the Roaring '20s, the crash and the beginning of FDR's first term in 1932, one man was *the* mayor of Portland.

That man was, by all accounts, the most colorful and popular person ever to hold the office. He was George L. Baker, affectionately called "Our George" by his

In 1898 the flambouyant showman was first elected to the City Council. Periodically in and out of office, he served 11 years. Using his theatrical flair and commissioner's credibility, George got the top city post in 1917.

A poster (left) for Baker's stock company also pushed his council candidacy. Mayor Baker and the council in 1919.

constituents and referred to with equal affection as "Big George" by the media.

George Baker was a native Oregonian born in The Dalles on August 23, 1868. His formal education ended at the age of nine when he left school to help support his family.

But humble beginnings did not deter young George. In those early days his burning ambition was to become an actor. He got as close as possible by taking a job tending animals for Cordray's Theatre.

From there his star rose rapidly. Within three years, Baker became assistant manager, then manager, of Heilig's Marquam Grand and subsequently owned two theaters. Although never himself a stage performer, the future mayor launched the Baker Stock Company in 1905, which, for more than a decade, brought big-name stars to town and was acclaimed for its repertory cast.

Over the course of the 16 ensuing years, "His Honor" exuded Portland positive if not Portland perfect. Kim MacColl in his *Growth of a City* points up the corrupting influences including questionable police conduct and condoned Ku Klux Klan activity while still according personal praise to the man.

Despite these shortcomings, George Baker remains undiminished. His infectious style made him not only "Our George" but also "The Kissing Mayor." At every official opportunity he planted a big juicy one on any worthy female within smooching distance.

During Mayor Baker's administration, the Public Auditorium was built, Bull Run Reservoir expanded, the waterfront reclaimed for public use, and Portland tourism promoted by a man who loved his city and knew that making news would help it grow.

Answer: Originally at the S.E. corner of 3rd and Yamhill (1890-96) it operated at Washington and Park through 1904.

City Hall: Carson to Riley (1933-1949)

June 20, 1984

Mayor Earl Riley poses at his desk. What did Carson and Riley do after leaving office? (Answer below cartoon.)

In January 1933, Joseph K. Carson, Jr. began the first of his two terms as mayor of Portland. Carson was 41 years old and had been practicing law locally for 16 years prior to his election. He was active in clubs and organizations, a WWI veteran and a well-regarded member of the social and legal establishment.

In 1938 both voted against a Housing Authority for Portland, which would have meant federal funds to build homes for low-income families. To Carson, Riley and their peers, this was tantamount to socialism. Anyone who supported such proposals was a radical, perhaps even a communist.

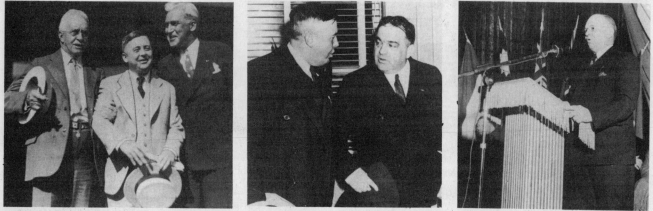

1933, Mayor Carson with Governors Cross of Connecticut and McAutt of Indiana (left). With New York Mayor LaGuardia (center). Riley giving war-effort speech, 1943 (right).

In January 1941, Earl R. Riley began the first of his two terms as mayor of Portland. Riley was 41 years old and had been a member of the City Council for 12 years prior to winning the mayor's race. He was actively involved in numerous local organizations and a well-regarded member of the social and political establishment.

Riley served as commissioner of finance during Carson's administration. They knew one another well and shared similar political viewpoints. For them the best interests of the community and the best interests of private enterprise were one and the same. They served the latter faithfully. In a nutshell, they were an integral part of the "old boy" system.

Only with wartime needs was the Housing Authority of Portland (HAP) finally established in order to develop the Vanport and Guild's Lake projects. After the war, when Washington urged that Vanport be retained as low-cost housing, Riley's administration argued for conversion to industrial use. The flood of '48 settled the question.

Paradoxically, they called forth every influence to assure federal money for Bonneville Dam, completed in 1937. Then, with equal fervor, fought off efforts to put the electrical power in public hands with a PUD (public utility district.)

To be sure, Portland's commitment to public interests has improved since those times. But how much, really?

WE'RE EARL AND JOE AND, YOU OUGHT TO KNOW, WE STAND FOR 16 YEARS OF STATUS QUO!

THROUGH THE GREAT DEPRESSION

PAST WORLD WAR TWO...

WE PAVED THE WAY FOR PORTLAND'S PRIVILEGED FEW!

Klooster '84

Answers: Carson was a captain in WWI and later U.S. Maritime Commissioner. Riley became a Packard auto dealer.

Portland police: Building the bureau

October 17, 1984

The police bureau's main transmitter in 1949. Who invented the device? How much did it initially cost? Where were receivers installed? (Answers below cartoon).

The history of Portland's police, related in *Round the Roses* the past two weeks, is a story of shortcomings. But as the city changed, so did the bureau.

Where once there was an unsalaried marshal with a couple of part-time deputies, a force of 375 men had evolved by the 1920s. In 1927 Portland was the first city in the U.S. to have 100 percent of its police officers complete a training course.

The nation's first police radio system was put into operation by the Portland bureau in 1932. The value of this instant communication became quickly evident.

leaders urged Commissioner Dorothy McCullough Lee to challenge incumbent Mayor Earl Riley.

Riley and his predecessor, Joe Carson, had maintained the status quo for 16 years, most of which time the bureau was under the stewardship of popular Chief Harry Niles whose tenure (1934-1946) was second only to that of Leon Jenkins (1919-33) and (1946-48).

Lee swept into office on the strength of her clean-up campaign and installed State Police Superintendent Charles Pray as the new chief of police. Even though the city's first woman mayor experienced a stormy adminis-

Traffic car with roof-mounted emergency equipment in 1940 (left). Roll call and inspection, early 1950s (right).

Retired veteran officer and police historian Ralph O'Hara reflected on the force in 1942, his first year, "We got $160 a month and it was obvious that corruption was widespread."

Kimbark MacColl notes in his *Growth of a City* that "the salaries of the top-bracket police official in San Francisco was practically double those of Portland . . . yet 55 percent of the (Portland) bureau was in the top intelligence bracket. Los Angeles . . . placed only 10 percent in the top group."

Continuing payoffs and the resulting proliferation of gambling and prostitution set the scene for change. In 1948, shocked by the revelations of a City Club report, local

tration, her efforts marked the turning point in the bureau's policies and practices.

In the late 1940s incoming officers received 24 classroom hours of training. Today, every cadet undergoes an intensive 16-week course, including rigorous physical conditioning, investigation techniques and knowledge of the law in the complex "post Miranda" legal environment.

The 1950s and '60s were a building period as the bureau was finally becoming better equipped, trained and paid. The members of today's 710-person force (including 70 women officers) are dedicated professionals whose jobs are more difficult and demanding than ever before.

Answer: Two Portland engineers put it into headquarters as a free experiment in 1932. Receivers took up most of the patrol car trunk space.

Portland's Fire Dept: The modern era

May 27, 1985

The Jay W. Stevens Emergency Car began operation in 1939. When was its predecessor put into service and for which Portland mayor was it named? (Answers below cartoon.)

The adoption of a civil service system in 1903 marked the turning point in the Portland fire department's transition from pioneer patronage to a professional public entity.

Over those 52 years firefighting had always been an honorable and respected, even an elite, calling. During the department's first 32 years, it was entirely volunteer and the companies were, in effect, civic service clubs like today's Lions, Kiwanis and Rotary.

Sportsman's Club fire, 4th & Morrison, 1949

With the change of city government structure to a commission system in 1913, the fire and police departments became bureaus under the Commissioner of Public Safety. Civil service had set salaries and physical standards. The new City Council set about the task of running the city like a business. And fire losses were bad for business.

While upgrading of equipment and training techniques continued to be emphasized, a new idea was given particular priority—fire prevention. In 1915 an unprecedented program was implemented with the appointment of Battalion Chief Jay W. Stevens as fire marshal to head up the new Fire Prevention Division.

Public awareness of fire hazards and safety precautions were promoted. Clean-up and fix-up campaigns were launched. Results were immediate. In the first year, fire losses dropped by a half-million dollars and false alarms were reduced by 85 percent.

Stevens soon moved on to manage the Pacific Coast Fire Underwriters Inspection Bureau, leaving a legacy of trained inspectors, a top-notch arson squad and well-developed inspection and community education programs to his successor, Edward Grenfell.

Not to be outdone, Fire Marshal Grenfell convinced the City Council to enact an individual liability law in 1918. This law put teeth in the enforcement of stricter codes, subjecting flagrant violators to stiff penalties.

Grenfell was also in the forefront of a campaign to remove hundreds of dilapidated buildings during the '20s. In 1928, his dedication was rewarded with elevation to chief engineer (Fire Chief), a post which he held for 30 years.

Despite the Depression, bureau programs expanded during the '30s. The war years posed serious problems with the influx of 75,000 wartime workers living in overcrowded conditions and a 50 percent reduction in trained personnel due to military inductions.

Following the war, Chief Grenfell initiated major revamping efforts, including the three platoon/60-hour work week. In 1957, new Chief Harold Simpson launched further modernization and consolidation, reducing the number of stations from 38 to 30, and districts from five to four.

Today, Chief Ken Owens commands a highly trained force of 888, operating from 39 stations in seven districts (including annexations) to protect 375,000 citizens and 115 square miles of property.

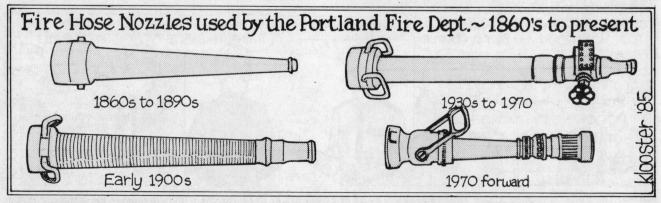

Fire Hose Nozzles used by the Portland Fire Dept. ~ 1860's to present

1860s to 1890s

1930s to 1970

Early 1900s

1970 forward

Klooster '85

Answers: The George L. Baker Emergency Car, a new 1933 Lincoln, was the fire bureau's first rescue vehicle.

Portland water: Bullish on Bull Run

February 11, 1987

Mt. Tabor Reservoir No. 6, Sept. 11, 1925. Why is No. 2 no longer in use? What happened to the original pipeline? (Answers below cartoon).

On Jan. 2, 1895, Bull Run water arrived in Portland. A 35-mile pipeline was in place (two-thirds of it over wilderness terrain); a four-reservoir, 66 million gallon storage system was operational and engineers were declaring Portland's water works one of America's great technological wonders.

The Portland Water Committee's 10-year odyssey to provide a public water supply was over. But it was only the beginning of the Bull Run story. The city was destined to double in size during the next 20 years and double again within another 40. Expansion projects spanning the first six decades of the 20th century would increase daily water delivery tenfold.

Mt. Tabor Reservoir No. 5, 1911.

Within months of the project's completion, another problem had to be overcome. Hillside instability and resultant landslides behind reservoirs No. 3 and No. 4 in City Park and subterranean water pockets beneath them took nearly 10 years to correct. This was the Water Committee's last major undertaking.

The 15-member group that had brought Bull Run to fruition was replaced by a five-man Water Board under a new city charter in 1903. First priority for the board was the battle to protect the watershed from encroachment. It was one step forward, two back in the struggle to hold the line against cavalier federal government policies.

In 1911, the first of several expansion projects was completed under the direction of Frank Dodge and David D. Clarke, who had taken over the superintendent and chief engineer posts, respectively, in 1897 following the death of Bull Run's "father" Col.

Isaac Smith. Conduit No. 2 which fed two new reservoirs, No. 5 and No. 6 at Mt. Tabor, added a capacity of 124 million gallons —almost twice the original storage.

When Portland adopted the commission form of local government in 1913, the Water Board became a bureau and, after an in-depth evaluation of municipal services, it was praised as the city's most efficient and corruption-free department. Superintendent Dodge died in 1914 and was replaced by Lawrence Kaiser who held the post for 33 years.

During Kaiser's administration, the Water Bureau entered its dam-building era. By the mid-1950s plans were underway for a major dam that would create a manmade lake in the watershed. But the specter of shortage demanded a stopgap measure. In 1917 a small dam was built at Bull Run Lake enlarging it to a 3 billion gallon reservoir. Kaiser then pressed forward with his longer range program.

A new headworks was ready in 1921 with a third conduit completed four years later. When Bull Run Dam No. 1, a 200-foot-high, 600-foot-long, state-of-the-art concrete structure, came on line in 1929, it boasted a 10 billion gallon reservoir (later called Lake Ben Morrow after the Chief Engineer responsible for its construction). Conduit No. 3 delivered its water at a rate of 75 million gallons per day (MGD).

By the mid-1950s, water needs of the city as well as tri-county areas that the Bureau had committed to serve, necessitated a third Bull Run blockbuster. Dam No. 2, creating a 7 billion gallon reservoir, took seven years from inception to dedication on May 1, 1962. The project had its problems — flood damage during construction, a strike, and a major design change from earth to rock fill. It even had bad water, temporarily, until an algae infestation was cleared up.

Following in the footsteps of its predecessors, today's Water Bureau continues to get top marks for system operation and quality control. Its latest addition, a 50-million-gallon, covered reservoir (one of four planned for the site) was completed in 1981 on Powell Butte. And a 100 MGD, groundwater (aquifer) complex will soon be available for backup.

Regarding the ongoing struggle to ensure the integrity of the source, that Bull Run story is still being written by bureaucrats, politicians and public advocates in Portland, Salem and Washington, D.C.

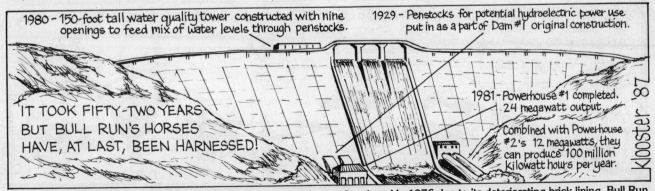

1980 - 150-foot tall water quality tower constructed with nine openings to feed mix of water levels through penstocks.

1929 - Penstocks for potential hydroelectric power use put in as a part of Dam #1 original construction.

IT TOOK FIFTY-TWO YEARS BUT BULL RUN'S HORSES HAVE, AT LAST, BEEN HARNESSED!

1981 - Powerhouse #1 completed. 24 megawatt output. Combined with Powerhouse #2's 12 megawatts, they can produce 100 million kilowatt hours per year.

Klooster '87

Answers: Completed in 1894, the 20 million gallon reservoir was abandoned in 1976 due to its deteriorating brick lining. Bull Run conduit No. 1 was cut off in 1952 when No. 4 was completed.

Portland airports: The Columbia 'Super'

April 4, 1984

This dramatic photo was taken at the "Super" on March 2, 1952. What was the occasion? (Answer below cartoon).

In the great American tradition of progress, the old makes way for the new and nowhere has this been more true than in aviation.

Portland's first airport, Swan Island, saw 14 years of duty, from 1927 to 1941, until it was phased out by the new Columbia "Super."

In 1936, the landfill site skirting Marine Drive behind the Columbia levee had been proposed and construction began the following year. The airfield was not fully operational until May, 1940, when the major runway, 8,800 feet long, received its surface of Gasco Roadbinder — a product of Portland Gas & Coke Co.

On October 14, 1940, Mayor Joseph Carson formally

craft until after the war when the lumbering DC-4, a made-over military transport, went into service. Planes were slower, stops far more frequent than today, but it was still the fastest way to go.

On May 30, 1948, the Vanport Flood inundated the entire field. At first, service was switched to Salem and then the airlines took over the Troutdale facility. It wasn't until October that they were able to occupy the "Super" once again.

Northwest, having added "Orient" to its name because of the Alaska-China service, began flights to Hawaii in 1948. By the early '50s, connections to anywhere in the U.S. were frequent.

Architects' renderings of the United building, the proposed Northwest facility and the only portion that was built.

dedicated Portland-Columbia Airport and the $200,000 United Airlines facility with passenger terminal, administrative offices, maintenance hangars and flight kitchen.

United and Northwest were the first major carriers to offer service out of the "Super," considered at the time to be one of the finest airports in the country. West Coast Airlines built an adjacent facility in the late '40s. Pan Am operated from United's building and Western from Northwest's.

The 21-passenger DC-3 was the principal commercial

The fast, four-engine, 65-passenger DC-6 and other luxury airships like Boeing's Stratocruiser and the Constellation were winging their way coast-to-coast and around the globe.

The popularity of air travel was growing faster than the most optimistic predictions. Portland-Columbia, renamed "International," was no longer held in high regard and a vast expansion program began which would bring Portland into the jet age. (Concluded on Pg. 81).

Answer: It was the 25th Anniversary of commercial aviation in Portland.

Early Portland: Tales of the mails

September 9, 1987

Main Post Office from North Park Blocks, ca. 1925. What was the most expensive 19th century mail delivery? (Answer below cartoon).

In Medieval Europe, mail service was the exclusive province of royalty and governments. Couriers in the pay of kings were the original letter carriers. When less lofty citizens got into the written communications habit, more plebeian methods of delivery had to be employed.

Public gathering places — inns, taverns and coffee houses — were designated as mail drops by the English. The American colonies adopted a similar practice. As early as 1639, a Boston tavern became the official royal repository for overseas mail. The doorstep service we take for granted was still more than a century and a half away.

Pioneer Post Office and Courthouse, ca. 1880.

With the redoubtable Benjamin Franklin as the American republic's first postmaster general, the foundation of an efficient postal system was laid. Franklin and his successors established regular postal routes, scheduled service between major cities and permanent post offices. But things were a bit different on the frontier.

Mail from the east took months to arrive in the Oregon Country by ship. Arrangements for pickup by intended recipients were informal at best. A relative could be long gone before word reached a Willamette Valley settler.

The Oregon Territory's first post office began operation at Astoria in 1847 with Oregon City following shortly after. That year also saw the introduction of another unique English innovation — the self-adhesive postage stamp. Portland had to wait two more years, until Nov. 8, 1849, for its first post office; Oregon's third.

Thomas Smith was appointed as the town's first postmaster. He set up office in a log cabin at the southwest corner of Front and Washington. For the next quarter of a century, patrons had to play the game of post office Portland-style, as in "where's the post office?" The place depended on the postmaster. During those 25 years, there were nine local postmasters and 13 different locations.

In 1875, Portland's postal hopscotch ended with the establishment of the post office at what today has proved to be one of the city' most durable and prized historic edifices. The Italianate revival building at Southwest Fifth between Morrison and Yamhill, now called the Pioneer Post Office, is, in the words of Oregon Historical Society Executive Director Thomas Vaughan, "the oldest and finest public building we have in the Pacific Northwest . . . a monument of the highest consequence."

Forty-one years of mail passed through its portals as the facilities of this combination post office, federal court and customs house struggled to stay apace with the rapidly growing needs of a burgeoning metropolis. Completion of the transcontinental rail connection in 1883 brought the latest in mail service — sorting enroute. When East Portland and Albina merged with Portland in 1891, their post offices became the first branches.

Residents of Eastern cities began hearing the postman knock as early as 1794. It wasn't until the late 1860s that Portland had grown up enough to merit home delivery. In 1896 Congress enacted rural free delivery and the Portland Post Office had the service on line within four years.

In 1916, when the new federal building was dedicated at Northwest Broadway between Glisan and Hoyt, Portland had 41 branch stations. Located across from Union Station, with loading docks and large sorting areas, the new main post office lent 20th century efficiency to handling an ever increasing volume of mail.

Today's modern facility, replete with the latest in automated equipment, opened in 1962 directly across the street from the "Old Main." This year it celebrates its 25th Anniversary and will expedite an estimated 1.7 billion individual pieces.

BY STAGE, BY RAIL, BY SHIP, THE MAILS INEVITABLY MADE THEIR WAY TO PORTLAND!

U.S. MAIL

THEN... CAN YOU TELL ME **WHERE** THE POST OFFICE IS LOCATED?

Klooster '87

Answer: The Pony Express initially charged $5.00 per letter. It operated for 15 months in 1860-61 and lost $200,000.

City Streets: By the names and numbers

September 16, 1987

The original 16-block Portland townsite plat. Why were the blocks so small and streets so narrow? (Answers below article.)

You're walking along the sidewalk next to (Multnomah) Civic Stadium and come to the corner. You look down momentarily and something unusual catches your eye. Embedded in the concrete curbing is the name "Chapman St." You look up at the street sign. It says "S.W. 18th Ave." You've just experienced a little piece of Portland history.

The same scenario is repeated in unexpected spots around the city where sometimes far more perplexing permutations occur curbside. Particularly on the East Side. It's one thing to note that a named street was changed to a numbered avenue and that, in the process, Chapman (he was an early Portland town-site promoter) has been erased from the map. It's quite another to unravel the complex chain of events that eventually led to Portland's current name and address system.

Eugene Snyder's 1979 book, "Portland Names and Neighborhoods: the Historic Origins," does just that and covers the evolution of districts, name origins, the ones that were lost and why. For all the details, I highly recommend it. If, however, you don't have time for the full treatment, this article traces the highlights.

Let's start at the beginning. The *very* beginning. Francis Pettygrove and Asa Lovejoy's original 1845 town-site plat. It had just 16 blocks, 200-feet square separated by 60-foot wide streets, and only three north-south streets — Front, First and Second. The nine east-west streets began at Washington and ended at Jefferson. All have retained their names to this day.

It is logical to assume that Pettygrove and Lovejoy were instrumental in this street-naming process and that they borrowed from a widely-used Eastern system for which Philadelphia was the prototype. Sequentially numbered streets intersect randomly named streets. Trees and presidents predominate along with "Main" and "Front" where a river is involved.

This system prevailed as the town grew with the notable exception of Captain John H. Couch's subdivision. It was in 1865, 20 years after he filed his claim, that the affluent sea captain-turned-merchant/banker decided to develop it. Then, being the precise mariner, he insisted that the street grid be laid out to coincide with True North. Since Portland's grid paralleled the river, the 21-degree angle in north-south streets at Ankeny, was the result.

At the time, Ankeny was dubbed simply "A" and Couch sequentially lettered all the other east-west streets in his plat earning it the nickname, "The Alphabet District."

The great consolidation of Portland, East Portland and Albina in 1891 not only created overnight a city of some 70,000 citizens encompassing 25 square miles, it also posed a dilemma in street names. Since tract developers selected their own, many as a dozen "A" "B" and "First" streets now existed in the "new" Portland

For several months, a Streets Committee tackled the task of overcoming this confusion. Eventually, a list of recommendations (based primarily on the Chicago plan) emerged. One name would follow one street across the city. The oldest name would be preserved. Base lines would divide the city into quadrants and buildings would be numbered out from the baselines. North-south streets would be called "avenues," east-west streets would be "streets" and diagonal highways would be designated as "roads." Lastly, 100 numbers would be allocated per block rather than the traditional 20.

The "avenues" and "100" numbers recommendations were both rejected along with certain name changes which would have eliminated streets such as "Hawthorne" and "Holladay." Couch's alphabet streets were given alphabetic names for local luminaries, his own being prominent among them.

On the West Side, compass designations were simple. There were none. But the East Side had to endure the most complicated aspects of the plan. South of Ankeny, all streets duplicated on the West Side carries "East" in front of them. All those north of Ankeny added "North" at the end as well. Where there was no duplication, there was no designation at all.

In 1910, a radical proposal to eradicate all names and create only numbered streets and avenues (Burnside becoming "Central" being the lone exception), was soundly rebuffed. The 100-numbers-per-block came up again but got buried in the public outcry against the "all numbers" plan.

Finally, in 1933, the current system was adopted. N.E., S.E., N.W. and S.W. quadrants plus North, named streets, numbered avenues and the new "100" address numbers. That's when Chapman Street became S.W. 18th Ave. and a legion of East Side names dropped by the wayside.

There were some special exceptions. Neighborhood fan clubs saved S.W. King St. and S.E. Peacock Ln. We still boast Barbur, Columbia, Hawthorne, Portland, Powell, Sandy, Terwilliger and Willamette Boulevards. Despite a primarily pragmatic bent, Portlanders have never been known for doing everything by the numbers.

Answer: Called "dollhouse" blocks by some architects and planners, the configuration maximized the corner lots that could be sold.

City Hall: Her Honor Dorothy McCullough Lee

August 29, 1984

Her honor in 1948 at a *New York Herald-Tribune* forum, where she was a speaker. Do you recognize the fellow on the far right? (Answer below cartoon.)

Portland's first woman mayor was a lifelong pioneer on many fronts. Her insistence on using both her maiden and married names became her trademark.

Born in Oakland, Calif., Dorothy McCullough earned her law degree at Berkeley in 1923 and was admitted to the California bar. Coming to Portland with her husband, Scott Lee, the following year, she set out to find a position with a local law firm.

five years, she was urged to run against incumbent Mayor Earl Riley in 1948.

Riley had maintained the status quo throughout his administration. The repercussions were a corrupt police force and proliferation of vice. Lee ran hard on a clean-up ticket and was swept into office.

During Lee's single term she fulfilled her campaign promises in spades. A new police chief was installed and a

(Lft) Pro-tem judge in 1940. (Ctr) the black community honors her support in 1952. (Rt) Convair named for McCullough Lee in 1949.

"They told me it couldn't be done," Lee said. "But I had come from San Francisco where it had been done." Rebuked by the established firms, she hung out her own shingle. After only two years in practice she launched a political career that spanned the next quarter of a century.

In 1928, "Dottie," one of only three women lawyers in the state, made her second try for the Oregon House of Representatives, becoming the first female to ever hold the office. After just two terms she successfully ran for the Senate, serving until 1940.

Lee's public career continued apace with her appointment as a pro-tem municipal court judge in Portland that year. In 1943 the City Council chose her to fill out the term of a disqualified commissioner. Making a mark over the next

new order quickly prevailed. Gambling, prostitution and the police bribes which bought their toleration were no more. The city should have been ecstatic.

However, Portland's new squeaky clean image, with an outspoken woman at the helm, was too much too soon for the conservative, male-dominated community. In her reelection bid Dottie was drubbed by Commissioner Fred Peterson.

Returning to private practice, her ex-honor was subsequently appointed to two federal boards. She taught at Warner Pacific and Portland State colleges. Dorothy McCullough Lee devoted her life to public service and led the way for other women in the political arena. When she passed away in 1981, her adopted hometown noted her accomplishments, but only in passing.

Answer: It's none other than Lyndon Baines Johnson, Democratic congressman from Texas. Next to him is James G. Fulton (R-Pennsylvania).

City Hall: Four years with Fred

January 16, 1985

The 88-year-old elder statesman of Portland politics. What key bond issues were passed during his administration? (Answers below cartoon.)

The chronicling of past events would be much more colorful if key participants could be interviewed. That opportunity, when it arises, cannot be passed by, particularly when the interview is with Portland's oldest living ex-mayor.

Fred L. "Pete" Peterson, our 40th mayor from 1953 to 1957, refers to himself as an "ex" rather than "former" mayor because he lost his reelection bid instead of declining to seek office again.

he won the first of three terms as a city commissioner.

In 1952 Peterson was encouraged by local businessmen and political leaders to challenge incumbent Mayor Dorothy McCullough Lee. Her community support having eroded, the city's first female mayor was defeated handily by the former pharmacist.

It is often said that everyone in Portland knows everyone else. As the city has grown so has the circle of power, but

Commissioner Peterson inspects 1949 Sunshine donations (left). Mayor Peterson attends opening of ex-Mayor Riley's Packard dealership, 1953 (right).

At 88 the elder statesman of Portland politics still remembers friends and opponents, relationships and events of almost a half-century ago with clarity and candor.

Prior to entering politics, Peterson was a pharmacist, having taken up his father's profession. He had moved to Portland from Minnesota in 1902 at the age of 6 and grew up in the Lents district.

As a student at the old Washington High School, Pete took an early interest in public affairs. He recalls debating the issue of private vs. public power, taking the side of the private sector which he advocates to this day.

By 1941 he had become a well-known civic leader, presiding over the Breakfast Club and maintaining an active involvement in the Rotary, Masons and Shriners. That year

during Peterson's 16-year public career, everyone who counted formed a close-knit, if not always compatible, nucleus.

Paradoxically, it was Peterson who had brought McCullough Lee into public life by backing her City Council appointment in 1943 to fill the term of disqualified Commissioner Ralph Clyde.

At the end of his first term, the popular mayor was ousted by the even more popular Sheriff Terry Schrunk. As Pete puts its, "Terry was unbeatable and the Democrats knew it." Even though the mayor's post is officially nonpartisan, in practice party politics always play a part. "And," he relates, "I was the one who taught Terry how to prepare a budget. That's gratitude for you."

A POLITICIAN HAS TO KEEP THE WORLD IN PERSPECTIVE!

WHEN YOU'RE IN OFFICE, EVERYONE IS TRYING TO COURT YOUR FAVOR!

BUT, IF YOU LOSE THE ELECTION, YOU GO BACK TO BEING A PHARMACIST!

PRESCRIPTIONS

Klooster '84

Answers: The Memorial Coliseum, OMSI and the public docks expansion project.

City Hall: Sheriff Schrunk takes charge

June 26, 1985

Schrunk's 1956 campaign poster. What was the significance of the slogan "End The Confusion"? (Answers below cartoon)

A 32-year-old naval lieutenant, who narrowly escaped death during an 18-month tour of duty in the Pacific, came home to St. Johns in mid-1945.

Carrying shrapnel in his back that would plague him the rest of his life, Terrence Doyle Schrunk was one of the fortunate WWII vets who had a job to return to—that of Portland fireman.

The Stayton farm boy, descendent of 1844 Oregon pioneers, had moved to the North Portland community in 1921 at eight years of age. He attended Roosevelt High and Columbia University (now University of Portland) where he played football, leaving in 1935 to join the fire department.

Portland Mayor Schrunk receives key to city from San Francisco Mayor George Christopher.

The necessity to quit college and go to work during the depths of the Depression did not deter young Terry from completing his education, however. Over the course of seven years, attending night and summer classes, he earned a B.A. degree in economics and political science from the University of Oregon.

Schrunk rose rapidly through the Portland Fire Bureau

ranks after his return. Over the next four years he attained the level of captain and the position of state firefighters' lobbyist during three legislative sessions. In October 1949 he was asked to handle a political hot potato and accepted the considerable challenge.

Multnomah County Sheriff Mike Elliott had just been ousted in a recall election and the Sheriff's Department was at an all-time low in morale and public esteem. Sheriff-appointee Schrunk knew the difficult task he would have to tackle. Taking immediate charge, he cleaned up the department, gaining high administrative marks in the process.

The 1950 election saw him sweep into office, defeating his opponent by the largest margin in Multnomah County history. Again, in 1954, he won overwhelmingly—three to one. And that victory prompted his candidacy against incumbent Mayor Fred Peterson two years later.

The sheriff's popularity made him, in Peterson's own words, "unbeatable by anyone in town" and, indeed, Schrunk won the 1956 contest handily. But he was not invulnerable and his second year in office was surrounded by scandal.

Accused of accepting a bribe from north-end gambling and night club interests while he was sheriff, the episode took Mayor Schrunk to Washington, D.C., for an appearance before the U.S. Senate's McClellan Committee on Teamsters racketeering.

Schrunk's career hung in the balance when a subsequent vice trial was convened in Portland. In June 1957, after exhaustive testimony, he was acquitted.

This draining experience would have devastated many but Schrunk seemed not to allow it to diminish him at all. With a clear track ahead, he began setting goals for his city—new directions designed to bring Portland greater exposure and status.

(Four-term Terry - Pg. 80)

MAYOR SCHRUNK, AFTER FIGHTING THE WAR, FIRES, AND CRIME, THIS JOB MUST SEEM **TAME!**

ARE YOU KIDDING? NOW I'M BATTLING THE MOST **FORMIDABLE** FOE I'VE EVER FACED!

WHO'S THAT?

THE **PRESS!**

Answer: It was a device to create the question, "Is there confusion and uncertainty in City Hall now?"

City Hall: Four-term Terry Schrunk

July 3, 1987

With Mrs. Hubert Humphrey Oct. 1967 What cutting criticisms were aimed at Mayor Schrunk? What did he consider his greatest failures? (Answers below cartoon.)

From March through June 1957, Mayor Terry D. Schrunk's job was on the line. Accused of accepting a bribe from north-end gambling interests while he was Multnomah County sheriff, Schrunk was subjected to a congressional inquiry and local indictment.

In office for less than a year, the former war hero, fire bureau captain and county sheriff had built up an excellent reputation in public service. Leaders of labor and business stood behind Schrunk. When he was acquitted, the headlines stated, "A man terribly wronged."

Vindicated, the mayor proceeded with his plans for the city which included building its prominence nationally and internationally. On the international front, Schrunk was a leader in fostering closer ties with Japan. In November 1959, he and his wife Virginia, headed a delegation to the Land of the Rising Sun.

Mayor Schrunk dedicating Memorial Coliseum, Sept. 1962

In 1960 Terry easily won a second term and his initial efforts were followed by Portland's playing host to the Japan-American Conference in 1961 and the 1963 Rose Festival appearance of Sapporo's Rose Queen. Schrunk was instrumental in the establishment of our sister city relationship with that Japanese city.

The opening of Memorial Coliseum in 1962 was another highlight of the mayor's second, four-year stretch. The groundwork for this important addition to the civic inventory dated back to the administration of his predecessor, Fred Peterson, and Schrunk made certain it came to fruition. Schrunk decided to seek a third term in 1964. The opposition was weak and the way seemed clear. So he went for it and won.

Pollution was a key problem to be addressed in the mid-'60s and Mayor Schrunk worked with Governor Tom McCall in setting stricter standards. Cleaner air and the resurrection of the Willamette were the results. Urban renewal also held a high priority. The South Portland revitalization we now point to with pride had its roots in this administration.

In 1968, despite recurring health problems, three-term Terry made the decision to try and duplicate Mayor George Baker's feat and run for a fourth. Times were good and he encountered only token opposition.

Terry's fourth term was punctuated by his election as president of the U.S. Conference of Mayors in 1969 and chairmanship of the Executive Committee of the Japanese-American Conference of Mayors and Chamber of Commerce Presidents.

The term also saw adoption of the Downtown Plan in 1970 and continuing deterioration of the mayor's health. In November and December of 1971, he had surgery and announced that he would not seek reelection. In April and again in October 1972, he suffered progressively worse heart attacks. His retirement dinner in December was attended by more than a thousand admirers.

Schrunk's advice on Portland's economic development continued to be sought after he left office. He became a member of the Chamber of Commerce board, serving until his death on March 4, 1975, at age 61.

MAYOR, THE COAST GUARD SAYS THERE'S AN ENTIRE **FLEET** OF JAPANESE SHIPS ON ITS WAY TO PARTICIPATE IN THE ROSE FESTIVAL!

TERRY D. SCHRUNK
MAYOR

DARNED CRASH COURSE IN CONVERSATIONAL JAPANESE. I THOUGHT FOR CERTAIN I TOLD THAT ADMIRAL TO COME **NEXT** YEAR!

Klooster '85

Answers: It was said he was dull and inarticulate. He was unable to achieve a city-county merger or elimination of the city commission system.

Portland airports:
The 'International'

April 18, 1983

Boeing's 707 was the first jet airliner. When was it introduced? What was its range and passenger capacity? (Answers below cartoon.)

In October, 1955, the Port of Portland formally announced plans for extensive expansion of the airport facilities along the south shore of the Columbia as a result of studies begun in 1946.

Acres of drainage and landfill were required for the 11,000-foot main runway which still serves today's largest aircraft. The modern terminal building was dedicated on August 24, 1958. Total outlay exceeded $9 million.

troversial aspect involved changing the main runway from an east-west to a north-south configuration.

This proposal, which meant filling a porton of the river to Government Island, saw such tremendous opposition from environmentalists, Vancouver residents and a congressional contingent headed by Senators Magnuson and Jackson of Washington, that it was abandoned in 1973.

Speculation persists that the Washingtonians plotted to

Special "bright" lighting at new terminal, June 1958.

Within five years, however, it was evident that the terminal could not accommodate increasing demands. The first commercial jet airliner, Boeing's sleek 707, had revolutionized air travel with vastly increased range and passenger load.

By the mid-60s Alaska, Northwest, Pacific Northern, Pan Am, United, West Coast, Western and General were serving almost one million passengers annually out of Portland International — double 10 years prior.

A master plan was developed by the Port of Portland to project and prepare for future needs. Their objective was to put meaning in the name "International."

The $78.1 million program undertaken in 1971 was the largest in the Port's then 80-year history. Its most con-

prevent Portland from becoming an important aviation center. But renovation of the existing field proved entirely satisfactory and expansion of the terminal, completed in 1977 at a cost of $17.7 million, nearly doubled its size.

"Airport closed due to fog" was an all-too-often announcement in the '60s. With the advent of sophisticated landing instruments this problem was minimized and the "International" came to earn its reputation as an ideal major metropolitan airport.

Current capacity is 5 million passengers annually. In 1983, 4,538,579 passed through its gates, beating the 1979 pre-recession record. The Port currently has plans on the drawing board to meet needs to the year 2000.

Answers: Pan Am's New York to Paris run, October, 1959. 4000-mile range. 219 passengers.

City Hall: The Goldschmidt legacy

October 29, 1986

Mayor Goldschmidt with Commissioner Mildred Schwab. What national honors did he earn while in office? (Answer below cartoon.)

Portland was ready for a new face at City Hall in 1972. During the last year of Mayor Terry Schrunk's four terms, traditional values nationwide were questioned as never before and in the forefront of the challenge was the younger generation.

City Commissioner Neil Goldschmidt, then 31, had been in the thick of this changing scene for almost eight years when he made his bid for the mayor's office. The Eugene native's political science diploma from the University of Oregon was less than a year old when he went to Mississippi (in 1964) at the height of the Civil Rights movement.

Goldschmidt with Japanese school children during Sapporo goodwill visit, 1974.

From there Neil went on to earn his law degree at the University of California's Boalt School of Law in Berkeley. Coming to Portland after graduation in 1967, the 27-year-old attorney worked in legal aid for the next two years. As a community activist, he gained grass roots support to run for the City Council in 1970.

Beating out incumbent Mark A. (Buck) Grayson, Goldschmidt played a visible role on the council. When Schrunk finally vacated the city's top post, Neil's youthful vigor and dynamic public presence made him a front-runner. Against seven opponents, he won with 57 percent of the vote in the primary.

At 32, Mayor Neil Goldschmidt was the youngest person to gain office since the city adopted the commission system in 1913. Only William S. Ladd, who became mayor in 1854 at 27, and Henry Failing, who was 29 when he began his first term in 1864, were younger.

During his first term, Goldschmidt's priorities were the budget, crime, jobs and public transportation. He was the primary force behind the Transit Mall, completed in 1978, and the principal opponent to the so-called Mount Hood Freeway.

Despite the young mayor's successes in holding the line on tax increases, instituting efficiencies in city government, attracting new businesses to the area and bringing about an across-the-board decrease in felony crimes, the transportation projects remain points of controversy to this day. But, with the perspective of a decade, his decisions on both the Transit Mall and the Mount Hood Freeway, would appear to be coming out on the positive side of the ledger.

Initial plans for the light-rail system were laid during the second Goldschmidt term. Of all his local efforts, this has been the most controversial and costly. Only now can we begin to evaluate the results. They don't seem nearly so dire as critics predicted. In fact, after another decade, we may consider MAX one of our most valuable public assets.

Action is bound to create controversy. Do nothing and there's not much people can say one way or another. The current statehouse occupant is case in point. But, the young man who sat in the second floor office at 1220 S.W. Fifth between 1973 and 1979 didn't let any cobwebs accumulate. The Crime Prevention Bureau, Neighborhood Watch and Victim's Assistance Programs were Neil's creations. Pioneer Courthouse Square and Waterfront Park owe their existence to his efforts.

In July 1979, President Carter tapped Goldschmidt as his secretary of transportation. With Neil's involvement on the local level, Jimmy must have felt he'd learned something about the subject. In 1981, he joined Nike, Inc. as vice president of the international division. Now, Neil Edward Goldschmidt wants to be governor of Oregon. If he is elected, there's one thing we can be assured of not having — inaction!

Answer: National Jaycees' 10 Outstanding Young Men In America, 1973. *Time Magazine's* "200 Faces of the Future," 1974, B'nai Brith Torch of Liberty Award, 1976.

The Interstate: Over the rivers

October 12, 1983

The twin Interstate Bridges, looking North to Vancouver. Which are the most and least traveled of our freeway system bridges? (Answers below cartoon.)

It was February 14, 1917, and Portlanders could now get to nearby Vancouver on the newly completed Interstate Bridge. Built at a cost of $1,750,000, it was a joint venture of Multnomah and Clark(e) counties. A huge celebration heralded the opening of the "engineering marvel of the Northwest."

The true wonder is how much further technology had advanced 65 years later in the design of the Glenn L. Jackson Memorial Bridge, an impressive work achieved for $175 million, exactly 100 times more than its early 20th century counterpart.

approved the Federal Highway Program. Despite the Interstate connection, counties were forced to foot the bill.

The Marquam Bridge created even more controversy. But public outcry and derision (trestle, erector set) was too late. The momentum of design approval, bids and funding earned Portland a $14-million double-deck overpass to link up I-5 in October 1966.

If the much-maligned Marquam was mistake-riddled, the Fremont made up for it. References to a bridge of that name at that location go back to 1931. With an unpleasant precedent to overcome, public pressure demanded design

A 1973 aerial view of the complete Interstate complex encircling downtown Portland.

The "second" Interstate bridge, a seven-million-dollar clone, was opened on July 1, 1958, and the original was promptly closed for reconstruction, including the addition of a hump which added clearance and made the two exact duplicates.

In 1960, when the work was complete, a controversial 25-cent toll was imposed. The only one on US99 between Canada and Mexico. This was a result of bad timing. Construction had begun only a few months before Congress

integrity and got it in the $82-million tied-arch beauty completed in late 1973.

People's Day on the Bridge, November 11, 1973, drew more than 20,000 to walk the sleek, soaring span — 175 feet above the river.

Because of these bridges, the Interstate encircles and circumvents River City, speeding our car-centered society to its many and varied destinations.

Answer: 24-hour two-way traffic counts: Interstate-89,750; Marquam-86,600; Fremont-63,000; Jackson-38,000.

The Portland Chamber: Business wise

November 26, 1986

Dickwin D. Armstrong, the Portland Chamber's first Executive Director at his introductory press conference, 1980. How many members does the Chamber have? How does it operate? (Answer below cartoon.)

The Portland Chamber of Commerce has been in the business of local business development for the past 96 years. Its predecessor, the Board of Trade, was formed in 1870 by local leaders to address pressing problems confronting the city's economic growth. Dredging the Columbia's entrance, completing the rail connection, building better dock facilities and setting grain standards were the priorities.

Original Chamber bldg., Third and Stark, 1893 (demolished 1934).

By 1890, when the Portland Chamber was created to succeed the Board, those initial goals had been accomplished. Oregon products were in international demand and shaping a world-class port became the newly incorporated Chamber's paramount consideration. In 1891 the Port of Portland was established as a state agency to coordinate river navigation needs with the federal government.

At the forefront of the effort were the most noted names of the day — Ladd, Corbett, Failing, Ainsworth, Kamm,

Dekum, Dolph, Pittock, Reed and a young entrepreneurial dynamo named George B. Markle Jr. Though Markle made and lost a fortune during only eight years in Portland, he left an indelible mark.

Owing primarily to his personal enterprise, the Chamber constructed an impressive, eight-story edifice at Southwest Third Avenue and Stark Street. Completed in 1893, while Markle was its second president, the Chamber of Commerce Building (later the Commerce Building) stood for 40 years as a symbol of economic power throughout the Northwest.

The Chamber's efforts helped ensure the success of the Lewis and Clark Centennial Exposition of 1905. Oregon's greatest-ever promotional event was the single most significant factor in doubling Portland's population during the decade.

The Commercial Club of Portland and the Chamber merged in 1915 and offices were moved to the Oregon Building at Southwest Fifth Avenue and Oak Street. Through the 1920s the combined organization placed primary emphasis on attracting new people to the area.

From 1929 to 1931 they operated out of the Multnomah Hotel. That year the old Art Museum building at Southwest Fifth Avenue and Taylor Street was purchased by the Chamber. It was to be their home for the next 53 years.

Predictably, top business and financial executives have dominated the roster of Chamber presidents as the organization helped guide Portland's progress over the past nine decades. In 1980, the group's first executive director, Dickwin Armstrong, was hired to augment full-time staff capabilities, planning and directing overall objectives.

That year the Portland Chamber was accredited by the Chambers of Commerce of the United States; one of only 412 of the nation's more than 4,000 chambers to earn the honor. In December 1984, a handsome, new headquarters building was dedicated at 221 N.W. Second Ave. in Old Town, reflecting a determined commitment to action in the '80s and beyond.

Answer: Approximately 3,200 member firms plus individual memberships. There are 22 committees and task forces divided into five action groups.

4. LIVING & LEARNING, PRAYING & DYING

Laurelhurst from an elevation of 5000 ft.

Portland Style

Neighborhoods, districts and towns, schools, churches and cemeteries — all possess a sense of permanence in the midst of a constantly changing society.

Yet, neighborhoods do change, sometimes with almost imperceptible slowness; in other instances, almost overnight. World War II brought a dramatic, new racial configuration to Portland's near Northeast. The Vietnam War did the same thing for the eastern end of Rose City Park. The close-in Southeast is seeing a revitalization because of good housing values. Nob Hill/Northwest has become the height of chic with the post-hippie establishment and prices have been escalating accordingly.

Since the article on Hollywood appeared, the district's most enduring eating establishment, Yaw's Top Notch, has been leveled to the ground. A set of golden arches now marks the spot.

Nor are institutions of higher learning immune to instability. Had Albany College not survived by the skin of its teeth in the early 1940s, there would be no Lewis and Clark College atop Palatine Hill today. In the early 1970s, University of Portland struggled through difficult financial times. Following the Vanport Flood, it looked as if the Extension Center that later evolved into Portland State would fold. A little luck, a lot of hard work and belief in something very worthwhile made each emerge stronger and better than before.

Houses of worship fell on hard times during the 1960s and 70s. But the edifices endure, elegant reminders of a society once staunchly Christian. In downtown, only the Old Church, of all its elaborate, wooden Carpenter Gothic contemporaries, survives. The next generation, constructed of sturdier stuff, dots downtown with stonework and steeples. Out in the neighborhoods, newer faiths have taken over older structures.

Local burial grounds have come in for their share of problems as well. Progress has threatened pioneer cemeteries. Lone Fir, in the heart of the Buckman district, languished in neglect for years, and stately Riverview suffered a sensational grave robbery. All these tales are told by simply turning the page.

At home in River City: Early elegance

(Part one of a four-part series)
January 8, 1986

James B. Stephens' home, built circa 1862-64, is the oldest surviving residence in Portland. Where is it today? (Answer below cartoon.)

Within a quarter century of the first rough log cabin's appearance at First and Washington in 1845, residences with a touch of class were being erected on the edges of what today is called "Old Town."

Since Portland's early elite built their elegant homes close to the action, eventually the action overtook them. William S. Ladd's mansion at Broadway and Columbia is now the site of the

Full block Victorian residences ca. 1880.

Oregonian Building. The estate's carriage house across the street still survives. The Public Service Building at S.W. Sixth and Taylor now occupies the property where Henry Failing's home once stood. Lincoln High School replaced Jacob Kamm's Italianate residence which is the only close-in survivor, having been moved to Eric Ladd's "Colony" at 19th and Jefferson in 1950.

Henry Corbett's home, which originally occupied the block betweeen Fifth and Sixth, Taylor and Yamhill, was the longest lived of its contemporaries. To the embarrassment of local leaders, the widow Corbett's cow grazed blithely in its half-block pasture until 1925 when the Pacific Building was constructed on the spot. The mansion itself survived until Mrs. Corbett's death in 1936.

By the mid-1880s, stately Italianate mansions lined the South Park Blocks and ornate Queen Anne edifices out in the "West End" (near Northwest) took up entire blocks. The Couch family compound consisted of four square blocks, part of which was later donated to Trinity Episcopal Church.

Fashionable ladies paraded in prancing carriages from N.W. 26th and Northrup (N) to West Park and Montgomery. Portland was being favorably compared with major Eastern cities such as Boston, New York and Philadelphia as well as the only other West Coast city of any note at the time — San Francisco.

Although the slopes of the West Hills were being assailed with construction in the early 1880s, the first hilltop dweller was George B. Markle, Jr. in 1889. Markle came from Pennsylvania with a fistful of coal mining money, started up several successful companies, including the first, and only, cable trolley line, and ended up losing it all in the Panic of 1893. A "panic" differs from a depression in that it doesn't last as long. But, for the overextended Easterner, it was long enough.

Markle's Portland Heights mansion was merely the precursor of an energetic wave of development that would eventually sweep over the entire expanse of the West Hills and their approaches. The earliest such enterprise was launched by *Oregonian* publisher Henry Pittock and William S. Ladd's brother-in-law, James Steel, in 1888.

Fulton Park, the residential district on the slopes behind Macadam Avenue and Johns Landing, was Portland's first suburban tract home development. In 1888 it was still outside the city limits while conveniently served by two rail lines. One thousand four hundred lots were offered at prices ranging from $50 to $500, depending upon location and view.

"Here is undoubtedly the best opportunity the man of small or large means will have to secure a good suburban home on the confines of Portland," stated *The West Shore* magazine in its issue of August 14, 1888.

This was only the beginning, as residential developments would soon be burgeoning at the loftiest levels of Portland's westside skyline.

Answer: Originally at the foot of Stephens Street just above the Willamette's east bank, it was moved to S.E. 12th and Stephens in 1902.

Northwest 19th: Gingerbread grandeur

September 30, 1987

Jigsaw gingerbread gone wild. Mayor William S. Mason's residence built in 1892 at 651 Irving Street. Where is 651 Irving? (Answer below cartoon.)

A man's home is his castle. The more successful the man, the more impressive the castle. Residences as symbols of stature. In the late 19th century, Portlanders of prominence epitomized this principle. Between 1880 and 1900 some of the finest private homes on the Pacific Coast were carefully crafted in the northwestern corner of the rapidly growing river city.

Eclectic, uniquely Northwest versions of the Victorian era's noteworthy architectural styles — Stick, Gothic, Queen Anne and Italianate — combined to create a splendid showcase on a series of previously undeveloped avenues. The primary thoroughfare of this exclusive enclave was 19th Street — an elegant promenade of gingerbread grandeur stretching from C to M Streets.

Richard Knapp residence, 17th & Everett, 1882.

Captain John Couch, a pivotal figure in the evolution of early Portland, owned the land claim on which the city's first distinguished residential district was erected. Though Couch died in 1870, a decade before the earliest of the grandiose domiciles appeared, his wife and family set the tenor for the entire neighborhood's development.

During the 1880s, the extended Couch-Lewis-Flanders-Glisan clan built substantial homes on a group of adjacent properties encompassing the blocks from E to J (the alphabet streets did not acquire names until 1891) between 19th and 20th — a five-block family compound.

In contrast to the tree-lined look of Nob Hill and vicinity today, 100 years ago it was almost barren.

Many a mansion stood starkly alone, the sole occupant of an entire block. Meticulous landscaping, a low hedge or wrought-iron fence and a curving drive leading to a handsome porte cochere lent design to the surroundings. But the trees were saplings, the streets unpaved and the sidewalks wooden. It was the edge of town, albeit the gilded edge, mirroring a metropolis still in the making.

Grand homes graced not only 19th and 20th but 17th and 18th streets as well. In fact, the single residence considered by many to be the grandest of them all took up the block between 17th and 18th, Davis and Everett. Richard Knapp, partner in Knapp, Burrell & Co., built the elaborately detailed, richly appointed Queen Anneish mansion in 1882 for the previously unheard of price tag of $80,000.

The wholesale machinery executive and his wife incorporated exquisite materials — lavish wood, spectacular stained glass and artistic metalwork — into the interior finishing. To top off their unparelleled showplace, the Knapp's imported the finest European and Oriental furnishings and objet d'art. The home survived until 1949 when it was dismantled piece by piece. Windows, doors, mantels, fixtures — all were sold to eager buyers. The property is now the playground of St. Mary's School.

Only former governor and mayor George Williams' grandly gabled residence at 18th and Couch, the imposing Levi White mansion on 20th between Glisan and Hoyt, and a handful of others were worthy rivals to the Knapp house.

Of the several dozen high-Victorian residences that dominated the district before the turn of the century, almost none remain today. The boldly designed, Captain John Brown house originally on Everett Street is probably the most outstanding example.

We may lament the loss of so many grand dames and wistfully dream of even one still standing on its full block perhaps as a museum and park. But there is consolation in the fact that a number of smaller, distinctive homes from the period still dot the district. It's an afternoon well spent simply strolling along those streets and happening upon them.

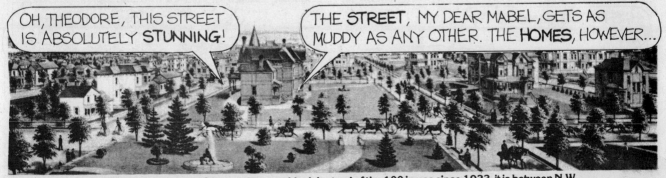

Answer: Under the old address system of 20 numbers per block instead of the 100 in use since 1933, it is between N.W. 20th and 21st.

At home in Portland: On the heights

(Part two of a four-part series)
January 15, 1986

Dorr Keasey's advertisement for Kings and Arlington Heights, 1912. Whose home was completed in 1914 at the highest point in the area? (Answer below.)

In the five years following the 1905 Lewis and Clark Centennial Exposition, Portland's population increased almost 50 percent to 210,000 and real estate business was booming. East of the river, farmlands were being subdivided in anticipation of working-class needs. Buckman and Sunnyside were under development with Ladd's Addition and Laurelhurst soon to follow.

West Hills residential expansion was almost as pervasive. What it lacked in numbers it more than made up for in snob appeal. Getting to the top was being taken literally where one's own residence was concerned.

Portland Heights from S.W. 16th, 1906 (left). Westover Terraces under construction, 1911 (right).

Homes of some stature had been ascending the slopes west and southwest of downtown since the 1880s. But their placement was without planning until realtor Dorr Keasey came on the scene. In 1905 his D.E. Keasey & Co. began offering view lots along a series of terraced streets traversing to the top of Portland Heights.

This development would be but the first of four ambitious "Heights" projects spearheaded by Keasey with the backing of prominent Portlanders. Next were Kings and Arlington Heights flanking West Burnside on the north and south, respectively. The twin undertakings, cleared and graded between 1910 and 1912, represented a half-million dollar syndicated purchase from the Amos King estate.

Keasey & Co. promoted its latest venture, largest in the city's history, based on the success of Portland Heights. "In 1905, while we were selling choice lots...from $1,000 to $2,000, we predicted that within five years (they) would sell as high as $10,000. Today you will find our prediction verified."

Unfortunately, the going was a bit rougher for Kings and Arlington. Engineering problems with the steep slopes proved costly to correct and a recession at the outset of The First World War slowed progress.

A neighboring tract just to the north came into existence as the result of its contribution to Portland's largest ever landfill. Between 1910 and 1913 the former Guild's Lake area was transformed into dry land as the Westover Terraces were being carved from the hillside above. Corbett, Ainsworth and Ladd family interests were involved as well as the ubiquitous Mr. Keasey. Even though well designed, Westover, like Kings and Arlington, languished in under-development until after the Great War.

Eventually, however, Keasey's immodest promotional proclamations would prove true. His time frame may have been a bit short but, by 1919, business began bustling along the Heights and the Terraces. Lots, originally priced at $1,000 to $3,500, were going for up to $5,000.

By the mid-1920s, Portland's affluent had forsaken the flats and taken to the heights. Despite the drawbacks of occasionally icy streets and lack of public transportation, nothing could beat the view from the top.

Answer: Henry L. Pittock's mansion and 46-acre estate at the top of Imperial Heights just west of Kings Heights.

Laurelhurst and Ladd's Addition

(Part three of a four-part series)
January 22, 1986

The Joan of Arc statue at Coe's Circle, 39th and Glisan, was contributed to the city by Dr. Henry Waldo Coe in 1925. What else did the local physician give to Portland? (Answer below cartoon.)

Were it not for William Sargent Ladd, two of Portland's most interesting and attractive neighborhoods would not exist. Mr. Ladd, who emerged from the city's early power struggles as one of its richest citizens, was directly responsible for Ladd's Addition and indirectly, but crucially, the catalyst for Laurelhurst.

Ladd platted his "Addition" in 1891, patterning it after Washington, D.C.'s diagonal streets and traffic circles. It is the only X-shaped neighborhood in Portland, which contributes to quiet streets, making a residential haven on the edge of a light industrial district.

"A neighborhood of rose gardens" has often been applied to Ladd's Addition. A neighborhood of avid admirers in residence is also apt. Ever since its earliest development, beginning some 10 years after Ladd's death in 1893, this has been a proud place with an ethnic mix. Italians and Chinese, living side by side, more than once

Ladd's Addition before 1919

banded together to stave off commercial encroachment on *their* Addition.

Ladd himself ensured longevity for the area when he deeded Ladd's Circle to the city in 1891. The one stipulation stated that if the Rose Garden was removed or significantly altered, the property would revert to his heirs. A 1917 plan to eliminate the circle was quashed by that clause.

The one commercial building on Ladd's Circle has led many lives. As the office of the Ladd Development Corp., it saw the tract through primary development in the 1910s and early '20s, then went from an ice cream parlor to a dance studio, a beauty shop to a cleaners and finally the Ladd Circle Grocery.

The grocery is the only business in Ladd's Addition. It, St. Philip Neri Catholic Church, and the Chinese Baptist Church have become integral parts of this unique neighborhood.

The much more extensive Laurelhurst district stretches from N.E. 44th to S.E. 32nd and Stark to Sandy Blvd. and the Banfield Freeway. It was laid out in 1905 on what had been W. S. Ladd's 400-acre dairy cattle breeding farm, Hazelfern.

That land was just waiting to be turned into what promoters called the "Pasadena of Portland." And, once the trees grew along its curving avenues, Laurelhurst fulfilled that promise. Development of the entire district was spread over more than 20 years. One of the area's most notable residences, Lebanese Consul Robert Bitar's 23-room Mediterranean villa on the northwest edge of Laurelhurst Park, was completed in 1928.

Ladd's Farm, circa 1900

Just down the street from the Bitar mansion is the charming Laurelhurst Club. Originally a tennis club, it now serves as a community social hall. The park property was purchased in 1909 from the Ladd estate. A $92,000 price tag bought 31 acres with a swampy bottom which was transformed into a manmade lake that is the centerpiece of a true treasure in city parks.

Although a small concession to commercialism was allowed at 32nd and E. Burnside for the Piggly Wiggly Market and Smith's Drugs in the 1930s, Laurelhurst, sometimes by neighborhood association action, has retained its original residential character.

NOW THE FUN BEGINS, **LADS!**

Klooster '86

Answer: Dr. Coe donated three other statues: George Washington (N.E. Sandy & 57th), Abraham Lincoln and Teddy Roosevelt (South Park Blocks.)

Alameda and Eastmoreland

(Part Four of a four-part series)
January 29, 1986

The 1909 "gold" brochure for Eastmoreland. What characterized neighborhood cohesiveness in recent decades? (Answer below cartoon).

In the first 10 years of the 20th Century, developers launched Kings and Arlington Heights and Westover Terraces on the westside; and Irvington, Rose City Park, Laurelhurst, Ladd's Addition, Alameda and Eastmoreland on the eastside.

The latter two, both platted in 1909, were the east-of-the-river equivalents of their up-market West Hills cousins. Alameda Park, as its promoters dubbed the district, was part of an 1859 donation land claim owned by William and Isabell Bowering. the key quarter section (160 acres) ran from the present-day N.E. 24th and 33rd to Fremont and Prescott.

Early Alameda Prince residence, 1918

When prominent politicians Joseph Dolph and John Mitchell bought that quarter section for $2,400 in 1871, it was undoubtedly considered a fair price. In 1879, Dolph, who had bought out Mitchell in 1875, sold to Abraham Buckman for $3,900.

The next transaction did not occur until 29 years later when, in 1908, Sarah Buckman sold 40 of the 160 acres to a Mr. H.L. Hamblet for $37,500. Hamblet was the agent for the Astoria Title & Trust Co., owned by E.L. Ferguson who, with farsighted planning, had formed the Alameda Land Company 18 years earlier.

Ferguson and Hamblet filed the Alameda Park plat on Feb. 1, 1909, and proceeded to grade the streets along the crest of the 250-foot-high plateau called Gravelly Hill. In 1883, Fremont Street had been widened and extended east to Sandy Road and the 1870 county road, now 33rd, was much improved. Adding to the area's accessibility, the Broadway Bridge would be completed in 1913.

The stage was set and promotion began in earnest. "A Fitting Homesite—A Golden Investment," headlined an Alameda Park brochure. "The largest restricted residence section upon the Pacific Coast," the copy continued, "Apartment houses, flats, hotels and stables are taboo, likewise people of undesirable colors and kinds." The racial exclusionary clause was removed from deeds in 1923.

Most of the fine residences along The Alameda and adjacent avenues were completed by the late 1920s. Eastmoreland's odyssey was more protracted. Initially a "restricted" residential area like Alameda, the primary focus of promotion for the former Ladd's Crystal Springs Farm was Reed College.

The Ladd Estate Company, headed by the late William S. Ladd's son, William M., emphasized the fact that fine institutions of higher learning across the country had been the catalysts for the creation of quality residential environments adjacent to the campuses.

Modest success for the still-very-suburban subdivision was stalled during the war years. With sales still sluggish in 1923, Laurelhurst developer Paul C. Murphy bought the Ladd Estate Company and three years later resold it to the Eastmoreland Company, an investment group made up of residents who were bolstered by the opening of the Ross Island Bridge in 1925.

The Crash of '29 and the Depression made their venture a losing one. Not until 1948 could the district finally declare that all 1,270 original lots had been sold. By then, Eastmoreland residents knew they had something very special.

Answer: The Eastmoreland Community Club (now Neighborhood Association) has successfully fought railroad and commercial intrusions.

Portland prestige: Dunthorpe & Assoc.

April 23, 1986

Lloyd Frank's Fir Acres estate, now Lewis and Clark college. who were the most prominenet architects of Dunthrope-Rivera residences. (Answer below cartoon).

The Alameda crest conveys class. Oswego offers luxury living at Lakeside. Eastmoreland exudes arboral affluence. The view from those various Portland "heights" is indeed valuable. But, for the epitomy of palatial, no place in Portland outdoes the Dunthorpe district.

William and Mary Jane Torrance's 1850 donation land claim, which encompassed Riverwood, Riverdale, Palatine Hill and part of Dunthorpe, created the catalyst for the area. Torrance and Milwaukie founder Lot Whitcomb had established the Taylor's Ferry to Macadam Road in the early 1850s, connecting the eastside town with Military Road and the Tualatin Plains. Macadam was, according to conflicting reports, paved either with planks or logs (corduroy).

to prominence.

William S. Ladd and Simeon Reed had bought several hundred acres south and west of Riverview Cemetery for iron-ore speculation. Ladd's son, William M., platted 125 acres of these holdings for upper Dunthorpe in 1916. His Ladd Estate Company also held the property which soon after became lower Dunthorpe. Henry Ladd Corbett, platted Riverwood/Abernethy Heights in 1909 and grain merchant Peter Kerr built his Scottish baronial mansion (now the Episcopal Diocese) over the next two years. Kerr's brother, Thomas, became his neighbor along with wholesale grocery magnate Cicero Lewis's sons, C. i iunt and Faber Lewis.

In 1920, William M. Ladd completed his 16-acre Dunthorpe

(left) Kerr estate, Riverwood/Abernethy, 1911, (center) The White House, Riverwood, 1890s, (right) Ladd estate, Dunthorpe, 1920.

At Riverwood, where the road ended, the area's first opulent symbol appeared in the mid-1870s. A dazzling white roadhouse, rising four stories above the Willamette, became well-known throughout the Northwest. Originally called "White House Bob's" for its first flamboyant proprietor, the facility came to full flower under the ownerships of gas company co-founder H.C. Leonard, who had purchased the Riverwood/Abernethy Heights properties in 1869. The White House, a combination hotel, gambling casino, dining place and dance hall, featured a race track on its landscaped grounds and remained popular until destroyed by a fire in 1904.

By the mid-1890s the Portland and Willamette Valley Railway made 14 trips daily between Portland and Oswego. Eleven stations were established along the route. Five of them served the little riverside settlements of Riverwood, Riverdale, Rivera and Elk Rock.

Second generation wealth was responsible for bringing the area

estate and secured its exclusivity with restrictive covenants on the district—swine and goats prohibited, minimum house cost $3,000, no advertising signs, no persons of African or Mongolian descent, no selling of liquor.

Hamilton Corbett's stately French chateau was a classic addition to the district but department store scion Lloyd Frank's Fir Acres was the pinnacle. With Palatine Manor as its Elizabethan tudor centerpiece, Frank's terraced, 64-acre estate was completed in 1924 at a cost of $1.3 million. Now the location of Lewis and Clark College, it epitomizes elegance among Dunthorpe dream homes.

Today, the largest estates are subdivided and many fine residences have passed from generation to generation. Though few live in the aristocratic splendor of their forbears, Dunthorpe-Rivera still represents the ultimate in status and prestige—Portland style.

NO MATTER **HOW** WELL YOU DO...

THERE'S ALWAYS SOMEONE WHO DOES IT **BETTER!**

Peter Kerr

Lloyd Frank Estate-Fir Acres

William M. Ladd

Klooster '86

Answer: A.E. Doyle, Wade Pipes, Herman Brookman and U of O School of Architecture Dean Ellis Lawrence.

River City status: Waverley Heights

August 20, 1986

William MacMaster's second Heights home, Ravenswood, 1923. Who was Ardgour's architect? What other prominent architects designed Waverley residences? (Answers below cartoon.)

The history and evolution of the Waverley Country Club, recounted on August 13, and the Waverley Heights residential area are inextricably intertwined. The leading citizens who founded the original Portland "Waverly Links" Golf Club in 1896 were responsible for the development of this exclusive residential district.

Finding their little nine-hole course at 27th Avenue and Powell Street inadequate, club members negotiated to purchase 80 acres along the Willamette from Joseph Lambert in 1898. This farm land was part of the 1850 Henderson Leulling donation claim and subsequent Luelling-William Meek partnership that produced Portland's first orchards and nursery.

Early Waverley Heights' estate Voorhies mansion, 1914

Although a townsite called Cambridge, laid out in 1890, encompassed the Waverley property, the Panic of 1893 stymied lot sales and further development was effectively eliminated by the golf course. In 1901 the Waverly Association bought the remainder of Lambert's adjacent property, bringing their ownership to 250 acres. For many years after, a few isolated lots, the result of purchases during the Cambridge Town promotion, dotted the links. Golfers simply played around these homesite hazards.

But the way was now clear for development of a different dimension. On March 14, 1903, Waverly Heights was platted with 16 lots on the 60-acre hillside south of the then nine-hole Waverly Club course, which included present day Garthwick, and east-of-the-riverside garden farms leased by Joseph Lambert to a group of Italians. The latter property would become the site of the club's present 18-hold course in 1913.

Eleven buyers, primarily Waverly Club members, snapped up 15 of the wooded properties, William MacMaster, Waverly and Arlington Club president, was the first to put a permanent residence on his property. Ardgour, the MacMaster's sprawling Tudor home, was built in 1907-08.

By the early 1910s a number of handsome homes had joined Ardgour on the Heights. The name Waverley, with the "e," was officially adopted in 1913. The John Latta residence completed in 1912 was called "The Highlands," and that's how the Latta's mail was addressed. The post office was obviously more indulgent in those days.

During the same period, Sarah Heard "Sally" Lewis of the Couch-Lewis clan had her home built in a Japanese motif and filled it with oriental antiques. Another Waverley founder, Walter J. Burns, constructed a Scottish-style country retreat, "The Latch," in 1912-13.

Looming large on 10 acres of hilltop, the Voorhies mansion stood from 1914 until it burned in 1967. Gordon Voorhies was a Waverley and Arlington clubber, as well as a member of the Portland Polo Club which played its matches on the field just south of the Waverley clubhouse. Another polo player, Sherman R. Hall, purchased the southern portion of the Voorhies property in 1915 and built the "Pink Palace," destined to become the most imposing estate ever on the Heights. In the early 1920s its new owners, the Henry F. Chaneys, expanded the surrounding property to 30 acres and added an indoor pool, a stable and barn, tennis courts and a ballroom.

Over the years almost all of Waverley's original 16 plats were subdivided and developed. Ardgour was torn down and replaced with another tudor home in 1937. The Pink Palace, minus most of its grounds, has been completely restored. Waverley Heights may not have the servants and splendor of its halcyon days but it remains an address of distinction.

Answers: David C. Lewis designed Ardgour; Morris Whitehouse, The Latch; A.E. Doyle, the Voorhies home; Ellis Lawrence, The Pink Palace, Jamieson Parker, several homes.

Old Multnomah: Unincorporated character

April 16, 1986

Nelson Thomas's General Store, now the Thomas Bldg., built in 1914 at S.W. 35th and Multnomah. Who cleared the adjacent land? (Answer below cartoon).

Unlike other commercial centers on Portland's perimeter, such as St. Johns and Sellwood, Multnomah never sought city status. Like Hollywood, its development began shortly after the turn of the century. But its outlying southwest site was not yet in the path of progress.

In May 1891, West Portland pioneer T.A. Wood initiated the area's suburban growth when he established the West Portland Motor Railroad. The steam train ran until 1899, when it was succeeded by the Oregon Electric Line which set up a station in 1908 at the current intersection of S.W. 35th and Capitol Highway. At the time the district was dominated by wooded hillsides and dotted with farms. Capitol was called Slavin Road for Hillsdale settler John Slavin.

streetlighting, sidewalks, a baseball field, even a local band. In 1915 the recently named Capitol Highway was "macadamized," becoming the U.S. Highway 99 west connection to Salem and causing a one-block commercial-center shift.

Natural gas and electric service took another year to reach the unincorporated community. By then, the post office was serving 2,000 citizens. In 1921 they could attend the area's first church and join the new Orenomah Masonic Lodge. Two years later they were able to deposit their dollars at the Multnomah Commercial and Savings Bank founded by Henry Raz.

Although the bank succumbed to the depression, it had a few headline-grabbing highlights during its heyday. In 1925, teller Walter Raz was relieved of $1500 by an armed robber.

Old Multnomah's main street, Captiol Hwy., early 1920s (left) and today (right).,

Oregon Electric dubbed their suburban station Multnomah, which comes from the Chinook word "nematlnomaq" meaning "down the river." C.B. Woodwarth platted the townsite as a little commercial core sprang up around the station. Residents erected a post office the same year as the station, and followed with a general store. The store featured livestock feed, which remained a popular item until 1919 when John and Jennie Denley's Milk Ranch, with 100 head, discontinued operation.

Pride in the district was exhibited early by residents and business owners. In 1911 they banded together to form the Multnomah Improvement Club, which immediately launched into community projects worthy of its name—

Raz set off a silent alarm wired to ring at the Twentieth Century Grocery across the street. The clerk hurried over to investigate and was held up along with the customers.

The Multnomah Community Club was founded in 1938 and captured the Rose Festival Parade President's Cup two years later. The 1940 post office estimate of customers served was 15,000. Suburban spread continued unabated as the area was annexed to Portland over an eight-year period from 1954 to 1962.

Despite loss of business to shopping centers and an ongoing influx of newcomers, Multnomah has managed to retain the traditional friendliness and cohesive sense of community that gives it a unique, district identity.

Answer: The six Magetti brothers, woodsmen and settlers of 1891, cut Multnomah's last stands of virgin timber.

Hollywood: Heyday of the district

August 31, 1983

This giant milk bottle was at the corner of the Steigerwald's Dairy building. Where is it? What is there now? (Answers below cartoon.)

Ah, memories of Hollywood. No, not movie stars and fancy cars, but standing behind the counter stools at the "second" Yaw's Top Notch, opened in 1936, waiting to sink my teeth into one of their incomparable burgers accompanied by a lemon coke and followed up with a slice of custard pie. Mom always chose the chili.

Savoring the batter-dipped prawns at the Pagoda — high

no drive-in! By the mid '50s, their "third" location, which took up the entire block, had become the "in" place for us Grantonians as well as interlopers from other schools. No problems, though. Yaw's supplied their own police patrol to keep things placid — all off-duty Portland officers headed by Bob Svilar, the Tootsie Roll cop (he gave them out by the handful.)

N.E. Sandy Boulevard at 40th looking east, January 12, 1941 (the day I was born.)

ceilings, divider booths and a full wall Oriental mural. Shopping at the "second" Hollywood Fred Meyer with its snazzy new rooftop parking lot. And catching the latest cinemascope release at the fabulous Hollywood Theater (the closest we got to the real thing).

The original Top Notch, launched in 1926, and the Hollywood, opened in the same year, are among the district's oldest businesses. But not *the* oldest. That distinction goes to Paulsen's Pharmacy. Same location, same name, since 1923.

The Pagoda is still there, remodeled just like Yaw's. In fact, Hollywood has four Chinese restaurants including Chin's Kitchen. Best take-out in town since 1949. These aren't plugs, they're facts. Yaw's hamburgers are still the same. The only ones anywhere I wouldn't sully with catsup. Family patriarch, Win Yaw, so the story goes, collaborated with E.E. Franz to develop the first hamburger bun.

But Yaw's itself isn't the same without a counter and stools. And

Hollywood was basking in its heyday. The second-largest shopping district in Portland next to downtown. In many ways it *was* like a little town. Harold Kelley, the affable appliance man, was even named the unofficial mayor. Kelley, who started his business in 1931, is the last remaining founding member of the Hollywood Boosters.

As he tells it, the district was originally called Rose City Park after the trolley line that was responsible for the growth on Sandy Boulevard. By the early '20s the "street-car suburb" was booming.

When the Boosters Club was founded in March 1934, it was agreed to officially dub their district "Hollywood" for the highly visible theater landmark. The district held sway, virtually without competition, until 1960 when Lloyd Center opened.

Even with the eventual loss of some retail outlets, it has taken change in stride and remains a vital part of the city. Portland's own Hollywood. A unique entity. A bit of irreplaceable Americana.

Answer: The tower at the corner of N.E. Sandy Blvd. and 37th, which today features 7Up, was also a Pabco paint can.

Separate cities: East Portland and Albina

March 12, 1986

N. Vancouver and Russell in Albina, ca. 1900. How did the town get its name and how was it originally pronounced? (Answers below cartoon.)

In 1891 the great consolidation among Portland, East Portland and Albina took place. It was encouraged by almost all concerned, little frogs acquiescing to bigger ones and expanding the size of the pond in the process. It was also the beginning of the long-standing westside superiority complex.

The town of East Portland had a considerable history in its own right before the municipal marriage. It could, for instance, boast the first white settler in the entire area—Etienne Lucier, a retired Hudson's Bay fur trapper, who built a cabin in the vicinity of East Morrison and Grand.

townsite, he and his wife both lived to see East Portland's greatest early triumph over the otherwise dominant westside when the first transcontinental train chugged into town on September 11, 1883.

The opening of the Morrison Bridge in 1887 heralded the demise of the ferries and the separate cities. Across Sullivan's Gulch the fledgling town of Albina welcomed the new river span almost as enthusiastically as its neighbor to the south.

Incorporated in the same year that the Willamette's first bridge opened, Albina's brief history had been essentially

Looking east to Albina and East Portland, ca. 1891

Although Lucier stayed only a year, he realized a profit by selling to another John McLoughlin man named Porier. Fifteen years later, McLoughlin, representing Porier's estate, sold the squatter's rights to recent overland arrivals, James and Elizabeth Stephens.

In June 1845, the Stephens took up the 640-acre land claim extending for a mile along the Willamette and back to the present day 20th Avenue. It was directly across the river from the townsite claim filed by Asa Lovejoy and William Overton just a few months prior.

James Stephens increased his eastside holdings and established a lucrative ferry service at the foot of Stark Street in 1856. East Portland, which he laid out in 1850-51, extended from A to U streets (Glisan to Hawthorne) and from the river to 12th Street. It was platted in 1861 and incorporated in 1870.

Although a sawmill, a railcar shop, orchards and other farmland remained the primary commerce of Stephens'

that of a company town. It was totally controlled by Englishman Edwin Russell, former U.S. Senator George Williams, and the extensive Albina railyards owned by the Oregon Railway and Navigation Company. By 1891 westside interest had already become pervasive in both eastside towns. The strings of the gas, electric and trolley services were pulled from downtown Portland. East Portland's city council approved virtually every franchise from across the river.

The combined coffers of the two little cities weren't substantial enough even to replace the rickety wooden bridge over the glorified gully separating them. Small wonder then that Albina voters approved the merger three-to-one and their East Portland counterparts doubled that margin. With consolidation came Portland's most dynamic period to date as its size multiplied four-fold accommodating unprecedented population growth over the next two decades.

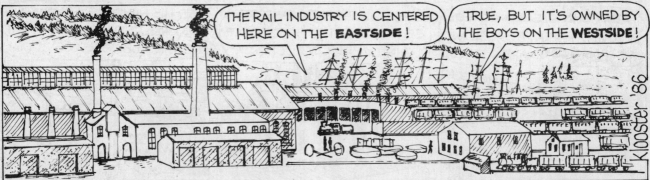

Answers: It was named for Edwin Russell's wife and daughter, both named Albina, who pronounced the name Al-bean-ah.

Separate cities: Old Sellwood revisited

March 19, 1986

Campbell's General Store, housing City Hall, no longer stands at 536 Umatilla Ave. What's the best way to see Old Sellwood's surviving structures? (Answer below cartoon).

The roots of Old Sellwood go back almost as far as those of its more prominent Willamette neighbors. It began with Henderson Luelling, a pioneer of 1847 who brought with him 700 fruit tree seedlings, berry and grape vine cuttings and peach pits. From this nucleus, Luelling, originally a North Carolina nurseryman and orchardist, established Oregon's first nursery on the donation land claim he took up the year following his arrival.

The next step in Sellwood's evolution has an interesting twist. Two brothers, the Reverends John J. and James R.W. Sellwood, both Episcopal ministers, were enroute to Oregon in 1856 via the Isthmus of Panama. Unfortunately for the Sellwoods, an internal uprising was underway in that Central American country's capital and the brothers were caught up in a riot during which John sustained serious injuries.

Tacoma Avenue, looking east from the Sellwood Bridge, 1928.

The reverend was subsequently awarded $10,000 by the Panamanian government. Although John never fully recovered, the substantial sum allowed him to pay $5,400 to the Luelling family in 1866 for 320 acres—half of the original land claim—north of the Milwaukie townsite.

In 1882 Sellwood sold the little, unincorporated farming community to developer Thomas A. Wood and *Oregonian* publisher Henry Pittock for $32,000. The two partners formed the Sellwood Land Company, named in honor of the previous owner, and began to tout Sellwood as a workingman's residential community the following year.

To serve new residents, a commercial district was rapidly growing along S.E. 13th. As an additional inducement, promoters guaranteed to supply ferry service from Portland for two years. In 1887 the city of Sellwood was incorporated. Its offices occupied the second floor of Campbell's General Store on Umatilla Avenue. Sellwood prided itself on being the first Oregon town to have paved streets and to establish a community center which carries forward to this day as a part of the Portland Parks Bureau.

The 1890s were an active time for Sellwood. In 1893 the town merged with Portland. The same year trolley service was initiated by the East Side Railway Company. Service came over the Madison Bridge, through the Brooklyn District and Sellwood to Milwaukie where the line's main shops were situated.

In 1897 Dr. John J. Sellwood, his grand uncle's namesake, founded the Sellwood Hospital on S.E. Harney between 13th and 15th. The central district encompassed some sixteen blocks from 12th to 15th and Umatilla to Nehalem serving the surrounding areas of Ardenwald, Westmoreland, Bybee and Garthwick.

Saloons and restaurants along 13th experienced a substantial loss of business in 1909 when the City View Park Race Track was torn down to make way for the new Sellwood Park. But the Oaks Park, opened in 1905, was just coming into its height as the eastside's most popular amusement attraction.

Through the 1920s such industrial firms as Oregon Worsted and Eastside Mill and Lumber kept Sellwood active. In 1925 the new Sellwood Bridge ended the era of ferry service and gave new importance to Tacoma Street. The major connecting routes, Milwaukee and 17th, built up their commercial activities accordingly, leaving 13th to a subsidiary role.

In the mid-70s, S.E. 13th saw a resurgence as antique shops sprang up along its length. Today, Old Sellwood's Antique Row attracts shoppers from throughout the Portland area.

REV. JOHN J. SELLWOOD GOT A TOWN, A PARK, A BRIDGE AND A SCHOOL NAMED AFTER HIM

HIS BROTHER, REV. JAMES R.W. SELLWOOD GOT TO BE RECTOR OF TRINITY EPISCOPAL CHURCH!

AND HIS NAMESAKE GRANDNEPHEW DR. JOHN J. SELLWOOD GOT MOST OF THE PUBLIC RECOGNITION!

Residence of Dr. John J. Sellwood Founder of Sellwood Hospital

Klooster '86

Answer: As a research project in 1984, Sellwood Middle School students produced an Old Sellwood-Walking Tour map with key points of interest.

Separate cities: St. Johns and Linnton

April 2, 1986

St. Johns City Hall on Invanhoe St., ca. 1926. What was Ivanhoe formerly called? Which St. Johns streets still have their original names? (Answers below cartoon.)

Peter Burnett, a Tennessee-born lawyer, and Kentuckian Morton McCarver became partners in a donation land claim on the lower Willamette in 1844. They named it Linnton in honor of Senator Linn of Missouri who had introduced the "free land" bill in congress four years earlier.

Burnett and McCarver built a warehouse at their townsite and, both being legislators in the provisional government, persuaded that body to pay for improvement of a cow trail over the hill to the Tualatin Plains. But the trail was steep— almost impassable in bad weather.

With limited flat land for building expansion and limited enthusiasm from its absentee owners who preferred to

remain at Oregon City, it soon became evident that little would come of Linnton's bid for township supremacy. The call of California gold beckoned both founders in 1848. Burnett rose to become California's first American governor and McCarver was involved in the founding of Sacramento and, later, Tacoma.

Directly across the river from Linnton another tiny townsite had sprung up. Its founder, James Johns, had come to Fort Vancouver via California in 1843. The former Missourian, enticed by Burnett's enthusiasm, lived and worked on the Linnton claim from 1844 to 1847. That year Johns filed his own claim and, within three years, was operating a store and selling lots.

"Old Jimmy Johns" or "Saint Johns" as he was some-times called, also introduced a ferry service to Linnton in 1852 and ran it for more than two decades. Although considered eccentric and reclusive, Johns managed to

induce settlers to come to his town immodestly dubbed St. Johns. The town was officially dedicated on November 28, 1868.

Three years after Jimmy John's death in 1886, steam-powered street cars began service to the peninsula community. By 1890 they were making 10 trips daily to serve the 500 residents. In 1891 St. Johns was drawn into the great consolidation along with East Portland and Albina. But its still-rural residents balked at Portland's high taxes and petitioned the state legislature for separation in 1898.

Both St. Johns and Linnton benefited from industrial growth following the Lewis and Clark Exposition of 1905. Within five years more than two dozen companies— sawmills, factories, shipyards, and lumber operations—

(left)St. Johns, corner N. Jersey and Philadephia, ca. 1908. (right) Linnton central district, 1926.

lined the opposing waterfronts.

Taxes once again became an issue in 1911 as the St. Johns mill rate exceeded that of Portland. Voters approved the merger but local officials forestalled the decision. It took an amendment of the state constitution to bring the peninsula town into the fold. On April 15, 1915 the vote was 799 to 499 and St. Johns went from a city to a district. Linnton was annexed the same year bringing with it much of today's Forest Park.

The dedication of a soaring suspension bridge on June 13, 1931 symbolized the connection between the two north-end towns. Their heyday was World War II. Kaiser's Oregon Shipbuilding Corporation brought unprecedented but shortlived prosperity. Since then St. Johns and Linnton have been relegated to residential and local commercial roles based on a long, intertwined historical heritage.

Answers: Ivanhoe was formerly Eighth Street. All St. Johns street names were eventually changed after annexation to Portland.

Separate cities: Irontown evolves

April 9, 1986

Oswego Lake recreation area, 1923. What federal lake rights battle did residents finally win in 1975? (Answer below cartoon.)

The area we now call Oswego was originally inhabited by the Flathead clan. For centuries this Clackamas tribe held councils on the bluff overlooking the lake near Jantzen's Island. By the time the white man began laying claim to the surrounding land, no more than a hundred of them remained—their numbers decimated by the invaders' diseases.

In 1849 and '50 donation land claims were filed on all the riverfront property from Robinswood north to Forest Hills. Jesse Bullock's claim included the present day Marylhurst College campus. Albert Alonzo Durham's irregularly shaped parcel stretched from just south of Sucker (Oswego) Creek to the present "A" Street and included the west end of the lake, at the time referred to as Sucker Creek Swamp.

Oswego Iron Works, 1867, now George Rogers Park.

Durham dubbed the tract Oswego for his hometown in New York State. But, even after the lake took shape when a wooden dam was constructed to provide water power for a riverside sawmill, the name "Sucker" stuck. In 1913 it was officially renamed Oswego Lake.

Commercial development came slowly to the area. Iron ore, discovered in the adjacent hillsides during the 1850s, remained untapped until 1865 when a prominent Portland group organized the Oswego Iron Works. As with just about every major venture of the day, Henry Failing, Henry W. Corbett and William S. Ladd were key investors. In this instance, gas company founders Henry Green and H.C. Leonard joined them.

A smelting furnace was completed in 1866 and began production on August 24, 1867. Over its 28 years of operation, the facility produced some 43,000 tons of pig iron. Its history was beset with problems, however, and the company changed hands in 1877 when a syndicate headed by Simeon Reed, Henry Villard and Abbott Mills bought the assets and renamed it Oregon Iron Works. A third company, Oregon Iron and Steel, took over in 1882 closing 12 years later.

Although the dream of a "Pittsburgh of the West" never materialized, most of the ironfront buildings in Portland and Salem, and even some in San Francisco, were its legacy. The smelter's stone chimney survives today in George Rogers Memorial Park.

With the platting of the downtown district in 1896, Oswego entered its modern era. The town's first newspaper, the *Iron Worker,* was published by Herbert Gill between 1891 and 1897. The Oregon Portland Cement Co. began operation on State Street at the turn of the century. In 1912, noted local land developer Paul C. Murphy bought land along the northwest side of the lake, laid out the Lake Oswego Country Club, the Lake Grove Swim Park and promoted the choice lakefront lots with the slogan "Live where you play—come to Lake Oswego."

Such palatial properties as Carl Jantzen's island residence contributed to rapidly rising values in the 1920s and '30s. Lake Grove burgeoned during this period. The Red Electric line provided rail service from Portland to Newberg. The pattern of future progress for Oswego and environs can be summed up in the words of the 1910 Glenmorrie Estates promotional brochure, "The early location of the residences of many of the city's best families and seal of fashion, thus set, has ever been maintained."

IF OSWEGO IRON WORKS HAD BEEN **SUCCESSFUL**...

INDUSTRIAL WASTE NO SWIMMING

Klooster '86

Answer: Originally declared a public navigable waterway, congressional legislation revoked the unrealistic, century-old designation.

Little Russia: A lost community

August 19, 1987

Housing in Little Russia at Southwest Sherman and First. What is now located here? (Answer below cartoon.)

Oftentimes, intriguing queries about subjects not previously treated herein come to my attention via the Round the Roses mailbag. In most instances, lack of time or available information preclude further followup. Today's topic is an exception. Karen Gilbert of Portland has posed a question. This is my public reply.

"Where was a Portland district called 'Little Russia' located?" Gilbert asks, mentioning that her great grandparents lived there during the early 1900s. They were, she says, members of a German colony in Russia called Norka which apparently immigrated to Portland as a group.

Southwest First at Caruthers, ca. 1920.

Around Karen's question spins the tale of thousands of Eastern European emigrants, primarily Russian and Polish Jews, escaping oppression. During the 1890s, they swelled the ranks of new arrivals. They came to America seeking opportunity and religious freedom. They came to Portland seeking relatives and a place to stay.

The city's Jewish establishment, mostly Germans from Bavaria, steered these newcomers to a rundown, tenement district just south of downtown. The fact that the long-timers owned many of these buildings may have had something to do with their recommendation. But the message came through loud and clear that acceptance into higher social levels would have to be earned — the hard way.

As to the area itself, Little Russia consisted of several blocks at the northern end of old South Portland running roughly from Southwest Caruthers to Lincoln and from Hood to Second Avenue. Italian immigrants created their own community to the west and south of the Russians. With both Little Italy and Little Russia, no neighborhood in the city possessed a more distinctive ethnic identity. South Portland's commercial hub stretched along an eight-block segment of First Avenue from Grant to Porter. The main electric trolley line from city center to points south traversed the length of this strip. Throughout the district, kosher shops did a bustling business alongside Italian ones. The ultimate permutation was Colistro (a southern Italian) and Halprin's (a Russian Jew) Grocery.

Particularly for the Jews, their self-imposed Portland "ghetto" served as a haven of transition. A place to preserve old-world traditions while slowly adapting to a new language and culture. A half-dozen synagogues dotted the district. Well-to-do Jewish citizens sponsored the Neighborhood House, which assisted immigrants in adjusting to the American way of life.

The first generation may have benefited from this assimilation process but their offspring needed no such special attention. By the beginning of the 1920s, these easily Americanized youngsters were joined by native-born siblings in pursuing their own lives and careers. They took their toll on the cohesiveness of the community within a community that had thrived for 30 years.

When the Ross Island Bridge was completed in 1926, its western approaches cut through the heart of the old commercial area. The economic ravages of the Great Depression all but eliminated the remainder. Some of the most well-established businesses relocated to the eastside along Southeast 11th and 12th avenues adjacent to Ladd's Addition. Mostly Italian, the last of them did not disappear until the early 1960s.

During the same period, Urban Renewal obliterated the last vestiges of the old district. Today, Interstate 405 gouges its wide expanse across the spot where Caruthers once intersected First. The little "railroad" Victorians clinging to the sides of Lair Hill are the only reminders of South Portland's heydey.

These quaint, and now much sought after, residential gems may be the area's most fitting survivors. For Little Russia and Little Italy, though rich in colorful ethnicity, would never have made the landmarks list. (For related story see pg. 249.)

Answer: The site is now occupied by the American Park Towers, a high-rise residential complex.

Lewis and Clark:
Oregon Ivy League
November 6, 1985

Presidents John Howard (left) and Morgan Odell (right). When were their respective tenures? Who is the current president of Lewis and Clark? (Answers below.)

This is the first in a four-part series on Portland area colleges and universities. Chronologically, Lewis and Clark is the oldest of them as the direct continuation of Albany College, established in 1867. The fact that it is also my alma mater is merely coincidental.

As with many other private Pacific Northwest schools, Albany College was church sponsored. It took 13 years of struggle and setbacks before the Presbyterian Church succeeded in establishing its "collegiate institute" in the Oregon Country. Incorporation papers were filed in Linn County on January 31, 1867, and Lewis and Clark College, as its successor, is the state's oldest continuous corporation.

Albany College main building in 1892

Frontier children usually had limited formal education so institutions of higher learning had to prepare their own pupils. Thus the "prep" school or academy was an integral part of a stepping-stone system which saw little Albany open its doors to 40 students and graduate its first class of four young women in 1874.

Getting off the ground was only the beginning of a never-ending battle for money and qualified staff. Albany's first president and the town's Presbyterian minister, William Monteith, had donated the land on which the school stood. He was the first of 12 presidents over the next 30 years, all of whom had to find and supervise faculty, teach classes, raise money, pay bills and hope there would be enough left over to compensate themselves.

In 1892 the original building was nearly doubled in size. A dormitory building was obtained in 1901 to house 24 women. After World War I the business of education was on the upswing and other additions were made to the campus. The faculty was increased, the curriculum modernized and an intercollegiate athletic program was underway. But the Crash of '29 and subsequent depression caused the Presbyterian Synod to seriously consider a change.

Portland trustees urged that a branch of the college be established in the state's principal city. In 1934 the freshman year was offered at the Allen Building, S.E. 12th and Salmon. The sophomore year was added in 1935 and the junior and senior years in 1937. By this time the Portland unit boasted an enrollment of 182 and Albany, itself, had declined to 169. That same year a select committee surveyed the situation and recommended that the entire college be relocated to Portland.

In September 1938, the college began registration for its 72nd school year in rented quarters at S.W. 13th and Main. It had neither accreditation nor a president. Dr. Clarence Greene, Albany College president from 1923-28, temporarily resumed the post but, for the school to be accredited again, it had to have a permanent home.

During the next three years, survival was doubtful. But two things made the difference — a dynamic new president and a dramatic new campus. In late 1941, Dr. Morgan S. Odell, who had been a highly regarded professor at Occidental College for 10 years, accepted the challenge to revitalize the "Cinderella" school and Aaron Frank, president of Meier & Frank, allowed the college to acquire his deceased brother's fabulous southwest Portland estate, built in 1924 at a cost of $1.3 million, for $46,000 in back taxes.

Other prominent Portlanders, including lawyer C.W. Platt and lumberman Herbert Templeton, proved to be stalwart supporters of the renamed Lewis and Clark College as it entered a post-War era of growth and wide acclaim under Morgan Odell's presidency.

In 1960, Odell retired and was succeeded by then-37-year-old John R. Howard whose 23-year tenure saw the school gain international stature with more than half of its students spending a year overseas. In 1965, Northwestern College of Law merged with Lewis and Clark, bringing an additional dimension to the already rich academic fabric of what has become one of the West's finest liberal arts colleges.

COACH McCARTY IS IT **TRUE** THAT THE **FIX** IS ON SPORTS HERE AT LEWIS & CLARK?

I CAN'T DENY IT. A **FIX** HAS BEEN PART OF OUR ATHLETIC PROGRAM FOR ALMOST **FORTY** YEARS!

FIRST WAS DIRECTOR ELDON **FIX**. NOW THERE'S HIS SON, COACH DAVID **FIX**!

Klooster '85

Answers: Dr. Odell was president from 1942 to 1960, Dr. Howard from 1960 to 1983. James Gardner, a former Ford Foundation executive, is now president.

University of Portland: No bluffing here

November 13, 1985

Ceremonial procession (circa 1943). Who is the university's longest serving president? What is the special benefit of clergy as administration and faculty? (Answers below cartoon.)

It took the efforts of two major church groups over the course of more than three decades but, finally, Waud's Bluff, a commanding promontory overlooking the Willamette in North Portland, became the site of a noted Northwest university.

In 1890 the Methodist Episcopal Church in Oregon was having doubts about the continuing viability of its initial Oregon school, Willamette University at Salem. The church operated more than 50 colleges and universities across the country and local church leaders hoped to establish a new university in the state's leading city.

With incorporation of "Portland University" in early 1891, and appointment of a board of trustees replete with prominent Portlanders, an ambitious land development plan was launched to give stability and substance to the new school. Pioneer John Waud's bluff property and adjoining acreage belonging to his neighbor, John Mock, were purchased by an investment corporation. The entire parcel was dubbed University Park.

West Hall, first campus building, 1891

Enthusiasm ran high for the plan which brought with it construction of a five-story brick and stone structure—West Hall. This imposing "Richardsonian Romanesque" building, housed offices, classrooms, dormitory and meeting rooms. During its first few years of operation, both the university and the residential development appeared to be on their way to permanence and prosperity. But dissension in the church fractured the former as the depression of 1893 took its toll on the latter.

In late 1898 a merger move was attempted to bring together the church's three Northwest schools—Willamette, Portland and Puget Sound—at the Portland site under a new name. Consolidated University. At first the plan appeared to be headed for success but then Willamette backed out, followed, more relunctantly, by Puget Sound. Portland University closed at the end of the 1899-1900 academic year.

Enter the Catholic Church and the dream of its educationally minded clergy to create a "Notre Dame of the West." Oregon's Archbishop Alexander Christie invited Holy Cross teaching fathers to join him in founding a Catholic university at Portland in the tradition already established by that order. Christie arranged purchase of the former Portland University campus and the renamed, male-only Columbia (for the river) University opened on Sept. 5, 1901.

Primarily a "prep" school in the 1920s, Columbia joined with other Catholic schools to successfully defeat an unconstitutional Ku Klux Klan bill that would have required all Oregon school-age children to attend public schools. In 1929, Columbia's collegiate arm graduated its first four-year students. 1935 saw its official name changed to University of Portland to avoid confusion with the famous New York City school.

The Depression and war years were difficult for private colleges. Immediately following the war, however, expansion in enrollment precipitated a flurry of building activity which almost put U of P under when student body size plummeted again in 1950. The following year the university went co-ed. Football was dropped as an intercollegiate sport and the focus shifted to basketball, upon which a winning reputation has been built. Through the 1960s the university made its greatest strides in growth of curriculum and physical plant.

But change brought problems and by 1971 costs exceeded income. Only tremendous belt tightening saw the school through this traumatic time. By 1976, as the University of Portland celebrated its 75th Anniversary, it had emerged securely situated on The Bluff.

Answers: Rev. Paul E. Waldschmidt, president 1962-1978. Catholic clergy take no salaries, only expenses.

Reed College: A different drummer

November 20, 1985

Reed Football Team, 1920. What is the college's current intercollegiate sports status? (Answer below cartoon.)

Simeon Reed, a Massachusetts native, amassed a fortune in Portland river commerce, real estate and other investments during the late 19th Century. When he died in 1895, Reed requested in his will that part of the family wealth, to which his wife, Amanda, was sole heir, "contribute to the beauty of the city and the intelligence, prosperity and happiness of its inhabitants."

After some reflection, Amanda Reed drew up her own will stipulating that the estate be used to establish an institute of higher learning in Portland. Even though she recommended that it emphasize "practical knowledge," when Mrs. Reed died in 1904, the trustees she named had the power to determine the direction the school would take.

Eliot Hall, Reed Institute's first building, 1912, named for prominent trustee and Unitarian minister Thomas Lamb Eliot.

with assistance from the General Education Board, a national advisory group set up by John D. Rockefeller prior to the Rockefeller Foundation, it was finally determined that Portland needed a top-quality college of arts and sciences rather than a vocational school.

That was the mandate given to Reed's first president, Dr. William T. Foster, when he took the post in 1910. As the 31-year-old Harvard graduate saw it, preoccupation with intercollegiate athletics and social life was usurping the primary purpose of serious learning at American colleges and universities. His goal was to create a college that would be "an honest, sustained and adequate challenge to the best powers of the best American youth."

With the Reeds' endowment backing him, Foster was able to recruit a premium caliber and like-minded young faculty. As outsiders, however, they did not find easy acceptance among Portland's powerful. In fact, community involvement efforts, although initially accepted, were ultimately rebuked by Portlanders as Foster & Co. began to gain a local reputation for elitism, eccentricity and intellectual snobbery.

Coincidental with the negative attitudes of Portland's provincial establishment during the school's first decade, it received glowing praise from educators across the country. The conflict between college and community did not help Reed's cause when financial pressures mounted. By 1919 income yield from the Reed family real estate holdings was inadequate to meet the school's needs. Still a regional school, with 70 percent of its students from Portland, no local help was forthcoming with the unpopular president in office.

Faculty defection, dwindling funds and the ultimate affront to Foster's philosophy, an intercollegiate football team (short lived), led to his resignation in 1919. Over the next three years, Foster's successor, Richard Scholz, mended bridges, attracted new faculty and maintained the serious standards for which his predecessor had steadfastly stood. Scholz solidified the character of the school before dying suddenly in 1924.

While reputed universities such as Columbia and St. John's were still in the throes of building basic programs around the books of great thinkers, Reed's was already in place. Departments were reorganized and integrated into four cross-related divisions still used today. Such ongoing re-evaluation, experimentation and innovation has always been undertaken with the basic precepts in mind. Even when attempts at fundamental change came from within, as with President Dexter Keezer (1934-1942), they failed.

Today, in its 14th year under Paul Bragdon, who has served longer than any other Reed president, the college enjoys the greatest local respect it has ever achieved along with international acclaim for doing what it set out to do — provide an unsurpassed liberal arts education for a select few. Within that statement also lies the secret of Reed's survival. For, despite conflict and controversy, those select few have continued to seek it out.

Answer: Reed does not have intercollegiate teams in major sports but Watzek Sports Center is packed day and night.

Portland State: The commuter campus

November 27, 1985

The PSU 1965 College Bowl team thrashed all comers and broke every record on the NBC show. What would their answer have been to, "Where's the Vanport Rock?" (Answer below cartoon.)

They called it "the college that wouldn't die." It was originally conceived as an interim measure providing lower-level courses to the overload of returning World War II vets who could then transfer to other Oregon schools. But the Vanport Extension Center refused to go away, even after it was inundated out of existence by the most devastating flood in Portland's history. It survived, it thrived and eventually became Portland State College.

When a college entry-level summer session, to be held at the Vanport federal housing project, was announced in March 1946, 221 students signed up. By August, more than 1,200 had registered for admission in the fall. Ninety-four percent were veterans, many with families who found the availability of 690 apartments as appealing as the opportunity to pursue an advanced education.

students gathered at Grant High School to hear that the college would continue — "somewhere, somehow." The "somewhere" was a former Kaiser shipyard building which, although no more attractive than Vanport's pre-labs, actually provided more useable space. The "somehow" became more of a "try and stop us" as the determination of those involved proved infectious.

With federal government backing, the non-accredited "junior" college (average student age, 28) was granted a one-year continuance by the State Board of Higher Education. Legislation in 1949 established Vanport as Multnomah county's ongoing lower division extension center for the state system. The college "without a future" was given a long-term lease on life.

In 1952, it relocated to the former Lincoln High School building in the South Park Blocks. Dubbed "Old Main" and now called

Portland State's Park Blocks campus in the fall of '58.

Despite makeshift facilities and inadequate space, a groundswell of support grew from within for this unprecedented experiment. It was Oregon's first public junior college, meant only to operate for a few years. But students, faculty and administration, alike, had different ideas.

Going into its second year, the extension center was already being referred to as Vanport College. Curriculum was expanded in both the freshman and sophomore years, student government and activities were in full swing and almost 1,500 students were enrolled.

But that second school year was to be the last at Vanport. On Sunday, May 30, 1948, just nine days after its second anniversary celebration, the entire campus was obliterated by Columbia flood waters along with the homes of hundreds of students and the entire 647-acre wartime community that had once been Oregon's third largest.

The Wednesday evening after the disaster, more than 1,000

Lincoln Hall, the facility served as the college's multipurpose center until the early 1960s. Four-year, full accreditation was granted in 1955 and the school's name was changed to Portland State College by a vote of the student body. The nickname "Vikings" and the "Vanguard" newspaper were retained.

The dynamics of a state college within easy commuting distance for one-third of the state's population had not escaped educators. But their expectations proved to be far too modest. In 1960, Portland State's enrollment was 4,552. By 1970, that number had ballooned to 11,354 with a vastly expanded curriculum including doctoral programs that had seen the "college" become a "university" the year before.

For the fall 1984 semester, Portland State University enrolled 14,390: 10,245 undergraduates, 3,934 postgraduates and 211 doctoral candidates. The campus has grown from the projected four square blocks to 28, with far too few parking spaces.

Answer: Drowned at Vanport, resurrected at Oregon Shipyards, the Delta Tau Rho rock now has place of honor at Lincoln Hall.

Portland Churches: In the beginning

(Part one of a four-part series)
December 4, 1985

Portland's Catholic pro Cathedral of the Immaculate Conception, 3rd & Stark, 1860s. What is the oldest surviving church building in the city? (Answer below cartoon.)

When the first Christian ministers made their way to the Oregon wilderness in the 1830s and '40s, their mission was to convert the heathen savages. Methodist Jason Lee found little success and the Presbyterians, under Dr. Marcus Whitman, were massacred in 1847.

In missionary work, a house of worship was a luxury. But for the churchmen who came to serve the rapidly arriving faithful, it was the focal point of the flock. Jason Lee founded the first Methodist mission in 1834, 10 miles north of Salem. Nine years later, Lee's fellow reverend A.L. Waller erected the first church building in the Pacific Northwest at Oregon City.

Portland's initial ecclesiastic edifice was also Methodist. Rev. J.H. Wilbur became the first pastor of Stumptown's first church at Third and Taylor in 1850. General Stephen Coffin, an early developer, had purchased a bell to be installed on the town's first public building. But it was taking so long for one to be built that he gave the bell to the church.

The Catholics completed a modest parish on Sixth in 1851 but moved to Third and Stark within a few years. The Episcopals, who

dale, in 1851.

West Union in Washington County was the site of the Baptists' first Oregon meeting in 1844. A meeting house was built in 1846 and the Willamette Baptist Association was formed in 1848. Within two more years the association had a piece of property at Fourth and Alder, donated by the generous General Coffin.

Just two years after the Baptists arrived, Lewis Thompson of Kentucky brought Presbyterianism to Oregon. Eight years later, in 1854, Portland's first Presbyterian church was organized but it was another eight years before they had their own building. Like the Baptists, Portland's Presbyterians underwent long lapses during the 1860s and '70s without a minister.

Portland's Jewish population elected its first congregation officers in 1858. The Beth Israel synagogue was built in 1861 at Fifth and Oak with Rev. Dr. Julius Eckman as rabbi.

Unitarians and Lutherans came close upon one another's heels with the former incorporated on June 30, 1866. The organization promptly purchased a lot at Yamhill and 7th. In the fall of 1867, Unitarian Rev. Thomas Lamb Eliot arrived from St. Louis to begin

Left to right: 3rd & Taylor Methodist, 1850; Beth Israel Synagogue, 5th & Oak, 1861; Trinity Episcopal, 3rd & Oak, 1854.

had begun their local ministry the same year, occupied the first Episcopal church on the Pacific Coast at Third and Oak in 1854.

Congregationalists also arrived early. In 1844, their first church was organized. The American Home Missionary Society sent a Reverend Atkinson to Portland in 1848 and a church was built on property donated by another prominent pioneer, Daniel Lowns-

the longest-ever pastorate in Portland. The German Lutheran Church held its first services at Trinity Methodist in 1868 and two years later worshipers were in their own facility at Fifth and Taylor.

By 1870, a scant quarter-century after Portland's founding, its God-fearing citizenry was served by 16 churches representing 11 faiths.

Answer: St. John's Episcopal Church, 1851, originally in Milwaukie, is now a wedding chapel overlooking the Willamette at Sellwood Park.

Portland Churches: Oaks from acorns

(Part two of a four-part series)
December 11, 1985

The Old Church, last of Portland's elegant wood edifices, was built in 1881-82. Now a public meeting place, what faiths did it previously serve? (Answers below cartoon.)

The riverbank village of a few hundred inhabitants saw its first house of worship erected in 1850. That little Methodist church at the corner of Third and Taylor was shortly joined by a half dozen others. Two decades later the town boasted 9,565 residents and 11 denominations had put down roots in Portland with 16 churches among them.

Portland's most prominent families were predominantly Easterners steeped in Victorian values. Regular church attendance had a high priority. Religious leaders held positions of wide respect and considerable influence in the community. They used that influence to make estimable contributions to the welfare and betterment of its citizens.

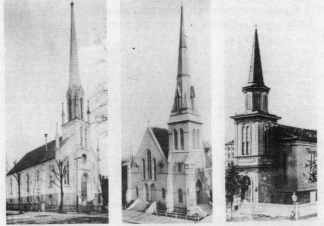
First Congregational, 2nd & Jefferson, 1875, Trinity Episcopal, 6th & Oak, 1873 and First Baptist, 4th & Alder, 1862.

Much of those good works emanated from the edifices they built. Although still wooden structures in the 1860s and '70s, churches were taking on an aura of permanence, even grandeur, with intricate stained glass windows, spires and soaring steeples.

In 1862 the Baptists, led by local layman Josiah Failing, built their first church on donated land at Fourth and Alder. By the mid 1870s, the dedicated efforts of several ministers had brought the struggling Baptist mission onto solid footing. In 1878, 22 westside members formed the First Baptist Church of East Portland. Establishment of local missions throughout the area soon followed.

Also, in 1862, the Most Reverend Archbishop Francis Norbert Blanchet moved his residence from Oregon City to Portland. With his arrival the Church of the Immaculate Conception at Third and Stark was elevated to the rank of Procathedral, remaining the area's only Catholic parish until 1874. That year, St. Francis of Assisi Church was completed at 11th and J (Oak) in the hamlet of East Portland. In 1879, today's Old Town landmark, the Bishop's House, was built adjacent to the cathedral.

Another substantial house of worship was completed by the Presbyterians at Third and Washington in 1864. Among its members were William S. Ladd and John Ainsworth with Dr. A.L. Lindsay, who established 22 churches, as pastor. Within 29 years, eight Presbyterian churches were flourishing throughout the Portland area.

The Congregationalists were fortunate to have the services of Rev. George Atkinson for 33 years. In 1871, the year before his pastorate ended, the First Congregational's new church was finished at Second and Jefferson. In the same year, Plymouth congregation was organized which Atkinson served until 1880.

Joining Temple Beth Israel, the city's original synagogue of 1861, was the stately Ahaval Shalom, organized in 1872. Rabbi Julius Eckman, who had been Beth Israel's spiritual leader from the outset, also spearheaded the new synagogue at Sixth and Oak with 50 male members.

Just down the street from Ahaval Shalom stood Trinity Episcopal, home to some of Portland's leading families. Within its walls the words of the Right Reverend Benjamin Morris, Bishop of Oregon, rang out from the pulpit. Morris, founder of St. Helen's Hall and Good Samaritan Hospital, is considered to have been one of the country's greatest Episcopal bishops.

On the eve of Portland's merger with East Portland and Albina in 1891, magnificent monuments of brick and stone were rising around the city. The list of religious denominations had grown far beyond the early arrivals. Lutherans rivaled in size some of their most prominent Protestant brethren.

Almost two dozen faiths, including splinter groups, had congregations in Oregon's major city. Quakers, Adventists, Mennonites, Christian Scientists and Latter Day Saints were among them. The unconverted Chinese had their temple. The wayward had their saloons. And, for everyone, the seemingly boundless beauty of the Northwest was just outside the door.

Answer: Originally Calvary Presbyterian, it became Emanuel Baptist in 1948 and was purchased by the Old Church Society in 1969.

Portland Churches: Enduring edifices

(Part three of a four-part series)
December 18, 1985

The First Congregational Church at S.W. Park and Madison. What does it have that no other downtown church has? (Answer below cartoon.)

Augmenting the momentum of their early establishment, Portland's prominent religious groups were planning major church building projects by the late 1880s. Within a half-dozen years (1889-1895), as many monumental houses of worship were erected in the Rose City.

St. Patrick's Catholic parish at N.W. 19th and Savier, the city's oldest church building still in continuous use, was built between 1889 and 1891. The Church of the Immaculate Conception, originally at Third and Stark, moved into an imposing new facility at N.W. 15th and Davis in 1895.

One of the Catholic Church's esteemed leaders of the day came to Portland four years later. The Most Reverend Alexander Christie left his post as Bishop of Vancouver Island in 1899 to become Archbishop of the Oregon Diocese. In 1923, just two years before his death, Christie was appointed Assistant at the Pontifical Throne — one step below Cardinal.

before it was replaced in 1906 with architect David Lewis' English Gothic masterpiece on N.W. 19th.

From 1899 to 1907, Temple Beth Israel had the good fortune to be led by a young rabbi who was destined to become, by many accounts, the most dynamic and pivotal figure in American Judaic religious history.

Dr. Stephen M. Wise began his rabbinical studies at 15, graduated from Columbia University in 1892 at 18 and received his PhD in 1901 while serving the Portland congregation. Wise more than doubled Beth Israel's membership during his tenure. Upon returning to New York, he formed the Free Synagogue and later founded the Jewish Institute. He was a lifelong supporter of workers' rights and had a profound influence on the status of American Jewry.

Equally passionate from the pulpit, if not as far as reaching in his impact, was Portland's Unitarian minister Thomas Lamb Eliot.

St. Patrick's, N.W. 19th & Savier, 1891; 1st Baptist, 12th & Taylor, 1893; Trinity Episcopal, N.W. 19th & Couch, 1906.

The Pacific Coast Council of Congregational Churches met at Portland in 1888. To a group of their members who climbed to Portland's highest point goes the credit for naming "Council Crest." In 1891, the First Congregational Church, with its white-capped, landmark bell tower, was completed at the corner of Madison on the Park Blocks.

Not to be outdone, the Baptists built their wondrous "White Temple" at Twelfth and Taylor in 1892-93 across from the First Methodist Episcopal Church which had been completed in 1889. Two blocks, south, at Twelfth and Main, stood Temple Beth Israel, with its minaret-topped twin towers. Completed in 1887, Portland's Jewish reform congregation mourned the loss of its second edifice, destroyed by fire on Dec. 19, 1923.

When Trinity Episcopal's splendid "Carpenter Gothic" structure was claimed by another conflagration in 1902, it took four years

The reverend and the rabbi shared the common causes of fighting corruption and injustice and their mutual respect reputedly forged a lasting friendship.

As Wise went on to his greater works, Eliot became a force in the Northwest and, among other things, was the catalyst behind and longtime trustee of Reed College. He lived to the age of 95, having earned the status of the Northwest's ecclesiastic elder statesman decades before his death in 1936.

By the turn of the century, Portland's religious community was established. In numbers the Methodists led the way. The Roman Catholics, Baptists, Presbyterians and Lutherans were closely bunched for second followed by a half dozen other denominations. In all, the year 1900 saw Portland with 43 different faiths, 121 churches, four synagogues and 18 missions serving a population of 90,426.

Answer: It is the only downtown church with a functioning bell.

Portland Churches: Keeping the faithful

(Part Four of a four-part series)

December 25, 1985

Westminster Presbyterian, N.E. 16th & Hancock. How many different denominations and churches serve the Portland area today? (Answer below cartoon.)

Shortly after the turn of the century, Portland's primary religious groups — the Methodist-Episcopals (the three Methodist sects would not merge until 1939), the Catholics, Baptists, Jews, Lutherans, Presbyterians, Episcopalians and Congregationalists — could all boast spectacular churches to match their community status.

As the city expanded, the churches followed. First into the eastside neighborhoods which, by the 1920s, represented 80 percent of the city's population. Then, out to the suburbs as Portland's metropolitan area began to emerge in the 1930s.

Few churches could equal or even approach the grandeur of the Baptists' "White Temple," Trinity Episcopal, First Congregational, First Presbyterian or Temple Beth Israel, however.

Temple Beth Israel, N.W. 19th & Flanders, 1928

Not that several eastside edifices weren't noteworthy. Centenary Wilbur Methodist at S.E. 9th and Pine was an early example, built in 1890 and razed in 1963 due to Columbus Day Storm damage. Westminster Presbyterian at N.E. 16th and Hancock, a stone stalwart of 1914 vintage, is also a significant structure.

But one place of worship outdoes all others east of the river as a singular statement. The Sanctuary of Our Sorrowful Mother, completed by the Catholics in 1924 is set among 58 serenely beautiful acres at N.E. Sandy Blvd. and 86th. The Grotto, a natural

cliff overhang, serves as the sanctuary's outdoor altar with the surrounding trees forming cathedral-like walls and the sky its ceiling.

Latter Day Saints, Portland Stake House, S.E. Harrison & 29th, 1929.

When Temple Beth Israel, at S.W. 12th and Main, burned in December 1923, the reform congregation marshalled its financial forces over the next three years to construct the dramatic, domed synagogue at N.W. 19th and Flanders, dedicated in 1928.

One story has it that the new Temple Beth Israel emotionally overwhelmed a former member of a German congregation when he stepped through its doors because of its similarity to his own Nazi-occupied synagogue.

Laudable among latter day edifices is the Mormons' Portland Stake House and Chapel at S.E. 29th and Harrison. Oregon's largest L.D.S. church was erected in 1929. The merger of two local conservative Jewish congregations, Ahavai Sholom and Neveh Zedek Talmud Torah, created Neveh Shalom and in 1963 an ultramodern complex just off S.W. Dosch Rd. was occupied. Two years later the orthodox Shaari Torah congregation completed its new synagogue at N.W. 25th and Lovejoy which also houses Hillel Academy.

The greatest problem facing most faiths in recent times is relevance to the younger generation in a rapidly changing world. As adherents have dropped away, the loss of financial support has meant difficult days for many local churches.

Whatever your own religious convictions during this holiday season, keep in mind those precepts common to all religions — love, peace and goodwill.

Answer: In the Tri-County metro area there are approximately 110 different religious faiths and more than 700 church structures.

Portland memorials: Lone Fir Cemetery

May 16, 1986

A 7-year-old child's epitaph (left). One of the few remaining Chinese grave stones (right). What happened to the hundreds of others? (Answer below cartoon.)

If cemeteries share one trait, besides being a final resting place, it's solitude. Not loneliness or melancholy, but tranquility. A peaceful, quiet and often strikingly beautiful setting.

I know of which I speak, having recently spent, for the first time, a fair amount of time striding over well-trimmed lawns and between marble markers in and around the Portland area.

Among these local plots of land, set aside to memorialize the dearly departed, one of the least known and most interesting is Lone Fir Cemetery. This close-in, Southeast Portland burial site is bounded by Stark, Morrison, 20th and 26th. Under its sod lie some of the area's earliest pioneers including a distant relative of mine who was originally owner of the cemetery property — James B. Stephens along with his wife, Elizabeth.

parcel was platted and filed under the title of Mt. Crawford Cemetery.

Lot 1, Block 1 was set aside for the Barrell family. Barrell donated Block 5 to the Fire Department in 1862 and sold two additional blocks to local Masonic lodges. Thirteen acres were added in 1865 and seven more the following year to complete the cemetery's current configuration of 30.5 acres.

In 1866, Barrell offered the cemetery to the City of Portland for $4,000 but the Common Council turned him down on the grounds that it was too far out of town. In fact, at the time it was more than a half day's journey for a funeral procession to set out from a west side undertaker, cross the river on the Stark Street Ferry, continue to the cemetery and return.

(left to right.) Shattuck Family marker. Soldier's monument, 1903. The MacLeay's $13,500 mausoleum, Tibbets' obelisk.

On the far eastern boundary of his farm, which was a pioneer land grant extending back from the Willamette, Stephens buried his father, Emmor Stephens. When he sold the property to Coburn Barrell in 1854, Stephens stipulated that Barrell maintain the grave.

Coburn Barrell honored that agreement and took it a step further. The same year that he purchased the property, a river steamboat in which he held a partnership interest exploded at Canemah, killing his partner, Crawford Dobbins, and David Fuller, a passenger.

Barrell had both men buried near the grave of Emmor Stephens and dedicated 10 acres as a cemetery. In August 1855, he bought 10 adjacent acres from his neighbors, the Murrays, and the entire

After the city declined the purchase, it was bought by private citizens and incorporated on July 16, 1866, taking a new name suggested by Mrs. Aurelia Barrell — Lone Fir Cemetery for the single fir standing near the cemetery's original group of graves.

By the early 20th century most of the plots had been sold and maintenance fell to owners and relatives of the many pioneers already buried there. By 1928 the cemetery was in such a state of deterioration that Multnomah County was granted custody of the property by special state legislation.

Under the county, Lone Fir has been restored to its former beauty, now boasts dozens of stately Douglas Firs, and is open daily from 10 to 4 for appreciation by all.

Answers: Once occupying the cemetery's entire south side, they were sent to China for reburial.

Portland memorials: The two Riverviews

May 22, 1985

Riverview Cemetery's Spanish American War Monument. What has been stolen, from the soldier's statue? (Answer below cartoon.)

Where Portland's West Hills curve back to the east, sloping steeply up from the Willamette, there is a commanding sweep of hillside. On this site, with its breathtaking panorama of the river and the the city beyond, Portland's pioneer elite chose to establish their private cemetery.

In 1881, a dozen families headed by the Corbetts, the Ladds and the Failings, founded the Riverview Cemetery Association. Portland's most prominent and powerful trio ensured the success of any local enterprise and Riverview was no exception.

The view from Riverview Cemetery looking north across Riverview Abbey to the river and downtown.

The group raised $130,000 within a year to start the cemetery which was incorporated on December 4, 1882. Thirty percent of receipts was earmarked for an endowment which continues to this day and currently exceeds $2,000,000.

Riverview burgeoned as the burial place of choice for Portland's preeminent citizens and their families. By 1900 the remains of more than 60 pioneers had been moved from Lone Fir Cemetery to Riverview. Such local names as Dolph, Failing, Flanders, Goodnough, Hoyt, Northrup, Skidmore and Terwilliger were significant among them.

The most sensational event to shock this otherwise serene setting was the grave robbery on May 18, 1897, of cemetery founder William S. Ladd's body. Diligent detective work on the part of Portland's finest led to its recovery and the arrest of four would-be-extortionists. To ensure that no such incident could occur again, Ladd's coffin was encased in concrete after being returned to its rightful resting place.

On the south and north sides of Taylor's Ferry Road the name Riverview is prominently displayed leading the casual passerby to conclude that this is all one large complex. But such is not the case.

On the south lies the family association's cemetery and mausoleum (indoor cemetery). On the north is the Riverview Abbey, a mausoleum, crematorium and mortuary established in 1916. It was originally built as an adjunct to the cemetery, but soon after became a separate entity, the Portland Mausoleum Co.

In 1930, W.R. Griffith & Sons, a concrete contractor engaged to increase the mausoleum's crypt capacity, took over its ownership. The Griffith family still operates Riverview Abbey and has continued to expand it over the decades.

The complex currently covers 3.5 acres on two levels. Stained glass skylights and magnificent marble stretch along a seemingly endless series of corridors named for flowers and trees. Almost 26,000 people are entombed here and 16 additional acres are dedicated to future growth.

Across Taylor's Ferry, on more than 350 meticulously landscaped acres, more than 50,000 have found their final home with room for as many more on undeveloped acreage to the south.

The two Riverviews may be separate, but together they make an impressive presence. Both facilities welcome visitors, whether to stroll through marble corridors or a pastoral park. Either way the experience is uplifting.

AN AFTERNOON AT RIVERVIEW IN THE 1880'S ~ FROM WEST SHORE MAGAZINE

Answer: The soldier's larger-than-life cast-iron rifle was taken in 1977 and has not been recovered.

Portland memorials: The Portland Memorial

June 5, 1985

Marble engraving has almost become a lost art. How many master carvers are there in the Portland area? (Answer below cartoon.)

Traveling along S.E. Bybee just before it makes the final curve south to merge with 13th Ave., a large sprawling complex of handsome buildings stands on the bluff above the Willamette.

The facades afford the casual observer no clue as to their identity. Is this combination of Victorian, Deco and Spanish, in the midst of a manicured garden setting, some millionaire's mansion done in an add-on eclectic style? Not quite.

A couple of discreet signs tell the tale. "The Portland Memorial," they state. "Mausoleum. Crematorium. Funeral Home." This facility is, in fact, the oldest of its kind in the Northwest (and the largest indoor cemetery west of the Mississippi).

It was begun in 1901, as a crematorium, by a group of Portland businessmen. The original Victorian building (perched right on the edge of the bluff closest to Bybee) is a columbarium—an indoor

Heathman, John Yeon, Rudy Wilhelm and Mayor George L. Baker.

The staff has a few favorite stories to tell. One is about Mayo Methot, who died in 1951. She was Humphrey Bogart's first wife and for years after her death a dozen roses arrived weekly to decorate the marble-covered niche she shares with her father and mother.

Another tale relates to the Rae Room, the most magnificent crypt on the entire 3.5 acre site. Two massive, free-standing sarcophaguses are side by side. On the right is George, who died in 1918 at 75. His wife, Elizabeth, 26 years his junior, is on the left. The beautifully vaulted and decorated, stained-glass-adorned crypt is opened only once a year—on Memorial Day. It seems no relatives would visit a man, even a very wealthy one, who'd run off with his maid.

A portion of the courtyard (left), Carrara marble statues (center) and a corridor on Memorial Day (right).

memorial for incinerated remains or "cremains."

More than 35 percent of people in the West opt for cremation today but it was less than 5 percent at the turn of the century. The Portland Memorial's founders reasoned that the benefits of an elegant and dry final resting place would appeal not only to future occupants but also to the relatives who could come to pay their respects and contemplate fond memories indoors.

Later owners added a mausoleum (indoor cemetery) in the 1920s and subsequent additions culminated in an eight-story building at the north end of the complex, four of which descend down the hillside.

As with Lone Fir and Riverview Cemeteries, The Portland Memorial is a treasure trove of local history. Among the nearly 58,000 permanent residents are such well known names as Zehntbauer and Jantzen, Amato, Franz, Shaver, Inman,

You can almost get lost in the labyrinthian combination of interconnecting buildings, halls, levels, staircases and corridors that comprise The Portland Memorial. Marble, brass, Italian statuary and stunning stained glass are everywhere. The new building has fountains that can be seen from several floors and panoramic views of the river.

The current owner, Jerry Westin, who bought the facility in 1979, has undertaken an ongoing program of preservation and expansion. Westin estimates that up to 120,000 can be accommodated with new additions and he wants more people to see this spectacular place. If you belong to a fraternal group, call and arrange a tour and get paid for coming. It's one of the ways The Portland Memorial promotes "pre-need." In other words, you shouldn't leave this last decision to someone else. Something to think about.

THIS STAINED GLASS IS SPECTACULAR. EVEN A **TIFFANY** FROM THE 20s

SUCH MAGNIFICENT MEMORIALS. BUT THEN, IT **WAS** BEFORE INCOME TAX.

Klooster '85

Answer: Only one: Carl Anacker. The only other local master marble carver, German born Julius Morains, has retired.

Profiles of long-time, local private enterprises

Collectively, this group of homegrown organizations represents most, but certainly not all, of the best that the Rose City has spawned. A number of important ones are missing. All this means is that I simply haven't gotten to them yet and there's more to come in future installments of *Round the Roses*. Though a few of the firms profiled here are no longer in existence, they made quite a mark in their day. Others have attained positions of national prominence.

Among those omitted that merit mention are the following major corporations: Chown Hardware, ESCO, Hoffman Construction, Leupold & Stevens, Pacific Power and Light, Portland General Electric and Reidel International. Important retailers and restaurateurs, past and present, include Ben Selling Clothiers, Fahey-Brockman, J.K. Gill, Hilaire's, Kelly's Olympian, The Old Country Kitchen, The Ringside and Henry Thiele's, Kelly's, by the way, has beaten out the White Eagle (unless some obscure unknown crops up) as the verified, oldest, continuous-operation restaurant in the same location. It has held forth on Washington Street since 1902.

Georgia-Pacific, the lumber giant, and Hyster Corporation, king of the fork lifts, made significant contributions to the Rose City. Since, however, both committed the ultimate effrontery by abandoning the area after having their headquarters here for umpteen years each, they were not given priority on these pages.

Now for a few updates. Lipman, Wolfe & Company's successor, Frederick & Nelson, stands empty on S.W. Fifth Avenue. Downtown store employees came to work one morning in October, 1986 and found the doors locked. No warning. No jobs. No class. Leave it to a Seattle-based outfit. There's a rumor that the old Lipman's owners might resurrect the ten-story, two-basement department store. But, no news, yet.

Local micro-breweries have begun fermenting some super suds since the 1983 *Roses* story on Blitz-Weinhard. It stated that "Blitz has been Oregon's only brewery since 1952." Other than that, its been pretty much business as usual with positive signs of an upswing in Oregon's economy.

Blitz-Weinhard: From Henry to Heileman

July 27, 1983

The spout opened. The mug filled and foamed with sparkling brew. Blitz's colorful neon sign was a Portland landmark. What happened to it? (Answer below cartoon.)

When Henry Weinhard established his first modest brew house just outside Fort Vancouver in 1856, he wrote the first chapter of an original Oregon story. The pioneer German immigrant had what it took to grow and prosper in those early entrepreneureal days.

Relocating his brewery to Portland in 1862, he became a pillar of the Portland establishment, directing the destiny of the business he built until his death in 1904.

Henry Weinhard would have been proud of his successor's resourcefulness in surviving Prohibition. Near beer and soft drink franchises kept son-in-law Henry Wessinger's ship afloat. In 1928 he negotiated a merger with Arnold Blitz of the Portland Brewing Co. The resulting Blitz-Weinhard Company was ready to resume business in 1933, when America's abstinence experiment ended.

brands, the Wessingers changed direction. Buying out other owners in 1974, the brothers launched what has proved to be one of the great latter-day success stories in America's brewing industry — Henry Weinhard's Private Reserve. The new "super premium," perfected in 1976, quickly showed the competition its heels.

It soon became apparent, however, that more muscle would be needed to maintain the momentum. In 1979 the brewery was sold to Pabst of St. Louis, which committed their resources, under the Wessinger's management, to the continuing development of Henry's Private Reserve.

By late 1982, Henry's was the talk of saloons from Seattle to San Diego. It was also at the center of a takeover try pitting "brand buster" Paul Kalmanovitz of General Brewing against G. Heileman of La Crosse, Wisconsin. The future of

Henry Weinhard (1832-1904), his City Brewery and his legacy, Henry's.

Since 1952, Blitz had been Oregon's only brewery, and grandsons Bill and Fred Wessinger, who assumed the helm in the mid-'60s, brought the fortunes of their flagship, Blitz-Weinhard, to its high point — selling one-third of all the beer in Oregon. But the hometown advantage didn't stop an onslaught of out-of-town competitors.

The national mega-brewers chipped away at Blitz's lead and, recognizing that they couldn't outspend the big

the brewery hung in the balance.

Although the boardroom battle was touch and go, Heileman finally gained control. Blitz is still in Portland. Henry's can be had in the best bars of ten Western states. And people are even starting to call it "Hank's." But Henry Weinhard wouldn't have minded. After all, it's good for business.

Answers: It was destroyed in the Columbus Day storm, October 12, 1962.

Meier & Frank: Meet me under the clock

July 27, 1983

Vacuum tube room, 1922. M&F's most famous employee was called "Billy" and he sold men's ties that year. Who was he? (Answer below cartoon.)

If customers of young Aaron Meier's general store at Front and Yamhill wanted to know the time, the 26-year-old German immigrant had to pull out his pocket watch. This shortcoming was remedied in a big way with the installation of what became Portland's most famous clock on the main floor of Meier & Frank's 14-story edifice at Fifth and Alder.

First 5th & Morrison building, opened 1898.

But more than a half-century would pass between the opening of that first 30-foot-by-50-foot retail establishment in 1857 and the dedication of "the largest store west of Chicago" in 1915. Over those years, Portland grew from a frontier village of some 1300 hardy inhabitants to a metropolis of nearly a quarter million.

Aaron Meier could scarcely have envisioned the heights his little enterprise would reach as he struggled to keep the business alive during its first decade. Shedding two partners in the process, he finally found the right combination. He met Emil Frank on a buying trip to San Francisco in 1870, and offered him a clerking job. Two years later Emil's younger brother, Sigmund, joined them. Thus was created Meier & Frank.

When Meier died in 1889, Sigmund assumed the helm and, since he had married the boss' daughter, Fannie, four years earlier, ownership was kept in the family. In addition to managing the store and masterminding its move to the present site, which later became the heart of downtown, Sigmund helped found the Portland Symphony and performed as lead violinist.

The new store, which would outdo and improve upon its five-story predecessor in every area of merchandise and service, was on the drawing board when Sigmund died in 1910. It fell upon the founder's son, Abe Meier, to see it through planning and construction over the next five years.

Abe's younger brother, Julius, took over the top post in 1930 and from 1931-34 shared his presidential duties with those of Oregon's governorship. As an independent, Meier swept the state and was an early force behind the establishment of our hydroelectric system. He also oversaw completion of the full-block renovation that brought the department store to its present configuration in 1932.

Crowded store during War Bond drive, 1944.

Leadership passed back to the Franks in 1937, when Sigmund and Fannie's son, Aaron, took the reins, holding them proudly and productively for 25 years. This period saw the Salem and Lloyd Center stores open with record sales. Julius' son, Jack, became president in 1964, marking 107 years as a family firm.

But the dynasty ended in 1966, when inter-family feuding opened the door for a stock battle between department store titans Broadway-Hale and the May Co. The latter emerged as victor and, to its credit, has kept Meier & Frank on a winning course to this day.

Answer: An itinerant theater troupe bit player named William Clark Gable, then 21 years old.

114

Northwest Natural: A gas since 1859

February 15, 1984

Part of Gasco's 36-motorcycle service fleet in 1920. What happened when a major generating plant fire occurred in 1956? How many service personnel are there today? (Answers below cartoon.)

When Henry Green and H.C. Leonard were granted a perpetual franchise to establish Oregon's first gas utility, early in 1859, they knew they had something good going.

The country's earliest gas works had been established in Baltimore in 1816, New York had had gas lights since 1829 and London beat them all turning on in 1812.

Shipping equipment 'round the Horn, it was more than a year before service began with just 49 customers. Leonard and Green's little utility, Portland Gas Light Company, was incorporated in 1862.

to take over the westside, eastside and St. John's operations.

Gas generation had evolved from an inefficient distilling process of carbonized coal to the controlled quality "blue or water-gas" method produced from crude oil.

Through the '20s and '30s, Gasco expanded its service throughout Portland into East Multnomah and Washington counties and down the Willamette Valley.

Secondary products were an important part of the company's business through the '40s. Briquets, benzoil

The 2nd Gasco plant at the foot of N.W. Everett operated from 1892 to 1913.

1868 was the first year gas was called upon for something other than lighting. The city's "common council" arranged for the company to keep the water hot in their horse-drawn fire engine boilers.

After extensive expansion and development, the company was sold in 1892. The group of new owners, who dropped "Light" from the name, was headed by Charles Adams and Abbott Mills (later president of the 1st National Bank).

The current company's direct origins can be traced to 1910 when Portland Gas & Coke Co. (Gasco) was formed

(which was used to make synthetic rubber during WWII) and Roadbinder, which surfaced the runways at Portland Columbia airport, were discontinued in 1956 with conversion to low-cost, clean-burning natural gas via the Canadian and Southwest pipeline networks.

As the newly named Northwest Natural Gas hit its hundredth year in 1959, an eternal gas flame more than 70 feet high burned at Oregon's Centennial Exposition.

Now, a quarter of a century later, the company is in its sparkling new "Old Town" building and serves 258,925 customers in Oregon and Southwest Washington. Happy 125th to Northwest Natural and the Beaver State.

Answers: From all over the West, 500 gas men flew to Portland to help restore service. Today there are 397.

The money merchants: First was first

October 2, 1985

First to offer night banking for WWII workers, what's another First National customer convenience first? (Answer below cartoon).

When Addison and Lewis Starr, mayor-to-be Philip Wasserman, Alexander Ankeny and Henry Eddy drew up the "Articles of Association" for the very first national bank on the West Coast, they chose July 4, 1865, as their charter date. It was a special Independence Day for Portlanders—a milestone in the city's continuing growth.

The founders petitioned the Comptroller of the Currency for the name, "First National Bank of Oregon." The comptroller was not so magnanimous. When the papers were returned, the name had been altered to "First National Bank of Portland."

Corbett Bldg. First Ave., 1871; First & Washington, 1882

Just four years later, two of the three richest men in town bought out First National's original owners. Henry Corbett and his brother-in-law, Henry Failing, increased the institution's capital stock from $100,000 to $250,000. The two could easily have started their own bank but, having been first in almost everything else, they probably wanted the prestige of the first "national" financial organization as well.

Honors for the first bank had already gone to the single wealthiest Portlander of the day, William S. Ladd, who founded his Ladd & Tilton Bank in 1859. Unlike Ladd's bank, which was a private company, the First National was subject to federal scrutiny from the outset. Ten months passed before the bank received its first currency issuance and opened on May 7, 1866.

Beginning business at 79 Front Street, a move was soon made next door to Portland's first brick building, owned by Mr. Ladd. In 1871, with Failing as president and Corbett, vice president, the First National Bank occupied the ground floor of Corbett's new building on First between Washington and Alder. Eleven years later they moved into the bank's fourth location and the first one it could call its own, a $125,000 three-story brick bastion at First and Washington.

Surviving a national depression in 1884 and the financial panic of 1893, which took seven local banks down in its wake, First National emerged as Portland and Oregon's largest banking institution. In 1903 Abbot Mills, a wealthy and well-connected Eastern financier who had come to Portland in 1889, succeeded Henry W. Corbett as president.

During Mills' 24-year tenure, he became one of Portland's leading citizens and guided the First National to even greater prominence. Pivotal to his success was investment in the city's public transit system.

In 1930 A.P. Giannini's Bank of America bought controlling interest in First National which it has retained ever since.

1933 saw passage of the Glass-Steagall Act allowing national banks to open branches in their respective states. By the end of that year, First National had opened 16 offices in nine communities. Expansion continued rapidly over the next four years. By 1937, the bank could boast 42 branches serving 35 Oregon cities and resources 250 percent greater than in 1932.

First National's leadership role in helping finance the state's growth marked the organization's progress through the war years and into the second half of the century. Solid top management took it to a billion-dollar year in 1959.

In 1964 the First National Bank finally got "of Oregon" on the end as its founders had intended back in 1865. The singular monument to the bank's place in Oregon's free enterprise system rose above the Portland skyline in 1972. Still today, at 546 feet, the now First Interstate Tower is the state's tallest building.

PEOPLE ASK ME HOW I DID SO WELL SO **QUICKLY** HERE IN CONSERVATIVE PORTLAND.

ABBOT L. MILLS President First National Bank of Portland (1903-1927)

WELL, MY FAMILY BACKGROUND WAS EASTERN ELITE AND MY **HARVARD** ALUMNI TIES HELPED.

THE **FIVE** MILLION DOLLARS I BROUGHT ALONG TO INVEST DIDN'T HURT EITHER!

Directorships:
OREGON RAILWAY & NAVIGATION
OREGON ELECTRIC RAILWAY CO.
OREGON LIFE INSURANCE CO.
PORTLAND CONSOLIDATED RAILWAY
PORTLAND GAS & COKE CO.
HOME TELEPHONE CO.
SECURITY SAVINGS & TRUST CO.

Klooster '85

Answer: The $5.5 billion, 167-branch First Interstate Bank of Oregon is part of a $40 billion, 930-office, 11-state network.

Portland Merchants: Olds & King

May 1, 1985

Oregon State College students, all summer employees, discuss back-to-school fashions from Olds & King's. Can you guess the year? (Answer below cartoon.)

Portland's most deeply rooted department store dates back to 1851. A consignment of stock to pioneer merchant Henry Corbett, which came 'round the Horn from the East Coast, comprised the initial inventory of the riverside village's first general store.

Within a year it became the McLaren store which it was called when John Wilson, later to become a prominent benefactor of the Portland Library, bought it in 1856. Wilson carried on the operation for the next 22 years.

Partners W.P. Olds and C.W. King bought him out in 1878, renaming the store after themselves. Apparently they held Wilson's ability in high regard for he stayed on as

"uptown" to S.W. 10th and Morrison. There a five-story, full-block, 240,000 square-foot facility, with a dramatic interior atrium, was completed in 1910.

Over the years the highly competitive Olds, Wortman & King's department store built its reputation on value for money. "We will *not* be undersold" was their motto. "The Store," as many loyal customers called it, was the first to install public phones and the first to hire women clerks.

Local ownership ended in 1925 when Lee Schlesinger, former manager of San Francisco's elite City of Paris, bought the business. There were several owners in the 1940s and '50s and, in 1951, Wortman's name was

Olds, Wortman & King's 1891 building at 5th and Washington (left).

comptroller for many years.

Olds & King's continued expansion called for several moves over the ensuing dozen years. They relocated to Third Avenue and then to three stories of a building at S.W. Taylor and First. In 1891 the firm occupied the first store built for them at Fifth and Washington.

It was also the first store to bear the name of H.C. Wortman, who had joined the company in 1880. Olds, Wortman and King remained in the four-story facility until 1903 at which time they took over their second custom quarters, the Exchange Building at 514 S.W. 6th, one of the city's earliest steel frame structures.

Just seven years later the ultimate move was made

exterior of 1910 building at 10th and Morrison (right).

dropped from the store title. Since the late 1930s only "Olds & King's" had been used in store promotion.

When the Rhodes chain took the reins in 1960, the Olds & King's name became history. Thirteen years later, Liberty House-Rhodes, a division of the Honolulu-based conglomerate, Amfac, Inc. closed the 10th and Morrison store permanently and converted their suburban outlets to the Liberty House name.

It took the ingenuity of Portland's Naito family to revitalize the property in 1976. A glittering shopping arcade was designed to maximize the effect of the five-story enclosed atrium and a great retailing tradition was brought back to life as the Galleria.

Answer: The photo was taken on August 30, 1939.

Portland merchants: Lipman, Wolfe & Co.

April 24, 1985

This 1912 newspaper ad invited fashionable ladies to the grand opening of Lipman, Wolfe & Co.'s new Fifth and Alder store. What was rival Meier & Frank's response? (Answer below.)

Side by side, cheek to jowl, two Portland department store flagships have competed for 73 years. The battle for customer bucks continues but, over the years, the names of the principals have changed many times. One of the marquees even bears a different banner these days.

The corner of SW Fifth and Alder is the scene of the confrontation. On the south side stands the venerable Meier and Frank Co., founded by pioneer Portland merchant Aaron Meier in 1857, at its present location since 1898.

Fifth and Washington entrance, 1956

Its across-the-street adversary, Lipman, Wolfe & Co., which today is Frederick & Nelson, relocated there in 1911. But the company dates back to 1850. In that year Solomon Lipman opened his first general merchandise store in Sacramento during its gold-rush glory. He was an instant success.

Over the succeeding 16 years he steadily built the business and then brought his favorite nephew, 18-year-old Adolphe Wolfe, on board to open a branch store of S. Lipman & Co. in wild and wooly Virginia City, Nevada.

Adolphe proved his worth over the next 14 years and, in 1880, they decided to expand into the promising Portland market. Wolfe established the first store to carry the Lipman, Wolfe & Co. name at S.W. 1st and Washington.

In 1892, the elderly Solomon Lipman sold his California interests and joined his nephew in Portland. They moved the store to the fashionable Dekum Building at Third and Washington, where it did a thriving business for 20 years.

At age 64, Adolphe Wolfe engineered the big move to Fifth and Alder. The new, 10-story, double basement facility made the corner the focus of downtown shopping. In 1925, Adolphe finally relinquished control of the company to National Department Stores of New York. Wolfe, a much loved and admired employer and civic leader, remained in a consulting capacity making regular office appearances until his death in 1934 at age 86.

He was succeeded by his own nephew, Harold Wendel, who saw the store change hands three times during a 40-year tenure. National sold to South American Gold and Silver, which in turn passed ownership to locally owned Roberts Department Stores in 1956.

The Roberts' reign was a good one for Lipman's. They transformed it into a superb, fashionably appointed specialty store. 1968 saw the 85-year-old Roberts' operation merge with Dayton-Hudson of Minneapolis with continued expansion to shopping malls and other Oregon cities.

In 1979, Dayton sold to Chicago's Marshall Field, spelling the end for the Lipman's name. Yet the spirit of the proud proprietors who built this enduring enterprise is not forgotten. And its successor, Frederick & Nelson, is a Northwest merchant name dating back to 1890. But that's a Seattle story.

Answer: Meier & Frank built "the largest department store west of Chicago" across Alder three years later.

Early eateries: Huber's since 1879

September 11, 1985

Jim Louie (1870-1946). How many turkeys did he feel you had to cook to become good at it? What is the popular Huber's drink he never made? (Answers below.)

The restaurant business is tough. Just ask anyone who's in it. Ten years is well established. Twenty-five is a fixture. So, at 106 years old, Huber's must be a monument.

Starting out in 1879 as the Bureau Saloon, it rapidly became a favorite watering hole for local luminaries. Original owner W.L. Lightner owed much of the credit for the saloon's success to Frank Huber, the affable, attentive and nattily attired bartender he hired in 1884.

Huber, who had spent several years behind the bars of other Portland public houses became sole proprietor of the Bureau four years later. Seeking additional ways to build business, he decided to offer a limited luncheon fare.

The place soon gained a reputation for quality which was

Interior of Huber's in the 1920s, now a national historical landmark.

provided by a young Chinese immigrant named Jim Louie. Louie had been a Portlander for 10 years when, in 1891, Huber stole the 21-year-old chef away from another establishment. It was the beginning of a family association with the restaurant that continues to this day.

During the fabled flood of '94, Jimmie enhanced his following by serving steamed clams and turkey sandwiches from a rowboat behind the counter of the flooded saloon. The following year found them in a new location at 281 Washington St. with the name officially changed to Huber's. Frank presided at the bar and Louie, by now a favorite of downtown businessmen, commanded the lunch counter.

In 1911, Huber's moved into its present home, resplendent in Phillipine mahogany, beveled mirrors and stained glass ceiling. With Frank Huber's sudden death the next year, management fell to Jimmie on behalf of Mrs. Huber. Assuming the proprietor's position as bartender, he carried on with the same dignity and demeanor that had been Huber's trademark.

Though he now had a young man prepare and serve the sandwiches, Jim Louie continued to cook the turkeys and hams himself, He took particular pride in his turkeys and the perfection that he was certain came only from long experience. "Cook 1,000 turkey, know a little bit. Cook 50,000 and know something about it," paraphrases his sentiments.

Although Louie and Mrs. Huber almost closed the saloon at the onset of Prohibition customers encouraged them to convert the operation to a restaurant. With an expanded menu, Huber's flourished and gained national prominence for serving turkey 365 days a year. Regulars referred to the restaurant as "the Chinaman's" or just "Jimmie's."

Mrs. Huber died in 1940 and Louie formed a partnership with her son, John. Six years later, following a full day of work at the place that had been his life for 55 years, Jim Louie died there. His nephew, Andrew, fell heir to Jimmie's half ownership and bought out John Huber in 1952.

Andrew Louie's sons, James and David, oversee daily operations today and Huber's enjoys a popularity as great as ever. Jimmie would have been proud of their efforts to carry forward the tradition. But he'd undoubtedly apologize for the fact that, with just a few thousand turkeys under his belt, the current chef is still only an amateur.

Answers: 50,000 turkeys. The currently acclaimed flaming Spanish coffee hadn't been created in Jimmie's time.

Fred Merrill: Wheelin' 'n' dealin'

November 11, 1987

The Multnomah Athletic Club "Early Birds," 1895. What caused the decline in the cycle craze a decade later? (Answer below cartoon.)

In the late 1890s, a new fad swept the country—bicycling. Outdoor-loving, exercise oriented Portlanders took to the trend with particular enthusiasm. Cycling clubs sprang up among the jaunty, young crowd. Otherwise dainty damsels could be seen pedaling tenaciously over hill and dale. The era of the highwheeler, the racer and the tandem was in full swing along the boulevards and byways of the Rose City.

By this time, of course, bicycling was nothing new. The first American manufacturer had begun turning out a variety of two wheelers in 1878. A young Portland entrepreneur named Fred T. Merrill had, himself, already been in the business for a dozen years when the craze hit. He recognized a golden opportunity and latched onto it.

Merrill's bicycle showroom, largest in the country.

Merrill was the exclusive Northwest dealer for the Rambler and Pacemaker brands. He had quite a reputation in cycling circles, having captured the Oregon State Bicycling Championship in 1884, the year before he opened the town's first retail outlet.

Seizing the situation, Merrill quickly opened a huge new showroom at Sixth and Alder. The 100-by-200-foot facility was the largest of its kind in the country. In 1898, the first full year of the five-year nationwide bicycling phenomenon, he sold 8,850 units— more than any other dealer in the Western United States.

If it had wheels and was recreational, Merrill somehow got involved with it. He sold trikes as well as bikes and, when the automobile began to make its appearance in Portland at the turn of the century, he became one of the town's earliest car dealers.

The two modes of transportation were more compatible than competitive. In fact, bicycle enthusiasts aided the cause of the motor car by lobbying for better road conditions. At the Oregon Road Club's 1896 convention in Portland, state Senator Joseph Dolph advised advance planning to secure funds from the state legislature. The first car would not arrive in Oregon until two years later.

While good-roads supporters continued their efforts, the cyclists got a new bike path from Portland to the Columbia's edge across from Vancouver. According to an *Oregonian* article, a summery Sunday afternoon might see as many as 3,000 two-wheelers on this route.

All the more business for Fred Merrill who, in addition to selling bicycles hand over fist, was busy running for a city council seat. He served three terms under the old ward system representing the Third Ward, which ran from the river to the city limits between Southwest Washington and Northwest Glisan streets.

This constituency included many businesses and Merrill became their favorite. Although an apparently honest politician, he operated under the old capitalistic principle that "what's good for business is good for society." Always pragmatic, it was his contention that drinking, gambling and prostitution cannot be eliminated; therefore, they should be licensed and controlled and made to pay their fair share of taxes.

At the same time he was lookng after the interests of the local business community, Merrill was watching out for his own enterprises. When he entered the auto arena, there were dozens of makes to choose from, many of which would fall by the wayside within a decade. He selected Ford.

Carrying the car connection a step further, in 1908 he built a mile-long, oval race track in northeast Portland. Speed contests were held there which attracted thousands of spectators into the early 1920s. It is now the "first nine" of Rose City Golf Course.

To cater to weekend motorists, he erected the 12-Mile House at what is now Southeast 232nd Avenue and Stark Street and even added a horse track next door. Merrill was one of those hardworking, hard-playing fellows for whom everything seemed to go right. In E. Kimbark MacColl's book *"Shaping of a City,"* he is quoted as saying that he wanted to be known as "one of the men who built Portland, made $1.5 million and spent it here."

Answer: Women of questionable character, wearing bright clothing and split skirts, took up the sport.

The Portland Symphony: Early orchestration

February 18, 1987

Willem van Hoogstraten conducting a 20-piano, 40-player concert, ca. 1935. What tragic occurrence brought him to Portland. (Answer below cartoon.)

Cultural considerations would seem to have held a low priority in a pioneer outpost barely beyond the basics. But Portland's early leaders were Eastern-born and bred. For them, the more refined aspects of proper Victorian society were important.

Little matter that theirs was a rough-and-tumble town. Those elements were relegated to the waterfront and the local elite had already headed for higher ground. The enjoyment of music, however, knows no barriers. Then, as now, the main difference is style.

While ordinary citizens stood in street corner saloons along Front and First avenues palavering over a pounding piano, River City's finest gathered at private homes uptown where they attentively took in the strains of a string quartet.

The Marquam Grand interior, ca. 1910.

Sigmund Frank was among the handful of amateur musicians who performed in those local parlors. A successful merchant and accomplished violinist, the soon-to-be department store mogul joined with other classical instrumentalists on June 15, 1866, to present Portland's first public concert. The site was the Oro Fino Hall on First Avenue and Wagner's "Tannhauser March" was among the pieces performed.

A town of only 6,000 could scarcely support regular concerts, much less a full-time orchestral group. But numerous performances attracted good attendance and several attempts to establish an orchestra were made over the next nine years until, in 1875, Portland's first Orchestral Society took root.

During the two decades that followed, devoted musicians found free rehearsal space, struggled to maintain a viable membership and shared equally in the profits from performances. Their efforts were rewarded in 1896 with the founding of the Portland Symphony Orchestra. By then, the city had grown to more than 75,000 and its leading citizens were immensely wealthy.

The new symphony joined a very exclusive group. Only five other major orchestras existed in the entire country and Portland's was the only one west of the Rockies until after 1900. Within three years of its establishment, an annual concert series was underway and, in 1902, the symphony went on tour for the first time, giving performances in Corvallis and Eugene.

Principal home of the local ensemble was the Marquam Grand Theater, now the site of the American Bank Building. Compositions by Beethoven, Schubert, Haydn and Mozart were performed under the batons of a series of "guest" conductors chosen from among well-known local musicians.

In 1911, the symphony went professional and embarked on a program that would see a full-time manager and offices, an expanded season, and subscription sales all put into place. By 1918, the orchestra had a permanent home base, the just-opened Civic Auditorium, where it gave the facility's first-ever performance.

The same year, the first resident conductor, Carl Denton, was hired. A graduate of London's Royal Academy of Music, Denton had a productive seven years in the position. In addition to performing the classics, he worked to popularize the works of American composers and added a chorus to the orchestral company. His successor, Willem van Hoogstraten, had the longest tenure of any resident conducter to date.

The European conductor came well credentialed. After attending the Conservatory of Cologne, van Hoogstraten conducted orchestras in Vienna, Salzburg, Berlin, Leipzig, Zurich, Oslo and Stockholm before becoming associated with the New York Philharmonic. Under his leadership, the Portland Symphony gained national recognition.

But the Great Depression put Portland's Symphony Society on the financial ropes. Support for the orchestra was suspended in 1938 and, with it, van Hoogstraten's services. For the next nine years, the Rose City would be without a symphonic season.

Tempo di Valse

Carl Denton (1918-1925)   Willem van Hoogstraten   (1925-1938)

klooster '87

Answer: Theodore Spiering, slated to succeed Carl Denton as resident conductor, died almost immediately after being appointed in 1925. Van Hoogstraten replaced him.

Oregon Symphony: Post-war counterpoint

February 25, 1987

Maestro Jacques Singer, Oregon Symphony Conductor (1962-72). What were the two most important occurences during his tenure? (Answer below cartoon.)

Discordant notes were played over Portland's classical music scene as the Great Depression drew to a close. The theme was "Hard Times" when the local Symphony Society disbanded in 1938 taking with it the orchestra's financial base. Although occasional performances, conducted by visiting impresarios, brought forth the faithful, nine years passed without a symphonic season.

Performers' view of Civic Auditorium audience.

Federal funding kept continuity in an otherwise sporadic situation. Works Progress Administration sponsorship of an annual "Stadium Philharmonic" series brightened Rose City summers as Multnomah (Civic) Stadium resounded to the strains of classical compositions. But it was the performers themselves who eventually pulled the Symphony back up by its own brass. In 1947, the Portland chapter of the American Federation of Musicians joined with a core of local supporters to resurrect and revitalize the Portland Symphony Society. New permanent conductor, Werner Janssen, was hired and the orchestra reorganized as a professional organization. Over the next 15 years, a succession of resident musical directors built on the base of their predecessors, each expanding the scope of the symphony.

When Maestro Jacques Singer took the conductor's stand in 1962, he had Janssen (1947-49), James Sample (1949-53), Theodore Bloomfield (1955-59) and Piero Bellugi (1959-61) to thank for molding an accomplished ensemble prior to his arrival.

Singer had made an early impact on the music world making his violin debut in New York's Town Hall at the age of 11. He then joined the Philadelphia Orchestra at 15, where his conducting abilities were soon recognized. Singer moved to Dallas in 1938 and, as conductor of that city's symphony, brought it national recognition.

During World War II, he served with distinction in the South Pacific then returned home to become director of the Vancouver (B.C.) Symphony in 1946. In the 1950s, Singer ranged the world as a guest conductor, receiving unprecedented ovations and lavish praise.

Over a 10-year tenure, Jacques Singer's dynamic presence and tremendous talent took the Portland Symphony to new heights. Under his guidance, all orchestra members were put under full-time contracts and the organization began annual tours throughout the state. In 1967, it reflected that expanded status with a new name—the Oregon Symphony Orchestra.

Throughout the following five years, premiere performances highlighted each Singer season. The symphony's inspired renditions of these premieres, as well as classical and contemporary works, reflected his conducting genius.

Singer's successor, Lawrence Leighton Smith, was introduced to Oregon audiences at the beginning of the 1973 season. Smith's credentials were already admirable by the time he became the symphony's eighth resident conductor. An Oregon native and Portland State University graduate, he debuted as a piano soloist at Carnegie Hall in 1962. Two years later he won the Dimitri Mitropoulos International Conducting Competition.

The New York and Los Angeles Philharmonics, the Minnesota Orchestra, Chicago's Grant Park Summer Orchestra, the Boston, Baltimore, Winnipeg, Tulsa, Austin, Phoenix and Pasadena symphonies all received the benefit of Lawrence Smith's gifted baton before he returned home. He also served three years as assistant conductor of the Metropolitan Opera and was on the faculty of several prominent universities.

When current conductor and music director James DePreist replaced Smith in 1980, he inherited the sometimes struggling but always proud past of the oldest orchestra in the West. DePreist has brought an international reputation to the position. He has continued the tradition of uncompromising excellence while serving as the chief spokesman for increased publc support.

Mastery of repertoire and inspired artistry mark the DePreist style that fills Civic Auditorium and other concert halls around the state. During seven sold-out seasons, he has elevated the Oregon Symphony to the first rank of American orchestras.

Answers: The name change from "Portland" to "Oregon" Symphony in 1967 and the complete remodeling of Civic Auditorium completed in 1968.

Oregon Historical Society: Himes time

August 5, 1987

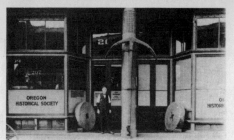

OHS temporary home (1914-17) at 205-7 Second St. Why did the Society occupy this location? (Answer below cartoon.)

On Oct. 18, 1873, a group of early Oregonians gathered at the home of Francis X. Matthieu in Butteville. Their purpose was to create an organization that would preserve the history they had had a part in making. The Oregon Pioneer Association, founded that day, filled the role for a quarter century.

During its first few decades, the association was vital and active. Its efforts to gather early maps and manuscripts, books and letters, relics and artifacts were invaluable. But the OPA had a fatal flaw. By the very limits of its membership requirements ("All comers to original Oregon prior to Feb. 14, 1859") it created its own eventual demise.

OHS museum in City Hall, ca. 1910.

At the association's annual meeting in 1928, the last three survivors of the Whitman Massacre were honored. By the late 1930s only a handful of members remained. The last of them, Mary Jane Clymer Taylor, died in March 1956 at 98. She had arrived in Oregon in 1858 as a baby.

Responsibility for pioneer history passed to the newly incorporated Oregon Historical Society on Dec. 18, 1898. The state-chartered body was charged with "the collection, preservation, exhibition and publication of material of a historical character, especially that related to Oregon and the U.S." *Oregonian* editor Harvey W. Scott became the society's first president. But its driving force for the 40 years to follow was George H. Himes.

Himes was a native of Pennsylvania who came to Oregon in 1853 when just a boy of 9. He apprenticed as a printer and bought a partnership of a Portland print shop in 1868. "Himes, the Printer"

produced flamboyant Western bard Joaquin Miller's first books and published numerous other early Oregon volumes over the years.

His keen interest in history gained Himes election as secretary of the Oregon Pioneer Association in 1886. He held the post for 53 years. When the Historical Society was created, George Himes was the logical choice as its first curator. He had already built a reputation for historic preservation work and extended the OPA's collection substantially.

Aided by University of Oregon professor Frederick Young, who became secretary and editor of the "Oregon Historical Quarterly," and assistant curator, John S. Greenfield, Himes ensconced the Society in its first quarters—3,300 feet of donated space at City Hall.

From its first year, the society emphasized the effort to designate and protect state historical sites. Public viewing of the collection and access to records was initially limited to afternoons two days a week but demand required expansion to a six-day schedule, Monday through Saturday from 1 to 5 p.m.

By 1916, the society's treasure trove had far outstripped available display area. Newspapers alone numbered more than 186,000, plus additional documents (13,507), books (14,028), pictures (6,775), lantern slides (854), pioneer relics (1,355), Indian relics (1,807), and pamphlets, letters, diaries, scrapbooks and maps.

In 1917, after two attempts at funding a new facility with bond issues failed, expanded space in the Public Auditorium was offered. Himes and his staff of five moved into what would be the Oregon Historical Society's home for the next 49 years.

George Himes died in 1940 at 95. The search for his successor ended in 1943 with the arrival of Lancaster "Jack" Pollard, who had developed a reputation as a historical writer, reviewer and critic on the *Seattle Post-Intelligencer*. During his 11 years as the Society's superintendent, Pollard authored several books and toured societies and museums across the country seeking innovations to apply locally.

When Pollard's successor, Thomas Vaughan, took the helm in 1954, an unprecedented period in the progress of the state's Historical Society was launched.

(The Vaughan era. — Pg. 123)

Answer: The city gave them a month to vacate their City Hall rooms. This was the best available on short notice and a limited budget.

Oregon Historical Society:
The Vaughan Era

August 12, 1987

These apartments once occupied the Oregon Historical Center site. Who designed the center? (Answer below cartoon.)

In June 1954, Thomas Vaughan, a 29-year-old Seattleite and recent doctoral candidate at the University of Wisconsin, became executive director of the Oregon Historical Society. Vaughan inherited an organization rich in memorabilia but lacking in wherewithal.

The Society's physical facility was a series of small rooms at the Public Auditorium. It had occupied them since 1917. There was no focal point for public interest. The young historian-administrator was, in his own words, "given free reign by a marvelous board of directors." He recognized, however, that things couldn't be changed overnight. Planning, patience and persistence became Vaughan's hallmarks, with a dash of brilliance thrown in.

Executive Director Thomas Vaughan in 1961.

Each year he went before the state legislature with persuasive arguments for an increase in the Society's annual appropriation. His articulate manner and slow, deliberate speaking style made him memorable. Eventually, his logic prevailed. Funding from both the public and private sectors grew and OHS programs were expanded.

During Vaughan's first decade as executive director, library acquisitions soared—books (175 percent), manuscripts (200 percent), film footage (600 percent) and photographs (800 percent). Commenting on his early emphasis toward building the society's photo and film collection, he says, "I just wanted to get as many as possible before any more were lost or destroyed.

Television's phenomenal success in the 1950s made it obvious that visual materials were the wave of the future. We worried about cataloging later."

Library usage more than doubled from 1955 to 1965 and so did the number of volunteers willing to aid OHS in its efforts. Vaughan's first major milestone was the Oregon Centennial Celebration in 1959. "In perspective," he admits, "it wasn't a spectacular event due to an unwillingness to commit substantial funding but we did attract regional attention and didn't lose money."

The monumental milestone of Vaughan's tenure to date has been the one which he made his primary focus for 12 years. In 1966, the Oregon Historical Center opened at Southwest Park and Jefferson. At last, the history of the Oregon Country had its showcase—a permanent home.

Once completed, the Center created a catalytic effort that was nothing short of synergism. Over the last two decades library holdings have skyrocketed—books from 31,000 to 70,000, photographs—800,000 to 2 million, film footage—500,000 to 6 million. During the same period, public usage of these resources has risen from 40,000 to 200,000 annually, volunteer ranks have swollen from 212 to 557 and OHS membership increased from 3,000 to 8,600.

When Tom Vaughan first arrived in Portland, a dedicated, overworked staff of five awaited him in their overflowing quarters at the Public Auditorium. Today's 72 full-time staffers are among the finest, if not *the* finest, group of historical specialists ever assembled anywhere.

Major exhibits, the new-age measure of museum stature, have garnered continuing acclaim for the state's society. last year's four-month-long Magna Carta show was a major media event that shattered all previous OHS attendance records. As Vaughan aptly points out, "such exhibitions tax resources and energies. Then the public expects more and better. If you jump 8½ feet, how about 9?"

Thomas Vaughan's goal is and always has been consistent high quality in whatever endeavor he or the Society undertakes. It's the Vaughan style reflected even in the search for his own successor. Though the 63-year-old executive director's retirement is still two years off, consideration of possible candidates will begin this fall. One can be assured that Tom Vaughan will play an important part in that selection.

Answer: Wolff/Zimmer/Gunsul/Frasca (now ZGF Partnership) were the architects. Pietro Belluschi was consulting designer.

124

OHSU:
A century of
medical education
April 15, 1987

The Medical Sciences Building, U of O Medical Schools' first structure on Marquam Hill, 1919. Where did its namesake, Dr. K.A.J. Mackenzie, live?

Oregon Health Sciences University marks its 100th anniversary on June 16, 1987. Known as the University of Oregon Medical School until 1974 and the University of Oregon Health Sciences Center until 1981, the nationally acclaimed school has come a long way in achieving that century milestone. And the embryo to which it owes its existence dates back even farther.

Willamette University in Salem established Oregon's first medical curriculum in 1865 but attracted no students until two years later. With limited facilities and few doctors in the small state capital, Willamette struggled for 11 years to maintain the department's viability, finally deciding to move it to Portland in 1878.

The Med School's home, 1893-1919. Northwest 23rd and Lovejoy.

With two hospitals and a much larger medical community from which to draw teachers and lecturers, the school could offer a comprehensive program to the 18 students enrolled that year. Though initial quarters were rooms above a livery stable at Southwest Park and Jefferson, they served the purpose for nine years. In 1887 a new building at Northwest 15th and Couch was completed to house the growing institution. It was to be a fateful year in Oregon medicine.

Disagreements split Willamette's medical faculty as the new facility was getting underway. A handful of key instructors resigned and enlisted the support of prominent local doctors in convincing the University of Oregon to set up a medical department at Portland. A charter was granted on June 16, 1887.

The University of Oregon Medical School began its first classes

from a former grocery store building moved to the property at Northwest 23rd and Marshall. Good Samaritan Hospital lent the land located next to a cow pasture. Dr. S.E. Josephi, the school's dean, and all members of the faculty cosigned a $1,000 loan for remodeling.

Two years later, street expansion necessitated a move one block south to Lovejoy. In 1893, the school got its first permanent home—an imposing three-story Victorian that occupied the quarter block on the 23rd and Lovejoy corner. A course in bacteriology was offered for the first time that year with students given the opportunity to view a tubercle bacillus through the Northwest's only microscope.

Two medical schools in Portland created keen competition for students and faculty. As a result, Willamette moved its department back to Salem in 1895. The demands of rapidly advancing technology strained the resources of both schools in the early years of the new century. U of O stepped up its standards, earning the American Medical Association's Class A rating in 1910. Willamette was rated Class C.

On September 1, 1913, the two schools merged, ending a 26-year rivalry and making the combined institution the only one of its type in the Northwest. It also had a new top administrator. After a quarter-century tenure, Dean Josephi, who had literally built the school from scratch, resigned. His successor, Dr. Kenneth A.J. Mackenzie, was a highly regarded faculty member. He immediately put new plans into action.

In addition to his university duties, Mackenzie had been chief physician for the Oregon-Washington Railroad and Navigation Co. The railroad owned 20 acres on the crest of Marquam Hill at the city's southern edge and the new dean saw it as the site for his school's promising future. One can only speculate why the O.W.R. & N. bought a hilltop for a proposed round-house but Mackenzie's request for its donation was approved within a year.

Overcoming considerable local resistance to such a remote location, Mackenzie enlisted the aid of department store tycoon Julius Meier in raising $25,000 to meet the conditions of a $50,000 appropriation from the state legislature. With this initial funding, construction of a medical sciences building commenced on May 1, 1918. Opened the following year, Mackenzie Hall stood alone on the hill for only a short time.

(The evolution of Pill Hill — Pg. 125.)

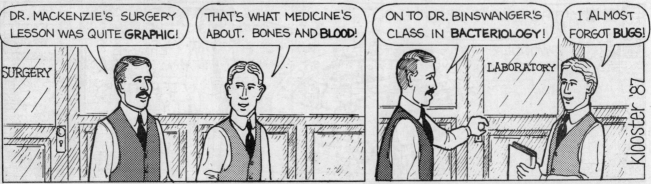

Answer: Mackenzie, prominent surgeon and the school's second dean, built a stone mansion, now the William Temple House, in northwest Portland.

OHSU:
The evolution of Pill Hill

April 22, 1987

U of O Med School Surgery Observation, ca. 1950. Who was the Marquam of Marquam Hill? (Answer below cartoon)

As Oregon Health Sciences University begins celebrating its 100th anniversary, its own "city on the hill" is tangible testimony to that century of accomplishment. From humble origins in a converted grocery store on Northwest 23rd and Marshall to completion of the first building atop Marquam Hill in 1919, the then University of Oregon Medical School gained in professional stature. But its 68 years on "Pill Hill" have seen the school's greatest growth.

Dr. Kenneth A.J. Mackenzie is the man who made the hill happen for his school while he was its second dean. He persuaded the O.W.R. & N. Railroad to donate the 20-acre site and convinced reluctant Portlanders to back "Mackenzie's Folly." Angina took the prominent surgeon's life in 1920 as construction of the Multnomah County Hospital was getting underway.

The Medical School in 1934.

Mackenzie's successor, Dr. Richard B. Dillehunt, shaped the school's next 23 years of dynamic development. "Dilly's" first step was to make certain that the second medical sciences unit was named Mackenzie Hall in honor of his predecessor. In 1924, a gift from the Jackson family of *Oregon Journal* fame enlarged the hillside campus by 88 acres.

The initial improvement to this newly acquired property, appropriately named Sam Jackson Park, was Doernbecher Memorial Hospital for Children. It was made possible in 1926 by a $200,000 gift from S.S. Doernbecher's children. Two years later the federal government erected its white-clad, Veterans's Hospital complex and, in 1931, the Outpatient Clinic was built with

$400,000 from the Rockefeller Foundation.

In 1939, the Medical School Library and Auditorium, along with the State Tuberculosis Hospital, rose on the hill—the result of private donations from Dr. John Weeks and the family of former governor Julius Meier. These additions highlighted the last years of Dillehunt's tenure. The school's third dean retired in 1943 due to ill health. Dr. David W.E. Baird then took the helm for 25 years, a term equalled only by the first dean, Dr. Simeon Josephi.

A University of Oregon grad, Baird's rule of thumb in decision making was "will it benefit the students?" During his administration, expansion efforts included the Crippled Childrens' Division (1954); the 14-story Medical School Teaching Hospital (1956), with the U of O Dental School's move to Marquam Hill coming the same year; the nine-story research building (1962); expansion of the library, a seven-story addition to the Outpatient Clinic and adjacent parking structure (1967).

Oregon's surgical superstar, Dr. Albert Starr, performed the world's first successful, artificial heart valve implant in 1960. Starr is only one of the volunteer instructors who have lent their skills and knowledge to the university over the years. When Dean Baird took office in 1943, he could count on the services of 102 unpaid professionals. By 1967, more than 600 part-timers augmented the full-time faculty.

During the 19 years since Baird's retirement, four highly qualified administrators have held the dean's post—Dr. Charles Holman (1968-75), Dr. Robert Stone (1975-79), Dr. Ransom Arthur (1979-80) and Dr. John Kendall, former chief of research for the Veterans' Hospital, who has been Oregon's top medical educator for eight years.

In 1974, the school was formally separated from its Eugene parent, taking on the name of University of Oregon Health Sciences Center. That appellation was changed to Oregon Health Sciences University in 1981 to more accurately reflect its independent status as an institution encompassing medicine, dentistry, nursing and research. Dr. Leonard Laster has been president of OHSU since 1978.

Portland's proud and prominent "Pill Hill" now boasts 26 buildings, a 500-member faculty, a new research facility—the Vollum Institute for Advanced Biomedical Research—a new V.A. Hospital and a worldwide reputation for innovative work in education, training, diagnosis, care and treatment.

Answer: Judge Philip A. Marquam was a prominent, early Portlander who once had extensive holdings in downtown, on the eastside and, originally, the sprawling hill property that bears his name.

The money merchants: Bank on U.S.

October 9, 1985

The Ainsworth Building became headquarters for U.S. National in 1902. Ainsworth Bank's founding was indisputable. What about U.S.? How large is it today? (Answers below cartoon.)

Seven Portlanders and two out-of-staters became the principals and directors of a new national banking corporation in Portland on Febuary 5, 1891. Donald Macleay, a sociable Scotsman who had already accumulated a "tidy fortune" as a local grocer, shipper and financier, convinced George W.E. Griffith of Kansas and the other initial investors to back the venture.

The combination created a financial institution comprised of such prominent Portland citizens as J.E. Hazeltine, Jacob Kamm, Rufus Mallory and Tyler Woodward, president of the Transcontinental Street Railway Co., member of the city council and second president, after Macleay, of the United States National Bank of Portland.

Exterior of U.S. National Bank's neo-classical edifice at Sixth and Stark.

Just two years after the fledgling financial institution opened its doors, the worse financial disaster in American banking history brought down seven local banks. But U.S. National was well financed and survived the Panic of 1893 to emerge as one of the primary contenders in the money marketplace.

In 1902 its merger with Ainsworth National made U.S. Oregon's second-largest bank, behind First National, and brought with it a new headquarters in the prestigious Ainsworth Building at Third and Oak.

Ainsworth & Co. had been formed as a private bank by sea Captain John C. Ainsworth in 1881. Nationally chartered four years later, it was, at the time of the merger, headed by Ainsworth's son, 32-year-old John C., who went on to guide the future course of U.S. for the next 29 years. During that time the modern banking industry took shape.

In 1907, the state formulated statutes to regulate the banks within its borders. Two-thirds of each bank's deposits had to be kept at other banks. The following year the National Monetary Commission was formed which led to the Federal Reserve Act of 1913. By instituting the "banker's bank" the government had a tool to control the money supply.

World War One shipbuilding helped buoy Oregon's economy and the big banks burgeoned. In 1917 U.S. merged with Lumberman's National, becoming the second-largest bank in the Northwest, and completed a new headquarters building at 6th and Stark. The A.E. Doyle neo-classical design received well-deserved praise and landmark status.

In 1925, takeover of the Northwest's oldest bank, Ladd & Tilton, vaulted U.S. National into the region's number one spot with resources topping $64 million. Two years later, Ainsworth joined forces with First National's Abbot Mills to guarantee the deposits of the failed Northwest National Bank.

When rival First National was bought by San Francisco-based Transamerica Corp. in 1930, U.S. responded with formation of the United States National Corporation to create an affiliate network. The Depression was bad for everybody including banks. U.S. saw its shares plummet from $405 to $30.

But they held their ground and went on to make a major contribution to the local defense industry effort during WW II. At the end of the war, E.C. Sammons succeeded Paul Dick as president and stewarded U.S. through a 15-year period of growth by acquisition and expansion, directing the bank's pioneering conversion to high technology.

LeRoy B. Staver shepherded the bank into the industry's most challenging era. Bank cards, diversification, competition from S & L's, pension funds and credit unions all contributed to the creation, in 1968, of the U.S. Bancorp, a holding company that has been the principal tool wielded first by Staver and, since 1974, by John Elloriaga to compete effectively.

Since the landmark deregulation legislation of 1980, U.S. has met the greatest challenge ever posed to traditional banks, becoming a regional financial services organization and announcing its position as Oregon's largest bank with completion of the dominating U.S. Bancorp Tower in December 1983.

Answers: After Donald Macleay's death, G.W.E. Griffith claimed the bank was his idea. Macleay's relatives vehemently disagreed. $6.7 billion in resources, 188 branches.

Miller's for Men: 100-year haberdasher

November 12, 1986

Miller's main store at Third and Alder, 1935. Which Miller never worked there? Who is the last person on the family's gift list? (Answers below cartoon.)

An illustrious list of Oregon companies has passed the hundred-year mark. But almost none have remained under continuous operation by the same family. Miller's for Men, the Portland clothing store which is celebrating its 100th birthday this year, is an exception. Alan Miller, the firm's current president, is its fourth generation family owner and manager.

Alan's great grandfather, Henry Miller, came to Portland in 1886 from his native Germany and opened a tiny, one-room men's hat shop that year on First between Couch and Davis. The riverside town was in the early phase of its greatest growth period and the little retail outlet then called simply "H. Miller" grew with it. Bringing his son, Alex, into the business in 1890, Henry renamed the company H. Miller & Son, moved up to Third Avenue and added accessories to the line of merchandise.

Alex had purchased the building on the northeast corner of the Third and Alder intersection in 1912 strictly as a real estate investment. The Kratz Saloon, which occupied the street level space, was a going concern. Dr. Wo, the Chinese herbalist on the second floor, was a long term tenant. But, Oregon went dry in 1915 and Prohibition took effect four years later. Without the saloon's rental income, Miller had to find another way to meet the mortgage payments. The additional store was his solution.

This new location became the site for consolidation of all the Third Avenue stores in 1926. Miller's remained a mainstay merchant there for more than sixty years until the property was purchased by the city for the Morrison Park East municipal parking structure.

Alex's son, Harold Miller, took the retail reins in 1933. Following

Miller's owners and tenures: Henry J. (1886-1906), Alex E. (1906-33), Harold J. (1933-70), Alan E. (1970-present).

A third name change and another location came eight years later. Moving across Burnside to Third between Oak and Pine in 1898, the newly dubbed "Miller Clothing Company" expanded into complete lines of work and dress clothing as well as shoes. In 1906, Alex Miller took over day-to-day management from his father.

The company employed a full-time tailor when it began to offer off-the-rack clothing. If the fit wasn't just right, exacting alterations ensured that it would be. Tailoring, in those days, meant more than hemming a cuff or shortening a sleeve. The customer would often end up with the next best thing to a custom-made suit. When the desired color or correct size wasn't in stock, special orders came across country via the transcontinental rail line.

Second-generation-owner Alex Miller obviously engendered the entrepreneureal spirit. He opened a branch store, the Eastern Hat Factory, directly across Third Avenue from his Miller Clothing Company in 1909. A third store, at Third and Alder, began operation in 1915. It was opened out of necessity rather than design.

World War II, the third-generation owner changed the name to Miller's for Men and modernized the merchandising concept to compete in the rapidly evolving, fashion conscious marketplace. Expansion, with its additional buying power, was another element in this strategy. Branch stores were opened in Oregon City, the Royal Building and the Sheraton Hotel at Lloyd Center.

Harold's son, Alan, entered the business in 1962 and became president in 1970. Four years later he launched a major branch at the new Washington Square suburban shopping center. In 1977, the downtown store was moved to its present location 726 S.W. Alder and all operations were once again consolidated there in September, 1986.

"The independent retailer has to specialize and offer extra service to successfully compete against the chains today," says Alan Miller expressing optimism about downtown's future particularly with light rail. "That's why we're one of the few stores that still has a full-time tailor."

For 100 years, Miller's for Men has kept pace with the latest in men's fashion trends! 1886 1906 1926 1946 1966 1986 Klooster '86

Answers: Founder Henry J. Miller. According to Alan Miller, dad is the last one on the list, particularly for clothing.

Franz Bakery: The good bakery

September 19, 1984

U.S. Bakery truck with Butter-Nut boy. Butter-Nut bread was Franz's flagship from 1909 to the early '60s. Where did the name come from? Why was it discontinued? (Answer below cartoon.)

In 1906, two enterprising brothers, Engelbert and Joseph Franz, purchased the little Ann Arbor Bakery at N.W. 16th and Glisan. Customers came from throughout the neighborhood and beyond to buy their bread unwrapped and oven-fresh.

The Franz brothers did so well that within a year they took over the considerably larger United States Bakery at E. 7th and Burnside. In the best American tradition, they set out to make it much more than a shopkeeper's business. Horse-drawn wagons delivered home-quality bread around Portland.

The three-quarter-block bakery in 1924

In 1912 the operation was moved to a much expanded plant on the edge of town—N.E. 11th and Flanders. The nature of the company was, by this time, primarily wholesale but many people still came direct to the bakery.

Engelbert and his family moved into living quarters on the second floor of the facility, looking after production almost around the clock. Here, in 1913, the current president, Joseph Franz was born in the then-bedroom that is now his office. Now that's a *family* business.

By 1920 the bakery covered three-quarters of the block and the wagons had been replaced by a fleet of 21 "modern" delivery trucks. Bread was packaged in a paper wrapper at that time and then in sealed waxed paper which prolonged freshness.

Completion of the new northeast corner addition came in 1947. The big bread loaf sign has been a landmark at 12th and Flanders since 1956. It was replaced with the pony-tailed polywrap loaf in 1967, heralding the end of waxed paper for Franz.

Joseph Franz, 72, has been a paid employee since he was 14. Working in almost every job in the bakery before going into management, Franz has insisted upon the strictest quality control, using the finest ingredients and old-fashioned methods. That means small batch baking and modernization has been adapted to assure this result.

Joseph's father, Englebert, can lay claim to inventing the first hamburger bun for Page Yaw's Top Notch restaurant in 1926. As a fitting tribute to his efforts, the continuing growth of the fast-food field has meant a burgeoning bun business for Franz.

The new addition at 12th & Flanders

From a few to more than 300, from one square block to four, from four employees to over 400, Franz today serves an area extending approximately 150 miles around Portland with a fleet of more than 200 trucks. The United States Bakery is a homegrown story that really grew up.

ENGELBERT **FRANZ**! RIGHT ON TIME WITH DELIVERY OF YOUR MARVELOUS BREAD!

AND JUST IN TIME TO TRY MY NEW SANDWICH. A STEAMED **HAMBURGER** PATTIE, CRISP LETTUCE, PICKLE RELISH, PICKLES, MAYO. WHAT DO YOU THINK?

IT LOOKS ABSOLUTELY DELICIOUS, MR. **YAW**.. BUT, WHERE'S THE **BUN**!?

klooster 84

Answers: One of the earliest examples of brand franchising, its Chicago owner sold the name to other nearby bakeries, limiting Franz to Portland.

Portland Merchants: Charles F. Berg

April 24, 1985

Charles F. Berg celebrates the firm's silver anniversary in front of the Broadway store. Who contributed the car? (Answer below cartoon.)

Before anyone had heard of the word *boutique*, Charles F. Berg was chic. The young Portlander who started his first retail business, a yardage goods store, in 1907 became the Northwest's premier women's clothing merchandiser.

Portland was a backwater of apparel awareness when Berg burst on the scene in 1922 with ready-to-wear. The off-the-rack concept caught on quickly among the city's cost- and clothing-conscious cognoscenti.

In 1930 Berg moved his business to Broadway, erecting a three story store that embraced art deco to the enth degree. The facade of this classic building at 615 SW Broadway is a downtown Portland landmark.

Berg, ever a promoter, took advantage of the opportunity. Nor is it known who designed the Broadway store's fabulous art deco window displays, but they rivaled their East Coast equivalents in every respect.

It was this striking attention to detail and quality in an always contemporary context that made Berg's the local fashion leader from the 1920s through the 1950s. Even with its founder's passing in 1932, the tradition was carried on by Charles' son, Forrest Berg.

Forrest became a noteworthy retailer in his own right, establishing the store as the place to shop for the younger set. Berg's Hi-Board was a hit for many years, consisting of

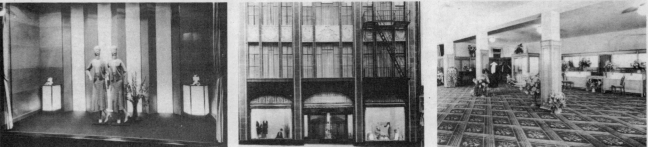

Art deco window display (left). Berg's magnificent main entrance (center). The expansive, flower-festooned second floor (right).

At a time when traditional retailers were still strictly business, Charles F. Berg was a hail-fellow-well-met who balanced a zest for life with good business practice. As the twenties roared, he was in the forefront of a flamboyant group the likes of which the Rose City had never seen before or since.

The Hoot Owls, an eclectic and unlikely group of friends from a variety of vocations, came together as amateur entertainers. Their hallmark was "hilarity and hijinx" and they were proficient enough at it, as musicians, singers and off-the-cuff comedians, to successfully air a weekly radio program over KGW Radio beginning in 1922 and continuing for nearly a decade.

No records remain to indicate whether or not Charles F. Berg Co. was a sponsor of this show, but the odds are that

representatives from each of the city's high schools who acted as consultants and models.

In 1960 a second store, dubbed The Dark Horse, was opened in the burgeoning suburb of Beaverton. The operation continued its winning ways through the '60s until, in 1974, it merged with Rusans of Spokane.

Each firm retained its own name and the Rusans/Berg connection continued until 1979, when both were sold to Vancouver, B.C.-based Mariposa and Gray's. The new owners brought down the final curtain on Portland's 60-year-old fashion firm in 1982 but its Broadway building still stands, resplendently refurbished, a symbol of an era and a tribute to its Portland proprietors—Charles F. and Forrest T. Berg.

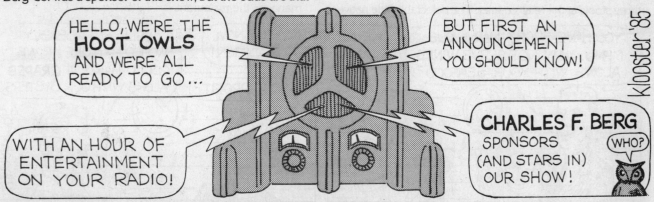

Answers: Berg's radio-show, the Hoot Owls, arranged the auto.

Early eateries: Dan & Louis Oyster Bar

September 18, 1985

Louis Wachsmuth III shows modern oyster farming technique. Who assisted them in research? What happened to the native Yaquina Bay oyster? (Answers below cartoon.)

Oregon oysters and the Wachsmuth family are synonymous. Four generations of Wachsmuths have been in the shell game. I guess they all said, "Shucks, this is for me."

All puns aside, if it were not for the efforts of these enterprising Portlanders, the tasty mollusks so prized by gourmets would probably no longer exist along our coast.

The story began in 1865 when great-grandfather Meinert Wachsmuth was shipwrecked off Yaquina Bay aboard the Annie Doyle. Her cargo was oysters. Having already been a sailor for nine years, the 23-year-old German immigrant decided to try his hand on land.

Yaquina Bay bivalve was the sought-after item. In fact, the demand for Yaquina oysters grew to such proportions that the Wachsmuths bought out the rights of the other oystermen in 1923 and obtained a near exclusive on harvesting of the bay's private beds.

But having the rights and having oysters were two different things. The native Yaquinas were barely surviving in a delicate environment threatened by sawdust pollution from upstream sawmills. The Wachsmuths went to court in 1930 and, although unable to gain a clear decision, public support was mustered for stricter controls.

Louis Wachsmuth Sr. (left photo) made Oregon oysters and his restaurant famous. Remodeled interior, 1939 (right).

Meinert went to work for the San Francisco-based Morgan Oyster Co., eventually representing their interests in the Northwest until he formed his own company in 1883. Taking up squatters' rights on oyster beds at Shoalwater Bay (Willapa Harbor, Washington), M. Wachsmuth & Sons became important suppliers to Portland.

Always innovative, they began transplanting Eastern oyster stock in 1895. The first-if-its-kind experiment proved highly successful.

Meinert's son, Louis, had gone to Portland in 1900 to work for the West Coast Oyster Company, a wholesaler. He subsequently operated an oyster house in Pendleton and, in 1907, opened a wholesale and retail seafood business, the Oregon Oyster Company, at 248 S.W. Ankeny in Portland.

In those days, the now-famous restaurant consisted of three stools at the retail counter. The delectable little native

Extensive replanting from Atlantic coast seed stock helped replenish the depleted supply and, in another unprecedented move, the company imported a top-quality Japanese oyster variety, the Kumamoto, which fully developed in eight months as opposed to four years.

In the decade from 1930 to 1939, the restaurant expanded 10 times. The last was a major remodeling that resulted in the varnished knotty pine nautical motif that has been the Dan & Louis trademark ever since.

Along the way, Louis, assisted by his sons, Louis Jr. and Chet, continued to build their oyster business supplying some of America's finest hotels and restaurants. In more recent years, the fourth generation has played a prominent role. Louis Jr.'s son, Louis III, has looked after the oyster enterprises in Newport and Olympia and Chet's son, Doug, manages the restaurant.

Answers: Oregon State University studies helped save the Oregon oyster industry. The little Yaquina is extinct.

Early eateries: Jake's famous crawfish

September 25, 1985

Today Jake's is the flagship of the McCormick-Western operation. What is the latest addition? What other new enterprise is growing rapidly? (Answers below cartoon.)

The corner of S.W. 12th and Stark has been home to Jake's, one of Portland's longest running restaurants, since 1908. In the local "same location" race, that puts it a close second to Dan & Louis (1907) and three years ahead of Huber's. However, since the Oregon Oyster Co. was only nominally a restaurant for a number of years and Huber's has a 13-year advantage as the overall oldest regardless of location, the venerable big three come close to a dead heat.

Small matter from the public standpoint because all have survived in a superior manner. Despite a complex evolution involving multiple owners, two dynamic periods have brought Jake's to its present pre eminent position.

The restaurant's roots stem from 1892 when Mueller and Meyer's bar-restaurant began business at 18th and Wash-

The bar and main dining room in Jake Freiman's day, 1910s and 20s.

ington. Its successor, the Quelle, (well or source in German) was founded by a Baron Schlenk at 2nd and Stark and moved to Jake's current location in 1908.

When the Quelle folded the following year, Jake Freiman, a well-regarded waiter, and John Rometsch formed a partnership to revitalize the business. Freiman's contribution was charisma and crawfish; Rometsch added a soft drink parlor in 1920 that kept customers coming during Prohibition.

Jake's position as out-front proprietor increased his popularity to the point where the restaurant was renamed Jake's Famous Crawfish that same year. It was Jake's taste

that made his place a classic. He created an elegant decor to accompany the delightful dining.

The eclectic collection he brought together transformed Jake's into a showplace. Chandeliers from an 1881 Portland mansion, the back bar's oak buffets shipped round the horn and a mini-museum of oil paintings, including Francesca Grothjean's "Villard's Ruins" which depicted the Portland hotel's foundation lying fallow due to lack of funds for completion.

After Freiman's death in 1932, the restaurant lost momentum until the end of Prohibition when it regained its role as a popular place to wet your whistle. Several owners kept the status quo over the next three decades.

Portland ad man Fred Delkin began to tap Jake's

potential but the restaurant savvy of transplanted Bostonian Bill McCormick, who bought out Delkin in 1971, took it to the top. After selling his San Francisco-based 18-outlet Refectory steak and seafood chain, McCormick concentrated his considerable talents on building a wholesale seafood business and his one remaining restaurant.

Today Jake's is *the* Portland place to go for in-crowd conviviality and first-class seafood. McCormick, aided by partner Doug Schmick since 1977, has extended his empire to eight restaurants in Portland and Seattle. Jake's wholesale Fish Company supplies the best fresh seafood daily to choosy clients across the country.

HI, MY NAME'S LARRY. I'M A LAWYER. MY SIGN IS LEO. THIS IS **BAR** PRACTICE!

HELLO, I'M SUSAN. I'M A PSYCHOLOGIST AND A SCORPIO. THIS IS SOCIAL THERAPY!

HI, MY NAME'S **LARRY**...

Klooster '85

Answers: The new Harborside Restaurant at River Place. Jake's specialty condiments and foods are achieving nationwide distribution.

Pendleton Mills: The wool to succeed

October 19, 1983

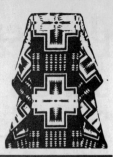
The Chief Joseph robe. How are 50 percent of these traditional blankets still used? In what other ways did Pendleton achieve early fame? (Answers below cartoon.)

The more that synthetic things pervade our lives the more we appreciate the natural ones. Nowhere is this more apparent than with apparel. Ever wear a double-knit Dacron on a warm, muggy day?

Pendleton Woolen Mills started out natural and has stayed that way. Even as the cost of producing a quality garment soared, the people at Pendleton refused to compromise. The policy of "not changing a good thing" has made the Pendleton label synonymous with wool and respected around the globe.

The company's origins are all Oregon. The story begins with Thomas Kay, a young Englishman trained in the family trade, woolen textiles, who came to the Beaver State in 1863 seeking his fortune on the new frontier.

Finding work at a Brownsville (Ore.) woolen mill, he stayed for 26 years, 23 of which he served as manager. Realizing a lifelong dream, Kay then opened his own mill in Salem. He was assisted by his daughter, Fannie, who continued her active participation even after marrying woolen specialty clothing merchant C.P. Bishop.

In 1909 the Bishops backed sons Clarence and Roy in purchasing a mill at Pendleton which had fallen on hard times. Thus began a family tradition now in its fifth generation.

Doing it all on their own, the Bishops have survived personal tragedy, the Great Depression, undercutting competition and inferior copies to emerge as a leader in the industry.

Today, Pendleton Woolen Mills, headquartered in Portland since the mid-20s, is co-managed by Clarence M. (Mort) Bishop, president, and brother Broughton H. (Brot) Bishop, chairman, sons of founder, C.M. Bishop.

Plants and distribution centers are as far flung as Nebraska, New Hampshire and Pennsylvania. The original mill at Pendleton is still in operation along with the largest mill, established in 1912 at Washougal, Washington. In addition to the home office, Portland has major processing and distribution facilities and three garment plants.

The first products, Indian robes and blankets, are still made in authentic patterns. Pendleton plaid shirts have never gone out of fashion since they became the lumberjacks' trademark in the '30s. The (19)49ers women's jackets set their own style and who can forget the hip-hugging, rally-girl reversible, pleated 100 percent Pendleton. Another original only-in-Oregon story.

The company's first mill at Pendleton, Oregon opened in 1909.

OH, RALLY SQUAD. BET I'D STILL LOOK GREAT IN THE OLD OUTFIT!

THERE'S THE SWEATER. NOW, WHERE'S MY REVERSIBLE PLEATED PENDLETON?

NEVER CARRY NOSTALGIA TOO FAR!

Answers: Ceremonial burial shrouds. Official 1932 Olympic team blankets. Early 20th Century China trade.

Jantzen:
A plan for
all seasons

July 13, 1983

This Jantzen diving girl is a classic collector's item. What is she? Why was the red-suited symbol of swimwear banned in Boston in 1924? (Answers below cartoon.)

Good fortune brought John Zehntbauer from Missouri together with Carl Jantzen, a Danish immigrant, in 1904. Design caused the two friends to join forces with John's younger brother, Roy, five years later to found the Portland Knitting Company.

Getting underway in early 1910, the Zehntbauers handled administration and sales, and Jantzen, production. Their first products were heavy woolen sweaters and hosiery which they retailed along with canvas gloves in their own store at SW 2nd and Alder.

1913 was a breakthrough year for the fledgling firm. Carl Jantzen had developed a special rib-stitch for sweater cuffs

The Jantzen diving girl, although modified several times over the years, has always worn red, and by the early 1930s was, according to a survey, "the seventh-best-known pictorial trademark in America."

Swimwear became Jantzen's only business and "the suit that changed bathing to swimming" ad campaign was their hallmark. Jantzen Beach Park, although a separate business, was designed to promote swimming. Besides, they needed a place to hold company picnics for the growing Jantzen employee family.

Always a trendsetter, Jantzen went international in the '20s, launched sweaters in the '30s, sportswear in the '40s,

Outdoor billboard posters of the late 1930s by noted illustrator, George Petty.

and a fellow Portland Rowing Club member requested a pair of trunks made from the same material. Soon, every member of the club had ordered a pair and the company decided to test and perfect the process to reduce weight.

By 1915, Portland Knitting found itself in the forefront of an eager and expanding new market. To complement their swimwear image a local artist created the now-legendary diving girl. The following year, despite Carl Jantzen's protest, his name became the company's trademark and, in 1918, the company name was changed to Jantzen Knitting Mills.

was computerized in the '50s and was among the first anywhere to have a non-smoking policy in their offices. The company diversified and expanded in the '60s, began trading on the New York Stock Exchange in the '70s, and was bought out in the '80s.

Out-of-state ownership hasn't affected local operation, however and Jantzen, Inc. (since 1954) continues swimming, sweating and sporting its way to success in one of the country's most competitive industries.

Answers: A hood ornament. Diving-girl decals were being pasted on windshields, hindering visibility.

The motorcar: Cranking up in River City

November 18, 1987

Chas. C. Fagan Co., Pierce-Arrow dealer, West Burnside and 14th Avenue, ca. 1925. What happened to this prestigious make? What occupies the location today? (Answers below cartoon.)

When the first horseless carriages creaked and chugged their way onto the American scene, they were dismissed as novelties —rich men's toys. How could such noisy, smelly, unreliable contraptions possibly replace the dependable horse and carriage as an everyday mode of personal transportation? So went the rationale.

Then, as more and more automobiles appeared on the main streets of cities across the country, reactionary segments of society began to perceive them as a threat to the status quo. Discriminatory, sometimes ludicrous, laws were passed.

One outrageous ordinance required the owner of an automobile, encountering a horse at an intersection, to stop, dismantle said auto and reassemble it on the other side. In Britain, an Act of Parliament decreed that "all self-propelled road vehicles must be manned by three people, one of whom should walk ahead waving a red flag of warning."

Fields Motor Car Co., E. Couch and Grand, 1925.

Rules governing the conduct of motorcars on Portland thoroughfares were not so onerous. As early as 1906, however, the city's auto owners found reason to protest one of them. On May 2, following persistent pressure from the Portland Automobile Club, the City Council changed the legal speed limit from eight to 10 miles per hour within the fire limits and 15 miles per hour in other areas under its jurisdiction.

The club's president at the time was Henry Wemme who had brought the first-ever car to Portland in 1898. An unabashed motoring enthusiast, Wemme's first car was a Locomobile which came by rail from Massachusetts. His second, a Haynes-Apperson out of Kokomo, Ind., was also the city's second auto. Other local Wemme firsts included Oldsmobile, Pierce-Arrow, Reo and Thomas Flyer.

During the first few years that autos were on the local scene, a major breakdown meant weeks or even months awaiting the arrival of a replacement part. Even then, if you weren't an adept do-it-yourselfer, a blacksmith was about the only specialist around who could perform repairs.

In 1903, the first few dealers opened up showrooms. Most of them also dealt in bicycles or carriages. Another five years and there were 30 dealerships including Auburn, Buick, Cadillac, Ford, Oldsmobile, Pierce-Arrow, Rambler, Studebaker and Winton. Fords sold for as little as $450. The regal Pierce commanded up to $3,650.

By the beginning of World War I, the Rose City could count 47 car dealers plus the Ford Motor Company's assembly plant at East 11th Avenue and Division Street. It operated through 1931. Clarence Francis, who had started out as a second hand dealer in 1905, opened his Ford agency at East Hawthorne Boulevard and 13th Avenue in 1914. He moved to his long-lived Grand and Hawthorne Street location in 1920. That same year, Wentworth and Irwin sold GMC trucks on the corner of Second Avenue and Taylor Street. Fields Chevrolet was holding forth at 14th Avenue and Alder Street. The former would buy out the latter.

The after-market aspect of the auto business really burgeoned after the Great War. Where there were but a handful of repair shops, tire dealers and auto supply stores in 1914, these listings far outnumbered dealers by 1920. As the prosperous '20s roared to their sudden end, Portland offered everything the auto owner could ask for in abundance — U-drive rentals and service stations, auto laundries and repair shops. The latter category took up almost two pages in the Polk Directory.

Automobile-wise, Portland was representative of the country as a whole and then some. A Northwest penchant for the outdoors brought on the autocamping craze accompanied by the push for better roads and more of them.

In the 1910s, America's love affair with the automobile was still only an ardent courtship. By the 1920s, it had become a serious involvement. And the best was yet to come.

FRANKLIN   DODGE BROTHERS   Oldsmobile

Nyberg   HUDSON MOTOR CARS   KNOX   LINCOLN   *Buick*   *Studebaker*

Stoddard-Dayton   MAXWELL   REO   NASH   *Cadillac*

Rambler   CHRYSLER IMPERIAL '80'   CHEVROLET   *Ford*   *Packard*

STANLEY STEAM CAR

Answers: An independent manufacturer, Pierce folded in 1938. The I-405 freeway.

Portland's own auto: The Beaver

November 25, 1987

The former Beaver State Motor Company plant in Gresham. What currently occupies the building? (Answer below cartoon.)

It wasn't actually produced in Portland proper, although they did have an office downtown. And there were, at most, four of them built. Nonetheless, the Beaver State Motor Company and its automobile, the stylish Beaver Six, makes for an intriguing tale.

During the first two decades of this century, hundreds of would-be motorcar magnates tried to cash in on what was clearly the wave of the future. In 1912, P.A. Combs, a successful automobile supplies and accessories merchant, obviously felt he could catch that wave. His enthusiasm must have been infectious because he convinced a number of substantial local citizens to become a part of the Northwest's first-ever auto manufacturing venture.

ORIGINAL BEAVER SIX CAR

The first (and only?) Beaver Six, completed Oct. 1912.

The good roads movement had gotten well underway. The Columbia River Scenic Highway was on the drawing board. Tens of thousands of Oregonians were already caught up in the motoring mania. The time was ripe. This was the pre-Detroit dominance era. Auto manufacturers were situated in a dozen eastern and mid-western states. So, why not Oregon? Think of the savings in shipping costs.

Combs and his colleagues selected a site in Gresham near the main rail line. What was to be Beaver State's first unit, a one-story, 60 x 200-foot, concrete and brick structure, was completed in March 1914. The first, six-cylinder, 45-horsepower, Beaver open touring car was already on the road with Mr. Combs at the wheel.

E.T. "Tom" Fletch, a twelve-year Packard employee, came out from Detroit to run the factory. A special Daimler-Lanchester worm drive gear was imported from England due to its perceived superiority. All other parts were fabricated at the factory. The company geared up for mass production amidst comparisons with the fledgling Ford operation of ten years prior and the fanfare of a public offering which raised $300,000 in capital.

Then, suddenly, the grandiose plan for Gresham to become the "Wheel City of the West" ground to a screeching halt. It seems that the Beaver's engine design was a smidgeon too close to that patented by Overland, and Toledo-headquartered Willys-Overland, Inc. cried "infringement."

Talk of a revitalized Beaver auto operation persisted for another three years but nothing came of it. Instead, the Beaver State Company converted its casting equipment to the manufacture of rail car wheels and sewer pipe. Later, drag saws, cement mixers and gasoline engines were produced. At one point, the firm employed up to 36 men.

The few Beavers that were built (conflicting information has it between two and four), all apparently passed into oblivion. One story says that a Beaver was being driven around the Gresham area until just before World War II. Another, more colorful account, was told by Portlander Ralph Coan whose father was a local bankruptcy trustee attorney.

Coan claims that his dad bought the one remaining car following the company's long protracted liquidation and the kids drove it until the tires gave out. Then it sat in their backyard for several years until, in 1929 as Ralph recalled, the senior Coan got fed up with seeing the old junker and built a bonfire under it. The aluminum body and oak frame melted and burned down to almost nothing.

A month following the fateful Beaver bonfire, according to Coan, a representative of tire tycoon Harvey Firestone came to his father's office prepared to pay $5,000 for the auto. Serious doubts, however, have been raised as to the authenticity of this offer and, in fact, that the destroyed car was even a Beaver. Antique auto historian Dick Larrowe of Corbett, who has painstakingly traced the Beaver's background found that Firestone was never a car collector and, furthermore, that the Beaver had an all-steel body and frame.

Larrowe also advises that the Portland area had at least two other attempts at motor car manufacturing. A cycle car, called the Portland and later, the Pacific, was produced locally around World War I. There is also evidence that one of the first buses in the country was made here briefly in 1903. As for the Beaver, if anyone can find one, Dick Larrowe is willing to pay $10,000 for it.

Answer: The Dean Company, 519 N.W. 11th Drive, is one of the country's largest manufacturers of high-quality wood veneer.

Fred Meyer: A My-Te-Fine merchant — Part I

November 23, 1983

Mayor Fred Peterson joins Eva and Fred Meyer for the Grand Opening of the Interstate store November 18, 1953, 30 years ago this month. How many people attended and what was the most popular attraction? (Answers below cartoon.)

No name is more well-known in Portland than that of Fred Meyer. And no business has contributed more to the city's economy.

The story of how this young man from Brooklyn parlayed horse-cart peddling into one of the country's greatest merchandising empires could fill a book. I'll attempt to give it some perspective in two articles.

When 19-year-old Frederick Grubmeyer came to Seattle in 1905, he was seeking Alaskan gold. He found it instead in groceries, a business learned back home from his father and seven uncles. Buying a Portland store, sight unseen, he arrived in town to find a sorry shop near Union Station.

Fred Meyer, Hollywood, mid 1930s. The country's first suburban "super"

In a manner that typified his life, adversity was turned into opportunity and Fred established a traveling coffee, tea and spice trade that extended to the surrounding lumber camps.

The declining downtown public market was his next step. Fred quickly became the proprietor of several specialty spaces, making each a separate profit center. The concept later formed the company's departmental philosophy.

When Fred G. Meyer married widow Eva Chiles, daughter of a Portland grocer, in 1920, he was almost ready to embark on his next phase of growth. The Meyers' union was much more than a marriage. It became a 40-year partnership.

Taking charge of several departments, Eva joined Fred in launching their flagship store at S.W. 5th and Yamhill in 1922. By 1930 they had four downtown stores in conjunction with Fred's brother, Harry, who later owned the now-defunct local Piggly Wiggly franchise.

Innovative "firsts" punctuated the Fred Meyer organization from the outset. First to offer one-stop shopping — a complete cash and carry food store — meat, produce, deli, bakery and canned goods under one roof. A concept some thought would never catch on.

The first self-service drug store in the world opened on Alder near Park in 1930, was followed by the "first" that was the prototype for all future Fred Meyers — the Hollywood suburban "Super."

Hollywood was an archetypical example of Meyer's ingenuity. Traffic congestion became a downtown dilemma in the '20s, heralding the ticketing era. Fred paid his customers' fines, finding in the process that many of them were Hollywood-Rose City Park residents.

His daring decision at the onset of the Depression to expand into the district proved prophetic. With free parking and complete self-service featuring "travel tray" carts and shelf pricing, the first one-stop supermarket in the country was an instant success, pumping new energy into the entire commercial community around it.

Walnut Park followed in 1936. Then came Stadium (1939), Foster (1940) and Rose City, the largest and most modern "super" in the U.S. (1949).

The early '50s saw Burlingame, Hawthorne, Interstate and Gateway join the fold, each bringing increased activity to surrounding businesses. Convenience, value and unbeatable prices under the My-Te-Fine label made "Freddy's" Portland's most popular place to shop.

By the time of Eva's death in 1960 at 72, the "mom and pop" operation had grown to 16 Portland-area outlets and $56 million in annual sales.

Her son, Earle Chiles, had become president of the expanding organization and Eve's Buffet Restaurants (the name she was known by) was to grow into the largest restaurant chain in Oregon.

Answers: 61,000 people. The Mutt Show was the feature event of several store openings.

Fred Meyer: A My-Te-Fine merchant — Part II

November 30, 1983

Rollin Killoran, Mktg. V.P. (lft.); Fred's stepson, Earle Chiles, president; and Meyer view the newest suburban store design in September 1959. Which stores used it? (Answer below cartoon.)

With Eva gone there were no more weekends at Mt. Hood for 74-year-old Fred Meyer. As much as business had always been FGM's life, it became even more so. The anagram FGM was only one of the efficiencies that was a company hallmark.

To this day the initials of administrative personnel are used in office correspondence and even in conversation. All part of Meyer's "ECRS" philosophy — eliminate, combine, rearrange and simplify.

The Beaverton store, largest in the chain. Meyer purchased the property 20 years before it was built.

With the working capital gained through a public stock offering, the company embarked on an unprecedented expansion program. The '60s saw a major thrust into Washington state with the purchase of Seattle's Marketing Drugs (1960), Round-Up Wholesale Grocery of Spokane (1964), Market Basket (1968) and the completion of Fred Meyer/Lynwood (North Seattle), as well as two Vancouver stores.

The modern genre of 160,000-plus square-foot super centers began in 1966 with the all-new Southeast store at 82nd and Foster. Totally redesigned inside and out, it set the pattern for all centers since, such as Tigard (1967), Longview (1973), Springfield (1977), Clackamas (1979), Tualatin (1980) and the largest ever at 208,000 square feet, Beaverton (1980).

Guiding the course of these quantum leaps was the founder. Just like Portland's first generation of entrepreneurs, Meyer was a pragmatic, laissez-faire capitalist. "There's no sense doing something unless you benefit," he said. "If you've worked for Fred, you've worked for the best," others said. His organization was regarded as a tremendous training ground for young managers.

Meyer's standards were stringent, his praise scant. As retired vice chairman and 30-year employee Rollin Killoran puts it, "When he said nothing, you knew it was a job well done."

If FGM was a demanding boss, he demanded the most from himself. This dedication, combined with an always inquisitive nature and the attitude that "anything, no matter how good, could be improved," earned him the accolade "one of the greatest merchants in America."

Doug Baker dubbed Meyer "the crafty old fox." And he was not without his detractors. Some called him cold and ruthless, saying he'd do anything to gain the advantage. But the praise far outweighs the criticism.

Fred Meyer insisted on buying Northwest products whenever possible and, in fact, saved many firms from going under while assisting a host of others in getting started. Giving generously to charity, he cared little for personal material possessions.

Meyer's life purpose was the building and bettering of his business. He died in 1978 at 92, having been the company's full-time working founder for 57 years. Only two months prior to his death, Meyer said, "There are so many more things to do. If only I had a little more time."

Fred Meyer, Inc. was then a 62-store, 11,000-employee operation with over $3/4 billion a year in sales. Its huge Clackamas distribution center was nearing completion. The bakery, dairy, central kitchen and drug manufacturing subsidiaries were among the largest of their types. The savings and loan had become, in only four short years, the fourth largest in the state under Meyer protege Gerry Pratt.

The Fred Meyer story is now being written by other men; not outsiders, but long-time employees who rose through the ranks, like Chairman Oran Robertson and President Cy Green. They met the demanding standards of the old taskmaster.

FGM would have been proud of them, though he might not have said so, as annual sales recently surpassed $1 billion and the 69th store, in Juneau, approaches completion.

Answer: Raleigh Hills (1959), Division (1959) and Oak Grove (1960).

Alpenrose: A 'dairy' old operation

August 17, 1985

Shetlands on display at Alpenrose Bowl. How did the little ponies lead to the establishment of Dairyville? (Answer below cartoon.)

Did you see the Shetland Shodeo this year? It was one mare-tossing, heel-kicking success the weekend of July 19-21 at Dairyland. No, not Disneyland but Dairyland, Alpenrose Dairy's fun-filled 52 acres, which is about as close as anything in Portland comes to the Magic Kingdom.

Great-grandfather Florian Cadonau, who carved his hillside dairy farm out of Portland's west slope wilderness in the late 19th century, would probably have difficulty believing what grew from the roots he planted.

The late 1950s saw the beginnings of what would eventually be dubbed Dairyland. Carl Cadonau Sr., Henry's son and current president, was the prime force behind these extracurricular activities. First came a Little League diamond, then a quarter midget track. A kid-oriented approach from the start.

Aided by his able assistant, Jessie Schuster, Carl saw things really take off in the '60s. As Alpenrose became a formidable force in the regional marketplace, Dairyland was constructed, encompassing a western town called Dairyville, a circus arena, two

Alpenrose employees pose for a group portrait at the original dairy farm, 1936.

Florian's son, Henry, grew up on the family farm and in 1916, at 23, decided to enter another area of the milk business. Purchasing a milk delivery route in East Portland, each morning he negotiated his horse-drawn wagon down the plank road from Hillsdale and over the Hawthorne Bridge.

Two years later Henry married Rosina Streiff, and the couple took over the entire dairy operation in 1922 when Henry's father retired. With knowledge of both ends of the business, they set themselves to building it. Their hard work paid handsome dividends.

By 1936, Alpenrose, the name Rosina gave the dairy when they assumed ownership, had eight delivery trucks as well as full-time farm and dairy crews. A fire in September 1943 prompted their move the following year from the original dairy site at S.W. 45th and Vermont to the present location on Shattuck Road, which was formerly the Elco Dairy.

They had 64 delivery routes by 1951. Ten years later that number had doubled and was augmented by 32 wholesale routes serving stores throughout the Portland-Vancouver area.

more Little League fields, Storybook Lake and facilities for groups to view a working dairy. The most unusual element is a world-class velodrome or bicycle racing stadium.

In 1970, David Newman, an electronics expert and antique collector from Astoria, was persuaded to bring his mechanized musical devices to a permanent home at Dairyland. This incomparable collection, along with some early autos and other memorabilia, comprise the David Newman Museum.

Today the fame of the fantasyland on Shattuck Road has overshadowed the dairy. But its cash flow keeps Dairyland going and allows it to be open free of charge each summer. And, at Alpenrose, fresh milk products are only the tip of the iceberg.

Or, perhaps more correctly, the ice cream berg. Because, since 1966, the Cadonaus have owned and operated the Baskin-Robbins franchise for the Pacific Northwest. They make it, in all 31 flavors, and sell it through the stores they own. The fourth generation of this homegrown family operation is now involved, assuring continuity in the quality and care that are Alpenrose and its Dairyland.

Answer: Shetland owner Clarence "Barney" Barnhart loved the Dairyland idea and gave the Cadonaus his little town shipped from Iowa.

Iron Fireman: Stoking the home fires

November 19, 1986

Iron Fireman facility on E. 17th, 1927. What totally unrelated product did they manufacture in the 1950s and '60s? (Answer below cartoon.)

Renowned industrialist Henry J. Kaiser coined the phrase "find a need and fill it." Portlanders T.H. "Harry" Banfield and C.J. Parker, who founded Iron Fireman Manufacturing Company, followed that philosophy and added their own innovations. For more than 30 years Iron Fireman enjoyed success nationwide owing to innovative enterprise and solid management on the part of its owners.

Local historian E. Kimbark MacColl profiled the company in his book "Growth of a City." The following account is based on information from MacColl's book and an interview with former Iron Fireman executive Joe Herron.

Banfield and Parker went into the construction business together in 1909 with a $700 combined investment. From that base they built a going concern over 14 years, acquiring a sheet-metal shop and then the company that would form their future fortunes.

through the Panama Canal. Along the way, their contracting company built the Vista Avenue Bridge and renovated the Broadway Bridge.

By 1928, Iron Fireman had become the country's largest manufacturer of automatic coal stokers for home use. That year Parker was killed and Banfield seriously injured in a plane crash. U.S. Bank vice president E.C. Sammons, who was the company's banking connection, accepted the position of chief operating officer and steered a profitable course over the next 17 years.

During World War II, Iron Fireman produced precision-machined military hardware. Western manager Joe Herron coordinated the effort working with such major contractors as Boeing. In 1945, Sammons returned to the U.S. Bank as its president becoming Portland's most prominent financial executive until his retirement in 1966.

(left) Stoker show a Multnomah Hotel, 1930. (right) Iron Fireman Complex on S.E. 17th, 1945.

When the partners took over the Portland Wire and Iron Works in 1923, they found an experimental coal stoker gathering dust in a corner of the building. At first glance this appeared to be an unlikely item for a Portland-based firm to produce. Its major markets were in the East and Midwest as were the conventional sources of its primary raw material, iron.

Here is where innovation came into play. With further study, they determined that the stokers could be manufactured less expensively in Portland due to lower labor costs and that large quantities of cheap scrap metal were available locally.

To overcome the considerable, cross-country freight rates for these bulky, one-ton objects, they shipped them

Harry Banfield was able to devote time to civic activities during Sammons' tenure at Iron Fireman. He served on the Docks Commission from 1930 to 1947 and chaired the state Highway Commission from 1943 to 1950. For his latter efforts, Portland's first freeway, the Banfield Expressway, was named after him.

When the company was purchased by California interests in 1962, there were no local counterparts of Banfield, Sammons or Parker to investigate alternatives and pursue diversification as the use of coal was overtaken by oil and natural gas. Iron Fireman became a pawn in an out-of-state game and it was soon nothing more than an admirable memory.

Answer: On-A-Lite Christmas lighting fixtures which could be placed anywhere on a light cord for indoor or outdoor use.

The money merchants: Ben's equitable

October 16, 1985

The Benj. Franklin's first home at Fourth & Oak, 1925. How did the S & L help save Portland's "Old Town"? (Answer below cartoon.)

In 1924, Ben Hazen, a young insurance man, took advantage of Portland's prosperous times and sold coin-operated savings clocks on behalf of a small savings and loan association.

It was the single most successful promotion they had ever conducted. But, since the firm had been unwilling to put up the money for the clocks, Hazen backed it himself. Consequently, he decided to start his own savings and loan.

Prominent downtown merchant Charles F. Berg encouraged Hazen to select a name with sizzle. Young Ben liked "Benj. Franklin" as the great American had signed his name to the Declaration of Independence.

"Thrift from Nature," Fourth & Oak window display. Woodpeckers embedded nuts in telephone poles (left photo). First branch at N.E. 39th and Sandy Blvd. in Hollywood, 1951 (right).

Opening at the corner of S.W. Fourth and Oak on January 17, 1925, Hazen had limited capital and only one employee. But he had his savings clocks and the '20s were roaring.

The fledgling firm and its founder rode the tide of the times, taking care not to let the sails out too far. With the crash of '29, 17 local S&L's went under. Only the Benj. Franklin and its estimable competitor, Equitable Savings and Loan Association, founded in 1890, survived.

Ben Hazen conceived the idea of a colonial motif for the company's offices during the 1930s. The concept was later carried out in all branches, most notably the Mt. Vernon look-alike in Lake Oswego and Russelville's Independence Hall.

Saving with Ben became a local way of life during WWII.

Afterward those savers became avid consumers. New homes and automobiles, unavailable in wartime, burgeoned loan business and the Benj. Franklin met the demand.

Branches were opened in suburban areas and the organization initiated its ongoing community involvement activities. Bob Hazen organized the GI home loan plan and served as a branch manager before succeeding his father as president in 1959.

During the '50s and '60s, Bob became as well known a TV spokesman as Ron Tonkin or Tom Peterson. Before relinquishing the reins in 1980, he saw the dedication of the 20-story Benj. Franklin Plaza for the bicentennial year and attainment of the billion-dollar asset mark the following year.

With congressional passage of the Depository Institutions Deregulation in 1980, the financial world changed dramatically. The Benj. Franklin assumed the role of a full-service bank throughout its 82-branch system in Oregon, Washington, Idaho and Utah.

The Benj. Franklin/Equitable merger in 1982 created the Northwest's largest savings and loan. The year following the acquisition, Dr. G. Dale Weight, a highly regarded Syracuse, N.Y., banker, assumed the CEO duties from Robert Downie. The new eastside Benj. Franklin Financial Center is nearing completion under his direction. This enduring example of core area redevelopment embodies the institution's commitment to its home city.

THE BENJ. FRANKLIN FEDERAL SAVINGS AND LOAN ASSN.

THIS NOTE MAKES US A LEGAL LENDER FOR ALL DEBTS, PUBLIC AND PRIVATE

B

ASSETS $3.8 BILLION

SINCE 1924
PORTLAND, OR

PENNY SAVERS EARN

FRANKLIN

Beny Franklin

klooster '85

Answer: It has been one of the most cooperative and generous lenders to historic preservation building owners.

Goodwill: Sixty years in the Rose City

May 20, 1987

Goodwill poster from 1927 brochure. How are Goodwills of America associated? How many are in other countries? (Answers below cartoon.)

In 1902, Edgar J. Helms, a Methodist minister in Boston found his own special way to practice "applied" Christianity. In simple terms, Helms used the old Robin Hood scenario — taking from the rich and giving to the poor. But the way he did it made the wealthy willing givers and the needy feel that they were earning their own way. It was the beginning of Goodwill Industries of America.

Discarded possessions were turned into jobs for the handicapped. The sale of mended garments, restored furniture, repaired toys and rejuvenated household items provided income for these workers and gave dignity to their lives.

The successful concept reached Oregon in 1926. George C. Todd was sent by the City Church Extension Society of the Methodist Church of Portland to study under Edgar Helms in Boston. Todd returned home to become the first executive director of Goodwill Industries of Oregon opening its original plant and store at Southwest Grant and First Avenue on June 1, 1927, with five employees.

• First Goodwill plant S.W. Grant & First, 1927.

Within four months, a drive was launched to place Goodwill bags in 7,000 homes. In January 1929, GIO joined the Community Chest, predecessor of United Way. The following year they moved into a new, two-story building in northeast Portland. In 1946, the current plant was purchased at Southeast Sixth and Stephens.

Other highlights of Goodwill's continued growth include Good Turn Day, begun in 1952, the opening of the Main Store directly across the street from the plant in 1957 and deposit boxes at supermarket parking lots, started the same year.

Since Goodwill's clerical training school, now the Vocational Training Center, began operation in 1971, increased emphasis has been placed on teaching office skills. State-of-the-art computers are used, backed by counseling and outside job placement. In 1975, the Salem Division opened — duplicating all of Portland's services. Collection Center trailers, known as Attended Donation Stations, were introduced the same year.

Financially self-supporting since 1943, Goodwill of Oregon is now a non-profit, non-denominational operation ranking ninth among the 176 Goodwills throughout the United States and Canada. In addition to its Portland and Salem plant operations, there are 11 stores and 34 donation stations. They combined to employ more than 300 disabled workers in 1986. The Training Center placed 47 persons in competitive jobs.

It's an eye-opening experience to see how private donations go from "junk to jobs." Last year 13 million pounds of discarded items rolled into the Portland plant. From the unloading area, a process begins whereby nothing goes unused.

Cardboard and foam rubber are bundled for recycling. Unsalable clothing is converted into wiper cloths — a $100,000 annual business in itself. Furniture is repaired, refinished and reupholstered. Goodwill even manufactures its own "Country Casual" line of sofas, tables, footstools and lamps.

All other items are separated out by specialists at various stations. There is even a Collector's Corner where sometimes rare and valuable pieces receive individual treatment.

Nor are Goodwill employees engaged only in these activities. Local firms employ the Contract Services Division for product assembly, packaging and mail order. Custodial Services contracts with outside companies, and food industry expert Elva Bennett prepares workers for restaurant positions.

Goodwill Industries of Oregon can point with pride to 60 years of accomplishments and look forward to many more based on a formula that will never become obsolete.

THE CHARGE OF THE BAG BRIGADE — FIRST GOODWILL GOOD TURN DAY DRIVE - 1952

Klooster '87

Answers: All Goodwills are autonomous but share promotional materials and management techniques through seminars. There are 45 Goodwills in 320 nations outside North America.

142

Grand Central Bowl: From aisles to alleys

June 19, 1985

Grand Central's newsstand, tobacco and sundries concession. Pall Mall, Camel, Chesterfield — 15 cents. What is the year? (Answer below cartoon.)

In 1930, at the onset of the Great Depression, the American public was forced to become cost conscious as never before. That year Fred Meyer made his initial expansion out of the downtown area, launching Portland's first "suburban super" in the Hollywood District.

That same year a group of enterprising investors made their bid to capture the close-in eastside shopper as they began construction of a full-block public market bounded by SE Morrison, Belmont, 8th and 9th.

Opening as the East Side Food Center in 1931, the market consisted entirely of independent vendors. There were a total of 44 stalls offering everything from produce to meats, baked goods to dairy products. Five lunch counters operated on the bustling main floor.

Grand Central and East Side signs both appear in this photo. SE 8th and Belmont, circa 1938.

When Ben Levin purchased the building at the end of 1944, he switched over to exclusive use of the Grand Central Public market name and expanded tenancy to its greatest level. In addition to the grocers, produce merchants and two meat markets, there was a variety store, newsstand, shoe repair, Routledge's Seed and Lawn Supply, Van Gorter's Deli and Kappel's Old Holland Bakery.

The basement area, which had been intended for underground parking, was occupied by Kappel's wholesale bakery operations, a discount shoe store, Day Music Co.

and Johnny Trulinger's 3,000-unit frozen food locker facility — largest on the West Coast.

Those lower-level operations were almost victims of the 1948 flood. Rising waters reached as far as SE 5th and seepage found its way into the building. But pumps running around the clock for several days averted inundation.

In the early 1950s, changes in shopping patterns began to erode Grand Central's business base. The opening of more suburban shopping centers, deterioration of the nearby Southeast residential areas and elimination of the street cars all contributed. By 1958 it was apparent to Herman Levin, who had taken over the building's operation when his father died in 1952, that he would have to seek alternatives.

He found what was to become the boom sport of the '60s — bowling. Grand Central seemed ideal in location and size for a bowling center. A friend from Vancouver had just jumped onto the bowling bandwagon, installing the Northwest's first automatic pinsetters in his new Crosley Bowl. So Levin followed suit.

Grand Central Bowl was launched in June of 1960. Sixteen lanes occupied the west half of the building with the 19 remaining retail tenants in the east half. But time had caught up with them. Two years later, the last of the retailers closed and Levin expanded to 28 lanes.

The heyday of ten-pin fever has subsided but, in the interim, Grand Central has become something of an institution. Open 24 hours a day, 365 days a year, the regulars — bowling leagues, pool players and restaurant patrons — will be helping new owner Stu LaGris (he bought out the ailing Levin in 1977) celebrate the center's 25th anniversary this month.

Last year, Stu decided to change the long-standing 365-day policy and be closed on Christmas. The only trouble was that he had to have new locks installed on the doors because nobody could find the keys to the old ones.

Answer: Photo is unidentified, so it's difficult to determine the exact year. Anyone for researching magazine covers? Probably late 1940s.

Coon Chicken Inn: It wasn't 'The Colonel'

September 26, 1984

Dishware from Mike Cramer's collection. These items fetch costly china prices. What other rare Coon Chicken collectibles does he have? (Answer below cartoon.)

When Seattle restaurant entrepreneur M.L. Graham launched his Coon Chicken Inn empire in 1931, prejudice probably never entered his mind.

Graham apparently had aspirations of a nationwide chain, as the facade of each facility prominently boasted "Nationally Famous — Coast to Coast." The grinning, almost grotesque head of a bald black man with porter's cap and winking eye formed the entryway. The door was in the middle of his teeth. Altogether an unforgettable sight.

Portland sold chicken pies for a quarter and deluxe Coon Chicken dinners for $1.25. By their last year, 1949, prices had risen to 40 cents and $2.50 respectively. Still a bargain in today's terms.

Although the Salt Lake City restaurant was staffed almost entirely with black waiters, this was not the case in Portland. The city's black population was very small until the influx of World War II shipyard workers. But with men unavailable for restaurant work, they switched to waitresses.

Nationally Famous — COON CHICKEN INN — 5474 Sandy Blvd., PORTLAND, OREGON.

This stereotypical imagery was employed merely as a clever means of selling chicken. And it did just that. Southern-fried Coon Chicken specials, chicken pie, noodles, livers, giblets and consomme. Even chicken salad and sandwiches. All from milk-fed chicken supplied by the Coon Chicken Poultry Farms.

Although chicken was the main thing, it wasn't the only food served. Hamburgers, chili, seafood, assorted sandwiches and desserts added diversity. Homemade pies, cakes, pastries and rolls came from the Coon Chicken Bakery. Their "Day and Night Delivery" was a popular feature.

The first year of operation, Graham's three restaurants in Seattle, Salt Lake City and at 5474 N.E. Sandy Blvd. in

Portland's Coon Chicken Inn was, by all accounts, a popular eating place throughout its existence. With a derby, a shoe and a jug forming other surrealistic facades along Sandy Blvd., it wasn't out of place.

Though gone for a quarter of a century, it remains a compelling bit of nostalgia, as local collector Mike Cramer can attest. Even better known for his Lewis and Clark Exposition souvenirs, Cramer has compiled probably the most complete collection of Coon Chicken Inn memorabilia found anywhere.

In April 1982, he attended a reunion of former Coon Chicken Inn employees, where much of this information was obtained firsthand. The reunion was held at, where else, the Prime Rib, 5474 N.E. Sandy Blvd.

Answer: Three sizes of menus, matchbooks, stationery, napkins, ashtrays and many other promotional novelties.

OLCC:
The green front turns 50

February 1, 1984

During WWII many items were rationed. What was the monthly Bourbon limit? How were servicemen treated stateside? (Answers below cartoon.)

Following 14 years of rum running, bootlegging and bathtub gin, the federal government finally relented and repealed the Volstead (Prohibition) Act of 1919.

It was left to each state to decide how they would make the transition. In Oregon a "blue ribbon" (perhaps a bit "blue nose," too) committee appointed by Governor Julius Meier recommended adoption of the "Quebec" system — state-controlled stores.

A special session of the state Legislature met in December 1933 to create the Oregon Liquor Control

A typical green front in the '50s.

Commission and the first stores opened on February 15, 1934.

The following month there were 24 stores (state owned and operated) and 130 agencies (operated by licensees). Sales in 1935 exceeded $6 million. Whereas anyone of age could purchase it, only those who belonged to private clubs could clink a glass of liquor in company with others outside of their own homes. Taverns then were allowed to serve only beer.

This situation prevailed until 1941 when the "bottle clubs" were established. Patrons brought in their own bottles containing the potable of preference and the club charged to serve it with a "setup" — glass, ice, mixer, water,

etc. It most assuredly was a strange setup.

Owing to Oregon's initiative process, the people put a measure on the ballot in 1952 abolishing bottle clubs in favor of "liquor by the drink," which took effect in May 1953. Within one year, 735 "dispenser" licensees were in operation.

By 1960, state stores were giving way to independent agencies, 35 to 143, plus 836 dispenser establishments accounting for OLCC sales of $49.5 million. The state's first self-service store opened in Lloyd Center.

State store #7, Medford, Oregon, in 1936.

A growing population meant increased sales — $81,500,000 in 1970. OLCC picture I.D., in effect since 1961, finally went by the wayside in 1979 owing to the new photo driver's license. 357,392 young adults from 21 to 26 years old had to pull out the blue and white card on demand during those 18 years.

No policing agency is going to win a public popularity contest but the OLCC's record over the last 50 years has been far to the plus side both in reasonable enforcement and contribution to state coffers.

Generating $150 million in sales from six self-service stores, 200 agencies and 1,268 dispenser licensees in 1982-83, the commission turned a $68,000,000 net profit.

Answers: Two fifths per month in Oregon. Many clubs were Off Limits or had restricted hours for servicemen.

Tektronix: Longtime leader, technologically

February 12, 1986

Tek founders, Jack Murdock (left) and Howard Vollum, with their first oscilloscope, type 511A (right). Why was it so successful? What does it do? (Answers below cartoon.)

When the subject of major Oregon companies comes up, the name *Tektronix* is, invariably, one of the first mentioned. Little wonder since the $1.4 billion international corporation, with more than 12,000 Oregon employees, is second only to the state, itself.

Founders Jack Murdock and Howard Vollum, who started out to build a better oscilloscope, personally supervised much of that growth. Murdock was active until a seaplane accident claimed his life in 1971. And Vollum, who relinquished his role as corporate board chairman in 1984, died on February 3, 1986, just nine days ago, at 72.

The two, both radio enthusiasts, met and became friends in the mid-30s. Vollum, a then recent Reed College graduate, set up a

The "assembly line" at Tek's S.E. 7th and Hawthorne plant in 1947.

repair shop in Murdock's appliance store at S.E. 59th and Foster Road. Their fledgling plan to design and manufacture electronics equipment was forestalled by World War II. When they began again in 1946, not only was their first oscilloscope better, it was less than one-third the cost of its closest competitor.

Within a year the young company had grown from six to sixteen employees. It went from the basements of the two partners' parents to Murdock's old store and, finally to a building at S.E. Hawthorne and Seventh.

Washington County was selected for the company's new plant in 1950. Choice of geographic area had been importantly influenced by a poll of employees, the majority of whom favored the westside.

The new, 23,000-square-foot facility at S.W. Barnes Road and Sunset Highway was designed for 200 workers. By summer, 1951, when they moved, Tektronix had 250 employees and immediate expansion was necessary. Five years later the Sunset plant

occupied 80,000 square feet with 50,000 more on the drawing board.

In addition to its leadership position in technology, "Tek" has been in the forefront of employee benefit programs. The Tektronix Employee Retirement Trust was established in 1953 as an investment entity separate from the corporation. In 1956 the trust purchased 313 acres in Beaverton on which Tek's single large complex was built over the next several years.

By 1973 that site had been stretched to its limits and the following year 265 acres in Wilsonville were acquired. The Information Display Group moved into its new Tek-Wilsonville plant in October 1975.

While Tektronix remains the world's leading manufacturer of oscilloscopes, they are only part of a product line, boasting more than 2,000 items. Seven "groups" or divisions comprise Oregon's largest corporation: Instrument Systems, Portables, Communications, Information Display, Design Automation, Electronic and Mechanical Components and Tek Research Labs.

Each applies advanced technologies — many invented by Tek — to the development and manufacture of electronic systems and components. As of January 1986 Tektronix, Inc. prepared to celebrate its 40th Anniversary with 20,094 employees worldwide selling its products in 70 countries.

The company's commitment to employee values was expressed by co-founder Howard Vollum thusly:

1. The individual has dignity and importance.
2. People are honest in a total sense.
3. Each person wants to do a good job.
4. No one has ever found the limits of human ability.

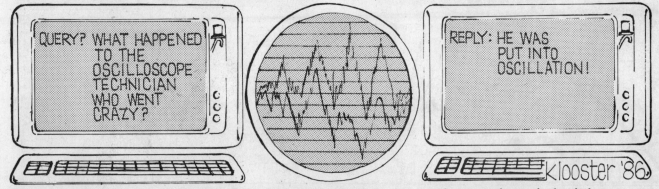

Answer: It was the fastest, most accurate and least expensive. Oscilloscopes observe and measure changes in electrical energy.

Viewmaster: A dynamic double take

February 12, 1986

How many scenes are on a View-Master reel? How many reels to a story? What well-known communications company now stands on the site of the original factory? (Answers below.)

What is the only entertainment medium in the world that has Mickey Mouse, Charlie Brown, the Muppets, the "A" Team, Sesame Street, the Smurfs, Star Trek and Michael Jackson all under contract at one time?

It's our own, homegrown, internationally known View-Master, the one-of-a-kind company that began manufacturing a little 3-D viewing device in 1938.

The company dates back to 1914 when Sawyer's, a photo-finishing firm, was founded in Portland as a producer of black & white postcards. The idea owes its origins to Sir Charles Wheatstone who invented the first stereoscope viewer a fully century before, in 1838.

Portland.

During World War II, Sawyer's View-Master produced training reels for the U.S. Army. After the war the company quickly expanded into Central and South America and introduced the first of its fantasy reels.

In 1950 they built a new plant in Beaverton and within a year had acquired the rights to reproduce all Disney characters and properties, an agreement that is retained to this day.

Sawyer's continued its growth through the '50s and into the '60s. Cartoons, top TV shows and movies were added to the viewer line. View-Master also introduced two-by-two inch

The first Sawyer's View-Master factory, late 1930s (left). A 1940 ad (center). The Beaverton (Progress) plant, 1962 (right).

Appropriate to its early scenic subjects, the two men who formed View-Master, Harold Graves, president of Sawyer's Photographic Services, and William B. Gruber, inventor of the stereo camera, met at the Oregon Caves. Sawyer saw Gruber photographing the tourist attraction and the two men struck up a conversation which led to a working agreement.

By Christmas 1939, the first viewers and seven-scene reels were on sale. The viewer was round, fitting the form of the reel, and the eye pieces looked like opera glasses. Today's reels and viewers are interchangable with those of almost 50 years ago.

In 1940 the novel new View-Master was introduced at the New York World's Fair. By the following year more than a thousand dealers nationwide were selling all the scenic reels that could be cranked out by the little production facility in

Pana-Vue scenic slides in 1960 and was giving Kodak a good run in the slide projector field.

The company's fortunes changed in 1966 when the families of the original owners sold out to GAF Corporation. The New York conglomerate dropped projector manufacturing and lent only nominal support to the View-Master, itself, which continued on its own momentum.

Fifteen years later, Arnold Thaler, a veteran of the big-time corporate world as group V.P. with the $5 billion American Home Products, took over the company in a leveraged buyout.

Over the past three years he has brought new vitality to his View-Master International using aggressive promotion and marketing savvy to make the most of this unique product. Just ask Mr. Spock, Mr. T., Michael Jackson or the (View) Masters of the Universe.

Answers: Seven scenes, two shots of each on opposite sides of the reel. KPTV Channel 12.

G.I. Joe's: A surplus of success

July 23, 1986

The original tent store on Union Ave. What did Ed Orkney use to detect painted-over copper? What was his employee philosophy? (Answers below cartoon.)

When Army Air Corps pilot Edward M. Orkney returned to Portland after World War II, he applied for civilian work doing what he was best qualified to do — flying airplanes. Unfortunately, thousands of other recently discharged Air Corps officers had the same idea.

Denied the chance to take to the airways again, the 30-year-old Orkney envisioned the stock market as a method to make the American dream happen for himself and his family. But he needed a nest egg, and the priority that veterans were given to purchase surplus military equipment provided the opportunity.

With borrowed money he bought 2,000 mummy bags from Fort Lewis for $1.50 apiece and then promptly sold them all on 82nd Avenue street corners at $12 to $15. Most of the profit went into the market and never came out again.

The first permanent G.I. Joe's on Vancouver Ave 1956.

Undeterred, Orkney once again took advantage of rock bottom prices on military materiel. This time it was hand tools, which resold to dealers within two months, and again his surplus profits saw the loss side of the stock-exchange ledger. Stung twice, it occurred to the young ex-aviator that he had made good money over the past year; it just hadn't been in the way he had originally intended.

For the next two years, Ed bought and sold surplus to dealers from Seattle to Los Angeles. Then, in 1948, he opened his first G.I. (Government Issue) Joe's store on Northeast Union Avenue near Columbia. That initial outlet was, appropriately, a series of surplus field hospital tents with plywood walls. Following an incident where vandals sliced through the tent sides, employees took turns sleeping in the store.

The disastrous Vanport flood gave the fledgling business a tremendous boost during its first year. Demand for blankets, field stoves and other camping equipment was overwhelming, but Ed didn't raise his bargain rates. Although wholesaling continued on some bulk items, the retail trade rapidly became the company's mainstay.

In 1952 G.I. Joe's moved to its first solid structure — an old building on North Vancouver and Schmeer Road. Square footage was doubled in 1956. In 1960 the Berlin Wall and the threat of war ended what had been a steady supply of military surplus. It was time to diversify.

With the growing availability of outdoor equipment from civilian manufacturers, it continued to be a key element in G.I. Joe's merchandising mix. But expansion into other areas made the company grow. In 1960 a separate building for sporting goods was constructed across the street and a third building for hardware was completed next to it in 1964.

Orkney's son, David, joined the company full time in 1971. David began making a nuts and bolts contribution to the business at 10 years old — literally putting the former on the latter. Having studied real estate in college, David headed up G.I. Joe's expansion effort that had been launched the year previous with the first satellite store —Rockwood at Southeast Stark and 184th Avenue. Under the younger Orkney's guidance, nine new stores have been launched; the most recent opening just this past March in Medford.

For the past dozen years Portland auto racing and G.I. Joe's have been synonymous. A relationship first formulated by David Orkney, longtime employee and now general manager Norm Daniels and First Interstate Bank's Bob Ames, has seen the company become the primary sponsor of the Rose Cup, the CART 200 and the G.I. Joe's Gran Prix, which will have its ninth annual run this weekend (July 25, 26, 27) at Portland International Raceway.

When Ed Orkney passed away in 1976, he left an admirable legacy for son David to carry forward. The little surplus store that started in a tent had grown into a multi-million dollar business. Last year the then 10-store G.I. Joe's, all-Oregon operation surpassed the $100,000,000 mark. David Orkney and his associates are currently laying battle plans to invade the Seattle-Tacoma area within the next two years. With a winning formula, there seems to be little doubt that they'll continue to have a surplus of success.

Answers: Orkney always carried a magnet. Take care of your employees and keep them. Most managers started in high school.

Christmas Northwest: Making seasons bright

December 17, 1986

Emery Neale with a favorite friend. In what other activity has Neale been a long-time winner? (Answer below cartoon.)

Outside the quarter-block building at 645 S.E. Ankeny St., an unassuming sign states "Christmas Northwest Corporation — Manufacturers Representatives." It only hints at the dazzling world inside. For company owners Emery and Mary Alice Neale and their employees, it's Christmas all year long. Christmas Northwest is the region's largest wholesale supplier of holiday lights, ornaments and decorations.

Showrooms filled with smiling Santas, impish elves, soaring doves, cuddly bears, coquettish dolls, prancing reindeer, marching soldiers, ringing bells and bangly bows, holly wreaths and artificial trees attest to 30 years of success in a unique Northwest business.

One room is devoted entirely to lights. Thousands of bulbs illuminate on demand. Large lights, tiny lights, blinking, twinkling, bubbling and flame-like, flickering lights. The industry that makes

Neale had begun selling the product several years earlier as a sideline. As a young sales rep for Holman Transfer Company, he worked on the Iron Fireman account. The Portland-based, national manufacturer of coal stokers owned the On-A-Lite rights but had not expanded distribution beyond a handful of major outlets.

Iron Fireman President Harry Banfield agreed to let Emery represent the product to all Oregon retailers that didn't already carry it. Within four years, he more than doubled sales and went on to become sole agent for On-A-Lite in the Pacific Northwest. In 1960, the Emery Neale Company provided all the outdoor "On-A-Lighting" for the newly opened Lloyd Center's first holiday season.

The following year, Neale, his wife and one employee moved into the Ankeny Street location the company has occupied ever since. Changing the name to Christmas Northwest in 1969, the Neales continued expanding and adding more lines until they took

(left) Christmas showroom; (center) Earliest artificial tree, Germany, 1914; (right) Easter and Halloween showroom.

Christmas bright has come a long way since a Japanese firm introduced a little, milky white, popcorn-shaped bulb back in the 1930s. According to Emery Neale, "today, the LED (light-emitting diode) light set is revolutionizing holiday lighting." Its bulbs never burn out!

More than 5,000 individual domestic items and 800 imported ones can be found in the Christmas Northwest catalogs. A subsidiary, Olympic Specialty Co., imports and markets the company's exclusive lines nationally. This end of the business takes the Neales each year to Hong Kong, Taiwan, Korea and, more recently, mainland China.

Quite an evolution from the one-man, one-room and essentially, one-product operation that Emery Neale, then 34, founded in 1956. That product was On-A-Lite, an innovative socket that allowed bulbs to be placed at any position along a light cord.

up every square foot of the building. Initially, they had operated from just two rooms leasing out the remainder to meet the mortgage.

The Easter season became part of the product lines in 1980 and Halloween followed in 1984. A separate showroom displays these two holidays which have grown to 25 percent of annual sales. Makeup kits are the single biggest seller.

Of particular pride to Neale is the company's own mini-museum — a collection of antique decorations and prewar light sets. The oldest ornament is from 1860. If imitation is the sincerest form of flattery, the Neales should feel sincerely flattered. In the last decade, two unrelated companies, Christmas Southwest and Christmas Southeast, have set up shop copying the Christmas Northwest concept in their own areas.

'Tis the night before Christmas at Christmas Northwest. The showrooms are brimming with their season's best. Ornaments and gift wrap, they're all on display. Wreaths, cards and candles add to the array.

Christmas lights twinkling all over the place. And brightest of all is each happy face. These folks are preparing to send up a cheer. 'Cause they're already selling for Christmas next year!

Kloster '86

Answer: Neale was a national collegiate tennis champion (1940s), Wimbledon Seniors' quarter-finalist (1967-68), three-time National Seniors' Singles champ (1966-68).

6. RIVER CITY RECOLLECTIONS

Social diversions and personal nostalgia

One of the prerogatives of being a columnist, as opposed to a reporter, is the latitude to engage in personal opinion, hearsay and whimsy. Whether the writer regales or repulses readers with such idiosyncratic indulgence, is the proof of popularity.

As a native Portlander, and a sentimental one at that, the opportunity to write about people, places, situations and events experienced first hand, is the wordsmith's analogy for the kid locked up in a candy store. It's just too tempting to resist going a bit overboard. On the other hand, interesting insights can be imparted. Even if you are already acquainted with some of the subjects, perhaps you will appreciate the perspective of this observer. Of all the stories in this book, these are the closest to my heart.

A history writer may get considerable satisfaction recounting times long past. But, there's still no substitute for being there — cheering wildly as Frankie Austin streaked around the Vaughn Street base path for an inside-the-ballpark home run; cruising Yaw's and the Tik Tok in my radically raked, fire engine red '50s Olds coupe; not missing a single episode of the Cinnamon Bear's Christmas time saga; joining the city's biggest residential traffic jam to take in the glittery show on Peacock Lane.

Since I wrote about Broadway's lights, the Hilton Hotel has changed its colors, or at least those on its lofty neon signs. The familiar, green glow they sported since 1963 has been changed to regrettable red a la the Marriott. Chinatown's lion-guarded gate, the product of Taiwanese artistry, has been installed. And the Morrison Bridge is all aglow thanks to the Electricians' Union. See *Symbols of the season* (December 29, 1984) where the idea of lighting all the Willamette bridges during the holidays was first recommended in *Round the Roses*.

The other stories that comprise this chapter are the stuff of someone else's memories. My amusement park was Jantzen Beach. My grandfather's were Council Crest and Lotus Isle. We shared the lone survivor — The Oaks. As for holidays of history, this writer has attempted to put himself in the place of those that lived them. I hope you enjoy the effort.

Portland Christmas: Symbols of the season

December 26, 1984

The West Hills martini glass. What was its special message to Jesuit High Schoolers from 1978 to 1980? (Answer below cartoon)

When you think of the Christmas season in the City of Roses, what images come to mind? Our own red-nosed Rudolph which first appeared on the White Stag sign at the west end of the Burnside Bridge in 1953? The neighborly residents of Peacock Lane who have given their special gift to Portland since 1935?

This year these festive classics have been joined by a new symbol of the season, one that appears destined to become a tradition — the Pioneer Square Christmas Tree, focal point of Portland's public plaza.

neighbor who had discontinued the glass after displaying it for several seasons. Dr. Cook has commendably carried on the tradition.

Another of Portland's most durable holiday happenings is probably the most difficult to coordinate and costly in which to participate. The Christmas Ship Parade or "Flotilla" has been organized annually by the Coast Guard Auxiliary for the past 29 years.

Walt Sheffield, owner of Sheffield Marine Propellor, has coordinated the colorful event since 1971. Each year,

The Christmas Flotilla off Marine Drive by Bart's Wharf. It began in 1956 with one boat.

The white lights of Jackson Tower twinkle brightly over the square's southwest corner. The illuminated Courthouse dominates its eastern flank.

Framed by the hills behind downtown, another familiar sign of the season stands out. The West Hills martini glass. The glowing glass, 10 feet tall, with olive, is the property of Dr. Gary Cook. But Cook, a local dentist, has owned it for only two years.

Monte "Buddy" Meadows Jr., son of the long-time Portland auto dealer, built it in 1978 while he was still in high school. Monte says it was originally set up as a signal to his Jesuit classmates — "Parents gone, party's on."

The younger Meadows also mentions that his martini glass was not the first. He picked up the idea from a

from December 8 to 23, a dazzling display of floating forms — a sleigh, church, star, tree, sternwheeler, to name a few — glide across the Columbia's nighttime waters.

From 20 to 30 boats bring their nautical light show, complete with prerecorded carolling, up the Willamette only one evening each season and it brings out the crowds. This year it was Sat., Dec. 22.

Each of these symbols adds its special couterpoint to the holiday celebration. Each takes time, effort and money to bring to us each year. So here's a heartfelt thanks to those generous people who make such marvelous memorabilia possible. Happy Holidays to them and to you all.

CHRISTMAS LIGHTS ON ALL THE DOWNTOWN BRIDGES, WHAT A WONDERFUL HOLIDAY IDEA!

THIS COULD MAKE PORTLAND FAMOUS!

ALL WE HAVE TO DO IS GET THE CITY TO COME UP WITH THE MONEY!

HO!HO!HO! WHOOP!WHOOP!

Klooster '84

Answer: Buddy Meadows Jr. lit it during the holidays when his parents were away as a signal to come up and party.

Portland Christmas: O Tannenbaum

December 15, 1984

Who claims bo have the largest Christmas tree? Where is it and where did it come from? (Answers below cartoon).

The community Christmas tree has been around for a long time in American cities large and small. But none has become more a part of its community than one that isn't a community tree at all.

The Lloyd Center Christmas tree, a promotional device, was the first of its kind in the country. When the nation's largest shopping mall opened in 1960, it was put on display that first Christmas.

Portland advertising man, Ron Schmidt, who was public relations director of Lloyd Center in its early days, recalls that Georgia-Pacific was the first supplier of the tree, with

Enquirer subsequently took all the credit for creation of the concept with attendant nationwide publicity.

Just this holiday season, the tree's unique, bolted-on branches came into play once again when Pioneer Courthouse Square personnel were given the bracket design and instructions on how to construct our new publicly-owned evergreen edifice. It was placed in a well specifically preplanned for it by architect Will Martin and his design team.

Unlike the Lloyd Center's tree, which is subsidized by the merchant association, the Pioneer Square tree became a

The 24th Lloyd Center tree (left); Pioneer Square's tree begins another tradition (right)

Publisher's Paper Company doing the honors in more recent years. A cream-of-the-crop selection is made six to eight months in advance of cutting.

Special brackets were designed to attach branches all the way down the trunk, thus creating the first-ever completely filled-in Christmas tree. The tallest one was 106 feet in 1976, with the average between 85 and 90 feet.

Ken Manske, Lloyd Center's public relations director in the mid-'70s, relates that the *National Enquirer* came to town asking about the technique to build the top-to-bottom tree. Center engineer Bert Smith showed them how and the

reality as a result of a cooperative effort from several sources.

The Association for Portland Progress was overall coordinator, Weyerhauser donated the tree, Meier and Frank and KGW co-sponsored the lighting ceremony, and contributions for the lights came from downtown building owners.

With both Lloyd Center and Pioneer Square, the Rose City now has two timbertopping tannenbaums to make our season bright.

Answers: The *National Enquirer's* tree at their headquaters in Lantana, Florida, grew up in Vernonia, Oregon. they say it's 126 feet tall.

Peacock Lane: A delightful gift

December 21, 1983

The annual children's Easter event. What other aspect of the lane was a gas in earlier times? (Answer below cartoon)

Traditions stem from many sources. School spirit, civic pride, religious belief. In all of them are found the roots of enduring observances, ceremonies and celebrations. But what about neighborliness?

Congeniality among people who live near one another (a custom which regrettably has waned) would hardly appear to form the foundation for time-honored traditions.

Yet this spirit of friendliness and cooperation is precisely what has created Portland's most celebrated Christmas street — Peacock Lane, an annual event whose origins go back almost half a century.

Ruth, traces the neighborhood's organized street decorating efforts to 1939 when residents got together for a street dance.

After the war, the lane's holiday extravaganza really took off. In 1947, the Peacock Lane Association was formed. The street dance continues to be held each August and 26-year residents Ed and Dorothy Hawes initiated a children's Easter Egg Hunt and Parade in 1960. Ed, at 77, has also just retired after 20 years as the lane's Santa.

Residents are justifiably proud of their annual gift to the City of Portland. And we obviously appreciate it. An

White Christmas on the Lane, 1978? No, it had melted by Christmas Eve.

The lane's longest and only original residents, Bill and Ruth Bonnett, moved into their newly completed home in March 1924. At the time, there were only seven houses along the two-block street which had been East 40th up until just a few months before.

The developer, so the story goes, had just returned from China and was so taken by the peacocks there that he petitioned for the name change to add distinction to the charming group of peak-roofed houses.

Bill Bonnett, 81, recalls that a number of houses were decorated as early as 1935 and his 92-year-old sister,

average of 4,000 vehicles visit each evening between 6 and 11 p.m. from December 15 to 31, according to association historian, Jon Christian. And that's not counting the thousands of pedestrians.

It is this sense of community that makes the loveliest light show in town even more special. So when you go to see it, keep in mind the spirit of giving that has made this neighborly Noel known throughout Portland and beyond.

Happy Holidays to everyone Round the Roses.

THANK YOU, NEIGHBORS, FOR WORKING TOGETHER TO MAKE THE LANE A SUCCESS AGAIN!

MADAM PRESIDENT!

EVEN THOUGH THIS PUBLICITY IS VERY FLATTERING, LET'S PLAY DOWN OUR **OTHER** ANNUAL EVENTS!

AFTER ALL, ONCE A YEAR IS ENOUGH TO HOST A **QUARTER** OF A **MILLION** HOUSE GUESTS!

klooster '83

Answer: Gas lights illuminated the lane and all the homes used natural gas.

Portland Christmas: The Cinnamon Bear

December 12, 1984

The now-Frederick & Nelson Cinnamon Bear. Where does he appear? How many are there? How many cinnamon cookies does he pass out? (Answers below cartoon)

There are few things more closely associated with a City of Roses Christmas than the kid-hugging cookie-giving Cinnamon Bear — a winning tradition for 47 consecutive seasons.

Lipman, Wolfe & Company, the downtown department store on Fifth between Alder and Washington for 67 years, introduced the bear and his holiday story in 1937 at the height of radio's dominance as a home-entertainment medium.

The tale, written by Granville Heish, was told in 26 installments of 15 minutes each. It centers on Judy and Jimmie Barton's search for a special family heirloom — the silver star that stood atop their Christmas tree.

It becomes a policeman's badge, is crushed into bits and restored by Melissa, Queen of Maybe Land.

The children and the Cinnamon Bear are put upon by pirates, waylaid by a witch and guided by a giant. It's the makings of an animated movie the equal of Disney at his best. In the end they meet Jack Frost and Santa Claus at the North Pole, recover the Silver Star and wake up from a wondrous dream.

Every year the tale has been retold and every year Paddy O'Cinnamon has played a prominent part in the celebration of Christmas around Portland. For the first 10 years he was a regular bear until, in 1947, Lipman, Wolfe designer Vernice Durand

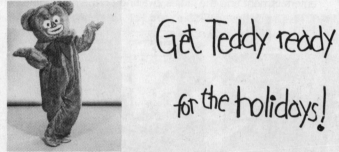

Paddy posing (lft.). and Teddy cartoon characterizations (center). At Doernbecher Hospital (rt.).

Children of the 1980s may have more entertainment options involving greater gimmickry, but nothing beats a good story — particularly a Christmas story. It wasn't aired on KKSN back then but any child or child at heart will enjoy tuning in at 6:45 p.m. now through December 24 as each succeeding episode brings Judy and Jimmie, aided by Paddy O'Cinnamon (The Cinnamon Bear), a step closer in their quest for The Silver Star.

The trio encounter an almost inconceivable menagerie of imaginary creatures along the way and are caught up in a series of adventures that rival Alice's wanderings through Wonderland: A Crazy Quilt Dragon perched on the cliffs above a Root Beer Ocean. Cruel King Blotto and his subjects, the Inkaboos; the strange inhabitants of the Island of Obi.

The star is swallowed by Wesley the Wailing Whale, juggled by Samuel the Trained Seal and swept up by Penelope the Pelican.

gave him the cinnamon-cookie look.

Seattle-headquartered Frederick & Nelson, which bought out Lipman's in 1979, has carried forward the tradition with enthusiasm. According to the bear's boss, Special Events Coordinator Cindy McBurney, young men and women "five-five to five-ten who work well with children and can tolerate heat" apply in droves for the opportunity to portray the cuddly bear.

Paddy makes special appearances at hospitals, including Doernbecher and the Emanuel Bear Clinic where toy bears are repaired at Christmas time. This year he was on hand to inaugurate Pioneer Square's first Christmas tree on November 23rd and helped Governor Atiyeh with the rotunda lighting ceremony on December 10th in Salem.

He's unique, he's ours, he's the Cinnamon Bear — an only-in-Oregon Christmas story.

Answers: All four Portland stores, Salem, Eugene and Corvallis, as well as special events. 30 to 35 bears. 8,200 dozen cookies.

Early Portland: Pioneer spirits

December 28, 1983

Erickson's extravagant exterior. Now being renovated by the Naito Brothers, it is scheduled to reopen in mid-May 1984. What will occupy the mezzanine? (Answers below cartoon).

If you find yourself downtown on December 31st toasting George Orwell's New Year, *1984*, take note of where you are. Across the street, down the block or on that very spot may have stood one of Portland's early saloons. In 1851, the year the city was incorporated, there were already two dozen.

Those bygone barrooms made today's toughest tavern look like a tea party. Counties set the rules for the purveyance of potables and corruption was the order of the day—a situation that prevailed until Prohibition which was imposed by legislators of the Beaver State, in 1915, four

mid-1880s, he set out to build "the biggest and best saloon in the world." 1890 was the first year it appeared in the City Directory along with more than two hundred local competitors.

By all accounts, Gus fully achieved his goal. Erickson's Saloon, occupying the entire block from N.W. 2nd to 3rd and Burnside to Couch, boasted the world's longest bar at 684 feet where 50 bartenders served 16-ounce nickel schooners. Workingclass and uppercrust alike availed themselves of the bountiful buffet, nonstop gambling, entertainment and the ladies awaiting on the mezzanine.

The Fountain Saloon, 2nd and Washington, circa 1890. No proper lady would set foot in such a place.

years before it took effect nation wide.

A little-known fact is that Oregon had once before tried total prohibition, the first in the country, from 1844 to 1849. Following its inevitable failure, saloons proliferated throughout the state.

Names such as Crystal, Pearl, Fashion, Mount Hood and Miner's Return marked the public houses of Portland's central district. They were places where a drink and a woman could be had for a price 24 hours a day.

The most famous and enduring of Portland's pleasure palaces was founded by Augustus "Gus" Erickson. In the

Erickson and his enforcers, including 300-pound "Jumbo" Reilly, kept order. Some illicit activities were obviously overlooked, however. Here, and all along the Portland waterfront, Shanghaiing was an ever-present danger for the unwary patron.

Old Gus sold out in 1913 and, himself, succumbed to drink. But the new owners expanded the establishment and its popularity. Only the power of Prohibition brought Erickson's incomparable era to an end.

But this was merely a temporary derailment in the continuing saga of downtown—always in the spirits.

Answer: The Advertising Museum, first and only one in the world, sponsored by the Portland Advertising Federation.

Portland New Year: Headline highlights

January 2, 1985

Combined masthead of the *Oregonian* and *Journal* on January 1, 1960. Why was this done and for how long? (Answers below story)

Nowhere are the changing times more pointedly portrayed than on the front pages of the newspaper. New Year's editions of Portland's papers provide a perfect example.

The first time an issue of the *Weekly Oregonian* fell on New Year's Day was in 1853 and the first one where I could find any reference to the New Year was Saturday, January 1, 1859.

January 1, 1910. The Aviation Age.

The editorial, headlined "Another New Year's Greeting," went like this: "That we may not be considered out of the ring in the cold formalities of the age, we hope you all may see many more New Year's days and that each will add materially to this one in the fulfillment of the stereotypical (sic) greating 'a happy New Year's to you all.'"

January 1, 1930. Ripley's Believe It Or Not.

Mid-19th Century editorializing obviously differed somewhat from its late-Twentieth Century counterpart.

The *Morning (daily) Oregonian* of Thursday, January 1, 1880, featured "Events of The Past Year" on the front page and continued inside. On January 1, 1890, a 32-page edition carried ads on half of the front page next to the lead headline, "TWENTY MILLION, Manufacturing Growth of Portland in the Past Year. INCREASE OF 50 PERCENT."

At the turn of the century the *Oregonian* proudly announced, "Year Just Closed Was The Most Prosperous in the History of the State." Pride in the city and state continued to be the primary focus at the onset of 1910. The New Year Annual featured the Deschutes River Valley and the development of N.E. Oregon. "Days of the Pioneer Stage Numbered" and "Oregon Forges to Front as Livestock State" were the headlines.

On the first day of the first full year under Prohibition, the *Oregon Journal's* January 1, 1920 edition proclaimed, "New Year's Given Rousing Welcome." "Another nail was driven in the coffin of John Barleycorn." Only 10 cases of drunkenness were reported. The past year had seen 43 traffic fatalities — a record. Oregon played Harvard at the Rose Bowl in Pasadena and lost 7-6.

The New Year in Nine Languages.

In 1930, January 1st fell in the middle of the week. Ten years of temperance was wearing thin as the cover story revealed: "High State of Revelry Beckons in New Year with Liquor Apparently Easy to Get." The *Journal* brought in 1940 with "Gorgeous Sunrise Heralds First Day of Year" and went on to chronicle the celebration of the night before. "Downtown streets were filled with honking automobiles and gay revelers."

A decade later Portland's public merrymaking was at its height: Honking autos and tooting Portlanders turned Broadway into a gay white way on Saturday night and 1950 came into town with a bang."

The temporarily combined *Oregonian* and *Journal* featured an eligible bachelor surrounded by single ladies for Happy New Leap Year 1960. In 1970 the *Journal* fawned over the year's first born. But the big news was, "Viet War Entering 10th Year."

And can you recall what the front pages said on New Year's Day just five short years ago? The *Journal* had a banner headline, "Happy New Year — On with the '80s." The *Oregonian* didn't even mention the new year until the sixteenth page.

Answers: The long-remembered Portland newspaper strike caused joint publication starting Nov. 11, 1959, through April, 1960.

Portland New Years: 1886 and 1936

January 1, 1986

On Friday, January 1, 1886, the *Morning Oregonian* reflected the New Year's mood of the community and state it served. The most important news was business news. Commerce came first and foremost and the first three columns of the front page were paid advertisements with the remaining four devoted to an extensive "REVIEW OF THE YEAR ... the general conditions ... throughout the Northwest . . . that accelerate or retard its progress."

The review, which continued throughout the paper, was prefaced with a description of pioneer "Characteristics and Traits" as compared to the inhabitants of Oregon 30 years later. "They were self-reliant ... grew no more than what they needed ... We now begin to see helpless people where formerly there were none."

Ads share spotlight with year-end editorial in *Morning Oregonian*, Friday, January 1, 1936

Henry Pittock's newspaper, under the editorship of Harvey Scott, strove to be the voice of Oregon. Stories of the past year covered Crater Lake, the Columbia Basin, the Coast and Eastern Oregon, as well as the Willamette Valley. The first issue of 1886 also offered a history lesson to readers. "The Historical Epochs of the Country Reviewed. THE MEN WHO MADE OREGON."

Events in Oregon of the half century prior had been adventurous and exciting, particularly to the Victorian mind in the midst of Portland's New England-style prosperity. For them the tamers of the wilderness were not flambouyant swashbucklers but practical leaders — men of substance and accomplishment who introduced civilization to the frontier.

Soldier/statesmen such as General Joseph Lane, Provisional Governor John Gaines and General Edward Hamilton were held in high regard along with missionaries Marcus Whitman and Jason Lee. The list of esteemed early settlers also included Governor Abernethy; Thomas Dryer, founder of the *Oregonian;* lawyer and politician James Nesmith; Republican leader Dr. James McBride and, of course, The Hudson Bay Company's Dr. John McLoughlin. Colorful mountain man Joe Meek was the only departure from this synopsis of solid citizens.

Fifty years later, the nation was slowly extricating itself from the grip of the Great Depression. On Wednesday, January 1, 1936, the headlines announced: "BABSON PREDICTS BRIGHT NEW YEAR. Outlook for Portland Declared Roseate. Business has made good comparison with rest of country." An interesting counterpoint to Oregon's present predicament.

Other items that merited front-page treatment included "NEW YEAR GIVEN NOISY RECEPTION." Portland night clubs were charging up to $15 a couple for partygoers! A story entitled "KID CUPID SOCKS MR. DEPRESSION" featured the fact that marriages during 1935 totalled 2,070 in Multnomah County — almost a 40 percent increase over the previos year. This, the article stated, "was a harbinger of prosperity's return ... along with a decrease in mortgate foreclosures."

Undaunted by the financial shortfalls of the day, advertisers were pitching their wares to what remained of the reasonably affluent. The 1936 Pontiac, "the Greatest 8 of its time, built to last 100,000 miles." Carried a price tag of $730. Up-market clothier Charles F. Berg was showcasing Chumley fur coats — $64 to $124. And, for shoppers across a broader spectrum, Meier & Frank's Storewide Clearance Sale was about to begin.

In the sports and entertainment worlds, the Rose Bowl game, pitting Stanford against SMU, was to be aired over KEX. And the Marx Brothers' *Night at the Opera* was in its second week at The Broadway. For immediate laughs, comic strip standouts included Li'l Abner, Moon Mullins, The Gumps, Gasoline Alley, Dick Tracy. Tarzan and The Captain and the Kids. An armless wrestler highlighted Ripley's *Believe It Or Not.*

The weather of 50 years ago also hit the front page: "RAINY NEW YEAR DEBUT PREDICTED." As we bid farewell to the driest year in Portland's recorded history, we might like to see that headline in today's paper. Have a happy and prosperous New Year — Round the Roses.

WE HAVE HIGH HOPES FOR OREGON IN 1886!

WE HAVE HIGH HOPES FOR OREGON IN 1936!

WE HAVE HIGH HOPES FOR OREGON IN 1986!

Answer: Nothing is wrong with it. Today's usage. "A new page to write your success on," is incorrect English.

New Year's Eve: December 31, 1918

December 31, 1986

Mayor George L. Baker (1917-1932). What still unresolved local issue was as controversial on the last day of 1918 as it is today? (Answer below cartoon).

Portland and the nation savored an especially sweet New Year's celebration at the end of 1918. Just two months earlier the "Great War" had ended and America's doughboys were headed home. Many of them would have to see in the New Year on the Atlantic.

"Warships Carry Troops — 16,375 Soldiers On Way From France" was but one of the war-related stories that punctuated the pages of local papers on Dec. 31. Some lucky Yanks had already arrived. Lt. James H. Wolford, a Roseburg native, recounted for *Oregon Journal* readers the fierce fighting at Chateau-Thierry, a pivotal part of the second Battle of the Marne that "turned the tide" for the Allies.

For the New Year's Festivities and a fitting start for 1919 serve the family and guests

WEINHARD'S APPLE JUICE

HENRY WEINHARD PLANT
Broadway 383
A-1172

Portland's New Year's Prohibition beverage

The same issue provided glimpses of Germany's fate in defeat. Headlines bannered, "Gloomy View of German Future — $129,000,000,000 (yes, billion) Indemnity Goes Beyond Anything Dreamed Of," and "Food Situation Grave." The seeds of suffering had been planted and their cruel yield would create fertile fields for a crop of unbridled power and prejudice in the years to follow.

Oregon, on the other hand, was looking forward to a bumper harvest from its farmlands and Portland projected an excellent business outlook in 1919. The faraway war had only a minimal impact on the Northwest's economy. The emotional implications, however, affected many lives throughout the region.

Oregonians in general and Portlanders in particular supported the war effort with uncommon zeal. Mayor George L. Baker, in the first of his four terms, personally provided the impetus for local conservation and recycling programs that overshadowed even our current ones. The city's Liberty Bond drives were among the nation's most successful.

Unfortunately, Portland's patriotic fervor manifested a sordid side. Across the country, citizens of German descent became suspect. Non-citizens were declared illegal aliens and severely restricted in their activities. Incidents involving unjust arrest and prosecution for "acts of sedition" marred Oregon's judicial record.

Even people in high places were not exempt. Popular Oregon Senator and former Portland Mayor Harry Lane was branded a sympathizer for his anti-war stand in Congress. Lane's untimely death in May, 1917, stymied a recall effort.

In a tribute to the first New Year's celebration clear of international conflict since 1914, an *Oregonian* editor sought to set aside the past with these words. "It is an unusual New Year. The old one saw the fluttering gasp of the war and the new one will see the return of the old practice of sitting around the sawdust box and telling yarns about the neighbors instead of saying harsh things about Kaiser Wilhelm."

The eve of 1919 saw a city ready to have "Fun By The Ton" as the Liberty Theater's ad copy promised. Temple Apollo invited partygoers to "Dance Tonight" to the music of Some Jazz Band for 50 cents per couple. The Cotillion Hall on Southwest 14th Avenue off Washington Street also enticed celebrants to "Dance in the New Year." At The Oaks, racing and exhibition skating accompanied a "Grand Masquerade."

Portland donned "her best togs" for a "rip snortin' time" on Dec. 31, 1918. But those who wanted to liven things up with a little libation had to obtain it under the table. Although national Prohibition was still another year off, Weinhard's Apple Juice was River City's official celebration beverage. Oregon had gone dry in 1915.

Answer: Dateline Portland: Dec. 31, 1918. "Move to join City and County begins. Three bodies at work on measure."

The Oaks: Down by the riverside
August 3, 1983

Why are these two vintage locomotives, the OWR&N (Union Pacific) 3202 and SP&S's 707, displayed at The Oaks? (Answer below cartoon.)

Jantzen Beach was big time and Council Crest was high time, but The Oaks is long time. This riverside amusement park, amidst a grove of stately oaks, is the oldest of them all. And the only survivor.

Built by the Oregon Water Power & Railway Co. for $100,000 and opened May 30, 1905, just two days before the Lewis and Clark Exposition, The Oaks Amusement Resort and Recreation Park was a going concern from the start.

Located "where rail and river meet," eastside trolleys carried 30,000 visitors to the park monthly during the summer. You remember summer. It began in June back in those days.

park, was its inspirational force. He introduced the summer concert series with nationally acclaimed bandleader John Phillip Sousa, which endured for a dozen years, and "The Last Days of Pompeii" Fourth-of-July fireworks extravaganza, a Portland tradition.

There's just not enough sunshine for a Disneyland or Great America in the Pacific Northwest, but The Oaks has adjusted. Its vintage roller rink attracts devotees year-round and the building itself rests on barrel pontoons so it will float in the event of a flood. The 1948 inundator (remember Vanport)) ruined the former floor.

The old gal may be a little aged around the edges, but her oaks are original and her carousel is incomparable.

The boardwalk (circa 1910) looking north to the great Natatorium (covered pool) on the Willamette.

The city's population doubled from 1905 to 1910 and 60 percent lived on the eastside. Parkgoers could stroll along the boardwalk at river's edge or take in the Jolly Gladway's creative coterie of rides and amusements — the jazz railway, cyclone coaster, monkey hotel, shoot-the-chute and the merry maze.

Had those original attractions been preserved, The Oaks would be a Northwest tourist must. Edward Bollinger, whose son, Robert, still owns and operates the

It's a magnificent menagerie of irreplaceable mounts. Not only horses, but lions, frogs, storks, cats, an ostrich, rooster and dragon bedeck this turn-of-the century "roundabout." Accentuated by a museum of weathered but wonderful murals, just coming to admire it is worth the trip in itself.

Portland's Little Coney Island has given us almost 80 years of entertainment. With our continuing support, we'll see it to 100 and beyond.

OAKS PARK ROLLER RINK

TED, YOU'LL LOVE SKATING AT THE OAKS, BELIEVE ME!

SKATING IS FINE, SHARON. IT'S **FALLING** I DON'T LIKE!

DON'T WORRY. I'LL HELP YOU!

I SUPPOSE NOW YOU'LL TELL ME I'LL HAVE NO PROBLEM WALKING ON WATER!

RINK

ROLLER SKATING

Klooster '83

Answer: They were part of the planned Railway Hall of Fame at Oaks Pioneer Park, which never materialized.

Council Crest: A top trade takes time

July 20, 1983

Why is '506' no longer at Council Crest? Last of the crest trolleys, Old '503' was displayed at the Oregon Electric Car Historical Society's Park in Glenwood for many years. Where are they now? (Answers below cartoon)

Talbot's mountain, as Council Crest was first called, after its original (1815) pioneer settlers, isn't quite lofty enough to merit that monicker. But it does deserve the designation "finest vantage point in Portland."

From the crown of its 1200-foot crest, five snow-capped peaks and 3000 square miles of territory can be viewed. In a time of fewer man-made diversions, the trek to the top became popular among locals and visitors alike.

tory led local citizens to advocate the purchase of the property as early as 1910. But buyout costs proved prohibitive and the amusement park, with its water chute roller coaster and lofty observation tower, continued to operate until 1929.

By 1936, public sentiment had mounted for acquisition of the Crest. The old park structures stood abandoned and the road was almost inaccessible. Both daily papers were peppered with articles and editorials deriding the

The Crest was very amusing in the early 20th Century.

A group of congregational ministers, in town for an annual council, made the journey on July 12, 1888. Having been advised that it had no name (sorry about that, Talbots), they gave it the one we know it by today.

The property was in private hands and its growing acclaim undoubtedly contributed to the decision in 1907 to build an amusement park on the uppermost 22 acres. With the improvement of the road to the top and the addition of an electric trolley line, Council Crest Park rapidly became a leading tourist attraction.

Portland's love affair with its most prominent promon-

deterioration and urging purchase.

After much council-chamber wrangling, a deal was struck with the owners. The city traded an old firehouse at 4th and Yamhill — prime downtown property — in exchange for Council Crest. A city park at long last and one whale of a deal considering comparative land values of the two properties today — 3 to 1.

Since then, its trolley cars have given way to buses. Its slopes are surrounded by upper-income inhabitants and its water tower is a graffiti mural. But the view is still the best this side of the Vista House.

Answers: '506' was vandalized and burned. '503' is on loan to San Francisco as a working attraction on Market St.

Jantzen Beach: Profits took the big dipper

July 6, 1983

The magnificent Merry-Go-Round lives on at Jantzen Beach Center mall. Largest ever built, how many horses does it have and for what event was it constructed? (Answers below cartoon)

For more than four decades the words "Let's go to Jantzen Beach" meant a fun-filled day for Portlanders, young and old. Opened in 1928, the Jantzen Beach Amusement Center featured the Big Dipper, pride of West Coast roller coasters; Dodge-Em, the ever-popular bumper car ride; one of the largest swimming-pool complexes in the country; the fabulous Fun House; and a giant, big-band-era ballroom.

My generation was the last to see the park at its height and we savored every moment, from cotton candy to kewpie dolls. In April 1959, an accidental death on the roller coaster embroiled the Hayden Island Development Corp. in a costly court battle. Just over a year later the Fun House and the Old Mill (tunnel of love) burned down.

The popular "Dodge-Em" bumper cars.

Nor did the weather cooperate. In August 1964, Les Buell, the corporation's general manager, lamented the cool and wet summers of the past two years. "We had over 4,000 at the pool this weekend and only 55 on the same weekend last year." Still, he expressed optimism about future prospects.

Despite hopefulness, however, the development of other Hayden Island potentials — a trailer park, marina and moorage — proved to be better investments. In August 1969, the final blow was struck. Freeway expansion plans doomed the Big Dipper and costs prohibited its replacement. On July 7, 1970, the fabled, 50-mile-per-hour hair-raiser was no more and with it Jantzen Beach Park. An era had ended.

Kids pool in front of two 500,000 gallon main pools

Yet the 42-year-old institution did not leave an empty legacy. Out of the rubble that was once a great amusement center rose a center of another sort.

On September 28, 1971, construction began on the new Jantzen Beach Center. Opening a year to the day later, the new eight-million-dollar shopping mall, restaurant and entertainment complex has been growing ever since.

Answers: 90 horses, including six kiddie ponies. The St. Louis Exposition of 1904.

Lotus Isle:
A bamboozle
that backfired

June 20, 1984

Al Painter Lotus Isle's dance-a-thon director, and contestants. What are the stories surrounding these promotions? (Answer below cartoon)

Last summer this column carried a series of articles on local amusement parks—the Oaks, Council Crest and Jantzen Beach. Interesting stories all.

But the tale of the one that was omitted—Lotus Isle—is perhaps the most intriguing. This amusement park was short lived. In fact, it was never meant to be built. Its promoters set out in 1929 to appear that they were planning a fabulous fun center just across the way from the new Jantzen Beach park, which was opened only the previous year.

Lotus Isle opened on June 27, 1930. Its 10 acres featured 40 rides and concessions, the gigantic Peacock Ballroom that could hold 6,600 dancers, accommodations for 15,000 picnickers and parking for 5,000 cars.

It appeared that Jantzen Beach was going to have a real competitor after all. But on August 28 tragedy struck. A young boy drowned after falling from the 3/4-mile-long roller coaster and the next day owner Edwin Platt committed suicide.

Picking up the pieces, new management put forth

The "bulldog" bumper car ride, Eiffel Tower neon sign and concessions at Lotus Isle.

The idea was to get the wealthy owners of Jantzen Beach to buy them out. But the bamboozle backfired. The Hayden Island group said there was room enough for everyone and welcomed the competition.

The would-be bilkers decided that the only thing to do was to scrape up the money and make the most of the Sand Island site (later called Tomahawk Island, just east of I-5).

As a legitimate venture the park was potentially viable. Since 1918 a popular bathing spot called Columbia Beach had operated on the north side of the Island. And the hoopla the promoters had put forth to the press peaked public interest.

another push the following season. A 100-foot-tall neon sign that could be seen for miles, a dance-a-thon promotion and "Tusko," the largest elephant in captivity, were new additions. But the 12-foot-tall, ten-ton pachyderm proved too unruly and the $90,000 ballroom mysteriously burned to the ground in a spectacular blaze on August 24.

The ill-fated park stumbled through one more season in 1932. Its assets were sold in bankruptcy early the following year. Pilings from the 700-foot-long tressle that carried cars from the mainland are all that remain of once-glittering Lotus Isle.

Answer: Questionable connections have generated conjecture about their operations and the ballroom fire.

Blue Lake: A park apart

September 2, 1985

Lifeguard Ollie Dick oversees Blue Lake swimmers, 1967. Who discovered lake dwellers of another era on this site? (Answer below cartoon)

Most teenagers don't think much about history. Particularly local history. When I was swimming and boating at our summer place on Blue Lake in the mid-1950s and early 1960s, no ponderings of its origins burdened my mind.

I knew that Mr. Welsh, who lived down at the east end of the lake, owned it and the property on the northern shoreline where he operated the private recreation park. We hung around the old wooden dock enclosure and watched cute girls in bathing suits. Then we went up and hung around the old wooden dance hall to watch cute girls in shorts and pedal pushers. One day I heard that Welsh had sold the park to the county.

Blue Lake Swim Center, ca. 1930.

Residents of Interlachen Lane, a narrow, deadend road that traversed the length of the oak-studded, sandstone shelf on the lake's south side, watched the new building activities with mild interest. Twenty-five years later, I reflect on the fact that it was history in the making. But, at the time, we were more concerned about the milfoil (a seaweed-like, leafy growth) which seemed to grow denser and encroach more closely to the shoreline every season.

In researching this story, all those loosely connected memories fell into place. The lake's role in Portland-area recreation goes back 30 years before I laid eyes on the place. In 1925, a group of Gresham businessmen envisioned an exclusive enclave—a private lake with a golf course skirting its shoreline. They called it "Fairview Country Club Estates."

The golfing never got off the ground, but a swimming dock,

bathhouse and dance hall were constructed. By 1928, when young Nicholas Welsh took over the boating concession, Blue Lake was already a popular spot. A few summer cottages had cropped up on the sandstone shelf where, after a 45 minute drive out the old Sandy Road, owners could relax in their rural retreats.

Welsh saw the future potential of this pastoral place and, over a number of years, acquired a large portion of the land adjacent to the lake's northern shore. He developed children's amusements, a food concession and shady, grass-covered picnic areas to go with the swimming facilities. The dance hall was replaced in 1930 after the original burned down.

For 30 years Nick Welsh owned this private park. It became a Portland-area institution. Then, in 1958, Multnomah County embarked on a park development program. They actually had extra money in those days. And Blue Lake Park became a prime candidate for public acquisition.

County estimates pegged the property's value at $240,000. Welsh's own appraiser advised him that it should be more like $350,000. The stalemate forestalled county plans for two years until a compromise was reached in 1960 and the park opened for the first time under county supervision that summer.

Over the next few years numerous improvements were made, including new concrete walkways for the swimming area and a bathhouse that could accommodate check-in for up to 1,800 swimmers. Additional property was purchased to expand picnic and parking areas.

County park superintendent W. R. "Tex" Matsler and Max Kilgore, the park's chief ranger, made Blue Lake their pet project. In 1967, three artificial islands were constructed just off the shoreline. Connected by arched bridges, they remained until 1979 when deterioration required their removal.

Other Matsler and Kilgore innovations included "Slurpy the Litter Eater," a refuse machine with taped voice and suction system, and "Old Blue," a talking, twisting dragon slide that had flashing eyes and emitted puffs of smoke.

Unfortunately, imagination couldn't overcome the milfoil problem. For four years the lake was closed to swimmers until the infestation was finally controlled. On Memorial Day, 1983, Portland's biggest swimming hole opened for business once again.

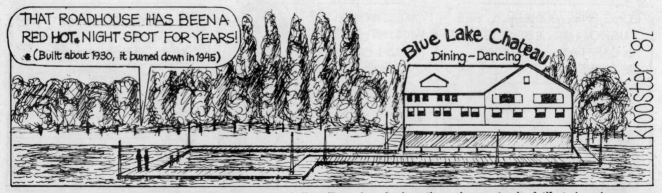

THAT ROADHOUSE HAS BEEN A RED HOT* NIGHT SPOT FOR YEARS!
*(Built about 1930, it burned down in 1945)

Blue Lake Chateau
Dining-Dancing

Klooster '87

Answer: Lewis and Clark's journals noted the lake and an Indian village along it where the park now stands. Artifacts have been discovered.

Lambert Gardens: A Portland paradise

July 9, 1986

Entrance to Lambert Gardens. What are the other famous, privately-owned Pacific Northwest gardens? (Answers below cartoon).

Descending a stone staircase from the Rose Garden to a sunken pool filled with water lilies, the viewer saw an endless illusion created by a huge paneled outdoor mirror. The Rainbow Garden consisted of a sweeping arched bed with multicolored flower rows against a wide curved wall. The Vest Pocket Garden utilized limited space to the ultimate, demonstrating another dimension of Lambert's design genius.

The expansive Italian Garden, one of the 10 Lambert Gardens.

A 400-foot long lawn, bordered on both sides by white walls, comprised the Canyon Garden. White flowers lined the length of the lawn leading to the multi-leveled Terrace Gardens beyond. Lawns, paths and bordered beds in pleasing patterns describes the Old Fashioned Garden. Informal Gardens for relaxing completed the floral fantasy. And flora was complemented by fauna, as pink flamingos, preening peacocks and crown cranes freely roamed the premises.

Gladiolas and azaleas, chrysanthemums and fuchsias, rhododendrons and tulips, dahlias and daffodils co-starred with the roses to create Lambert's paradise of flowers. Exotic trees and shrubs took no back seat, however. European smoke, Chinese silk, Japanese cherry, flowering crab and plum added their attributes.

From around the world they came to see this spectacular statement until its last season in 1968. Lambert Gardens stands prominently on the list of lost local landmarks that are fondly remembered by all who knew them.

An apartment complex now occupies the 30 acres on Southeast 28th Avenue and Steele Street, which were once a horticultural fantasyland. For almost 40 years Lambert Gardens was among Portland's top tourist attractions.

Andrew B. Lambert, a landscape gardener from Mobile, Ala. via Shrevesport, La., who migrated to Portland in the 1920s, was its creator. Each year thousands of visitors marveled at this magnificent group of gardens considered by many to be among the most beautiful in the world.

Lambert made this his life's work. Finding the City of Roses to have an ideal climate for the growing of a diverse variety of flowers, trees and shrubs, he used them in creative abundance throughout the 10 distinctive gardens that comprised those 30 manicured acres.

The Spanish Garden was surrounded by boxwood hedges, with a flowing fountain and pool as its focal point. Scarlet zinnias were the featured flower. Its immediate neighbor was the Italian Court, whose slender columns of arborvitae rose above horseshoe-shaped beds. The area was accented with stone benches and statues of Roman maidens. A stucco villa facade with iron-laced balconies stood at its edge.

True to the city that spawned it, Lambert Gardens raised roses in profusion. The queen of flowers had its own area with a 200-foot arbor. Hundreds of types and thousands of blooms adorned this two-level tribute to the family Rosaceae.

Answers: Butchart Gardens on Vancouver Island, B.C., and Pedersen's Rock Gardens near Redmond in Central Oregon.

Rose City Radio: The early ether

July 1, 1987

Oregon's first commercial radio station, KGW, squawked and squealed its way onto the airwaves on March 25, 1922. Then owned and operated by *The Oregonian*, the Portland station joined 76 others across the nation broadcasting over "the ether" (the so-called conducting medium for radio wave oscillation) for the first time that month.

Speaking from the station's studios on the top floor of the Oregonian Building at Southwest Sixth and Alder, editor Edgar Piper introduced the initial program which featured a live performance by Chicago opera star Edith Mason and remarks from the Rose City's own political showman, Mayor George Baker.

KGW broadcast of Coolidge speech, 1924.

With its solid financial support, KGW survived the industry's early days of experimentation and lack of regulatory guidelines. Many of the 508 stations that went on the air during that first year did not.

When KGW made its debut, there were perhaps 5,000 private receivers in Portland, many handmade, and less than a half-million across the country. Within five years, set ownership would soar to more than 10 million. Outside of two amateur stations, KGW had no local competition until 1925. That year Charles Myers, business manager of the Portland News, bought KQP and changed the call letters to KOIN. Offering only live programming, the new entrant focused on education and national news.

During the next year, KEX and KXL began broadcasting. The latter sent its signal out via a 10,000 watt transmitter—double KGW's power output. In 1927 KWJJ went on the air emphasizing sports and religion. Originally located in the Broadway Theatre Building, the station billed itself as "the Voice of Broadway."

In major markets, stations had proliferated. The resulting signal overlaps brought chaos to the airwaves, finally forcing Congress to pass legislation with teeth. The Radio Act of 1927 empowered the newly created Federal Radio Commission to apply the doctrine that "the right of the public to service is superior to the right of any individual to use the ether."

Comprised of five representatives, one each from the five radio zones in the United States, the commission standardized the broadcast band between 500 and 1,500 kilocycles. Station frequency designations were set at 50kc apart in each zone. A myriad of other conflicts, such as reduction of total stations in operation, had to be resolved over the ensuing years. But the basis for order was established and the battle to gain the ears of an awaiting audience got underway in earnest.

Locally, KGW went from under three hours of broadcasting per day during its first year to 23 hours per day the next. It pioneered a coast-to-coast hook-up to report presidential election returns and initiated remote broadcasts. When President Warren Harding spoke at Multnomah Field on July 4, 1923, KGW's microphones were there. Other remotes included regular Sunday broadcasts from the First Presbyterian Church and Symphony recitals.

In 1926, the Radio Corporation of America bought out AT&T's 18-station group and established the National Broadcasting Company. The advent of radio's first national network added a new dimension to program diversity. KGW became an NBC affiliate on Feb. 22, 1927.

Radio sorted out its priorities during the Roaring '20s. Stations originally owned by newspapers, hotels and department stores changed hands and became "publishers of the air" soliciting competitive advertisers. Regulation and licensing limitations enhanced the value of broadcast properties. Top talents threw themselves into a new world of innovation to create word and sound images of comedy, mystery and adventure. The ether was on the verge of exploding into its golden era.

(Rose City radio: Air for all ages · Pg. 165).

Answer: the building was damaged in the Vanport Flood on May 30, 1948 but survives today just north of P.I.R.

Rose City Radio: Air for all ages

July 8, 1987

Red's Gang, Musical Director Red Dunning and the KOIN Band, 1957. How long was the band a part of the station? (Answer below cartoon)

After the technological air was cleared by the Federal Radio Commission in the early 1930s, radio broadcasters concentrated on networking and improving what they were sending out over the ether.

RCA's National Broadcasting Company, began offering a plethora of new programming to affiliates of its Red and Blue networks. Its primary competitor, the Columbia Broadcasting System, pressed hard on the larger network's heels in the race to entice listeners.

KEX's new studio, S.W. 12th & Main, 1948.

Radio's most memorable productions — soap operas, mysteries and crime shows, situation comedies, variety programs and musicals, quiz shows, drama and adventure series — were the result. NBC's Blue Network introduced Amos and Andy and The Goldbergs in 1929. Other enduring comedies quickly followed. Fibber McGee and Molly, Burns and Allen and Jack Benny were but a few that soon became household names.

One of radio's all-time hits, The Lone Ranger, literally created a new network. First aired on Jan. 30, 1933, over WXYZ in Detroit, the masked rider of the plains, starring Bruce Beemer, was shortly picked up by other major independents. The following year, this small group started the Mutual Broadcasting System.

In Portland, five stations dominated the market. *The Oregonian's* KGW and KEX carried NBC's Red and Blue programming, respectively. Charles Myers' KOIN joined CBS, KWJJ

and KXL remained independents, offering audiences a wide variety of music, news and sports. Benson High School's KBPS, which began as KYG in 1923, also continues its long and impressive record of public service. It is the only AM station in the nation licensed to a school district.

In 1936, Portland's newest station, KALE, became a Mutual affiliate. With the backing of the *Oregon Journal,* Charlie Myers bought and merged KFJR and KTBR to create the new property. Pioneer broadcaster Ashley Dixon had founded KFJR in 1923. The Journal Juniors program began its long run on the station in 1926. KALE was a fixture on the Portland radio scene until 1948 when its call letters were changed to KPOJ.

By the mid-1940s, radio had reached its zenith. KEX joined the new ABC network, formed when NBC-Blue was sold. Legendary shows created by some of the country's most talented writers and performers captured large and loyal followings among all age groups. And, with little wonder.

Who could resist the spine-tingling suspense of The Shadow, The Whistler and Inner Sanctum? Or the never-ending battles against crime waged by Sam Spade, Ellery Queen, Boston Blackie and Mr. and Mrs. North? And let us not forget Mr. Keen, Tracer of Lost Persons, The Thin Man and The Fat Man, Gangbusters and The FBI in Peace and War.

Listeners loved the everyday foibles of Ozzie and Harriet and Our Miss Brooks, the pratfalls of Abbott and Costello and Jimmy Durante, the heartthrobs of Stella Dallas, Helen Trent and Young Doctor Malone. They thrilled to the adventures of Superman, Captain Midnight and The Green Hornet.

Luminaries of stage and screen starred on Lux Radio Theater, Gulf Screen Guild and Mercury Theatre of the Air, where Orson Welles shocked the nation on Oct. 30, 1938, with a mock invasion from outer space. Bing Crosby, Arthur Godfrey, Rudy Vallee, Kate Smith, Bob Hope, Eddie Cantor, Red Skelton, Don Ameche and countless other songsters and comedians owe their careers to the crystal set.

The airwaves of the '40s were filled with fabulous entertainment for the ears until a new and even more exciting medium began to fire the imaginations of performers, audiences and sponsors alike. Television would soon be on the scene reshaping America's habits and rewriting radio's role in society.

(Portland broadcasting: Getting channeled — Pg. 166)

Answer: KOIN's live musical ensemble, longest running of local radio bands, was on the air between 1926 and 1972.

Portland Broadcasting: Getting channeled

July 15, 1987

KPTV's Southwest 20th Place studios, ca. 1952. What important station, not mentioned in this article, went on the air in 1961? (Answer below story).

By the late 1940s television had reached most major American cities. Portland was the single exception. Along with numerous, smaller metropolitan areas across the country, it got caught in the FCC's four-year freeze.

From 1948-1952, the commission placed a national moratorium on the processing of new station applications in order to conduct studies and set standards that would eliminate signal interference. During the forced hiatus, radio made its last desperate effort to retain audiences. One gimmick, listener-participation quiz shows, gained popularity but was ultimately ruled illegal.

Mid-century proved to be pivotal for New York City. In 1950, the Big Apple's television viewers equalled its radio listeners for the first time. The networks were working feverishly to refine their programming lineups. Some of

KOIN-TV election central, 1956, with Rick Meyers, Johnny Carpenter and Chuck Foster.

radio's most successful shows made the transition to the tube. It was obvious to everyone in broadcasting that, when the freeze ended, the television would replace radio as America's primary entertainment medium.

Some doomsayers declared that radio would soon be dead. But cooler heads realized it would just take some experimentation with new directions. Whereas network affiliates had relied on slick shows and big names, independents had managed to attract listeners with news, music and another powerful audience builder—the local, on-air personality.

Pioneering the disc jockey concept was Portland's KWJJ, with its Jukebox Jamboree launched in 1948 to target teen-agers of the "Top 40" format that would dominate radio from the mid-'50s through the '60s.

Portland finally got its first television station on Sept. 20, 1952. KPTV was the first UHF station in the world. To receive

the Channel 27 signal, a special band had to be installed in TV sets of the time since they were equipped only with VHF tuners.

Portlanders flocked to appliance stores to see the flickering, black and white phenomenom. They watched test patterns. They even stared at the snow. And, undeterred by the additional cost for a UHF converter, they emerged as the proud owners of Zenith, G.E.s, Hoffmans, Philcos, Dumonts and Stewart-Warners.

KPTV hooked up with NBC and enjoyed market exclusively for just over a year. On Oct. 15, 1953, it was joined by KOIN-TV Channel 6. KOIN radio, a long-time CBS affiliate, continued that network connection with the new TV property. Mount Hood Radio and Television Company had bought the station the year prior from Marshall Field of Chicago. They won the nod for Portland's second TV outlet over Sam Newhouse's Pioneer Broadcasting which, at the time, owned KGW radio.

Newhouse sold to Seattle's Bullitt family in 1954 and their KING Broadcasting finally secured the Channel slot for KGW-TV in 1956. December 17 was the sign-on date. Meantime, the locally owned independent KLOR-TV had become the city's third station on March 8, 1955, broadcasting over Channel 12. KPTV and KLOR merged two years later at the older station's Southwest 20th Place facility. Channel 27 was abandoned for the better reception of Channel 12 at the top end of the VHF dial.

The same year it was purchased by Chris-Craft Industries, KPTV lost its NBC affiliation to KGW-TV in 1959, but immediately became ABC's local outlet. Seattle-based Fisher Broadcasting entered the Portland market with KATU-TV Channel 2 on March 15, 1962, and wooed ABC away within a year and a half. KPTV has been independent, award-winning and prosperous ever since.

Viewers were treated to a potpourri of memorable shows during the late '50s and early '60s including "Alfred Hitchcock Presents," "Dragnet," "The Lawrence Welk Show," "Gunsmoke," "The Mickey Mouse Club," "Perry Mason," "The Untouchables," and "Leave It To Beaver."

On the home front such local personalities as Gene Brendler, Richard Ross and Rick Meyers were forging long-term television careers. Bob Lynott was the most-watched weatherman, TV cowboy Heck Harper rounded up the kids after school, and the Ghouls, Milton and Tarantula, captured the latenight crowd with their spine-tingling, monster movies.

The tube totally engrossed a generation. Families restructured their lives around favorite shows. Radio retreated and gave thanks for the automobile. And color TV was still to come.

Answer: The country's 53rd educational TV station, KOAP, made its debut on Feb. 6, 1961 with studio, control room, tower and transmitter all atop Healey Heights.

Vaughn Street: Out to the ballgame
July 25, 1984

Opposing teams of Portland railroad officials in the 1890s called themselves the "Fats" and the "Leans". Where did they play? What was at third base? (Answer below cartoon).

America's favorite pastime found its way to Portland in the late 1880s. By the turn of the century, several "industrial" teams were active and from their ranks came many of the players who formed Portland's first professional baseball club in 1901.

The opening game of that first-ever season for the new Pacific Northwest League took place on May 22, 1901. The "Webfooters" won 8-6 in a rain-shortened game against Spokane and went on to take the pennant.

encircling the field. In a pinch it could seat 12,000.

The game's popularity prompted formation of a much more ambitious league in 1903. The Pacific Coast League with eight teams (the Portland Beavers, Seattle Rainiers, Oakland Oaks, San Francisco Seals and Missions (later the San Diego Padres), Los Angeles Angels, Hollywood Stars and Sacramento Solons) drew loyal fans for 50 years.

Rivalries developed. Players spent their entire careers with one club.

Vaughn Street Ballpark in 1951. Home of Portland baseball for 55 consecutive seasons.

The "baseball park" out on 24th and Vaughn was the scene of that initial contest. The four-block site was owned by F.I. Fuller's Portland Railway Co. and developed in a joint venture with C.F. Swigert's rival City and Suburban Lines. Both trolley companies stood to profit substantially from the ballpark traffic.

Fifteen hundred fans braved the weather to watch the competing "tossers" slog and slug it out that opening day, sitting in bleacher-style seats, some just completed, along the baselines.

In 1912, Vaughn Street, as it came to be called, was rebuilt into a fully enclosed, top-caliber ball park with covered grandstands the full length of the baselines and bleachers

This was top-notch AAA ball and it was the only game in town. Many PCL players went to the majors and many PCL teams could have given their Eastern brethren a tough go on a good day.

After World War II, the old wooden wonder was showing signs of wear. In 1947 the city threatened condemnation following a fire in the bleachers and there was considerable clamor for a new stadium.

Remedial measures and partial rebuilding saw Vaughn Street through eight more seasons until, in 1955, the franchise and the facility were sold. After 55 years and eight championships, the home of the "Lucky" Beavers was no more.

Answer: The old Multnomah Field, site of Multnomah (Civic) Stadium. A keg of beer.

The Beavers: Diamonds aren't forever

August 1, 1984

Action between Vancouver and Portland in 1959 at Multnomah (Civic) Stadium. who was the Beavers' all-time hitting leader? When was the stadium sold to the city? (Answers below cartoon)

The Portland Beavers got their name from a newspaper contest in 1908. Consecutively called the Webfooters, Browns and Giants before then, they all had one thing in common. Vaughn Street Ballpark was home. This classic stadium brought spectators close to the action and packed them in year after year.

In 1955, after 55 seasons, eight PCL pennants and six owners, a group of leading Portlanders spearheaded community ownership of the club. With hometown involvement came a new home stadium.

Several of the principal investors in the Portland Baseball

owned" operation bought it for $125,000, doubled their money by selling the property for industrial use, and spent $285,000 remodeling Multnomah Stadium.

Baseball fever ran high in the 1950s. Although the Beavers hadn't taken the pennant since 1945, their new facility was almost major league and the PCL was at its best. The team appeared to be poised for better things. Then fate stepped in and changed the face of the sport forever.

In 1959, the New York Giants and Brooklyn Dodgers moved their franchises to San Francisco and Los Angeles, respectively. In one fell swoop, major league baseball was

Two decades separated championship seasons for the Bevos. In '45 they won; In '65 they were runners-up.

Club, Inc. were also key Multnomah Athletic Club members and, in 1955, Multnomah Stadium was suddenly in need of a new revenue base.

Murray Kemp and his Multnomah Kennel Club had been the stadium's primary tenant since 1926. but MAC's demand for doubled rent plus a percentage sent Kemp out to East County and the facility was left with a few college football games and the Rose Festival to fund operations.

So, even though valiant old Vaughn Street was available for a song ($7,500 yearly lease), the new "community-

on the West Coast and the Pacific Coast League had lost two of its best teams and biggest draws—The S.F. Seals and L.A. Angels.

Considerable controversy and even some litigation went on in the wake of this unprecedented move. But, in the end, the new order prevailed. The Beavers, lacking a strong working agreement with a major league affiliate, made it to the playoffs only once between 1955 and the end of their 14-season community relationship in 1969.

New private ownership lasted until 1973, when AAA baseball left Portland.

Answers: William Bagnell—.391 in 1926. The Stadium became "Civic" in 1966.

Rose City Park: A child's playground
May 21, 1986

Rose City Park School was built in 1912. Where did graduates go before Grant High's completion in 1924? (Answer below cartoon)

The Rose City Park district is Portland's largest residential area. Its origins date back to 1907 when plats were filed encompassing Fremont to Hancock streets and 45th to 62nd avenues. Residential blocks were first developed adjacent to the Hollywood district marching eastward over the succeeding decades. By 1923, construction was 75 percent complete.

The boundaries of Rose City Park have been the subject of an ongoing dispute. In 1930, an *Oregon Journal* writer, Earl Goodwin, generously defined them as "Sullivan's Gulch on the South, Fremont on the north, East 33rd

Rose City Speedway, 1915

Avenue on the west and the City Limits (82nd Avenue) on the east." Today, that description is essentially accurate, although some would argue for 39th Avenue on the west giving deference to Grant Park. And the Hollywood Boosters understandably promote the individual identity of their district.

The significance of separate identities escaped this youngster and his contemporaries of the 1940s and '50s. For us it was simply a good place to grow up. Rose City Park meant the grade school at Northeast 57th Avenue and Thompson Street and the park bordering Northeast 62nd Avenue and Tillamook Street.

Rose City Park Elementary, a typical example of the red brick and white tile educational architecture that sprang up throughout the eastside during the 1910s and '20s, was completed in 1912. Almost from its opening, enrollment exceeded original design capacity; testimony to the stable, middle-class family environment surrounding the school.

Its faculty was dedicated and long-tenured; the type of

teachers that have a strong impact on evolving minds and bodies. Its gravel playground has taken an eight-decade toll on the knees and elbows of those ever active anatomies. "Rose City," as we called it, was also the principal meeting place of Cub Packs and Scout Troops; another important aspect of our adolescent experience.

Rose City Park, the alfresco variety, was our summer-long playground. A football-field expanse of grass, softball diamonds and sloping, shrub-covered hillsides were the locales where early peer-group encounters and childhood adventure fantasies were played out.

Rose City Park district, 1947

A popular race track once occupied the huge bowl which now embraces the first nine holes of the Rose City Golf Course. Millionaire bicycle retailer and city councilman Fred W. Merrill built the Portland Country Club with its mile-long dirt track in 1908. Horse races were initially run on the course. Then, as the Rose City Speedway, which operated until 1926, it was the site of auto and motorcycle races. Other events included a head-on locomotive collision.

The track's most memorable event took place on August 10, 1912. Walter Edwards lofted his aeroplane loaded with mail and made a 13-mile flight to Vancouver Barracks. Commemorated in the Smithsonian, it marked the Pacific Northwest's first airmail service.

We preteens stood on the grassy ridge separating our park playground from the first nine and imagined early speedsters going "like 60" around that long-gone track. Then, gazing to the east, we contemplated new adventures atop the stone-rimmed "Rocky Butte" looming in the distance.

Answer: Rose City students commuted to the old Washington High School established in 1908 at East 14th and Stark Street.

170

Rocky Butte: An adolescent's adventure

May 28, 1986

Hill Military Academy was founded in 1931. What is it today? (Answer below cartoon)

There were many worlds to explore for young Rose City Park residents of the late 1940s and early '50s. As children, our outside-of-school adventures were confined to the immediate vicinity. The Hollywood District was our downtown with its vintage 1926 movie palace, the Hollywood Theater, Fred Meyer's first suburban store, Penney's, Miller's, a throng of thriving specialty shops including Paulsen's Pharmacy, Joseph & Lucas Music Mart, Vic's Hobby Shop, The Hollywood Pet Gardens and that quintessential drive-in hangout, Yaw's Top Notch.

The stone-adorned summit completed in 1938.

But the rural experience was as intriguing as the urban one. The countryside was almost outside our back door. Rose City Park, and its adjacent 18-hole golf course, was an 80-acre adventure in itself.

Before the Mittleman and Binford apartment complexes were constructed east of 65th Avenue in the early 1950s, the area was open land. The yawning cavity of a gigantic garbage pit was its most notable landmark. A dirt road was the continuation of Tillamook Street to 82nd Avenue.

Bicycling brought a new dimension to our explorations. Once we were old enough to get our parents' approval for afternoon excursions, and even a time or two without it, small bands of buddies pointed their balloon-tired, single-geared Schwinns in the direction of Mt. Tabor, the Columbia River or Rocky Butte.

Mt. Tabor was a relatively sedate getaway. Homes have spread over its volcanic slopes since the 1920s. A trek to the Columbia-Super Airport at 47th Avenue and Marine Drive was another story. We stood on the levee for what seemed like hours between takeoffs to view DC-3s and 6s drone down the runway, roar skyward and make their lumbering climbs to altitude.

Of all our adventures, Rocky Butte was the best. No houses dominated its hillsides in those days. The only developments were more dour. At the bottom of a rock quarry on the southeast side, Multnomah County had constructed a stern stone fortress in 1940. Rocky Butte County Jail, or "The Butte," loomed below as we clambered over the King's Chair, a many-faceted rock formation protruding from the cliff above the quarry.

Speaking of stern, the solid structures on the butte's northern slope evoked more direct images. Hill Military Academy was established in 1931 by the sons of Joseph Wood Hill. The family owned the entire 1000 acres of tree-covered rocks and ridges.

Military drill and instruction, academics and athletics were the academy's curriculum, served up with a steady diet of discipline. Northwest families paid $500 for each son they sent.

These edifices aside, the major attraction was at the top. The Hills donated that high point to the county in 1935. Between 1937 and '39 a rock masonry ring was erected around the butte's summit by the Works Progress Administration. From this promontory one could enjoy the only, unobstructed 360-degree panorama in the Portland area.

After peddling up that pan-shaped peak, a preteen could savor the view from the top. That delight had only a short duration. We were soon distracted by the possibilities around us—a fortress to storm, battlements to defend. The Korean War was in full fury, and unaware of what war really meant, we romanced our mock battles for all they were worth.

Answer: Portland Bible College has occupied the site since 1982 and was preceded by Judson Baptist College.

Tik Tok: An orphaned intersection

November 14, 1984

Ben, Vic and Ocky Harris at the Tik Tok, circa 1957. What stood for 20 years across the street? (Answer below cartoon).

If you've never been caught by the traffic signal at East Burnside and 12th going west, you're better off. If you have, then you know it's one of the longest in Portland.

More times than I care to recall, I have found myself staring into that red light recently enhanced by the new U.S. Bancorp tower as a backdrop. Since the wait is infuriatingly protracted, my gaze wanders to the open lot on the south side of this desolate intersection. And I recall that it wasn't always abandoned.

The Tik Tok with its steaming coffee cup sign, early 1960s

Where only Pastor Allan Hamilton's Foursquare Church sign now stands as the single sentinel in a wasteland of graded gravel, once presided Portland's first and foremost drive-in restaurant.

We're talking be-bop and car hops, shakes, burgers and fries. We're talking deuce coupes, clean machines and cruisin'. We're talkin' the TIK TOK.

Founded in 1939 by Sherman G. Marriott (later of Marriott Hotel fame) and Horace C. Williams, the Tik Tok quickly became an in spot with the younger set. You could grab a seat at the semi-circular counter, resplendent in its gleaming linoleum, wait for a highly coveted booth or call in the order from your car.

I don't know whether or not the Tik Tok was the first drive-in but it surely must have been an early entry. Several sources have also said that Portland's first automatic car wash preceded the restaurant on the site. Anyone with further information or verification, please drop me a line at *This Week*.

By the mid-50s, the place had become a local landmark. Kids of all ages flocked from around the town to see and be seen at the Tik Tok. It was a mandatory stop on the cruisin' route which encompassed the Broadway and Sixth Avenue crawl, the Sandy Boulevard stop light to stop light tire burners and the mandatory Yaw's drive through. For the more adventurous, a jaunt over to Speck's at S.E. 52nd and Foster Road could be included. Serious hotrodders ventured all the way out to Jim Dandy's in Parkrose and, in those days, 82nd Avenue was reserved for heavy duty street drags.

In 1957, Vic, Ocky and Ben Harris bought the restaurant and maintained its momentum for another 15 years. The Harris brothers were Portland promoters and restaurateurs better known for their Three Star Restaurant on Barbur Boulevard. A hot spot through the 1950s and '60s, the Three Star introduced topless to town.

The Harrises closed down the aging dowager of drive-ins in 1971, citing costly repairs and a decline in business. Subsequently torn down, nothing has come along to stake a new claim at the focal point of today's five-way melee.

Personally, I think the Portland Development Commission ought to get behind a drive to transform this orphaned intersection into the Rose City's own Place de l'Etoile. Cars could plunge into the swirling merry-go-round and then, after a few circles, work their way outward to dart for their desired exit. A grand statue of famous old Portlanders might be erected in the middle.

Private funds could help complete construction. Who knows? It might even end up with a donor's name. How about Schnitzer Circle?

Answer: Scotty's Hamburgers, home of the 19-cent burger, was the Tik Tok's north-side neighbor beginning in 1961. It was torn down in 1981.

172

Downtown: The lights on Broadway

November 16, 1983

What chic new eatery has become the place to see and be seen on Broadway? What replaced Jolly Joan's?

Broadway has been Portland's downtown show street for more than 40 years. Over those years, as many as six motion picture emporiums have dominated the electrical extravaganza illuminating this thoroughfare.

Heading the parade is the Paramount (originally named the Portland), "the finest theater west of Chicago," built in 1928. Then comes J.J. Parker's Broadway, followed by the Fox and its dimunitive neighbor, the Music Box. The lavish, long-gone Liberty and the opulent Orpheum, negated by Nordstrom, completed the procession of film palaces contributing to the fluorescent fantasy.

In the 1950s and '60s Jolly Joan's round-the-clock coffee

cool, on the make, party time as phalanxes of cars crawled bumper to bumper up Broadway and down Sixth around and around bathed in the glow of those signs of the times.

Portland's promenade of spectacular signs has been dimmed of late. But things are looking up. The palatial Paramount will soon have a new lease on life as the Performing Arts (Schnitzer) Center, along with an entirely refurbished Heathman Hotel.

Theater mogul Larry Moyer's award-winning plan for remodeling the Broadway includes restoration of the neons to their former dazzling display. However, he still has to take the design from the drawing board to reality.

The lights on Broadway in the early 1950s.

shop was the street's late-night gathering spot. A diverse cross-section of Portlanders, from after-theater-goers to the Broadway gang, frequented the restaurant that featured a neon sign equal to any on the avenue.

Beginning in the early '50s, and for two decades to follow, the brightly lighted strip was the scene of a super, city-wide cruise-in on weekend nights. Especially during the summer. Hunkered-down hot rods arrogantly revved their souped up mills alongside "daddy's" wheels. Cases of Blitz and Oly were jammed into the backseat leg spaces. It was play it

Speaking of looking up, if you look up at night from Broadway, the Christmas-tree-bordered Jackson Tower will greet you adjacent to the Hilton's green glow.

Portland's first modern-era hostelry celebrated its 20th Anniversary this year and Sam Jackson's edifice, originally the home of his *Oregon Journal,* has graced the downtown skyline since 1912.

Revitalization is the byword for downtown these days and a brilliant counterpoint to this development will be the once-again-bright lights on Broadway.

Answers: The Manhattan-style Metro on Broadway is "in" with the trendy set. Morgan's Alley has occupied the site since 1969.

The catch-all category

Choosing chapter groupings for this book posed a few problems. Whereas most stories were naturals for their niches, a few defied easy description. As a result, this category was created.

The 26 columns thrown into this "pot" range the gamut of time and locale in Portland's past panorama. From the positioning of the Willamette Stone, which set the surveying standard for the entire Northwest in June 1851, to the Oregon Maritime Museum opened in November 1986. From the Stockyards to downtown to the Gorge and back again.

The Willamette Stone was stolen in 1987 for reasons unknown. Its only value is historic. As of November 1987, it had not been recovered. In 1985, Union Station's "Go By Train" neon was resurrected from more than a decade of darkness through the laudable efforts of the Pacific Northwest Chapter of the National Railway Historical Society. The cramped Schnitzer Concert Hall now has a better half. Its companion, the Portland Center for the Performing Arts, was completed next door in September 1987. But Larry Moyer still hasn't rebuilt his dilapidated Broadway Theater just across the street.

On the slopes of Mount Hood, Timberline Lodge celebrated its 50th Anniversary this year. A couple of years ago, Multorpor Ski Area got a new name — Mirror Mountain — and improved facilities. Back in Portland, Elks Lodge #142, which had been downtown since 1889, moved its headquarters to the Hollywood District.

In this Portlandian potpourri, the special stories for me are those written by my TAG (talented and gifted) students. Nine sharp kids (ages 13 to 18) put together three excellent articles. They appear on pages 201-203.

The Willamette Stone: Center of the Northwest

June 25, 1986

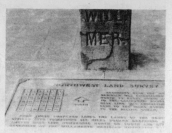

The Willamette Stone. How are the townships measured from it identified? (Answers below cartoon.)

The prospect of free land brought some 12,000 hearty pioneers overland to Oregon during the 1840s. Even though there was no certainty that they would be able to keep the land they were homesteading, these settlers were undaunted.

Ironically, their presence was a principal element of the events culminating in the treaty between the United States and Great Britain that established the 49th parallel as the international boundary. Physical possession carried greater weight than exploration and discovery.

The Stone's Base Line is the east/west measurement.

Two Missouri senators, Thomas Hart Benton and Lewis F. Linn, were the prime movers behind the land-grant legislation that hastened settlement of the Oregon country. In 1841 Benton pushed his Preemption Land Bill through Congress. Any U.S. citizen was given the right to settle on 160 acres of surveyed land. They could later buy the land from the government at a minimum fixed price.

When establishment of a price became the subject of controversy, pressure mounted to give the land to those who lived on and improved it. In 1842, Linn, with the support of Benton, introduced resolutions calling for termination of the shared-Oregon agreement with Britain and the granting of 640 acres to any white male resident who occupied and cultivated the land for five years.

Though these resolutions did not pass, they were the harbinger of what came to pass by the end of the decade. Following the resolution of the sovereignty issue in 1846, a territorial government was established two years later. It took an additional two years before the squatters were legitimized by the Donation Land Act of 1850.

A single man could claim a half-section or 320 acres, a married couple, a full 640-acre section. The wife was to hold the additional half-section in her own right. This was 62 years before women were given the right to vote in Oregon. The law also precipitated many otherwise unlikely marriages in a land where females were few and far between.

With the Oregon land act came the appointment of a surveyor-general and the tedious, but critically important, task of properly describing and recording all claims past, present and future.

A benchmark, a starting point from which the entire territory could be accurately surveyed, was essential. How that exact location was determined is uncertain. It was a high point above the dominant town in the territory. Population, commercial activity and land speculation would soon be centered there.

That spot, now indicated by a small concrete obelisk and commemorative plaque, is called the Willamette Stone. It is interesting to note that the east-west baseline set by that marker runs straight down Stark Street through the heart of the original Portland townsite. The north-south longitudinal line, known as the Willamette Meridian, is the other base measurement.

All the land, from the Canadian to Oregon borders, from the Pacific Ocean to Idaho, is divided into six-mile square townships from this point. Each township is divided into 36 one-mile sections of 640 acres. It is literally the center of the Northwest.

Answer: Townships are numbered consecutively beginning east to west on the west side of the meridian line and west to east on the east side. They are called "northings" north of the baseline and "southings" south.

The Great Plank Road: A wash out

October 21, 1987

Portland co-proprietor Stephen Coffin. When did he come to Oregon? Why is he wearing a uniform? (Answers below cartoon)

By 1851 Portland was well on the way to establishing itself as the region's principal port. The wharf at the foot of Washington Street, built by townsite promoter Francis Pettygrove five years earlier, buzzed with activity. Newer neighbors on either side enjoyed an equally brisk business in agricultural products, livestock and lumber.

For all concerned—middlemen, ship owners and farmers—future prospects couldn't have been brighter. The farmers from the fertile "Twality Plains," however were forced to contend with an ongoing irritant to fulfill their part of this commercial coalition. To reach Portland's warehouses and wharves they had to negotiate one of two steep, rutridden wagon roads.

Section of Canyon (Old Plank) Road, ca. 1880.

The first of these routes, barely more than a twisting pathway along what later evolved into West Burnside, was completed by Pettygrove in 1846. Three years later, tanner Daniel Lownsdale, who had recently purchased Pettygrove's Portland interest, opened an alternative connection which followed Tanner Creek up what is now Canyon Road.

Though Lownsdale's road was but a pair of wagon tracks, it had the advantage of being shorter and less arduous than Pettygrove's. Still, during bad weather, it too could prove impassable by anything with wheels. Continuing complaints about the road's condition went unheeded until the summer of 1850 when Portland's most serious competitive challenge was posed by a combined effort between the downstream townsites of Milton and St. Helens.

"The easist, shortest and best road from the plains to the river" was the way the enterprising proprietors ballyhooed their new route. Though actually 10 miles longer to Hillsborough (sic), it was in much better condition and had a considerably easier grade. Portland's principal owners—Lownsdale, builder Stephen Coffin and lawyer William Chapman—knew they must counter this threat.

Initially, they tackled additional stump removal, then invested in "corduroying" the worst parts of the Tanner Creek route (setting logs side by side) which created a firm, albeit bumpy, roadbed. Although these efforts made a substantial improvement, the trio decided that stopgap measures were not enough.

The previous year, William Chapman had hatched a half-million-dollar scheme to run a railroad to the valley. Though subscribed to $100,000, the Portland & Valley Railroad Company never got off the ground. In its place came the more pragmatic proposal for a plank road.

The Portland & Valley Plank Road Company received its charter from the Oregon Territorial Legislature in March of 1851. Stephen Coffin was charged with construction of the first-ever such undertaking in the Pacific Northwest. At the stockholder's first meeting on July 30, 1851, a schedule was set forth to complete 10 miles of planking by Nov. 1.

Confident that he could meet the ambitious goal, Coffin put a crew of 80 men to work and prepared six miles of roadbed for planking within a month. On Sept. 27, a festive ceremony with appropriate fanfare and oratorical remarks accompanied the laying of the first plank. Afterwards, a sumptuous banquet was spread out on the freshly placed planks.

Unfortunately, this elaborate event was no substitute for hard cash and only a couple of miles of planks had been laid when available funds ran out. Subscriptions were only promissory notes. Of the 40,800 pledged, less than $3,000 had actually been put up.

Before measures could be taken to collect more capital, winter set in and severely damaged the portion of the road already completed. *Oregonian* Editor Thomas Dryer cried "Incompetence!" and confidence in the project was irreparably undermined.

By April 1852, with $14,593 in expenditures and only $6,026 in monies collected, construction on the Great Plank Road ceased. But, the road to Sylvan was vastly improved and, even without planks, it helped Portland maintain its edge in the struggle for townsite superiority.

Answers: A pioneer of 1847, the energetic Coffin was a general in the Oregon militia and a key contributor to Portland's early success.

Early Portland: Bridging River City

August 10, 1985

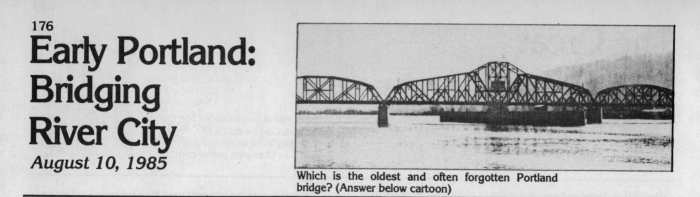

Which is the oldest and often forgotten Portland bridge? (Answer below cartoon)

Portland, East Portland and Albina were still separate towns when our first bridge, the Morrison, opened for business on March 2, 1887. And "for business" was just that because it was a toll bridge built by a private firm. People on foot were charged five cents, the same as sheep and hogs. Cattle and horses were 10 cents each. Two horses and driver was the highest, at 20 cents.

In 1895, the city, consolidated four years previously, bought the wooden structure for a princely $150,000 and promptly removed the toll. They also had to replace the

owned with the inevitable tolls. This time the city moved more quickly, buying the bridge in November of the same year for $145,000.

This shoddy, but profitable, wooden span had to be replaced in 1900. The second Madison Bridge, also of wood, was damaged by fire in 1902. Proving inadequate for increased traffic, it was replaced in December 1910 by the renamed Hawthorne. A steel single-lift span, this vintage structure has moss to match on its aged, but durable, median planks.

The second Morrison Bridge at its west approach, ca. 1915.

bridge ten years later with a steel swing-span type. The second Morrison was not the first steel bridge on the river, however. That honor went to the OWR&N (Union Pacific) Bridge, built by the railroad in 1888 and called the "Steel" because it was the first of its kind on the West Coast.

The Steel Bridge we know is the second one. Built in 1912, this classic double-lift span (two decks) is among a handful left in the world.

A third bridge, the Madison, came just four years after the Morrison. Completed in June 1891, it too was privately

With the addition of the first Burnside Bridge, a swing span costing $316,000 in 1894, traffic over the Willamette was served by four bridges. This status quo held until April 1913, when the first double-leaf bascule, the Broadway, with a whopping price tag of $1.6 million, went into service.

You are, of course, familiar with the double leaf bascule as compared with the single- or double-vertical lift span and the swing span. You aren't? Then refer to the cartoon below and stay tuned next week for another installment in this suspension-filled saga.

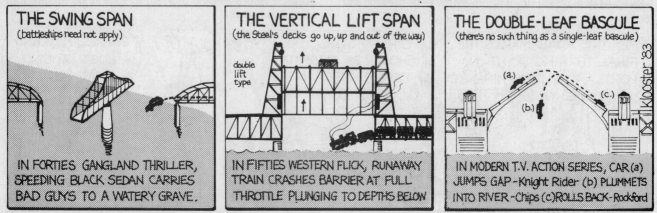

THE SWING SPAN (battleships need not apply)

IN FORTIES GANGLAND THRILLER, SPEEDING BLACK SEDAN CARRIES BAD GUYS TO A WATERY GRAVE.

THE VERTICAL LIFT SPAN (the Steel's decks go up, up and out of the way)

double lift type

IN FIFTIES WESTERN FLICK, RUNAWAY TRAIN CRASHES BARRIER AT FULL THROTTLE PLUNGING TO DEPTHS BELOW

THE DOUBLE-LEAF BASCULE (there's no such thing as a single-leaf bascule)

IN MODERN T.V. ACTION SERIES, CAR (a) JUMPS GAP—Knight Rider (b) PLUMMETS INTO RIVER—Chips (c)ROLLS BACK—Rockford

Klooster '83

Answer: The SP&S (now Burlington-Northern)R.R. Bridge, a swing-span completed in 1908, will soon be rebuilt under a federal program.

Skidmore: The Pharmacist's fountain

May 9, 1984

Sculptor Olin L. Warner with a plaster model of the fountain's maidens. What other works did he do while in Portland? (Answer below cartoon)

Stephen Skidmore was 12 when, in 1850, he came with his parents to Portland from Illinois. He loved his adopted hometown and saw it grow from a riverfront village of 800 to a thriving city of over 25,000. During that time his own hard work and enterprise (plus some prudent early real estate investing) brought him a sizable fortune.

Stephen G. Skidmore (1838-1883).

In addition to his retail drugstore, Skidmore's involvements in civic affairs were numerous, including service with Multnomah No. 2 Volunteer Fire Company, city councilman and Oregon representative to the Paris World's Fair of 1878.

At the time of his death in 1883, Skidmore was only 44 years old. He left an estate valued at $175,000 (the equivalent of at least $1 million today), out of which he bequeathed $5,000 to the city for a fountain where "horses, men and dogs" might drink.

The pharmacist's many friends took his bequest to heart. Five years and an additional $20,000 later, a local blue ribbon committee had made the fountain a reality. C.E.S. Wood, attorney, adventurer and one of Portland's most illustrious personalities, had provided the essential element—the artist, Olin Warner.

By 1886, when he accepted the Skidmore Fountain assignment, the 43-year-old New Yorker was one of America's foremost sculptors. The classically elegant work he designed and executed was heralded as a masterpiece by Eastern critics. "Too good for that provincial little town in the Pacific Northwest" was one comment.

Warner sculpted the 30-ton fountain in New York and had it shipped to Portland by rail. It got sidetracked in the process but, finally arriving, he supervised every step of its assembly and completed some of the delicate details here.

Various sites had been suggested for its placement but the then-center of town won out. That center was short lived as growth and floods moved the main action uptown.

Skidmore's fountain in its original setting, looking East

As fate would have it, the fountain was the rallying point for revitalization of the city's original hub which we now call "Old Town" and its donor, Stephen G. Skidmore, has achieved immortality far beyond that of those who made his dream a reality.

Answer: Medallion profiles of attorney C.E.S. Wood, Chief Joseph, and Moses, Chief of the Okinokans.

Early Portland: The Exposition Building

January 9, 1985

The destruction caused by the July 14, 1910, blaze. Why does this map of the stadium area look unfamiliar? (Answer below cartoon)

The largest building on the West Coast was completed at Portland in September 1889. It was located at the north end of the old Multnomah Field and took up the entire two-block area now occupied by the north end of Multnomah Civic Stadium, the Multnomah Apartments and the extension of Morrison Street later constructed in between.

It was 400 feet long by 200 feet deep with an interior main exhibit area three stories high. The full title of this magnificent edifice was the North Pacific Industrial Association Exposition Building.

The North Pacific Industrial Association Exposition Building operated between 1899 and 1910.

On May 5, 1891, the building received a fitting dedication. More than 15,000 Oregonians jammed within its walls to hear President Benjamin Harrison wax eloquent about the benefits of their new exposition center.

This project was the brainchild of an enterprising young Pennsylvanian named George B. Markle Jr. Unlike Portland's cautious founding fathers, Markle was a man of action willing to take risks. The North Pacific Industrial Association was but one of a dozen companies he had organized within three years after arriving in River City.

Heir to a coal mining fortune, Markle quickly got in with Portland's prominent people and enlisted the aide of downtown mogul Frank Dekum in launching the exposition plan. He bought the land and took out a personal mortgage for $62,000 to commence construction.

The finished structure was imposing. It featured iron and brick work, large glass areas, steel arches and fir trusses. Total cost to complete it was $150,000.

But Markle's whirlwind entrepreneureal maneuverings proved to be his undoing.. Caught by the Depression of 1893, his fortunes took a devastating downturn. He was involved in a scandal over misuse of public funds, lost his Portland Heights hilltop home, his wife and all his local holdings.

After just eight years, 37-year-old George Markle, Arlington Club member, business tycoon and community leader, left Portland forever with hundreds of thousands of debts behind him.

Its mortgage defaulted, the Exposition Building was sold to local investors and became an ongoing attraction. Its more than 250 exhibits brought visitors from near and far for 20 years.

Then, early on the morning of July 14, 1910, the aging giant was swept by fire which totally destroyed it and several adjacent structures. They included a dozen surrounding commercial buildings and the Multnomah Athletic Club's 10-year-old clubhouse and grandstand.

Answer: Chapman Street was changed to 18th. Morrison was extended to 20th. Washington St. segment is now W. Burnside.

The Customs House: Hail to the port

July 2, 1986

The grand staircase and vaulted ceiling in the foyer of Portland's U.S. Customs House. What does it look like today? (Answer below cartoon).

The last decade of the 19th century saw Portland firmly established as the principal port in the Pacific Northwest. Portland, which nearly doubled in size during that decade and would double again during the next, was busily engaged in world trade.

While Portland's export firms were shipping unprecedented quantities of lumber, grain and produce, its affluent populace eagerly awaited an ever-increasing flow of exotic goods from foreign ports. Payment of duty on these imports reached the point where federal customs facilities and a small group of agents were taxed to the limit.

In 1897, the U.S. Treasury Department made the decision to erect an enduring edifice to international trade through the Port of Portland, which had been established just six years earlier. The Treasury's supervising architect, James Knox Taylor, designed the U.S. Customs House, a handsome, full-block building bordering the eastern edge of the North Park Blocks.

U.S. Customs House under construction, 1898

The Custom House took four years to finish. Upon completion in 1901, it stood imposingly alone. Its four-story, pyramid-peaked eastern section was clearly visible from the waterfront eight blocks away. A time ball was erected atop a tower facing the river. For years the ball dropped precisely at noon so ships' captains, and any others who so desired, could set their clocks by it. Not until too many tall buildings obstructed the tower was it finally removed.

The government spared no expense with its second major Portland building. Its first, the Pioneer Post Office completed in 1873, had previously housed all federal functions. The new facility, fashioned in the Italian Renaissance style, featured a colonnade-fronted courtyard, a grand staircase, cast iron balustrades, brass fittings and oodles of oak paneling.

Much of that elegant paneling originally adorned two upper-story courtrooms. The Feds considered their Customs House to be an excellent opportunity to create a new local headquarters for the federal court. Local lawyers didn't agree. Such an outcry of objection arose from the legal community that they were never used. The reason? In those horse and buggy days, the Customs House was considered to be too inconveniently located.

As the role of the port and the methods of customs clearance changed, so did the grand house that the Treasury built. The courtroom paneling was covered over. A central court light well was eliminated. The building served a variety of federal tenants until, in 1968, the U.S. Army Corps of Engineers made it headquarters of their North Pacific Region.

In 1974 the U.S. Customs House was placed on the National Registry of Historic Places. Although the government has declared the building surplus property, its listing offers some safeguards against possible demolition. When and if such future endangerment might occur, this writer would be among the first to sound the alarm. The weight of concerned numbers vocalizing their views could make the difference.

Meanwhile, Portland can count the Customs House among a small but significant group of structures to be admired and appreciated.

Answer: The Customs House foyer was restored to its original appearance as part of a major renovation begun in 1976.

Union Station: Portland's Grand Central

November 2, 1983

Identify this imposing railway station done in the French "Grand Gare" style. (Answer below cartoon).

When Henry Villard's Grand Union Depot was at last completed in 1896, it was a very different edifice from the one initially designed in 1882 by New York architects McKim, Mead and White.

After Villard wrested control of the Oregon Central from Big Ben Holladay in 1876, he completed the Northwest's transcontinental connection, which just celebrated its 100th Anniversary. But, as fate would have it, the German financier's fortunes waned even more rapidly than they had

been located. But in 1893, financial concerns brought about changes in the million-dollar design.

Finally finished at a cost of $400,000, the station was Portland's transportation hub for more than 60 years. At its height, 74 trains came and went each day. During the war year 1944, it served more than 4.8 million passengers.

But, by the 1960s, train travel had declined drastically with the advent of modern freeways and the ascendancy of the airlines.

The original Union Depot design on the present site was scaled down in final execution.

risen. By the end of 1883, Villard was forced to relinquish stewardship of his Oregon and Transcontinental Company and construction of Union Station fell to new owners.

For reasons that remain unclear, both the original location (NW 7th and 8th between Hoyt & Marshall) and the design were changed. The project was awarded to the Kansas City firm of Van Brunt and Howe, noted for their railway terminals around the country.

Construction began in 1890 on its present site, fill land at the foot of NW 6th, where Capt. John Couch's Lake had

Last of the grand passenger trains, Union Pacific's domeliner "City of Portland" gave way to Amtrak in 1971. Today the station sees no more than twelve travel trains daily but they are a bargain well worth looking into. It's still a thrill to "Go By Train," as the sign on Union Station's 144-foot clock tower reminds us.

Despite changing times, this classic modified Romanesque landmark, with its massive tiled roofs and fine grillwork, remains as a symbol of an illustrious era in the evolution of Portland and the Pacific Northwest.

Answer: This is Villard's $1.5-million New York plan, next to the North Park Blocks.

Mount Hood: Pioneering the Peak

January 1, 1984

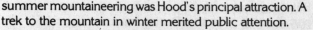

Mazamas on their favorite mountain. Where, when and by how many was the famed climbing club formed? (Answer below cartoon).

The wintry warrior was called Wy'East in Klickitat legend. Lieutenant William Broughton, one of Captain Vancouver's officers, named it "Hood" in honor of the British lord who plotted their exploratory voyage of 1792.

Lewis and Clark's journals refer to the majestic mountain by that name in 1805. Hardy Hudson's Bay trappers dwelt on its slopes as early as the 1830s. Overland pioneers of the 1840s and '50s knew their destination lay just beyond the lofty peak.

In 1849 federal troops bivouacked at "the *government camp* on the Camp Creek." Pioneer Oliver Yocum adopted it for his new townsite there and, despite objections from the Post Office, the name endured.

summer mountaineering was Hood's principal attraction. A trek to the mountain in winter merited public attention.

In 1887 the Oregon Alpine Club was formed and a spectacular illumination took place on July 4th. A party led by noted conservationist Will Steel set off 100 pounds of powder, emitting a minute-long red glow clearly visible in Portland.

Steel, most noted for his preservation of Crater Lake, spearheaded the formation of the Mazamas in 1894. During that period their activities centered around Cloud Cap Inn. Built by financier William M. Ladd and lawyer C.E.S. Wood, the rustic lodge was completed in 1889 at almost 6,000 feet on the mountain's northeast slope.

Mt. Hood's original retreat, Cloud Cap Inn, is maintained by the Hood River Crag Rats.

That irresistible urge "because it's there" compelled a quartet of climbers, including Henry Pittock, to conquer the then-thought-to-be 14,000-plus-foot, dormant acidic volcano on July 11, 1857.

Samuel and William Barlow blazed the mountain's southern route in 1845. Through bad repair and good, the Barlow Trail remained a private toll road for more than 40 years until good roads and auto enthusiast Henry Wemme bought the company and gave his state a generous gift.

From the time of the first ascent until the mid-1920s,

Also, due to Steel's efforts, the Cascade Range Forest Reserve was established in 1893. Split up into several "forests" in 1908 under the recently organized U.S. Forest Service, the Oregon forest became the Mount Hood Forest in 1924.

With the opening of the loop highway in 1925, a new era began. The Mount Hood Recreation Area was dedicated the next year "to be held for the use and enjoyment of the general public."

(Mt. Hood: Timberline tops 'em all - Pg. 182)

Answer: July 19, 1894, on Mt. Hood's summit by 193 stalwarts — 154 men and 39 women.

Mount Hood: Timberline tops 'em all

January 11, 1984

The Magic Mile chairlift, second built in the country, had lines in 1942. How long did it operate? Where was the first? (Answers below cartoon).

Skiing and Mount Hood are almost synonymous today. But the groomed slopes and smooth-operating lifts were part of a long process at Portland's winter playground.

References to 10-foot-long skis and head-high poles (early Norwegian-style cross-country equipment) go back almost to the turn of the century.

Though summer recreation far outstripped winter then, in 1903 a Mazama club member predicted that "soon more people would come to Mount Hood in winter." Soon,

The Government Camp Hotel, built by pioneer guide Oliver Yocum in 1900, and augmented by his protege, Elijah Coalman, was the only winter accommodation on the mountain. Coalman also built the original shelter at the summit.

In 1926, a Portland group's plan to put a tramway to the top and an enlarged hotel complex at Cloud Cap was stalemated in one of the earliest clashes between conservationist and commercial interests.

Timberline Lodge's fabulous front side, impressive inside and beautiful backside.

however, was more than 20 years off. The Mount Hood Loop Highway, opened on June 21, 1925, was the catalyst that made the mountain a place for all seasons.

The oldest ski area in the nation, Summit, sponsored by the then-Advertising Club of Portland, welcomed its first customers on December 11, 1927. It boasted warming huts, skiing and tobogganing slopes. Everyone had to walk up to earn the exhilarating trip back down. The area's first rope tow was installed in 1935.

The Cascade Ski club opened the original ski jump on Multorpor (MULTnomah, ORegon, PORtland) Mountain for the 1928-29 season. 1936 saw their first rope tows and two years later the adjacent ski area—Ski Bowl—opened.

Destruction of the Government Camp Hotel by fire in 1933 left no overnight facility for the increasing numbers of snow aficionados. FDR's Works Progress Administration filled the void in fabulous fashion.

Bringing together in Autumn 1936 an army of artisans in the finest crafts—woodcarvers, metal workers, stonemasons, painters, weavers, carpenters and furniture makers—the WPA created in less than two years (given a late fall in 1937) one of the most magnificent, and highest, mountain edifices on earth.

Timberline Lodge was dedicated by President Franklin D. Roosevelt on September 28, 1937 and opened to the public the following February.

(Mount Hood: Downhill dominates · Pg. 183)

Answers: 23 seasons. Opened in 1939, it was replaced in 1962. Sun Valley's chairlift was first.

Mount Hood: Downhill dominates

January 18, 1984

A typical Meadow weekend. What is the area's best season to date? What well-known winter area isn't for skiing? (Answers below cartoon).

The snow-covered slopes have lured skiers, and those who just dress the part, to Mt. Hood for nearly six decades. After World War II the sport grew greatly in popularity and Portland's winter playground, a mere 50 miles away, burgeoned.

Ski area operators responded with additions and improvements. Summit, oldest area in the country, installed a T-bar in 1959 and a chair lift as recently as 1980. Multorpor and Ski Bowl merged in 1962, putting in a double chair that season and a new chalet the next.

freed it of that burden.

Taking the peak's Indian name, Wy'East Lodge opened for the 1981-82 season. A handsomely designed day-usage facility, it had over 192,000 skier day visits last year—a record for Timberline.

In January 1968, the mountain's largest ski area began welcoming skiers to its slopes. Mount Hood Meadows featured two chairs, two rope tows, a T-bar and an attractive day lodge.

Today, Meadows serves 60 percent of Hood's skiers with

Timberline and its new companion lodge, Wy'East completed in 1981.

For the first 18 years of its existence, Timberline Lodge was a problem child. The logistics of managing such a large lodge halfway up a mountainside was no minor matter. Not until 1955 did the government find an organization equal to the task.

Richard Kohnstamm's RLK Co. has made the Timberline area go and grow ever since. Pucci was put in his first year, the Magic Mile was replaced in 1962 and the Palmer lift began operation in 1979.

The lodge, averaging near 90-percent occupancy in recent years, was never designed for heavy day use. The newest and next-largest structure on the mountain finally

seven double chairs. A new triple chair lift and a second day lodge are under construction.

The fate of ski areas is, of course, at the annual mercy of Mother Nature. Even though winter sports activity doubled between 1950 and 1960, the last decade's draw has depended on the weather. Combined skier usage for all Mt. Hood areas in 1979-80 was 538,724 while 1976-77 totalled only 218,116.

The operators are a stoic lot. This season looks great so far. Could always be better, but then, who wants traffic jams on the lift lines?

Answers: 330,000 in 1979-80. Snow Bunny Lodge, an overnight family facility, is run by the Commercial Club of Portland.

Forest Park: A natural evolution

March 5, 1986

This Douglas fir is the tallest tree in Forest Park. How large is it? When was it "discovered?" (Answers below cartoon).

The process which brought about America's second-largest city park preserve was long and arduous but the results were well worth the effort.

It began in 1897 when Scottish-born Portland entrepreneur Donald Macleay donated to the city a 130-acre parcel of undeveloped, timber-covered land in Balch Gulch. The intention was to log off the virgin timber and convert the property into a park. But an idea whose time had come intervened.

Two years later the City Parks Commission was formed and, led by Col. L.L. Hawkings, this nature-loving body looked upon Macleay's donation as a rare opportunity to preserve and protect a small segment of that primeval forest which once had embraced the entire landscape but which was rapidly falling victim to the ax and saw of population and progress.

Although a million-dollar bond issue was approved, the plan was never carried out. But other promoters of natural beauty and preservation kept pushing. In 1912 Chicago planner Edward Bennett's proposed Greater Portland Plan stated "the forest preserves are extensive in the large cities of Europe. The great woodland areas are the life giving elements of the city."

Owing largely to these recommendations and the efforts of local groups, no major subdivisions were platted in Forest Park after 1915. The city acquired 1400 acres by forfeiture due to unpaid property assessments for the construction of Hillside Drive which became Leif Erickson Drive in 1933. Some 1100 additional acres reverted to the county for delinquent property taxes.

The Clark and Wilson Lumber Co. donated 17.7 acres west of Linnton in 1927 and the A. Meier estate deeded 287.8 acres, now

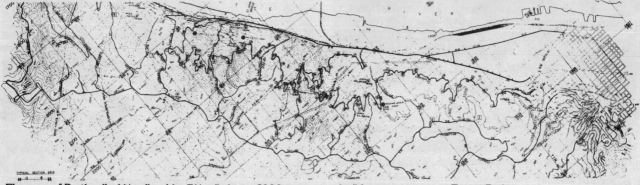

Fire map of Portland's 1¼-mile wide, 7½-mile long, 6000 acre natural wilderness preserve—Forest Park.

Macleay Park was the southeast anchor from which Portland's Forest Park took shape. At the turn of the century almost all of what eventually evolved into the seven and one-half mile long arborial sanctuary was in private hands. Its densely wooded northeastern edges along the present day St. Helens Road provided easy access for early exploiters and great, clear-cut swaths soon scarred the hillsides.

By 1903, when nationally known park planner John Olmsted came to town, Linnton had long been subdivided and cultivated farmland stretched up to Skyline Boulevard. Olmstead recommended that the undeveloped area above the river northwest of Guild's Lake be linked to a series of Hillside Parkways ringing the westside hills from St. Johns to Sellwood.

called Linnton Park, to the city in 1938. The following year George and Mary Holman gave Portland 52.4 acres north of Macleay Park.

Add to these acquisitions the Oregon Audubon Society's 30-acre Pittock Bird Sanctuary on Cornell Road and, bit by bit, Forest Park was slowly pieced together. But it took the action of a citizen's group to make the park a reality.

In late 1946 and early 1947, the Forest Park Committee of Fifty, a coalition of forty civic organizations and ten at-large members, convinced the City Planning Commission to recommend creation of the park to the City Council. On July 9, 1947, the council adopted a resolution to set aside 5,635 acres. Following fourteen months of hearings and city/county agreements, Forest Park was formally dedicated on September 25, 1948.

Answers: Found amidst a virgin grove in 1957, it is 7½ feet in diameter and 211 feet tall coming to a broken top.

City Park: When the old zoo was new

August 14, 1985

The main building of the old Washington Park Zoo, late 1930s. What now occupies this site? (Answer below cartoon).

With the Washington Park Zoo currently ranked among the top 10 in the country, it's difficult to imagine that at one time our city zoo was treated like an orphan and almost died of neglect.

Like so many other civic endeavors in pioneer Portland, the establishment of a zoo was more happenstance than planning. Zoos didn't make money. Neither did parks, for that matter. That's why the rapidly growing city had no park in 1871 and the idea of an animal exhibit remained 15 years away.

That year Amos King, whose land holdings extended into the heights behind the central district, sold 40 acres to the city for its first municipal park. Of course, its size was almost embarrassing and those citizens who lived close enough to enjoy it on a regular basis had substantial property of their own, but it was a beginning.

City Park circa 1900 (left). The zoo's bear grotto, mid-1930s (right).

In the early 1880s Richard Knight, a retired sailor-turned-druggist, began caring for an odd assortment of exotic birds and animals left with him by his fellow sailors. Knight kept this motley menagerie at his drug store on S.W. Morrison between 3rd and 4th and, as his collection grew, in a vacant lot next door.

By 1887, with the addition of an Alaskan brown bear and a grizzly, Portland's self-proclaimed "first zoo" had become both a success and a burden that Knight could no longer maintain. When he offered the entire assemblage to the city, the Common Council accepted and Portland acquired a zoo essentially by default.

The initial zoo compond was constructed in the 40-acre City Park on the site of what is now the westside city reservoir. Another ex-sailor, Charles Meyers, was the first park

and zoo keeper. Meyers' devoted efforts, until his accidental death in 1910, laid a firm foundation for the future expansion of both. He is also credited with creating the first barless sunken bear cage in the world which served as the model for the zoo's later bear grotto.

During Mayor Harry Lane's administration (1905-1909), the zoo fell out of favor. Lane advocated its eventual elimination but the predominantly native specimens continued to propagate, thus perpetuating their home. Ironically, the zoo acquired a lion, leopard and polar bear from the Lewis & Clark Fair during his first year in office.

The zoo hobbled along on minimal funding into the mid-1920s while the park saw refinement with statuary landscaping and the addition of the International Rose Test Garden. Moved to the top of the renamed Washington Park, zoo facilities were remote and inadequate. But the almost

abandoned orphan received enough support to survive and, in 1938, got its first full-time director.

Cary Baldwin had worked at Hearst's San Simeon Ranch and the San Diego Zoo. His 18-month tenure, before leaving to become director of the San Francisco Zoo, helped rebuild momentum which was carried forward by his successor, Arthur Greenhall, a reptile specialist. but both were hampered by lack of funds and council apathy.

It was left to Jack Marks, who became the Washington Park Zoo's third director in 1947, to pick up the post-World War II pieces. Facilities were deteriorated and there was no room for expansion. Putting patch on patch to serve the needs of some 300 species, Marks sought a new direction which meant a different location and an new zoo—a monumental task.

WHY ARE THEY LETTING THOSE ROSE FESTIVAL PRINCESSES GO IN WITH THE **BEARS**?

WELL, I HEARD THE ZOO WAS **LOW** ON MONEY.

BUT I DIDN'T KNOW THAT THEY'D RUN OUT OF **FOOD**!

Klooster '85

Answer: The Japanese Gardens were built on the location after construction of the new zoo.

Washington Park Zoo: High marks for the director

August 21, 1985

Packy, Portland's first baby elephant, doubled zoo attendance in 1962 over 1961. Who originally owned him? How large is the zoo's current herd? (Answers below cartoon).

In 1947, when Jack Marks took the helm as director of the Washington Park Zoo, he was well aware of its many inadequacies. Having worked with his predecessor for several years on the evaluation of possible sites for a new zoo, Marks made this his ultimate goal. But first he had to tackle more pressing problems.

Throughout the zoo's history its animals had never had more than token veterinary care. So Marks initiated an area-wide search which culminated in an on-call arrangement with two local veterinarians, Drs. Clifford Bjork and Walter Steele, who proved to be invaluable assets. Deaths among the zoo population declined dramatically as symptoms were spotted and diagnosed early.

During their tenures the two vets hired a young assistant, Dr. Theodore Reed, who eventually assumed primary responsibility for the zoo. In the process he gained an expertise that earned him the top veterinary post at the National Zoo in Washington D.C. and later its directorship.

Zooliner, June 29, 1958.

The relationship between Reed and Marks greatly benefited the Portland Zoo over the years. Only one example was the establishment of the chimpanzee colony.

With more specimens, however, the lack of space became a critical concern. Despite more makeshift fencing, dividers and enclosures, escapes were inevitable and deaths, particularly from males killing their newborn, all too frequent. But, with a barebones budget, patchwork was all that was possible.

The first stirrings of salvation for the struggling facility came in 1951 when the Portland City Club set up a zoo study committee. The resulting recommendations were that a new site be selected, a new zoo constructed, a zoological society formed and a zoo commission established.

After decades of council apathy and neglect, attitudes had finally changed. An ordinance was promptly passed to create a zoo commission of eleven members, all of whom apparently took their responsibilities seriously. Within a year, site selection had been narrowed to the city-owned West Hills Golf Course just north of Canyon Road, and a $3.85 million bond issue was on the November ballot.

To ensure passage of this vital measure an independent fund raising and promotional group, the Portland Zoological Society, was chartered on August 21, 1952. The group immediately initiated a continuing campaign to make the new zoo a reality.

Architect's rendering, polar bear exhibit, 1957.

Despite narrow defeat of this first bond measure, a major publicity coup kept the momentum going. With the enthusiastic support of Mayor Fred Peterson, Portland acquired its first elephant Rosy, from Thailand in September of 1953. A revised five-year zoo tax levy passed handily the following spring.

All involved individuals and entities sprang into action. Director Marks and the design team studied zoos and aquariums across the country. The initial exhibit list included more than 1,600 species. A four-mile railway train ride was part of the plan. Realities of cost increases resulted in the opening of what Marks called a "bob-tailed" zoo on July 3, 1959.

Many exhibits were yet to be completed and others had to await future funding. But the dream of Jack Marks and dozens of other dedicated Portlanders had come true. Marks had ventured to Antarctica the previous year to bring back the first of several groups of penguins, the new OMSI complex was drawing accolades across the way and, in 1962, Portland gained national prominence, zoologically speaking, when Packy became the first elephant to be born in the United States in 44 years.

Answers: Noted Northwest animal trainer Morgan Berry owned Packy's mother, Belle, and sold her to the zoo. Eleven elephants.

OMSI:
Scientifically "funtasticational"

September 4, 1985

Governor Paul Patterson with OMSI man, 1957. Character was created by Disney artist. What new technology for animated entertainment will soon visit OMSI? (Answer below cartoon).

It began in 1906 with a few dusty "don't touch" natural history exhibits hanging around City Hall. What it does today stimulates your synapses and you have a terrific time in the process. That's been true ever since the Oregon Museum found its first "real" home.

OMSI's predecessor was a still-adolescent and almost-abandoned 38-year-old when, on November 15, 1944, the Oregon Museum Foundation was incorporated. Nearly all artifacts had been stored away during the 1930s due to lack of funds but now the much desired museum was on the road to reality.

was a success. Only a year later the first planetarium in the Northwest was opened on the site. but by 1957 the Lloyd Corporation was on the move and, although a concerted civic effort to build a museum was underway, OMSI got left out in the cold a third time.

This predicament precipitated an unprecedented event. On August 17, 1957, the first ever museum raising was held. Orchestrated by OMSI Director Dr. Samuel Diack and assisted by volunteer union labor, the walls went up in one day and the publicity helped continue the push that saw formal dedication ceremonies take place on June 7, 1958.

OMSI's first home at 908 N.E. Hassalo (left). Planners with original museum model on site (right).

With Dr. J.C. Stevens as its spokesman, the message was carried to the state capitol and initial funding was obtained. Offices in the Portland Hotel, as well as a display area, formed the nucleus augmented by additional displays in the U.S. and First National banks.

But, private donations and new archaeological finds swelled the collection and these facilities were soon inadequate. By 1949 the fate of the grand old hotel was in serious doubt and it was apparent that the museum would once again be without a home. Enter Ralph B. Lloyd.

Lloyd offered a large old house, adjacent to the city blocks he would later develop into the Lloyd Center complex, as a new home for the museum that finally took on its official name, the Oregon Museum of Science & Industry, at the end of 1954.

From its opening on May 17, 1949, OMSI's new home

In 1960, the OMSI staff created a fund-raising auction concept that has since been copied across the country. Joining with the zoo, the first of eight ZOOMSI auctions was held that year. Going it alone from 1968 forward, the annual OMSI Auctions have been a hit ever since.

In addition to this benefit bash, individual donations have played a vital role. The Swigert family saw to it that construction continued in 1957 and Harry Kendall funded the planetarium, completed in 1967.

OMSI-goers have been treated to intriguing and informative traveling exhibitions over the years. From science fairs to agates and minerals, IBM to the Smithsonian, the Inventors' Expo to the Muppet Show, OMSI's a funtasticational place to go.

Note: Welcome to new and first female director, Marilynne Eichinger.

Answer: The World of Holography will be at OMSI from September 30 to October 30.

Washington Park: A lot is new at the zoo

August 28, 1985

Charlie, the zoo's dominant orangutan. How many of its kind are left in the world? Where do they originate? (Answers below cartoon).

Over the twenty-three years since Portland's first baby elephant, Packy, was born in 1962, the Washington Park Zoo has become North American headquarters for the Asian pachyderm.

What once was an international event became almost an annual occurrence as announcements of expectant mothers and impending arrivals flowed from the zoo's management offices. There were ten births in as many years.

Only sixty percent of the zoo's original master plan had been executed when the facility opened in July, 1959. But Director Jack Marks was relentless in his expansion and improvement efforts as was his successor, Warren Iliff, who came to Portland from the National Zoo in 1975.

Society in 1971, but civic donations remained an important factor.

In 1976 state legislation brought the zoo under the umbrella of the Metropolitan Services district. A five-year, $10-million levy was passed that year and the zoo's name was changed from the Portland Zoological Gardens back to its original one, the Washington Park Zoo, following a contest.

The form and function of a zoo have changed considerably since the early days. Once, merely caging animals so that the public could view them without fear of harm was considered adequate. Then, giving them an enclosure where they could stretch their legs a bit more freely, swing

The zoo's Alaska Tundra exhibit (left), the main entrance mural (center) and the Cascades trail head (right).

Marks' dream to develop a penguin colony ended in tragedy when all of the Adelie and Emperor penguins he had secured on three trips to Antarctica eventually succumbed to Aspergillosis due to their lack of natural immunity. Iliff made up for the loss by bringig in Humboldt penguins, a heartier species from Peru, and installing them in a controlled environment. The "Penguinarium" has become one of the zoo's most popular attractions.

The ongoing financial needs of the zoo and its neighbor OMSI, were given a big boost in the pocketbook with the 1960 launching of the first annual ZOOMSI auction. Primary funding continued to come from the City of Portland even after operation was taken over by the Portland Zoological

from a tree branch, swim in a pool or lounge in the sun represented a significant step forward.

Today, the zoo's new Alaska Tundra exhibit is the state-of-the-art in animal captivity. This elaborate recreation of each creature's natural environment is an exciting advance. The new bear facility, currently under construction, will add another dimension.

Combine these with the Cascades trail which takes visitors on a walk through a capsulized version of our own Pacific Northwest wilderness and you will see that the Washington Park Zoo offers a day of unique entertainment and information that truly earns it a high position in the nation's top ten.

Answers: Less than 5,000 orangutans exist in the wild. Their native habitats are the jungles of Borneo and Sumatra.

Lewis and Clark: The Centennial Celebration

June 13, 1984

This "Wild West" sculpture greeted visitors at the entrance to the 1905 Fair. Which famous American artist was its creator and what was it called? Answers below cartoon).

The seeds of Portland's greatest-ever civic undertaking were planted just prior to the turn of the century. Local business men felt that an international fair would showcase Oregon and Portland.

Despite doubters in this traditionally conservative city, the idea finally gained momentum. In December 1900, with the backing of *Oregonian* Editor Harvey Scott and banker Henry W. Corbett, the Oregon Historical Society proposed a "Northwest industrial exposition" to coincide with the 100th Anniversary of the Lewis and Clark expedition.

The nighttime electrical extravaganza.

With a half-million-dollar commitment from the Oregon Legislature, lobbyists tackled the more difficult task of securing federal funds. Following nearly a year of Capitol Hill politicking, a bill authorizing $2.6 million was signed on April 13, 1904, by President Theodore Roosevelt.

By this time more than two years of intensive planning had already gone into the project. After considering several possible sites, the Guild's Lake location in Northwest Portland was selected. Its 400 open, marshy acres were easily adaptable and close proximity to existing street car lines was a plus.

Once underway, the fair's scope exploded in extent. Emissaries were everywhere on both domestic and international fronts. The promotional outlay alone eventually totalled $114,000.

These efforts brought the participation of 18 states, 10 of which had separate buildings. California and Washington, recognizing the opportunity, put up exhibits almost matching the main halls in size and grandeur. Twenty-one foreign countries were represented in the European and Oriental buildings.

The primary architectural themes were Spanish renaissance and classical. Oregon's Forestry Building was the only total departure. The world's largest log cabin remained as the fair's sole survivor until, tragically, it burned to the ground in 1964.

During its 4½-month run (June 1-Oct 15, 1905), the Lewis and Clark Centennial and American Pacific Exposition Oriental Fair attracted more than 2½ million guests. 1.5 million of them paid (50 cents for adults, 25 cents for children) for the privilege.

The U.S. Government Exhibit, across the lake, largest building at the exposition.

Mostly from the West, these visitors were treated to a spectacular show, beautifully designed, smoothly run and, in the end, profitable for both the promoters and the city.

Even more significant, the benefits of the exposition extended throughout the Northwest. With its infinitely enhanced image, Portland's population nearly doubled in the next five years.

Answer: "Hitting the Trail" by Frederic Remington (1861-1909).

The Columbia Gorge: Viewpoints revisited

June 17, 1985

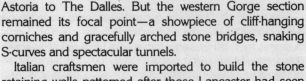

Dedication Day, June 7, 1915, at Crown Point. What was the highlight of this event? (Answers below cartoon).

To say that Portlanders appreciate the breathtaking natural beauty of the Columbia Gorge is an understatement. It's a love affair that's been going on since the days of early pioneer settlement. Today, the trip takes only a little effort. Pack a lunch, pile in the car and zip up I-84 for the afternoon. At the turn of the century it was an overnight outing.

In summer, the weekend paddlewheelers to Hood River were always crowded. Train passengers disembarked at the Oneonta Station for the trek back to Multnomah Falls. Some adventurous types took horse and buggy over a rut-filled road.

For the noisy, undependable, motorized contraptions, just beginning to make their appearance in Portland, the journey was all but impossible. But the automobile was the irrepressible wave of the future. In 1905 there were 218 cars in the state. Four years later, the number had risen to 552. It would increase fifty-fold by 1915.

Astoria to The Dalles. But the western Gorge section remained its focal point—a showpiece of cliff-hanging corniches and gracefully arched stone bridges, snaking S-curves and spectacular tunnels.

Italian craftsmen were imported to build the stone retaining walls patterned after those Lancaster had seen along the steep slopes of the Rhine River. The work was done with horses, mules and hand tools. When completed, except for paving, in July of 1915, the 20.47 miles from Chanticleer Inn to the Hood River County line were heralded as an engineering feat without rival in America.

One month later, the Portland-to-Astoria portion opened. The following year congress passed its first-ever highway funding legislation. Those dollar-for-dollar matching monies covered the costly tunneling at Mitchell Point and ensured completion of the entire highway in 1922.

The contribution of Simon Benson and his good friend John Yeon deserve special mention in this story. As county

Shepperd's Dell and Eagle Creek bridges show diverse arch styles at opening of highway, 1915.

In early 1909 word began to spread around local motoring circles about an ambitious plan to build a highway from Portland to Hood River. Noted construction engineer Samuel Lancaster, who had just returned from the first International Road Congress in Paris, was convinced that time-tested European techniques could overcome the Gorge's sheer basalt cliffs. He found an enthusiastic ally in Sam Hill, an eccentric, but visionary millionaire.

Hill's connections and Lancaster's credibility attracted a formidable group of local supporters. Lumber barons Simon Benson and John Yeon, *Oregonian* publisher Henry Pittock, *Oregon Journal* publisher C.S. Jackson, department store mogul and future governor Julius Meier, attorney Jay Bowerman and County Commissioner Rufus Holman lent their considerable clout to the effort.

Under Lancaster's guidance, construction began on the Columbia River Scenic Highway in 1913. The plan had been expanded to encompass a river route stretching from

roadmaster, Yeon supervised the highway's construction bringing it in below estimates submitted by private firms.

Erection of the elaborate Vista House atop Crown Point in 1918 was another matter. Whereas only $12,000 had been allocated for "a shelter" at the site, Yeon personally approved the almost $100,000 expenditure which led to this remarkable monument. Commissioner Holman had him fired for his unauthorized extravagance.

Benson, who was appointed first chairman of the State Highway Commission in 1917, had personally put more than $200,000 into the promotion of good roads. He purchased the properties at Multnomah and Wahkeena Falls to protect them from commercial encroachment.

When Benson resigned from the Highway Commission in 1920, Yeon assumed the chairmanship at the request of Governor James Withycombe. It was a fitting vindication of his Vista House decision and his role in creating the Northwest's first grand scenic highway.

Answer: President Woodrow Wilson pressed a telegraph key in Washington, D.C., that sent a cross-country signal unfurling the American flag.

The Columbia Gorge: Its highway and hotel

June 24, 1985

The Chanticleer Inn, oldest of the Gorge roadhouses. What happened to the Mitchell Point tunnel? How many visitors does Multnomah Falls have each year? (Answers below cartoon).

On June 7, 1915, Marmons and Reos, Franklins and Pierce-Arrows rumbled over the newly opened Columbia River Scenic Highway for the first time. Passengers in more than 2,000 automobiles would round the cliff-clinging route that day to marvel at the views and participate in the dedication ceremonies atop Crown Point.

The men who had made the highway happen—Hill, Benson, Yeon, Pittock, Meier and Holman—were on hand. Oregon tourism promoter without peer, Frank Branch Riley delivered an inspired oration to honor the accomplishment and the engineering genius of its designer, Samuel Lancaster.

Lindsey Inn, 35 miles from Portland

Most of them would gather at the site again, on May 5, 1918, for the dedication of the Vista House. The handcrafted stone jewel crowning the Gorge's most prominent point cost $100,000—eight times the amount originally budgeted. Though that immense overrun lost county roadmaster John Yeon his job, the result was clearly worth it.

Motorists were drawn to the scenic drive like bees to honey. Entrepreneurs quickly responded by erecting roadhouses along the route. The Chanticleer Inn at Corbett was the only pre-existing facility. The Multnomah Lodge and Lindsey Inn soon added their country charm to the scene.

During the summer of 1921, these rustic hostelries found themselves eclipsed by a new entrant in the competition for lodging and dining dollars. Lumber baron, civic benefactor and good roads promoter Simon Benson had outdone himself, spending $500,000 to construct the Columbia Gorge Hotel.

Situated on 40 wooded acres overlooking the Columbia just west of Hood River, the 42-room, tile and stucco villa was dubbed the "Waldorf of the West." Its crystal elegance, continental fare and impeccable service attracted the Pacific Coast's motoring elite. Illustrious guests included such stars of the silent screen as Rudolph Valentino, Clara Bow and Myrna Loy.

The hotel's General Manager Henry Thiele, destined to become a respected Rose City restaurateur, had been executive chef at Benson's flagship hotel on Broadway before accepting the new position. Columbia River salmon and Hood River apple pie emerged from his kitchen as haute cuisine.

For 30 years the hotel maintained its grand style until 1952 when different times and a changing society led to its demise. The Scenic Highway also saw significant change. Having proved inadequate for traffic loads of the 1930s and '40s, it was replaced by a new expressway in 1954. Portions of the old road were obliterated and other sections abandoned. The roadside inns closed.

On the cliff above Wah-Gwin-Gwin Falls, the aging hostelry hung on for 25 years as a retirement home for the Neighbors of Woodcraft. In 1977, it was purchased, along with 11 remaining acres, by a Portland businessman for $325,000. The new owner began extensive refurbishment but ran out of money and went deep into debt.

The ambitious project was resurrected in 1982 when two Seattleites, Boyd Graves and Peter McGary, assumed the $1.2 million SBA loan and poured an additional $750,000 into completing the restoration. Today, the Columbia Gorge Hotel is once again a sumptuous showplace offering superb dining and luxurious accomodations.

Following the lead of its renowned hostelry, the Scenic Highway will soon see a renaissance. It was designated a national engineering landmark in 1985. The same year, passage of the Columbia Gorge Protection Bill created a national scenic area that will be administered under a set of strict environmental standards.

The complex guidelines for this unique entity are still being formulated. But one thing is certain. The rich heritage of the Gorge, its highway and hotel has been recognized and, due to the keen concerns of several groups, should be well protected.

Answers: The multi-arched tunnel was blasted away by road-widening in 1965. 2.4 million visitors annually.

Expo and environs: No bum steers

June 18, 1986

The Red Steer Cafe was purchased and remodeled in 1984 by Barry and Marian Brownell. What was it originally? How long has it been there? (Answers below cartoon).

As undeniably eastern as Portland's founders and builders were, they molded a uniquely western metropolis. And that meant livestock—cattle, sheep, hogs and horses. Shades of Chicago and Kansas City. It was only natural that, as the city grew, so did a market for money on the hoof.

By the end of the new century's first decade, Portland's population had exploded to 205,000—the second largest on the Pacific Coast. Two years later, in 1912, a major stockyard was established on the south edge of the Columbia River by one of the country's most prominent meat packers. In 1917, the Chicago-based Swift & Co. added substance to their sprawling field of pens and fences by erecting an impressive three-story brick office building at its northeastern edge.

the Portland Union Stock Yards Company presided over independent brokers who created a long and lively period of prosperity through the 1930s.

Expo's only dark days had nothing to do with its original purpose. For five months in 1942, under Executive Order 9066, more than 3,500 Japanese-Americans were held at the euphemistically dubbed Portland Assembly Center awaiting completion of facilities at Hunt, Idaho, where they would be detained for the duration of World War II.

The popularity of the P.I.L.E. continued through the 1950s. But as market conditions changed, Expo had to change with them. Multnomah County purchased the facility in 1965, the same year that Swift shut down its packing plant at the western end of the complex.

The bright-red, Expo Center in 1935 with Swift & Co. plant in background.

As movement of Northwest livestock centered on the North Portland yards, the Pacific International Livestock Association decided to make it the home of their annual exposition. During 1921-22, the P.I.L.A. constructed the West Coast's largest livestock showplace. it was the beginning of an Oregon tradition that continues to this day. Grading of breeds to strict standards, coveted awards, prestige auctions and top-caliber rodeos all became part of the "P.I." or, simply, the "Expo."

The original buildings burned to the ground only three years after they were built. But the exposition was a going concern and a new complex, eventually painted a bright red, went up almost immediately. Swift & Co. was required to fivest itself of the stockyards during the same period and

The renamed and remodeled Multnomah County Exposition Center became home to the county fair in 1969, and other shows requiring extensive square footage began to take advantage of the favorable rates and 5,000-car parking lot.

Today, the Expo Center hosts such popular annual events as the Home, Boat, R.V., Antique and Agricultural shows. The Dog Show is Expo's oldest "tenant" and the Auto Swap Meet drew more than 50,000 attendees last year.

Cattle and sheep are still sold at the adjacent yards in quantities up to 1,500 weekly for each as the "Expo" maintains its unique role in Portland's scheme of showplaces.

WHAT WAS THE BIGGEST BOMB THAT EVER PLAYED THE **EXPO** ARENA?

KANSAS CITY **BOMBER** WITH RAQUEL WELCH FILMED HERE IN 1972!

Klooster '86

Answers: Built in 1908 as the offices for Swift & Co.'s stockyard operations, it bacame a restaurant in 1917.

Elkdom:
A proud brotherhood in Portland

March 6, 1985

Elks Convention parade down Broadway, July 18, 1947. What is the Oregon Elks' most prominent charity? What role do women play in the order? (Answers below cartoon.)

America's largest homegrown fraternal order was a rapidly growing 20-year old by the time it reached Portland in 1889 and the Benevolent and Protective Order of Elks soon became a significant factor on the local scene.

A group of New York City actors, musicians and other theater people had formed a social club called the "Jolly Corks" in 1868 for the purpose of mutual fellowship and supportiveness. Its popularity caused the club to grow so quickly that a more dignified name was soon demanded.

The founders decided that something distinctively American was called for — something like the proud Buffalo, the industrious Beaver or the noble Elk. The Elk won out and the organization became noted for its benevolence to members and their families and its increasing role in community service.

In the Victorian era, such virtues were both admired and emulated. The order expanded rapidly into major eastern cities and then across the country. By the time it reached Portland, the local lodge was the 142nd.

served the lodge for 17 years until, in December 1923, a structure considered to be the finest owned by any fraternal order in the country was completed.

The million-dollar Elks Temple at S.W. 11th and Alder served almost 6,000 brethren at its height and was the focal point of the 1925 National Convention. But this expansive edifice was to have a short tenure. With the onset of the Great Depression, membership plummeted to a low of 450 in 1932. The lodge lost both the building and its garage a block away on 12th.

Recovery came slowly with a new building at S.W. 16th and Morrison acquired from the Concordia Club. It served the lodge for 35 years until 1963, when a modern facility was built across the street, which has been home to B.P.O.E. 142 since.

Portland hosted the national convention for a third time in 1947, witnessing a changing organization. Postwar members represented a broader cross-section of middle America. Where power and influence once combined with conviviality, patriotism and civic mindedness, primarily the latter was left.

Elks Temple at 11th and Alder: Main Ballroom (left), Dining Room (center), Lodge Meeting Room (right).

Many of Portland's most prominent men — doctors, lawyers, business leaders and public officials — became Elks. The city's original Street Fair and Carnival, predecessor to the Rose Festival, was begun in 1900 by a group of Elks.

B.P.O.E. Lodge 142 enjoyed such success in the early years of the century that it was chosen to host the 1912 Elks' National Convention or Grand Lodge Reunion. To gauge the order's continued growth, the Oregon City lodge, formed the year before, was the 1189th.

Having doubled and redoubled its membership, the Portland lodge had to find ever-larger quarters. In 1906, after several moves, they constructed their own $80,000 building at S.W. 7th (Broadway) and Stark — current site of U.S. National Bank. It

Today, the Elks, along with other fraternal orders, face a critical new challenge in Oregon and across the nation. Their contributions are overshadowed by a public conception of chauvinistic clannishness and self-serving motivations.

The compelling question asked by younger people is: Are they relevant? Yet, the Portland lodge still boasts 2,600 members. Other local area lodges, such as Gateway, Milwaukie and Oregon City, which celebrated its 75th anniversary on March 4th, are still doing well in spite of the economic environment.

True, more Elks are over 50 than under, and their image is not big-city vogue. But soon more than half the population will pass the half-century mark and most of them don't commute.

ONCE WE WERE THE BIGGEST GAME IN TOWN. NOW SOME SAY THAT WE'RE AN ENDANGERED SPECIES.

DOES COUNTLESS HOURS AND $2 MILLION DONATED LAST YEAR BY MORE THAN 90,000 OREGON ELKS SOUND LIKE EXTINCTION?

B.P.O.E.

Klooster '85

Answers: The Elks Eye Clinic. The women's auxiliary, formed in 1906 locally, is vital to the organization.

PP&L:
The Lincoln
steam plant
April 10, 1985

One of the Lincoln plant's three steam-driven turbine generators. When was it last used? Where was the only other downtown steam and power plant? (Answers below cartoon.)

Near water's edge at the south end of downtown stands a solid link to Portland's past. Many people wonder, "Just what is that big old building?" Others who are aware of its purpose know only the half of it.

It's called simply "the Lincoln plant" and it was built in 1917-18 by Northwestern Electric Co. (which merged with Pacific Power & Light in 1947) to produce steam heat and electricity for downtown.

The site at the foot of Lincoln Street was selected for its immediate access to water for cooling the giant turbine generators and for the adjacent sawmills which supplied cheap hog fuel (wood chip waste) to fire the furnaces.

Lincoln plant in the late 1920s   Fuel conveyor system

A mountain of the stuff stood alongside the plant until 1967 when conversion to natural gas was completed. This was the last step in a transformation that had originally seen the plant topped by 180-foot-tall smoke stacks and later by squat, cylindrical filters.

Many who are familiar with the plant think its sole purpose has always been to provide steam heat for downtown buildings. But through the 1920s and '30s three gar-

gantuan generators that now stand idle supplied one-third of the city's electric power.

Those generators sprang to life once again after the calamitous Columbus Day storm of October 1962. With major transmission lines down, the central city would have gone without power for days had it not been for this powerful backup system.

Downtown's dwindling steam heat needs no longer require all six of Lincoln's cavernous dutch ovens and boilers. PP&L's customer base has declined steadily since the late 1960s due to the self-contained design of new high-rise buildings.

Reluctantly, the company decided to discontinue its heavily subsidized steam service on a phase-out plan calling for complete shutdown in 1986.

Where once the bustling plant was surrounded with sawmills and served by a battalion of barges, it now stands stoically among stately poplars. At its height a crew of 70 was fully occupied in its operation. Now a handful of old timers keep things running smoothly.

Lincoln's destiny is tied to the new south waterfront project, RiverPlace, rapidly taking shape on its northern flank. Seattle-based Cornerstone Development Company has the option to take over the property and the plant. The question as to whether the old leviathan will be leveled or renovated remains unanswered.

Whatever is done won't be easy or inexpensive. If you ever need a bomb shelter, the Lincoln plant would be one of Portland's best. In the floods of 1948 and '64 it was surrounded by water and suffered only a little leakage.

Here is an early 20th-century industrial statement — a concrete-and-steel monument to the harnessing of steam power that hopefully can be preserved.

Answers: The hydroelectric-restricted drought year of 1973. In the basement of the Pittock Block until 1965.

River City:
The scandalous spans
August 17, 1983

What do the Aberdeen (Wash.), Sellwood and Bull Run bridges have in common? (Answer below cartoon.)

An ambitious bridge-building project begun in the early '20s, the Sellwood, the replacement Burnside and the Ross Island, proved to be Portland's own "over-Watergate."

Responsibility for local bridge construction and maintenance had been placed under county jurisdiction in 1913, so awarding of contracts fell to the county commissioners rather than the City Council, whose constituency would be the primary beneficiaries of the new bridges.

The triumvirate of commissioners, upon whose collective heads condemnation rained when the scandal came to light, included Dow Walker, former MAC manager and popular personage about town who had come to public office with the backing of the Ku Klux Klan. His insurance company stood to benefit substantially from the construction bonding.

part of the old-boy system, played a careful hand. The Sellwood Bridge plan, well underway before they came on the scene, is poignant testimony to the self-serving environment of the times. At $541,637.99, it may have seemed to be the last of the bargain bridges, but this narrow, two-lane span was obsolete when completed in December 1925.

The new Burnside, on the other hand, was a state-of-the-art, double-leaf bascule with a 68-foot-wide roadway ringing in at $2,964,647.09 when dedicated on May 28, 1926.

Last of the three, the Ross Island entered the scene that December and cost a million dollars less ($1,937,468,.44) than the Burnside even though it was over twice as long (1891 ft.) and twice as high (129 ft.). No opening mechanisms meant less cost and more acclaim for its attractive lines.

Burnside Bridge dedication ceremonies, May 28, 1926

Commissioner Charles Rudden found that one construction company seemed better suited than its competition. His reasoning had little to do with their bridge-building capabilities. Commissioner R.H. Rankin was the third collaborator in this corrupt collusion. As Kimbark McCall states in his estimable *Growth of a City,* "In 1924, the entire board was recalled for improperly awarding three Willamette River bridge contracts."

The new board of Multnomah County Commissioners, no less a

The modest praise accorded the Ross Island was overshadowed only 4-1/2 years later by Dr. D.B. Steinman's stately St. John's Bridge. Even though he also designed the Golden Gate, Steinman considered this Gothic towered beauty, dedicated in June 1931 during Rose Festival, to be his masterpiece. Carrying a price tag of $3,911,634.78, it was our spendiest span to date but had not a hint of scandal.

Answer: They all utilized materials from the original Burnside Bridge.

1927:
Lindy launches
local aviation

March 28, 1984

Fashionable Portland ladies disembark a United airliner in 1932. How did the famous airline come into being? (Answer below cartoon.)

On May 20-21, 1927, a daring young aviator achieved an unprecedented feat — flying solo in a sleek, custom-made monoplane, dubbed the "Spirit of St. Louis."

Twenty-five-year-old Charles A. Lindbergh made the longest (3,614 miles) nonstop flight in history—a trans-Atlantic crossing from New York to Paris in 33-1/2 hours.

Following a grand tour of France, Belgium and England, the new international celebrity launched into a nationwide flying junket which found him approaching Portland's Swan Island Airport on the afternoon of September 14, 1927.

mogul Julius Meier's yacht for the trip across the river to the Battleship Oregon, anchored at the downtown seawall completed the previous year.

From there the procession through downtown was greeted with as much enthusiasm, if not numbers, as Lucky Lindy's New York reception where an estimated 4.5 million — the largest crowd in the Big Apple's history — had been on hand.

At Multnomah stadium, in accordance with Lindbergh's request, school children and their escorts were given

Journal headlines, September 1, 1927. A $90,000 Ford Tri-motor warming up at Swan Island Airport, October 8, 1931.

In anticipation of Colonel Lindbergh's arrival, thousands of spectators blanketed the hillsides overlooking the small spot of land on the Willamette's eastern edge which was the site of Portland's infant airstrip. Thousands more lined downtown Broadway awaiting the grand parade.

At 1:59 PM, one minute before its scheduled arrival, the silver, single-engine plane, built by Ryan Airlines of San Diego at a cost of $10,580, touched down smoothly and was greeted by 400 local dignitaries.

Accompanied by a select few including Mayor Baker and Governor Patterson, Lindbergh boarded department-store

preference to hear his address. Along with VFW members, they comprised most of the 30,000 who heard the man, characterized as America's last true hero, speak for the cause of aviation.

That night he was guest of honor at a banquet at the Multnomah Hotel where he slept for 13 hours. Lindy still had a month left on his 22,000-mile 83-city trek.

Portland responded to the call by completing a state-of-the-art terminal at Swan Island in 1930. The Rose City had entered the aviation age.

Answer: It was formed in 1931 as a Boeing subsidiary, buying out Pacific Air Transport and Varney Airlines.

The Public Market:
A three-block bust
December 10, 1986

The Yamhill Public Market, ca. 1920. At its height, how many producers used it as a retail outlet annually? What famed merchant got his start there? (Answers below cartoon.)

Today's Yamhill Marketplace recalls the popular farmers' produce market which drew throngs of shoppers to Southwest Yamhill between Third and Fifth avenues through the 1920s. Its Euorpean, open-air atmosphere made the Yamhill Public Market a major attraction for tourists and locals alike.

As much as Portlanders supported the simple, sidewalk-stall strip brimming with bargains on fresh fruits, vegetables and flowers, their planning commission had different ideas. Deeming the congested and unsanitary area inadequate for expanding public needs, the commission indirectly endorsed a plan to build its replacement, the Portland Public Market Building.

success of this new, utility certificates-convertible-to-bonds approach hinged on a Depression-era, Reconstruction Finance Corporation loan. The additional $775,000 enabled construction to be completed.

From ground breaking to opening day, the Portland Public Market Building took only five months to finish. Ready for operation just prior to Christmas 1933, the cavernous, concrete structure never gained its anticipated acceptance from merchants or customers. Despite three acres of free parking, convenient layout and the latest in modern displays and equipment, within two years the $1.4 million complex was on the verge of total collapse.

The Public Market Building and the Battleship Oregon, 1928. Interior view, Christmas, 1933.

Originally conceived in 1923 as a five-block long behemoth, by 1927 the building had been scaled down to a mere three-block monolith stretching along the waterfront from Southwest Salmon Street to just south of Morrison. Four years later the location was given the blessing of the Portland Chamber of Commerce paving the way for its consideration by the City Council.

Financing such an immense project, the largest-ever public market in the country, became a complex undertaking. It was further complicated by powerful local self interests that stood to gain substantially from the sale of the blocks involved. Accusations of bribery led to indictments alleging, on the one hand, payments to Mayor George Baker and other city commissioners to vote for the new Front Street location and, on the other, to back retention of the existing setup.

The Portland Public Market Company's initial private stock offering failed to materialize, primarily due to the 1929 crash, and a public-funding scheme was devised. Paradoxically, the eventual

Embroiled in litigation, burdened with liens and assessments and abandoned by an antagonistic City Council that denied any commitment to take over ownership, it was impossible for the market to continue operation. In the end, only the property owners, the designers and contractors profited from Portland's biggest boondoggle.

During World War II, the Navy leased the building and, in July 1946, the *Oregon Journal* bought it for $750,000. The now defunct, evening daily operated from the oversized space for 22 years until, in 1968, they sold to the city for $1.3 million.

Using monies from the U.S. Bureau of Outdoor Recreation and the State Highway Department, the building was demolished the following year along with the adjacent riverside expressway, Harbor Drive. In their place, the Waterfront Park was created finally fulfilling the recommendation of the Bartholomew Plan, a much-heralded master scheme for riverfront improvement, presented in 1932, paid for by the city and, then, ignored.

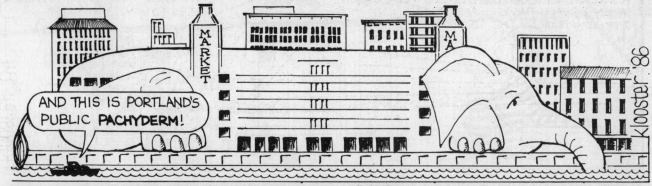

AND THIS IS PORTLAND'S PUBLIC **PACHYDERM**!

Answers: Approximately 75,000 different growers and other producers. Fred Meyer.

River City: Bridges of another color

August 24, 1983

What is the origin of these chalk murals that decorate pillars of the Lovejoy ramp? Were they done by some talented transient? Did you know they were there? (Answers below cartoon.)

In 1961, color coding was recommended for Portland's bridges. Enigmatic as we often are, a sizable group pushed pastels. Now, it's one thing to suffer grim grey and boring black but, quite another to love a lavender-laced Burnside. We might, however, revel in a rose-tinted Ross Island.

Impressionistic indulgences aside, the county did commission a color consultant to study the situation. His recommendations went well beyond black and grey but were more pragmatic than pastel.

— before the county finally won out.

No such battle took place over the same color for the Burnside. The amount of metal surface (the only areas painted) is minor. Today, both bridges badly need fresh coats.

The once-vibrant Ross Island has also faded. Oregon is responsible for maintaining it and the St. John's, as both are part of the state highway system. What is Mediterranean blue really like? Look at the city's recently repainted watermains along the Ross Island's upper sides.

Downtown bridges, July 17, 1963. Note that the Hawthorne is still black.

The selected colors and timetable for painting were: 1962 — Broadway (Golden Gate red) and Sellwood (green); 1963 — St. John's (green) and Hawthorne (yellow-ochre); 1964 — Burnside (yellow-ochre); and, lastly, 1967 — Ross Island (Meditterranean blue).

The plan also called for placement of placards at all bridge entrances stating "Willamette River." They were installed immediately to inform any visitors who might otherwise think they were venturing into Vancouver.

The colors were not without controversy. Enough Portlanders found the thought of observing an ochre Hawthorne objectionable and created a color controversy for months — from yellow-ochre to green and back again

Notice something missing in this colorful tale? The modern Morrison, completed in 1958, already wore its shiny silver coat. The Steel, owned by the Union Pacific, was not part of the plan. I'm told it wouldn't have mattered anyway because only black graphite will stick to its surface.

The somewhat-bedraggled black behemoth will be renovated next year to accommodate the new Light Rail system. New paint, too? The county says 12 years is maximum durability. They redid the Broadway in '78 and it looks great. Almost went to white but that was $75,000 more.

As of this writing, the Sellwood's new paint job is in progress. Perhaps with better times and bigger budgets, the Willamette will soon be resplendent with brighter bridges.

Answers: No transient, Greek immigrant and railroad watchman Ted Stefopoulos rendered them in the late 1940's.

History afloat: The Maritime Museum

November 5, 1986

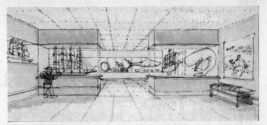

Rendering of Maritime Museum interior. What happened to the Battleship Oregon? (Answer below cartoon.)

On October 30, 1986, a long-overdue addition to Portland's already admirable list of public resources became a reality. It's the Oregon Maritime Center and Museum, an institution that promises to become one of the waterfront's most interesting attractions.

The Smith Building seen from the Battleship Oregon Memorial.

Situated in Old Town's historic and handsomely restored Smith Building at 111 S.W. Front Ave., the museum features nautical artifacts and memorabilia collected through the efforts of a blue ribbon organizing committee over the past half-dozen years. The center aspect of the facility indicates its function as an important resource for maritime research.

The concept was first conceived 22 years ago when, despite a determined drive, would-be organizers were unable to coalesce all the logistics. Revived in 1980, the idea gained new momentum under the guidance of a dedicated group headed by Dr. Everett Jones as president and retired Navy Captain Bill Peterson, vice president.

The executive board includes Mayor Bud Clark and a flotilla of ship's captains and business executives. The executive board, chaired by oil company owner John A. Carson, boasts such local business luminaries as Frank Chown, Ward Cook, Sam Naito and Knute Qvale. The public sector is represented by Senator Bob Packwood, Judge Lee Johnson and Port of Portland Executive Director Lloyd Anderson. Architect Brooks Gunsul provides the design expertise. Strong support has also come from the Nautical Society of Oregon and local yacht clubs.

The 114-year-old Smith Building (1872) is an ideal home for the center and museum. Waterfront Park and the Battleship Oregon memorial are just across Front Avenue, Saturday Market is only a block away and the Oak Street MAX station, two blocks.

Ship models, diving gear, nautical artwork, brass instruments, plaques, sextants, bells and wheels are among the rare pieces on display. A copy of the outstanding film of World War II shipbuilding in Portland, produced by the Kaiser Foundation, has been secured and will be shown several times daily in the center's presentation room.

Long-term goals go beyond maintenance and upgrading to the possible dream of acquiring an early ship to be restored and moored along the seawall. The center may qualify for federal grants depending on membership and donation levels achieved.

During the late 19th and early 20th centuries, Portland was one of the most important seaports on the West Coast. The evolution of River City and the region's inland shipping are inextricably tied. Since the lamentable demise of the Battleship Oregon in 1942, the city has had no focal point to feature that fact.

Meanwhile, maritime museums have sprung up in Seattle, San Diego, Honolulu, Monterey and Astoria joining the only pre-war facility in San Francisco. It's high time Portland had a place to highlight its nautical history — The Oregon Maritime Center and Museum. Welcome aboard.

Answer: A floating waterfront museum from 1923 to 1942, it was sold back to the Navy during World War II for salvage and scrap. Visit the new Maritime Center and Museum for its complete history.

TAG director isn't playing games

July 11, 1984

When Bob Siewert began his education career with the Beaverton School District, he never imagined that it would one day lead to administering the most ambitious advanced student program in Oregon's history.

A Northwest native (born in Oregon, raised in Washington), Bob attended Western Washington State College in Bellingham and received his degree in special education from Portland State University before taking that first post.

Arriving at Beaverton for the 1972-73 school year, Bob worked with handicapped children at schools throughout the district. He was then asked to head the program called "talented and gifted" which was a forerunner of today's revitalized state plan. At the time there was no Oregon Department of Education budget for enrichment courses and the local school district had earmarked a portion of its own funds for this effort.

Courses for students with exceptional abilities had been offered during the late 1950s and early 1960s through Ford Foundation grants statewide. By the end of the 1960s, these monies were almost depleted and it was only through the initiative of such progressive school districts as Beaverton's that some programs survived.

In 1977, after almost a decade without an advanced education program, the state Legislature appropriated $1 million for "Talented and Gifted" grants. The then-31-year-old special education administrator applied for the position as director of Oregon's new TAG program and got it.

That million-dollar budget covering the 1978-79 school year kicked things off with a bang. Programs were put into place in districts large and small — throughout the state.

But just as TAG started to soar, its wings were clipped by the recession and resulting budget crunch. The next allocation was cut in half — $500,000 for each of the following two years, 1979-80 and 1980-81. The 1981-82 and 1982-83 school years suffered even further reductions, down to $333,500 for each. As a result it was necessary to cut the state TAG staff by one-third.

This year 96 of the state's 309 school districts offer TAG courses and more proposals are being received than ever before. But with a current budget of $345,000, only one-fourth of these grant requests can be funded.

Siewert chairs a committee that decides which grants are approved and which aren't. "Far more proposals have merit than it is possible for us to support," says Bob. As he puts it: "This area of education is on the fine edge of the 'must dos' and 'we'd sure like tos.'" Even with the budget limitations, TAG presents exciting challenges for bright kids who are ready and eager to progress at an accelerated pace.

Although TAG progams span the spectrum of elementary and secondary grade levels, most are aimed at grades four through nine. Courses are primarily in academic disciplines — the sciences, math, history and literature. Students enter the program through teacher recommendations and can request evaluation. High school students have found the apprentice programs and out-of-school courses conducted by volunteers to be most valuable.

As a special education coordinator, Bob Siewert has always placed particular emphasis on community involvement. "Business and professional people give students direct contact with what will be asked of them in the real world," stresses Siewert.

Over the past three years at Sellwood Middle School, fifth-through eighth-graders have been involved in a unique program under Portland Public School District TAG Coordinator Sue Parker.

It is called "The Sellwood History Project" and has encompassed in-depth research into the evolution of that old eastside community, including interviews with long-time residents and historical education tours. The project culminated in a festive celebration of the school's 100th anniversary.

Jefferson High School is another beneficiary of Portland TAG funds. "Jefferson is what we call a 'magnet' school," related the state director. "Students from all over the city take advantage of its performing arts emphasis but they must also meet all the secondary curriculum standards."

The Rose City's claim to *Fame* predates TAG by three years and requires a considerably larger commitment than the state funds can meet. The local district digs deep to support this special school and the opportunities it offers.

As the economy improves, there are some encouraging signs from Salem. During the last session there was even a suggestion for a state math and science "magnet" school.

Now that would be a strong signal to high-tech execs of Oregon's willingness to plan for the future. A special school directed to augment and hone the technical aptitude of students from around the state.

"But," notes Siewert with a hint of hopefulness, "nothing has happened, yet." Meanwhile, he and his trimmed-down staff continue their lobbying efforts to recapture, if not exceed, the lost budget. "I'd like to see at least five to 10 percent more for next year just so we can maintain what we have," he adds.

When the figure $100,000 was mentioned, Bob replied that all borderline grants turned down this year could have been funded with that much additional money.

So there's the bottom line. Although prognosticators say we're on the road to recovery, increases are still hard to come by. When the fiscal mood does change, each of us who is interested in the future of Oregon should contact our legislators and encourage them to get behind the Talented and Gifted Program. The rewards will come in the form of long-term dividends that are worth far more than money

★ ★ ★

Community involvement in TAG means a personal commitment as this writer discovered. It also means a special sense of satisfaction. Over the course of four months I met every Friday (except spring vacation) with three student groups from Lincoln and Grant high schools and Beaumont Middle School.

Each group, two writer-researchers and a cartoonist, were asked to select a Portland subject, research it, find visual materials, write the story and draw an accompanying cartoon. The finished product would be an article in the same format as my weekly column, *Round the Roses*. The rewarding results are on the next three pages.

Story by Julie Ducher
and Melanie Morris
Cartoon by Michael Riley

White Stag skiwear in
the late 1930s. What
other unique outdoor
wear did the company
make? (Answer
below cartoon.)

White Stag: Wearing well for 100 years

This year marks the 100th anniversary of White Stag. The Portland-based company has grown from a small sail-making business into a very large organization that manufactures sportswear, recreational and athletic products worldwide.

Founded in 1884 by Henry Wemme as the Willamette Tent and Awning Company, the business was sold to Max Hirsch in 1907. Harry Weis, who had worked for Wemme, eventually became his partner.

outerwear for loggers and mill hands.

In 1929, after the company moved back a block to First Street, the founder's son, Harold S. Hirsch, chose the brand name "White Stag" for their new clothing and skiwear lines, the first in the world made specially for the sport.

"Hirsch" in German means a male deer or "stag" and "Weis" means white. To promote the new name, Mr. Hirsch made use of a sign on the roof of the building. The sign, which dominated the riverfront skyline, consisted of an

Hirsch made sails for ships like this. The landmark sign originally identified the second home of White Stag.

The business was originally located on the edge of the river. The firm repaired and made new canvas sails for clipper ships that came from Boston and New York 'round the Horn. The ships docked at Portland because it was the only fresh water harbor on the Pacific Coast that could accommodate ocean-going vessels. The ships were put into dry dock where barnacles would die and then could be easily scraped off the wooden hulls. At the same time the local sail loft company was busily at work on the sails.

Early in the century the company's name was changed to Hirsch-Weis Canvas Products to reflect its principals. The product line was expanded beyond ship outfitting to

outline of Oregon with White Satin Sugar written inside. White Stag converted the map into a sign for themselves.

When the song "Rudolph the Red-Nosed Reindeer," came out in the early 1950s, Mrs Hirsch hit upon the idea of putting a red nose on the stag every December. The tradition caught on quickly and each holiday Portland awaits the arrival of "Rudolph's Nose" with great anticipation. In 1977 the company merged with Warnaco. Over the past 100 years it has grown to international status — from a small canvas company to a corporate conglomerate.

Dutcher, Morris and Riley are students at Lincoln High School.

Answer: Workmen's canvas rainsuits dipped in paraffin were nicknamed "tin pants" because they stood by themselves.

Story by Amelie Hastie
and Joel Martin
Cartoon by Shanon Playford

John Reed and Louise Bryant set Portland on its ear with their radical views. What memorabilia of Louise is now in the Oregon Historical Society? (Answer below cartoon.)

John Reed: Never a hometown hero

Once upon a time, in a land removed from where you now sit only by years, a fellow named John Reed was raised. "Jack," as he preferred to be called, was no typical Portlander. In fact, he despised Portland and Portland returned the favor. You see, Jack was a communist, an atheist and an advocate of free love.

He came from one of the city's first families. His grandfather, Henry Green, founded the Gas Company, and it was at "Green Gables," one of Portland's stateliest homes, that Jack spent his younger years.

In fact, after Reed's graduation, his father was supportive of his lifestyle in Greenwich Village. A letter from C.J. to a friend in New York read: "Get him a job. Let him see everything. But don't let him be anything for awhile. Let him play."

And "play" he did, or at least that's what those proper Portlanders may have thought of his aiding in the cause that led John Reed to become a hero.

Before leaving for Russia in 1915, Reed returned to Portland. While here, he met writer Louise Bryant and fell in

Jack Reed at his typewriter (left). The staircase of his Portland home (center). his tomb marker, 2nd name, in the Kremlin wall (right).

His father, Charles Jerome "C.J." Reed, was a prominent businessman who became U.S. Marshall and later president of the Arlington Club.

Jack's independence was apparent even in childhood. Always chafing at the bonds of authority, he joined the 14th Street Gang as a boy.

Going off to Harvard didn't change things. Jack became one of the leaders of a revolutionary group which advocated overthrowing the U.S. Government.

Although this certainly wasn't following in his father's footsteps, C.J. Reed did not attempt to put a halt to his son's freedom of thought and action.

love. Louise left her husband to live with Jack in New York.

During his visit Reed proclaimed that Portland was "dull as ever" and announced, "I don't ever again want to live there." Portlanders had had enough of Reed, too. One wealthy man was quoted as saying that Reed was "a radical of the worst sort."

This radical's life ended in 1920 much as it had begun — surrounded by the elite. But these were quite a different elite than those of his hometown. They were the leaders of the Russian Revolution who lie buried beside John Silas Reed in the Kremlin Wall, far, far away.

Answer: The Society has some of her furniture left in Portland when she went to New York.

Story by Amy Moorman
and Margaret Richen

Cartoon by Chris Soentpiet

The elegant Lloyd's Golf and Country Club, which is now Sweet Tibbie Dunbar. What caused the end of the golf course? (Answer below cartoon.)

Sweet Tibbie Dunbar: From tee to tea

Ralph Lloyd, an engineer at the University of California, first came to Portland in 1911, immediately after graduation. Following financial difficulties, he returned home to the family's cattle ranch in Ventura County, north of Los Angeles.

Rumor had it that there were oil deposits in the area. Young Ralph drilled on the family property and discovered deep oil wells which assured him of lifelong financial security. This enabled him to return to Portland, his favorite city.

regarding what improvements could be made in the coffee shop. He must have been impressed by the recommendations because Mr. Ireland took over immediately and the name was changed to Ireland's.

After Mr. Ireland assumed management of the coffee shop it was much improved. In fact, so many people went there that, in 1936, Lloyd agreed to expand and include more parking in the back, thereby eliminating part of the driving range. Again, in 1948, Lloyd wanted to clear away more of the driving range; this time to build apartments.

Views of Lloyd's Golf Course. Benson High School in background (left). Sullivan's Gulch fairway (right)

In 1928 he purchased a large tract of land in East Portland from Holladay Addition to Sullivan's Gulch. His original plan for this land was to build new municipal buildings for the City of Portland.

Although the plan was never developed, on one section just south of the gulch, he built Lloyd's Golf Course and Country Club in 1932.

This deluxe, exclusively male club, was equipped with a sauna, tennis courts and a small coffee shop. The coffee shop was, for the first two years, run by a Mr. Parsons. However, Parsons left when it was determined that his management was losing money.

Lloyd consulted a restaurateur named Elston Ireland

Three years later, just as these plans were taking off, the government intervened and took over Sullivan's Gulch to turn it into the Banfield Expressway. Lloyd received generous compensation for the loss of his land and Ireland's restaurant, now fully expanded, remained under Mr. Ireland's management until he retired in 1974.

Far West Services leased the building from the Lloyd Corporation, remodeled the interior, creating an English inn atmosphere, and changed the restaurant's name to Sweet Tibbie Dunbar after a poem by Robert Burns.

Moorman, Soentpiet and Richen are students at Beaumont Middie School.

RALPH LLOYD'S RISE FROM COLLEGE TO COUNTRY CLUB!

Answer: Concerned about damage because of high winds, Lloyd eliminated golfing and the driving range.

Police Sunshine Division: Playing Santa year-round since 1923

December 5, 1984

Sgt. Mike Salmon, Sunshine Division Commander. When did he begin this one-of-a-kind job? (Answer below article.)

Bringing a brighter Christmas to less fortunate Portland-area families is the goal of the 62-year-old Portland Police Bureau Sunshine Division. The origin of this unique organization dates back to 1922 when, just before Christmas, a devastating fire swept through the home of an Albina district family.

A beat patrolman, whose name has been lost to time, heard about the family's plight and decided to lend a helping hand by taking up a collection among his fellow officers.

One of the officers, who was touched by his fellow patrolman's good intentions, related the story to a member of a local group called The Hoot Owls. A civic-minded club of sorts, The Hoot Owls were comprised of talented Portlanders who aired a weekly radio program over the newest station in town, KGW.

Hoot Owls in the midst of harmony and hijinks for KGW Radio with Charles F. Berg, prominent Broadway clothier, in the center.

Prominent businessmen such as clothier Charles F. Berg and professional entertainer Mel Blanc, a native Portlander, headed up the cast.

The tale of the Albina family and the local cop was told by the Owls on their next evening's show. At the conclusion of the program, the group members descended from the station's studios in the Jackson Tower to the lobby where they were mobbed by a multitude of listeners bearing gifts and donations.

Needless to say, everyone was overwhelmed by the magnitude of the response to this call for contributions and a down-on-their luck family had a much happier holiday season.

Over the following months the idea of a police-sponsored organization to benefit needy families took hold. The next Christmas, 1923, the Portland Police Bureau sponsored its first official drive to collect food and deliver it to families in the Portland area.

The Hoot Owls continued their on-air support and Captain Carrol Tichenor (who had been appointed commander of the division that first Christmas) began devoting full time to the task two years later.

The division quickly gained strong community support. In 1932, one of the worst Depression years, more than 3,000 families received food baskets and other necessities.

Of the many ways that the Division has been benefited over the years, boxing matches through the 1930s and '40s played a prominent part. More well-known is "Can Day," initiated in 1939 by the Paramount Theater and subsequently adopted by other local theaters. A can of food bought the price of admission.

The can donation and the sports connection survive to this day on behalf of the Sunshine Division. Both the Portland Trail Blazers and Winterhawks presently sponsor "Can Days."

For the past seven years the Sunshine Division has been headed by Sergeant Mike Salmon. Commander Salmon is the eighth Portland police officer to hold the post since Captain Tichenor took up the challenge in 1923. He did a 12-year tour of regular duty before joining the special division in 1977.

Originally Sunshine was dispensed from the second floor of the police bureau's old Eastside precinct at SE 7th and Alder. But, with the onset of the Depression, the division's needs multiplied and it moved to a warehouse at 38 NE Russell which was home for more than 40 years.

Today, Mike and his full-time staff of four "civilians" operate from a 30,000-square-foot warehouse and office located at 687 N. Thompson just east of Interstate. The division relocated to this new facility in 1974, having once again outgrown its quarters.

Although many people don't realize it, the Sunshine Division operates five days a week, 12 months a year. And, like the city bureau that backs it, the division responds rapidly. Food baskets, bedding, clothing, even furniture are kept on hand at all times. When a call comes in, a Sunshine employee or volunteer delivers the requested items no later than the next day. No government agency or other organization is prepared to act so swiftly.

During the holiday season the division's tradition of giving shifts into high gear. Approximately 2,200 food boxes are packed for families in the local delivery area and up to 1,000 for delivery by other cooperating police agencies in outlying communities.

An average of 60 to 70 police reserve volunteers and their families help with preparations every day during the week and a half prior to Christmas. Sixty trucks, driven by Teamsters on their own time, deliver the boxes with the help of Boy Scouts who accompany them and take the much-appreciated donations right to the family's doorstep.

When you pass those Sunshine barrels set up at supermarkets throughout the Portland area, put a food donation inside. If you have something bigger call the Sunshine Division at 287-1294. They'll be glad to come and pick it up. You'll bring a ray of Sunshine into someone's life.

Answer: Salmon did a 12-year tour of regular police duty before taking over the Sunshine Division in 1977.

8. ON A BLOOMIN' SOAPBOX

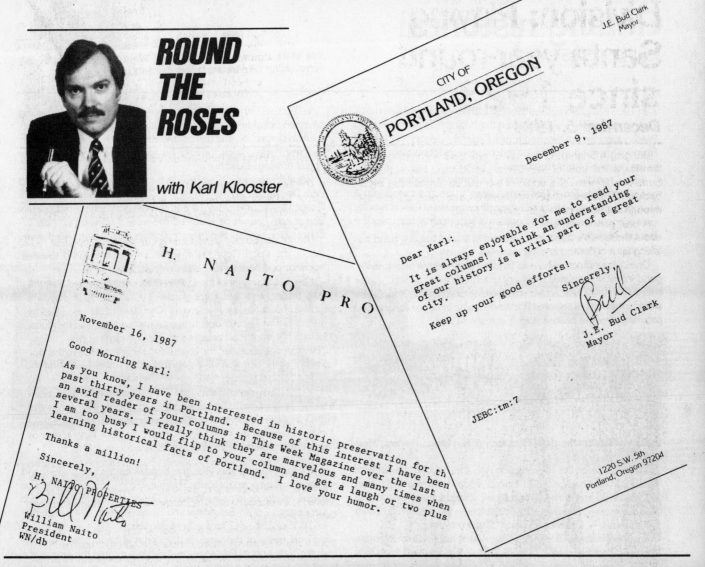

ROUND THE ROSES

with Karl Klooster

J.E. Bud Clark
Mayor

CITY OF
PORTLAND, OREGON

December 9, 1987

Dear Karl:

It is always enjoyable for me to read your
great columns! I think an understanding
of our history is a vital part of a great
city.

Keep up your good efforts!

Sincerely,

Bud

J.E. Bud Clark
Mayor

JEBC:tm:7

1220 S.W. 5th
Portland, Oregon 97204

H. NAITO PRO

November 16, 1987

Good Morning Karl:

As you know, I have been interested in historic preservation for th
past thirty years in Portland. Because of this interest I have been
an avid reader of your columns in This Week Magazine over the last
several years. I really think they are marvelous and many times when
I am too busy I would flip to your column and get a laugh or two plus
learning historical facts of Portland. I love your humor.

Thanks a million!

Sincerely,

H. NAITO PROPERTIES

Bill Naito

William Naito
President
WN/db

In Lownsdale Square

Those of us in a position to make our voices heard, if only on a local level, constantly harangue at those who are in a position to right wrongs. Whenever possible, we wave warning flags in the hope of nipping injustice in the bud. Now and then, the effort pays off. A worthy cause prevails and it makes up for all the failures and disappointments.

Editorially speaking, my beat is history - preservation, place-names, the past as it relates to a present context. Mostly, I combat complacency — an all-too-often ambivalent attitude towards galloping greed. If a building, a bridge, a statue, a school or other structure with landmark potential is threatened, you'll see me speak up. If significant architectural changes are planned for public places, I want to make certain they're the best that they can be.

Some of the stories in this chapter have had positive outcomes. One remains to be resolved. Thanks to Yamhill Marketplace developer Bob Stoll and other investors, the Police Bureau Building has been handsomely remodeled for office use. The "Miracle on Morrison," on the other hand, has yet to happen. Now dubbed Pioneer Place, downtown's largest ever single project has been pared down but its striking glass pavillion will make this a true show "place" once completed.

Given a three and one-half year perspective, Pioneer Courthouse Square seems to be fulfilling its promise as a public space and outdoor entertainment place. Young people with purple hair may make it their hangout but that's no problem. In fact, it adds color to the collage. The loss is the untimely death of the square's designer, architect Will Martin, killed while piloting his vintage plane in the Grand Canyon.

Preservation Week: Getting historical

May 7, 1986

The Vista House on Crown Point. What was the controversy surrounding it? (Answer below cartoon.)

In 1966 Congress passed the National Historic Preservation Act. This landmark legislation created the National Trust for Historic Preservation and authorized a new Federal Advisory Council on Historic Preservation to screen federal projects for possible threats to the nation's historic resources.

To underwrite these programs, Congress authorized income generated from federal offshore leases to be channeled into a Historic Preservation Fund. These actions provided the catalyst for unprecedented activity in restoration of historic structures over the last two decades.

In Portland the league has been instrumental in placing nineteen buildings under conservation easement, which protects them in perpetuity, and has contributed to such important sites as the New Market Block, the Elks Temple, Charles F. Berg's and the Postal (Failing) Building.

Local Preservation Week events include the Ankeny Arcade and Park Dedication on May 11 at 11:30 a.m., the annual Columbia Gorge Day Tour on May 12 and the Oregon School of Design's Beaux Arts Ball which wraps up the week's activities on May 17. Other tours, exhibits and presentations make an event-filled week.

Preserved landmarks (left) Princeton (Elks) Bldg., (center) New Market Theater, (right) Charles F. Berg's.

At the time of the Preservation Act, the National Register of Historic Places had only 800 listings. Today there are more than 40,000, including some 1,200 historic districts. Establishment of Portland's two downtown historic districts — Skidmore/Old Town and Yamhill — was a direct result of this movement.

National Historic Preservation Week was instituted to celebrate the heritage embodied in these buildings. It takes place from May 10-18. Statewide activities are scheduled under the sponsorship of the Junior League of Portland and the Historic Preservation League of Oregon in conjunction with the National Trust.

The Historic Preservation League is Oregon's watchdog organization in the ongoing battle to prevent indiscriminate destruction of historically significant structures. The pursuit of that goal has taken Preservation League Executive Director Eric Elsmann from Astoria's John Jacob Astor Hotel to Crater Lake Lodge, from the Vista House at Crown Point to the Pittock Estate's Gate Lodge.

For the first time this year, the Kendall Estate at S.E. 39th and Taggart will be open for tours. This handsome 1889 Romanesque revival residence is now owned by Del and Linda Pearson. Tour Times are 12-5 on Saturdays and Sundays, May 10-11 and May 17-18. Call 234-1242 for further information.

Focal event of the week is the Portland Landmark Commission's 10th Annual Preservation Awards honoring the past year's outstanding local achievements in renovation and restoration. This year's theme, "Back to the Future," features a DeLorean Time Machine. A new Light Rail car will also be on display at the Centennial (Gevurtz) Building, 210 S.W. Morrison, where the event takes place on May 15 starting at 7:30.

The list of luminaries includes Senator Bob Packwood, National Preservation Action President Nellie Longsworth, Mayor Clark and Commissioner Strachan. Call the Planning Bureau, 796-7700, for details.

IF YOU GO **BACK** TO THE FUTURE,

HISTORIC PRESERVATION WEEK ~ MAY 10-18

WILL YOU COME **FORWARD** TO THE PAST?

Klooster '86

Answer: Commissioner Rufus Holman fired County Roadsmaster John Yeon for spending $100,000 to build it when $12,000 was budgeted.

Historic Preservation Week: May 9-16

May 6, 1987

Crater Lake Lodge. What has become of the Historic Preservation League's efforts to prevent its destruction? (Answer below cartoon.)

It's that time of year again when, across the country, our architectural heritage holds the spotlight. In cities large and small, preservation groups plan and coordinate week-long programs to promote awareness and appreciation of structures that represent the best surviving examples of their types.

Accumulatively, they chronicle the history of a community and a culture. Separately, they are unique period pieces—often striking, sometimes spectacular. Commercial, residential and industrial edifices, bridges and fountains, even entire districts, have found their way onto landmark lists owing to the efforts of locally based organizations.

The Hollywood Theatre, 1926, before the big sign

In the Beaver State, the most active force in this ongoing endeavor is the Historic Preservation League of Oregon. During this year's Preservation Week, the HPLO has put together a full and exciting calendar of events.

The Hollywood District takes center stage for opening-day activities in Portland. Sparked by the district's longtime promotional group, the Hollywood Boosters, merchants are gearing up for the celebration on Saturday, May 9. Attired in period apparel,

they will be lining the sidewalks with sale merchandise.

That evening, from 7:45-10 p.m., the Hollywood Theater will host the week's premier event. Mayor Bud Clark will issue an official proclamation and unveil a plaque signifying historic registry for the majestic old movie palace. Following the ceremonies, there will be a showing of *The General* starring Buster Keaton, a classic silent film released in 1926—the same year the Hollywood opened.

Opening-night attendees are encouraged to come dressed as their favorite movie stars."Best Costume" will win two nights at Rippling River Resort. Admission is $5 per person, popcorn and soft drink included. A vintage film series will then run at the Hollywood throughout the week.

MAX is the connecting link for Preservation Week in the Portland area. Gresham, its eastern terminus, is going all out to emphasize the week. The town has chosen "Tracks of History" as its celebration theme focusing on the history of older communities served by the light-rail system.

The week's second showcase event is the Portland Landmarks Commission's 11th annual Preservation Awards Ceremony. The public is invited to Montgomery Park (the former Montgomery Ward Store at Northwest 24th Avenue and Vaughn Street) at 7:30 p.m. on Thursday, May 14, when the Commission will announce those buildings singled out for recognition of excellence in restoration and renovation during the past year.

Guided tours and open houses are being held throughout the week. In addition, brochures have been prepared for self-guided walking tours of four areas—Yamhill, Skidmore/ Old Town, Terra Cotta (downtown) and the Hollywood District.

Shows and exhibits, displays and dinners, all with historic themes, will be happening in the Willamette Valley, along the coast and in the southern and eastern extremities of the state. Albany, Ashland, Astoria, Aurora, Baker, Brooks, Brownsville, Eugene, Florence, Forest Grove, Gearhart, Government Camp, Independence, John Day, McMinnville, Newburg, Oakland, Oregon City, Salem, Seaside and the Dalles have events on tap.

The list of contributors, sponsors and cooperating organizations is long and laudable. But, the lion's share of credit should go to the Historic Preservation League, its executive director Eric Eisemann and his staff, and, especially, the dedicated core of volunteers around the state. In many ways, this special week is a tribute to them.

Answer: Both houses of the Oregon State Legislature have unanimously passed a "memorial" to Congress recommending that the lodge be restored for the lodging and dining on its present site at the rim.

Preservation Week: Eastside emphasis

May 13, 1987

The WPA's stone fortress encompasses J.W. Hill Park atop Rocky Butte. What happened to the property deed? (Answer below cartoon.)

Over the years, East Portland has had to play second fiddle to its big brother west of the river. After being absorbed (merger is the more polite term) along with Albina in 1891, East Portland was no longer a municipal entity. The eastside's destiny was in great measure determined by westsiders. The former may have had the population but the latter had the money.

During this year's celebration of National Historic Preservation Week currently underway, the eastside is finally getting its due. The week's Opening Ceremonies were held on Saturday, May 9, at the historic Hollywood Theater in the heart of the shopping district that was once second only to downtown. Merchants along MAX from Hollywood to Gresham are taking part in the weeklong festivities.

To further emphasize the east-of-the-river connection, a photographic exhibit entitled "East Side Style" is on display at the Old Town headquarters of the Historic Preservation League of Oregon (26 N.W. Second Ave.). It features 50- to 100-year-old buildings located in central southeast neighborhoods.

Grand Avenue, looking north, early 1930s.

Primary credit for the show, scheduled to run through July, goes to the Central Eastside Preservation Project. This grassroots group, which focuses its efforts on documenting and protecting the area's rich architectural heritage, is funded by a Metro Arts Commission Grant with additional support from the Hawthorne Boulevard Business Association.

Public advocacy of eastside historic preservation is not limited to the close-in core, however. Recently joining the ranks of citizen-involvement groups is the Rocky Butte Preservation Society. This organization, which just began gearing up within the last six months, is vitally and vocally concerned about the future of the promontory that affords one of Portland's most sweeping and spectacular panoramas.

The Hill family owned the entire 1,000-acre volcanic vent until 1935 when they donated its highest point to Multnomah County as a park in honor of patriarch Joseph Wood Hill. The Hill estate still owns the steep slopes and slighly lower bluff surrounding the stone fortress at the summit for which the Butte is famous.

It is that "lower bluff" just south of the rock-ringed top which has prompted area residents to action. Local developer Carlo Ottoboni has an option on the parcel and plans to build nine homes there. The Society is concerned about what future individual owners might do to their "private" property.

From the standpoint of public interest, Rocky Butte has special protections not applicable to many other areas. It is designated as an Area of Significant Environmental Concern. Any proposed structures are subject to public design review and must comply with restrictions on height, colors and changes in the natural surroundings.

The ideal scenario would be outright public purchase of the hillside property as a buffer zone. Unfortunately, the city of Portland is in no position to allocate such an expenditure. So, the society sees its immediate role as that of tenacious watchdog working to ensure maximum protection through the SEC review process.

Within the limits of governmental impartiality, the city of Portland is proving to be a laudable friend to Rocky Butte and, thus, to the Society. After Multnomah County approved deeding Joseph W. Hill Park over to the city last year, Commissioner Mike Lindberg made a personal commitment to upgrading the facilities in recognition of their importance as a major regional attraction.

Lindberg quickly put the Parks Department and Street Maintenance Bureau to work. Marked improvements in general appearance of the park and roadway condition are already evident.

To learn more about the Rocky Butte Preservation Society's efforts and objectives, attend their Preservation Week presentation on Saturday, May 16, 10 a.m. on the second floor of the Portland Building. For more information call Ken Benshoof (254-4467) or Mary Goldberg (255-0179).

EAST SIDE STYLE

1932 Packard Deluxe Eight Victoria Conv.

Wilbur Reid Residence - California Bungalow Style

klooster '87

Answer: After Multnomah County decided to give the park to the city of Portland in 1986, they were unable to locate the original deed. It still hasn't been found.

Awards Night: Preservation Week

May 27, 1987

The Dekum, S.W. 3rd and Washington. What did original owner Frank Dekum insist on in its construction? (Answer below cartoon.)

You were cordially invited to the 11th Annual Preservation Awards Fete of the Portland Historical Landmarks Commission at Montgomery Park on May 14. If you didn't attend, you should have. This was the night when the best of the best were honored. It's a highlight of Historic Preservation Week.

The setting was, fittingly, one of the 10 award winners. It was Montgomery Park, the former Montgomery Ward building, another restoration triumph for those unparalleled champions of local preservation—Bill and Sam Naito.

Prior to the presentation, the winners were known only to a few insiders—Landmarks Commission members, key Portland Development Commission staffers and, so they would be certain to attend, the property owners, themselves. Anyone leaking prior information to the press would be labeled a preservation pariah.

This writer wasn't about to violate an 11-year-old tradition. Better to wait for the public moment elaborately orchestrated by Landmarks Commission Chairwoman Susan Seyl with the assistance of Mayor Bud Clark.

Seyl arrived at the podium in a dump bin, propelled by attendants on roller skates. That was the way workers got around on the upper floors of "Monkey Ward's" nine-story, 800,000 square-foot warehouse. Clark, sporting a bright-red polo shirt and a giant, red rose, put the city's blessing on the event.

Commissioner Earl Blumenauer, whose office oversees the Planning Bureau, lauded the professionalism and tenacity of preservationists in pursuing their purposes before the City Council. Then, the audience was regaled with a slide-show presentation of the best since 1977.

But enough of the preliminaries. Eight Certificates of Merit, one plaque (the Commission's highest honor), and a special recognition award comprised the main event. On the west side, the Nicholas-Lang Residence, 1884, a three-story, Portland Heights "American Vernacular" house; The Town Club, 1931, a Romanesque villa at the top of Southwest Salmon, for its new elevator tower addition; and the Police Block, 1912, at Second and Oak, remodeled for offices, received certificates.

The First Presbyterian Church, 1887, won for ongoing, fine maintenance and upgrading of its steeple. The Chinese Consolidated Benevolent Association and the Portland Development Commission were singled out for—the new Chinatown Gate.

As expected, the Naito Brothers' Montgomery Park project was another winner. Credit goes to SERA Associates for the spectacular atrium that is now the focal point of Ward's 1920 vintage, former West Coast catalog distribution center.

H. Naito Properties scored a special coup for The Dekum Building at Southwest Third and Washington. The recent renovation of the seven-story, atrium lobby of this 1892 Richardson Romanesque classic and the faithful retention of its overall original character captured the Landmark Commission's coveted plaque.

Osborn Hotel, S.E. 2nd & Ash.

East of the river, the Second Empire-style, Osborn Hotel at Southeast Grand and Ash, 1890, was recognized for its handsome remodeling. And, the Ladd's Addition Conservation District Advisory Council also came in for certificate commendation owing to their dedication in protecting Portland's first planned neighborhood.

The one-of-a-kind "Nellie" Award finished up the evening's festivities. It was presented to Nellie Longsworth, president of Preservation Action, a Washington D.C., based lobbying group, in recognition of her work since 1975.

Answer: Dekum demanded that all Oregon materials be used including Siskiyou sandstone and bricks from a Newburg kiln.

Old Town: On its last legs

January 23, 1985

Billboards had replaced buildings at the southwest corner of S.W. Front and Morrison in 1930. Which outdoor advertising company owned them and where did it start? (Answers below cartoon.)

Fate placed the Skidmore Fountain at the epicenter of Portland's original central district. If other factions had won out in 1883 and the pharmacist's fountain had been situated farther uptown, preservation of the historic area in which we take so much pride today might never have come about.

By the mid-1880s Portland had already outgrown its roots. The First and Ankeny intersection was surrounded by

automobile brought with it the greatest demands. From the late 1920s onward, older buildings were relentlessly razed.

The collonades of ironfront arches along Front Street went by the wayside in the late '30s and early '40s. By 1949, everything on Front from the Steel Bridge south to Burnside had been leveled to make way for the new riverfront drive.

Developers chipped away at buildings and blocks along First and Second avenues over the next 20 years, leaving

Front Ave. looking north to Burnside Bridge, 1932 (left). Front Ave. north to Steel Bridge, 1949 (right)

backwater businesses still doing well but destined for a downhill skid which beset the area for the next eight decades.

Construction of the finest ironfront and terracotta facades reached its zenith in 1889. By then, more than 200 ironclad edifices occupied the blocks bounded by Yamhill and Glisan, First and Third.

Buildings from the 1860s and '70s, including a number of survivors of the great fire of 1873, hung on until the 1930s and '40s. But, as the downtown's center of activity moved farther from its original core, the old district deteriorated through neglect.

An era of progress and expediency called for change. Modernization was the byword and the advent of the

gaps and gaping holes, empty lots and parking pavement. In the developers' defense, many of the ancient denizens were beyond repair but many others were sacrificed senselessly.

Only a few dozen pre-Twentieth Century stalwarts remained in the early 1960s when the first embryonic stirrings of revitalization began. Over the next decade a few more were lost but the trend was slowly changing and the Skidmore Fountain area was the focal point for this change.

By the early 1970s, the tide had turned and the new watchword was restoration appended with "tax credits." At the forefront of the new wave, as one of its earliest and most avid advocates, one name stood head and shoulders above the rest. That name was and is — Naito.

Answer: Foster and Kleiser, now the largest outdoor advertising firm in America, was founded in Portland in 1901.

Old Town: The new look is Naitoesque

January 30, 1985

Bill Naito with an 1890 map of Portland in his office. What did he do during W.W.II? Where did he attend college? (Answer below cartoon.)

By 1957, the district we now call "Old Town" had been almost totally abandoned by mainstream business interests. But Hide Naito and his sons, Bill and Sam, recognizing opportunity where others saw only further decline, bought their first building in the area that year—the Fleischner-Mayer Block at N.W. First and Davis.

Portland's original central core represented much more than a business investment for this enterprising family, however. It was a commitment to their community.

stake in Old Town's future. The Bickel and Skidmore blocks were bought in the late '70s and the Erickson Hotel and Hirsch-Weis building, now the headquarters of Norcrest China Co., came in 1981.

In recent years, Bill Naito has assumed the role of family spokesman and has emerged as Old Town's most avid promoter. Respected for other successful ventures such as The Galleria and McCormick Pier, Bill's innovative ideas are given careful consideration by other civic leaders.

Naito properties (lft. to rt.) The Hirsch-Weis (White Stag) building, Fleischner-Mayer (Butterfly) building. The Bickel Block and Import Plaza. The Norton House and the

Norcrest China Co., the glassware importing firm that was begun as H. Naito & Co. in 1938, had prospered despite its discontinuation during World War II when the family "evacuated" to Salt Lake City to avoid the deplorable Executive Order 9066 under which most Japanese-Americans were detained throughout the war.

With their company as the foundation, the Naito family began to build a real estate empire. Bill Naito places 1963, when they bought the Globe Hotel and opened Import Plaza, as the pivotal year. Then, in rapid succession, over the next decade, acquisition of the Foster Hotel, the Merchant Block, Norton House, Shoreline, Phillips and Pomona hotels followed. The Dekum Building was a significant south-of-Burnside purchase.

By the early 1970s, the Naito family had a substantial

Persistence and patience are also a part of Bill's considerable repertoire. In the early '70s he and some associates proposed a tourist-attracting trolley system for Old Town. Unable to gather enough interest, he waited.

When the Light Rail Plan became a reality, Bill bought four 100-year-old Brill trolley cars in Oporto, Portugal. The cars, identical to those used on Portland's old lines, are stored at the Trolley Park in Banks, Oregon, awaiting opening of the Light Rail. The plan is to run them during off hours on a downtown-to-Lloyd Center loop.

Portland owes a great deal to this family and we can be thankful to have the energy and enthusiasm of Bill Naito working daily on deals that are uncanny combinations of business acumen and civic betterment.

WHY AM I SO INTERESTED IN **RESTORING** OLD TOWN?

AN OLD JAPANESE PROVERB SAYS "HE WHO PRESERVES TRADITION WILL LIVE **LONG** AND **PROSPER!**"

JUST ASK MY DAD. HE'S **NINETY-FOUR** AND WE'RE STILL WORKING FOR HIM!

Klooster '85

Answers: Naito joined the U.S. Army Nisei (Japanese-American) 442nd Division and became a translator, Reed College.

Old Town: The Police Bureau: Building — Part I

October 24, 1984

The imposing Police Bureau building front facade. What is required to prevent its being torn down or altered? (Answer below cartoon).

Since this column is devoted to telling tales about those thrilling days of yesteryear, only occasionally does the opportunity arise to present the present.

Over the last three weeks, the story of Portland's police agency, from 1851 forward, has unfolded in this space. For 70 of those years, one building was the focal point of the bureau's activities.

That building, at S.W. 2nd and Oak, was completed in 1913: the year the form of Portland's municipal government was changed to the commission system; the year the name of the Metropolitan Police Force was changed to the Police Bureau.

Architect George "Bing" Sheldon and his SERA Associates were commissioned by the city to analyze the buildings (there are three) on the block and make recommendations. SERA found the 1913 building to be structurally sound but badly in need of repair.

The adjacent quarter block to the west, built in 1944, is, they concluded, hardly worth saving. But the gray cement half block on the north, although shoddy, is solid as a rock. It was built to accommodate the addition of up to six more stores.

SERA has suggested renovation of the original bureau building for offices and ground-floor retail with conversion

The Police Bureau building, second on the site, completed in 1913.

The north addition circa 1955.

Just over a year ago, the imposing, four-story brick building and the glum, gray structures clinging to its flanks saw their last roll call and booked their last suspect. Giving way to the gleaming new gem called the Justice Center, the block suddenly became something of a white elephant.

Althought the For Sale signs went up before the doors closed, this is no ordinary piece of property ready for a quick sale. Police headquarters is a link to the past, a part of Old Town, and the eventual fate of the block will have a significant impact on the surrounding area.

of the remaining three-quarter block to city-owned parking. Anyone who has tried to park in the vicinity on a Friday night would agree. But Mayor Ivancie had a different idea.

Reasoning that selling this choice site to the highest bidder would generate a nice chunk of change, he proposed that the profits be earmarked for the Performing Arts Center. Preservationists weere caught in a bit of a dilemma: How to protect the 1913 building from the very real possibility of demolition while agreeing with the critical need of additional funding for the Paramount's transformation. (Continued · Pg. 213).

MAYOR IVANCIE, WHY DID THE CITY BUILD SUCH AN **ATROCIOUS** ADDITION TO POLICE HEADQUARTERS?

IN THE FIFTIES THE PHILOSOPHY WAS "**FORM** FOLLOWS FUNCTION"

SO, HOW ELSE WOULD **YOU** DESIGN A COMBINATION JAILHOUSE AND PARKING GARAGE, CAPABLE OF FUTURE EXPANSION, ON A ROCK BOTTOM BUDGET?

PARKING ENTRANCE

klooster '84

Answer: Its owner (currently the City of Portland) must apply for historical landmark status.

Old Town: The Police Bureau Building - Part II

October 31, 1984

This 1944 building at S.W. 3rd and Oak will probably be replaced by parking. What city department and commissioner has responsibility for the police complex? (Answers below).

The Portland Police Bureau's headquarters, occupying the block bounded by S.W. 2nd, 3rd, Oak and Pine, has stood empty since January of this year.

Its three buildings, built in 1913, 1944 and 1955, were interconnected over the years with a labyrinth of doors and corridors in a losing battle to make the complex serve the bureau's growing needs.

Since the bureau's move to the new Justice Center,

economic expediency. In this instance, financial considerations are an especialy important element since profits from the sale will go to the Performing Arts Center.

However, it appears that a benevolent buyer has been found. After discussion with several prospects, Coldwell Banker's Jon Torgeson seems confident that a group of investors, headed by attorney Bob Stoll, is prepared to do the job right.

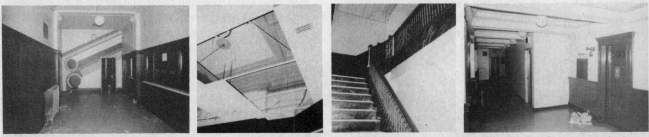

(lft.) Old and new in 1913 lobby. (lft. ctr.) Courtroom ceilings were concealed. (rt. ctr.) Original stairway (rt.) 2nd floor connecting hallway.

attention has focused on the fate of the 1913 building. Although just outside the boundary of the Skidmore-Old Town Historic District, this classic, five-story Italianate structure forms an important link between the Skidmore and Yamhill districts.

Parking lots, checkering the adjoining blocks, give mute testimony to the loss of dozens of late-19th- and early 20th century buildings, making this survivor all the more valuable.

Historic landmark status would have ensured the retention of its facade, but the city, wanting to keep their options open, did not make application. After all, a prospective buyer might be turned off by the prospect of having to renovate the old relic, rather than raze it.

As with so many Old Town buildings in the past, the fate of Police Headquarters has been left to the vagaries of

Stoll, developer of the Yamhill Marketplace, has indicated to this writer the group would retain the 1913 building with its original facade, and remodel the interior for offices. Remember that the buyers are under no restriction in regard to preservation.

The north side half-block structure would also be retained with the hope that preservation tax credits can be applied due to the contiguous nature of the complex. Stoll notes that a brick facade, compatible with the 1913 building, appears to be a logical way to go. The badly deteriorated southwest corner will probably be replaced with parking. No one will lament its loss.

If the Stoll group can reach agreement with the city early in November, a landmark, although as yet an unofficial one, will be saved and an estimable part of Old Town may yet be integrated into the Skidmore Historic District's boundaries.

Answers: The Department of Public Utilities, headed by Commssioner Margaret Strachan.

Old Town: The Chinese connection - Part I

September 5, 1984

Chinese shacks and vegetable gardens occupied this Salmon Street site until 1909. What has been there since? What did the Chinese think of Western farming? (Answers below cartoon).

The promise of riches lured thousands of adventurous Chinese across the sea to Mei Kwok (America) in the mid-19th Century. California's gold fields proved, however, to have as many pitfalls as rewards. Racial and cultural differences bred blind prejudice. More than a few "Chinamen" were forced to abandon the dream of Gum-san (the Gold Mountain).

Many returned home, a significant number settled in San Francisco and a few sought a more hospitable haven in K'o-li-chin (Oregon). In 1850 there were just two Chinese in the entire territory but within seven years enough had come to work the mines that they were considered a threat.

railroad construction, in the late 1860s.

Chinatown had grown to 500 by 1868 and to over 700 the next year. It began on Alder between 1st and 2nd, eventually expanding along 2nd from Taylor to Pine. Forty Chinese laundries dotted the city by 1872. Later that year the first Chinese theater opened.

In December 1872 a fire gutted two downtown blocks. Blamed on neglect in a Chinese laundry, this incident precipitated actions by the City's Common Council deliberately calculated to create hardships for the alien enclave.

Orientals were banned from work on publicly contracted projects. The Cubic Air Ordinance made it illegal to occupy

A Chinese funeral procession up Second, north from Alder, 1873. Exterior of Joss House, 1882. 2nd, south from Washington, 1890.

The Oregon Territorial Legislature passed a bill to tax all Chinese miners and the Constitutional Convention barred them from owning real estate or mining claims.

By 1860, Portland's 2,000 residents included 27 Chinese. The "Celestials" were vilified as corrupt, immoral — a species of low cunning.

Continuing condemnation intensified as Portland's Chinese community grew. The real controversy centered around cheap labor. A fair wage to a Chinaman was an insult to an American. Yet they worked hard for it, finding their way into the local iron, paper and textile industries, as well as

living quarters with less than 550 cubic feet of space per person.

On August 3, 1873, the most disastrous fire in Portland's history destroyed 20 square blocks. It was obviously arson aimed at Chinatown. The fire skirted that district, but the die was cast. Harassment, legal and otherwise, beset the Celestials.

In 1882, the National Exclusion Act prevented further immigration of Asians. But more than 100,000 Chinese were already in America, nearly 10,000 of them in Portland.

Answers: The Multnomah Athletic Club and Field. They found it very untidy and inefficient.

Old Town: The Chinese Connection—Part II

September 12, 1984

Five tunnels converge in the Elephant & Castle basement, 2nd & Washington, once the heart of Chinatown. What was their purpose? (Answer below cartoon.)

Portland's Chinese community was well established by the mid-1880s with more than 5,000 residents. That figure nearly doubled when seasonal workers, particularly in the fish canneries, returned for the winter.

The dream of returning home in financial triumph was shattered by those idle months when savings were eaten up simply surviving. Discrimination, abuse and exploitation were a way of life.

Anti-Chinese agitation reached its zenith in 1886. Driven from almost every town in the Northwest, the beleaguered Chinaman found his last stronghold in Portland. Despite diligent efforts throughout the decade to rid Oregon of the "Celestials," Chinatown survived.

Tong Wars were waged in Portland. Three secret societies, the Hip Sing, Suey Sing and Bow Leong, engaged in recurrent encounters involving control, honor or both.

In February 1917, early in his first administration, mayor George Baker called for a crackdown which brought more than two dozen arrests. Continued effort eventually put an end to this oppressive era.

The predicament of the Chinese, even those who were citizens, was caused by unjust legislation. They could neither vote nor own land. As a result, Chinatown was perpetuated as a concentrated insular community far longer than it would otherwise have been.

Suffrage was restored to Chinese-Americans in 1927 but

Chinatown gambling raid, 1922 (lft.). New Year's celebration, 1931 (ctr.). Bulletin board, 1937 (rt.).

Over the following few years, hundreds did depart, as much out of despair as coercion. This defection, coupled with natural deaths and no new immigration due to the exclusion laws, caused the Oriental population to dwindle dramatically by the turn of the century.

Although today's enlightened attitudes would abhor the actions of our 19th Century ancestors, they were not entirely without cause. Criminal Tongs were an early element in the community controlling prostitution, gambling and opium. And more than once violence broke out among competing hatchetmen, or "highbinders" as they came to be known.

Their numbers, though few, were a pervasive part of Chinatown. Except for the most flagrant activities, they were largely ignored by the police. From 1905 to 1920, a series of

it was not until 1946 that the property ownership law was at last repealed. With changing conditions came the slow disintegration of the original Chinatown. Its community diminished as families dispersed throughout the city, and Chinese businesses found the area north of Burnside more suited to their needs.

By the mid-1950s there were few reminders of the once-thriving district. The Golden Dragon Restaurant at Third and Stark is today the sole survivor of the community within a community that at one time had extended almost solidly along Second Street from Pine to Taylor. It was a community full of tradition, history and conflict. An important part of the story of Portland's Old Town.

Answer: Although they may have been used for shanghaiing, they were built to bring and store goods from the waterfront.

What's in a name: Sauvie or Sauvie's

October 23, 1985

Sauvie, Oregon's largest island. What secret did it hide from Oregon's earliest explorers? (Answer below cartoon.)

That pastoral and serene 15-mile-long, four-and-one-half-mile-wide stretch of land at the mouth of the Willamette is the subject of this week's discourse. To many it wouldn't matter what name it was given, and there have been several, so long as it's there—a nearby retreat from hectic city life.

Its earliest inhabitants, Chinook Indians, called the island Wapato or Wappato for the wild potatoes that once flourished along its marshy edges, attracting waterfowl by the millions. In their journals, on November 5, 1805, Lewis and Clark described the birds as "Emmensely (sic) numerous and their noise horrid."

The legendary explorers were not the first white men to set foot on Sauvie's shores, however. As early as 1792, British Naval Lieutenant William Broughton viewed Mt. Hood from the island and named it for Lord of the Admiralty Samuel Hood.

Also referred to at various junctures as Multnomah and Wyeth (for an early settler, Nathaniel Wyeth, who established a trading post, Fort William, on the island). The present name derives from a French-Canadian, Laurent Sauve.

Historical Society, is Sauvie's oldest surviving structure.

Later construction of levies held back all but the worse of the watery rampages, allowing full utilization of this prime bottom land. The island's narrow northern half consists of little lakes and lowlands which today are a haven for more than three dozen duck hunting clubs.

But what of the island's name? Sauvie's, with the possessive "s," was the one universally used during my childhood. That is how it was referred to in articles and notations through the 1950s. A book on the island's history by Omar Spencer is entitled *The Story of Sauvie's Island*.

How, then, did we end up with the decidedly dissonant clashing of two vowels. Sauvie Island rather than the euphonic and generally accepted Sauvie's Island? For the answer to that question I turned to Lewis McArthur, long-time member of the Oregon Geographic Names Board. Mr. McArthur cites two critical criteria.

One, the federal government's board of geographic names has a policy of eradicating possessives wherever possible and, two, the island never belonged to Sauve.

Sauvie settler Jonathan Moar's grave in 1915 (left). James Bybee's home, oldest on the island, built in 1858 and since restored.

Upon his retirement as a trapper with the Hudson's Bay Company in 1838, Sauve was given land on the island by John McLoughlin and operated a small dairy. His name subsequently became associated with the entire place.

Despite its susceptibility to flooding, early farmers worked fields throughout the southern portion of the island's 24,000 acres. Pioneer settlers such as James Bybee, Jonathan Moar and Edward Morgan left their mark from the 1850s onward. Bybee's home, now owned by the Oregon

Therefore, despite common usage or what to many sounds better, we have Sauvie. Of course, we also have John's Landing, Taylor's and Boone's Ferry roads, Gale's Creek, etc., all of which once belonged to the persons memorialized. But, the apostrophes are excluded.

So much for that little rondelet of research. It'll always be Sauvie's to me. Now let's move on to Multnomah, I mean, "Civic" Stadium. Civic, you say? Where is that? Pondunk, Peoria, Poughkeepsie? Oh. . . Portland.

Answer: The island's bulk divided the Willamette's outlet into two smaller streams, concealing the river's true size.

Pioneer Square: The sum of its parts

April 11, 1984

The square's focal point is its fountain. What is beneath it? How did the designer and the contractor fair on the project? (Answers below cartoon.)

At long last "The Square" is open. Dedication day, with its speeches and festivities, is history. Portland's Pioneer Courthouse Square is ready to become a part, hopefully a very meaningful part, of this metropolis.

The idea of a grand piazza dates back more than 11 years to October 1972, when the Portland Development Commission focused on this choice chunk of real estate as part of the Downtown Plan.

The story of the site was related in *Round the Roses,* Dec. 7, 1983. When the 80-year-old Portland Hotel was demolished in 1951 to make way for Meier & Frank's parking

funding of some $7 million. The value of scores of volunteers' time and company resource contributions is inestimable.

Until Friday, April 6, the average passerby could only gaze through a cyclone fence at the incomplete work. Pillars that support nothing. Even one that lies fallen. A broad expanse of brick. A small iron gate.

Pioneer Square's principal designer, local architect Will Martin, prevailed over 162 competitors from across the country. His concept is an individualistic expression that cannot escape controversy.

Will Martin's Pioneer Courthouse Square is a spatial experience inspired by European plazas.

garage, its loss was much lamented. To help create this legacy the department store giant gave $500,000, setting the tone for a community wide effort.

Downtown merchants expressed concern over the loss of parking. Multi-levels beneath the square were suggested. But funding sources barely met basic needs as original cost estimates doubled and completion took two years longer than projected.

Land and Water Conservation, Urban Mass Transit Authority, Housing and Urban Development grants, Portland Development Commission allocations and public donations (primarily brick sales) comprised the square's

There are few trees — little comforting coziness. This is *not* a park. It's a square meant to have, made to endure with brick, tile and bronze. And now that it's ours, what of this place?

Do its many intriguing elements combine to make a whole? Are they synergistic — more than their sum? When the purple-checkered fountain is flowing, when the deli is dishing up its delights and Tri-Met is dispensing its tickets, when the events and activities are underway, will the people be drawn to this square in the very heart of the city?

That's history yet to be written.

I BUILT THIS CHESS BOARD ON MY OWN TIME. THIS IS FOR PRIDE NOT WAGES!

I'VE REALLY BECOME ATTACHED TO THIS PLACE, WORKING ON IT, HARRY!

YEAH, EVEN THAT FUCHSIA FOUNTAIN GROWS ON YOU AFTER AWHILE!

HEY, NEW YORKERS DIDN'T LIKE THE STATUE OF LIBERTY WHEN IT FIRST ARRIVED!

Klooster '84

Answers: Tri-Met's downtown ticket offices. Both firms lost substantial sums during their four-year involvement.

Downtown: Miracle on Morrison Street

December 14, 1983

The Goodnough and Corbett buildings. Why will these relics be razed? (Answer below cartoon.)

The '70s saw considerable change in Portland's downtown core area as the city took aim at the revitalization of sagging sales.

The Galleria (1974), the new Nordstrom (1976), the transit mall (1977) and Frederick & Nelson (1978) all enlivened downtown and helped head off the flight of dollars to the suburbs.

As urban renewal and historical preservation, begun in the early 1960s, gained momentum, a master plan emerged in 1972, under the Goldschmidt Administration.

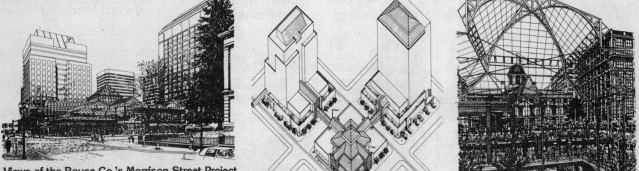

Views of the Rouse Co.'s Morrison Street Project

The Portland Development Commission adopted a Downtown Plan which called for enhancement of the retail core. The 1974 Urban Renewal Plan added impetus through eminent domain.

In 1978, attention focused on S.W. Fifth and Morrison. The so-called 100 percent corner. That intersection is considered to be the epicenter of downtown traffic activity where, in 1985, the Light Rail will cross the mall. It became the pivotal point of a three-block development concept presented by the Cadillac-Fairview conglomerate.

The Canadians' proposal was ultimately rejected, but the Morrison Street Project — the most ambitious civic plan ever undertaken (others had been conceived early in this century) — was not to be denied.

In August 1982, the call went out for new proposals. As Chris Kopca, the commissions's project director stated, "Only a dozen or so companies in the country could put this together for us."

Three contestants — The Rouse Co., Wright Runstad and the Williams/DeBartolo joint venture — submitted imaginative, thorough proposals, demanding a long and difficult selection process. The Rouse Company's inspired "pavillion" plan, with turn-of-the-century design touches, eventually emerged as the winner.

The three-block, 2.7-acre project encompasses retail, hotel and office components with 800-plus underground parking places.

Portlanders may call this the "Pavillion Project" when the multifaceted glass gem facing Fifth and Morrison begins to take shape. It will be a fitting successor to those vintage landmarks, the Corbett (1907) and Goodnough (1891) buildings.

Anchor retailers have yet to be determined but, whether a Saks, Neiman-Marcus or Magnin, it will be a wise retailer that comes to the same conclusion that Sigmund Frank did in 1898. Fifth and Morrison is where the action is going to be — again.

Answer: Each competing designer concluded it was not feasible to retain them.

River City: The Freeway Follies

October 5, 1983

Squatter's shantys in the early 1942. Where were they located? (Answer below cartoon.)

Oregon joined the freeway generation in 1955 when the Banfield was opened to serve Portland's rapidly expanding eastside suburbs. At the time, making your way out to 82nd via Sandy, Burnside or Powell was a stop-and-go ordeal.

On the Banfield you were there in no time except, of course, during rush hour. Fifties planners couldn't predict the extent of continued growth which, today, often results in the accursed commuter crawl.

To aid city access for North Portlanders and Vancouverites, as well as speed interstate travelers on their way, the "Minnesota" was completed in 1965. The "what?" OK. I'll begrudgingly admit that it's called I-5 North.

entire load, are lightly traveled these days.

Public tread met the pavement of the George P. Baldock Memorial Freeway in 1962. Politicking Portlanders could conduct capital city business in the morning and be back in time for lunch at Jerry's Gables or Dan & Louie's. Around the flanks of upper I-5 South have flourished Tigard and Tualatin. It was Oregon's big link in the Interstate.

When homeward-bound commuters head west, they travel into the sunset and *on* it. State Hwy. 26 wasn't always a freeway and isn't part of the Interstate system but, without the "Sunset," Beaverton and environs would be the staging area for an around-the-clock traffic jam. Even with it, tie-ups

I-5 North at the Portland Blvd. overpass, 5:15 PM Monday, Sept. 26, 1983. / Union Ave. and Portland Blvd. 5:25 PM

For some unknown reason, unlike its fellow freeways — Banfield, Baldock and Sunset — the nickname Minnesota (the street it eliminated) didn't stick.

Our first state-of-the-art artery, I-5 North, is up to six lanes wide, designed for safety and totally immobilized if an accident occurs. Shades of L.A. When the backup is long and prolonged, as it often is, the clever commuter heads for the nearest off ramp and takes North Interstate or Union Avenue. The two thoroughfares, which once carried the

still plague the upwardly mobile minions.

Finally finished last February, I-205 is the last link in the chain of the freeways round the Rose City. Now Portland has another thing in common with Salem and Eugene. You can drive by it and never see it.

But I-205 will alleviate some of the problems on I-5 and those infernal 18-wheelers can skirt around our edges at 70 all the way. The multi-ramped monument to motoring is complete.

ROSE CITY RADIO TIME IS **5:25**. NOW FOR AN UPDATE FROM PAT PROCTER IN THE **KGX** TRAFFIC COPTER!

HOW'S IT LOOK UP THERE, PAT? HAS **I-205** HAD ANY EFFECT ON **I-5** NORTH?

klooster '83

DEFINITELY, RANDY. NOW THE BACKUP IS ONLY **3** MILES INSTEAD OF **5**!

ℓ☆✲ @#⑧

Answer: Sullivan's Gulch at Grand Ave. The Banfield Freeway eliminated this hobo haven.

The convention center: A public proposal

March 26, 1986

Memorial Coliseum, dedicated in 1962, is the city's most ambitious public project to date. Was it built on public property? What might we call the over-the-freeway center? (Answers below cartoon.)

The Olmsted, Bennett, Bartholomew and Moses plans for central city development and improvement, introduced between 1904 and 1944, were recounted in this column during February. Each contained elements that could have given the city distinction. None were ever effectively implemented.

Today, we are faced with a vital decision that may mean the difference between dynamism and mediocrity for Portland in the 21st century — the building of a major convention center.

In mid-April the Regional Committee on Convention, Trade and Spectator Facilities will select a site from among only four currently being considered. This decision won't guarantee that

slope is owned by the state and the north side was deeded to the city by the Lloyd Corporation in 1958. Thank you, Lloyd Corporation.

Although such a structure would cost more than those already proposed, the savings on land cost would more than make up the difference. And the location is unique. Situated over the gulch, it would link the north and south halves of the eastside core area and provide the catalyst for growth on the under-developed south side.

The site is closer to downtown than any other proposed — right in the heart of the central city plan. It has direct airport access and is just four blocks from light rail. With the ability to build part of the

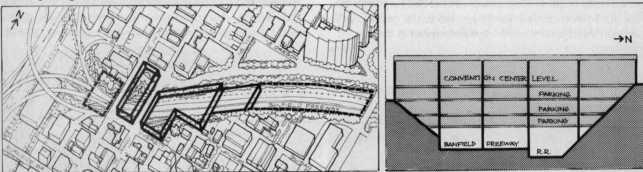

Location of the proposed "over the freeway" convention center (left). Schematic section showing parking levels (right).

one of the four proposed sites — Memorial Coliseum, Holladay/Union, Union Station, or South Waterfront — will be developed. But it's a significant step in that direction.

As critical observers have pointed out, "Each proposal has its problems." And, in each instance, private property must be purchased at substantial cost. Furthermore, the property will then be removed from the tax rolls. Most importantly, none of the proposals have physical uniqueness either in site or basic design. In other words, they don't stand out.

An alternative and, until now, unpublicized proposal from Portland architect Robert Mickelson, AIA, does stand out. Instead of building on a sprawling 10-block site, Mickelson, 52, a former associate partner with Zimmer Gunsul Frasca who is currently project architect on the BPA building, suggests spanning the convention center and parking facility over a freeway. On public land. Zero acquisition cost.

Sound intriguing? Wondering where he has in mind? Try Sullivan's Gulch from the Union Avenue viaduct east. The south

facility below grade, Mickelson envisions a low-profile configuration on varying levels to avoid the monolithic look. And the concept is expandable all the way up to 12th Avenue. There would even be room for an over-the-freeway domed stadium. Lots of parking directly underneath the action. You heard it here first.

But that's getting way ahead of present reality. Who would design this one-of-a-kind facility? I say, let them compete. Robert Ridgely, Bud Clark, Dennis Buchanan, and Lloyd Anderson, who spearhead the Regional Committee, are eminently capable of putting together an excellent competition.

Whether or not this over-the-freeway idea is considered, a convention center with character could be the catalyst whereby major hotel chains would make commitments to Pioneer Place, the KOIN-TV Center and the proposed Northwest Natural Gas hotel site. Regardless of how the decision goes in April, Robert Mickelson has given the City Hall some of that public input they asked for on this important issue.

Answers: The coliseum was built on private property purchased with public monies. Sullivan Center is my name contribution. Yours?

Rose Buds: Past, present and future

May 14, 1986

Doc Harry Lane, mayor of Portland (1905-1909). What did he do after his term of office? (Answer below cartoon.)

In 1904, Dr. Harry Lane became Portland's first populist mayor. This mild mannered physician rose to the office out of concern for the people and contempt for the corrupt system that was ruling his city. Doc Lane was elected by his eastside constituency. Eighty percent of the population was on the eastside. Eighty percent of the wealth was on the westside.

When Lane took office, plans for the Lewis & Clark Exposition were in place. Despite the fact that it was the most successful event ever held in the Pacific Northwest, he was denied access to the power circles. Still he fought for the public interest throughout his two terms occasionally winning small battles but always stalemated in the war.

with both inherited and new problems that affect Portland's present and future. But he is only one of five voices on a council. He, like his predecessors since 1913, is not a chief executive but rather the chairman of a committee.

Despite the often complicated position of compromise that the mayor must contend with, he is still expected to provide leadership and direction. Bud Clark has already shown his ability to act as the city's spokesman in the nationwide battle for bucks. Here is a man who obviously wants to make something happen in Portland. But, without broad-based support, his effectiveness will be diminished.

Clark may not be the consummate politician or a seasoned, back room favor swapper. He may, in fact, have

(left) George L. Baker, 1917-1932, (center) Dorothy McCullough Lee, 1948-1952, (right) John E. "Bud" Clark, incumbent.

Another populist mayor, George L. Baker, rose from a humble childhood in The Dalles to become a successful theater owner and councilman before taking the top post. "Big" George played the power game while still serving the city. His popularity earned him an unprecedented four terms (1917-1932) at the helm of City Hall.

Portland's first female mayor, Dorothy McCullough Lee, was elected in 1948. Even though she had been an attorney, pro tem judge, commissioner and was probably the most qualified person ever to hold the office, the mid-century male chauvinist mentality effectively stymied her efforts to stimulate growth. Lee did, however, clean up corruption, firing the chief of police in the process.

Today, we have the most recent "Bud" in this rose bush of revels — John Elwood Clark. Currently, Clark must deal

entered the office as an idealist, but that is not all bad and certainly not without precedent in this city that so many say sets its own style.

Speaking idealistically, we may not be able to control what goes on across the country, but we do have the capability to control our own destiny. And, if we're talking trickle down, as goes Portland so goes Oregon. With the imminent withdrawal of federal funds, the local fountain better begin flowing soon.

If public and private interests can set aside their own myoptic agendas, if the media can be convinced to substitute support for cynicism, it can happen. Let Bud bloom and help him tend our still green garden. We'll put bouquets on our tables and, not incidentally, plant the seed for future "Buds" to blossom.

Answer: Lane was elected Oregon's junior senator in 1913 serving until his death in 1917.

Bud Clark: Burned by Brokaw

October 1, 1986

Mildred and Bud on a happier occasion. How many other women have served on the city council? (Answer below cartoon.)

Members of the local advertising/communications community look forward to the Portland Advertising Federation's annual kickoff meeting. A major industry figure is featured highlighting the club's programs for the coming — September to June — year. What does this have to do with history? Well, this week's column is a commentary on yesterday's news. And, as every good journalist knows, yesterday's news is ancient history.

On Thursday, Sept. 18, Tom Brokaw, 47-year-old anchor of the NBC "Nightly News," was the big draw for the PAF's 1986-87 season opener. Brokaw's appearance was hyped by local broadcast and print media. Anticipated turnout was so great that the location from the club's regular meeting rooms at the Portland Center Red Lion to the ballroom of Conrad cum Barron's local

as he is with a Goose Hollow regular. Little did he know, though some say he should have suspected, that the nationally known newsreader sharing his hospitable table would compromise the confidence. Putting it bluntly, Bud was burned.

To publicly parrot such a tongue-in-cheek quip suggests, at the very least, insensitivity. It's disappointing to think that a man of such stature could so disregard the people and place where he was being treated as an honored guest. Tom Brokaw took advantage of a mild indiscretion of the moment for the sake of levity at someone else's expense.

The narrowminded will undoubtedly make the most of an otherwise innocuous incident. Supercilious sensitivites have been rankled. But, if I had a dollar for every off-color comment I've heard

Mayor Bud (the host) Clark, Commissioner Mildred (the innocent victim) Schwab, T.V. Tom (the guest) Brokaw.

outpost. To accommodate the $1.8-million-a-year media superstar's schedule, the date was even switched from the usual Wednesday meeting date to Thursday.

And T.V. Tom did draw. Almost 800 people showed up at the Hilton to hear NBC's main mouthpiece. But his present speech to the assembled multitudes is only incidental. It was an impromptu remark that left River City reeling.

By this time just about every local citizen knows essentially what Brokaw said or rather what he said that Mayor Bud Clark said about Commissioner Mildred Schwab. Clark's off-the-cuff comment was as politically inappropriate as Neil Goldschmidt's "nowhere" remark about Bend. The definitive difference is that one was made during the course of a private conversation and the other was a public statement.

Engaged in informal patter on his homeground, the mayor was probably as unpretentious in the presence of the beguiling Brokaw

about La Grande Dame Schwab, I could be basking in the Bahamas at this moment.

As for the principals, neither party seems to be diminished. Bud apologized; Mildred accepted. Though she can hardly be expected to forget, she has apparently forgiven the faux pas. From everything I can glean, Clark has considerable regard for Schwab's abilities. Nor does the estimable commissioner underestimate the people's politician who elevated local grassroots politics to a new level.

Brokaw behind them, these two inimitable individuals will continue to tackle Portland's problems elbow to elbow in the council chambers; trying to make miracles when there aren't enough mirrors to go around. We may not agree with their style, but they have substance. Tom Brokaw exhibited neither. Would he have reiterated a denigrating remark about a fellow NBC colleague while addressing a New York City Ad Club? I wouldn't bet on it.

Answer: In addition to incumbent Margaret Strachan, the other women have been Dorothy McCullough Lee (1943-49) and Connie McCready (1970-79) both of whom became mayor.

9. DISASTER STRIKES

Local losses from fire, water, wind and the hand of man

If only Portland still had the Battleship Oregon majestically moored on the waterfront adjacent to the newly risen RiverPlace. If only the Corbett mansion still stood in its Victorian grandeur where the abandoned bus depot now languishes ingloriously. If only the Hoyt Hotel were still going strong with Gracie Hansen presiding over the Roaring 20's cabaret. If only the opulent Oriental Theatre hadn't been torn down to be replaced by a slab of asphalt. If only the largest log cabin in the world hadn't burned to the ground. If only . . .

Fantasies of a Portland history buff gone wild. What showplaces these lost landmarks would be had they survived. How they would enhance the city and add enticement to tourism literature. But, they are gone and an important lesson can be learned from their loss. The dedicated group of civic minded citizens that saved the Pittock Mansion from the wrecking crew learned it well. The Historic Preservation League of Oregon teaches it daily.

Speaking of destruction, it is not only the hand of man that lays waste the landmark. Mother Nature's irresistible fury makes manmade devices appear puny by comparison. The devastation that fire, wind and water have unleashed upon Portland is recounted in this chapter. Relive the Vanport Flood of '48 and the Columbus Day Storm. Discover how disaster was dealt with in the 19th Century. Read on before the earthquake hits.

Portland disasters: The Great Fire

February 27, 1985

The heart of Portland in 1873, looking northwest up Washington from the top of a building at Front. What new ordinances were enacted following the fire? (Answers below cartoon.)

The summer of 1873 was a scorcher in Portland. In the central district, wooden buildings, lined up like dried-up matchsticks, were a fire waiting to happen. And early on the morning of August 2nd, it did.

Started in the storerooms of Hurgren and Shinder, a furniture shop at 170 First Street near Taylor, the disastrous blaze was most likely the work of arsonists or "incendiaries" as this particularly heinous form of criminal was called at the time.

St. Charles at Front and Morrison. As they worked feverishly to soak the roof and walls, the totally engulfed Kellog Hotel next door collapsed on itself, saving its neighbor. Following 12 hours of exhausting effort, the fire was finally checked.

Whether or not greater preparedness would have limited the extent of the damage is debatable. But Mayor Henry Failing must have been haunted by such thoughts. Having defeated Philip Wasserman that June, Failing curtailed efforts then underway to augment the department's

August 2, 1873, aftermath: St. Charles Hotel, Front and Morrison (left). Near 3rd and Taylor (right).

Before it was finally checked, the conflagration had consumed 22 central city blocks — almost 1.25 million dollars of the city's $9 million total value. More than 90 families were left homeless, scores of businesses destroyed, and the once-proud, all-volunteer fire-fighting force was brought to its knees.

Help was summoned from as far away as Eugene, with departments assisting from Vancouver, Oregon City, Salem and Albany. The raging inferno could only be stemmed by sacrificing buildings as fire breaks. But some were considered too valuable to lose without a fight.

A combined force of Portland and Salem redshirts made a stand at the city's finest hotel, the four-story, stone-faced

apparatus. His actions had been taken in light of the economic recession gripping the country that year.

There obviously was much to be concerned about in the wake of such unprecedented devastation. The mayor set up a relief committee comprised of prominent citizens to assist the destitute families and businesses. The victims formed their own self-help organization.

To aid in recovering their losses, the latter group sought financial aid from outside Portland. But local leaders steadfastly refused to cooperate with this course of action, citing civic honor and pride. Pulling itself up by its own bootstraps, it took many years for Portland to fully recover from the Great Fire of 1873.

Answers: Erection of new wooden buildings was curtailed, awnings were eliminated and street blockage was prohibited in the downtown area.

Portland disasters: The Flood of '94

March 20, 1985

The fire department demonstrates its waterborne equipment at 2nd & Oak during the 1894 flood. What watersport did Portland's Chinese community devise? (Answer below cartoon.)

Portland promoters called it "A Carnival of Waters" and published a photo-filled booklet carrying that title. Advertisements of prominent local businesses were interspersed with a story about Portland's tradition of floods. The city made the most of an unpleasant situation.

The flood of 1894 was the granddaddy of a series of Spring "freshets," June rises that had plagued the town since its earliest days. In 1853, 1854, 1862, 1871 and 1880, years of heavy snowpack, sustained warming trends triggered rapid runoff and the river rose slowly yet relentlessly over a period of several days.

Water stood three feet deep on Front Street and extended back to Fourth. For 18 years, the highwater mark on Ladd & Tilton's Bank at First and Stark was thought to be unsurpassable. The 1880 flood fell about a foot short. But then came 1894.

On May 17th, Northwest weather turned warm and stayed that way. The Columbia, swollen by its rushing tributaries, left the equally engorged Willamette with nowhere to go but up. Train service was discontinued on May 27th. The river kept rising day by day, foot after foot.

On June 6, the official peak of 33.6 feet was reached. The

1894 flood — Dekum Bldg. at S.W. 3rd and Washington (left). S.W. Front and Ash looking south (right).

The floods of 1861 and 1890 were exceptions. Unlike their slowpoke siblings, these raging torrents brought sudden destruction in their wakes. 1861 was a warmer winter which wreaked havoc along the still sparsely populated riverbanks. By 1890 the well-developed waterfront suffered considerable damage when incessant warm rains over a three-day period put the Willamette on a rampage.

Every winter of substantial snowfall posed the spring flood threat. In 1862 the first of the high June rises had caught merchants unaware and they paid for it. In subsequent years they were prepared to move their merchandise to higher ground or upper stories.

The rise of '71 caused little problem and the '76 inundation set a new record at 28.3 feet with minimal loss.

1876 mark was eclipsed by five feet and 250 city blocks were affected, stretching up to S.W. 6th and Washington and N.W. 10th and Flanders.

With no way to predict when the water would recede, the city of 90,000 carried on as best it could. The bridges were left open. Every boat or reasonable facsimilie was put to use. Businesses operated from their second floors. A floating bar carried on a flourishing trade.

In the same way it came, day by day, little by little, the water gave way. It was a month before the Willamette once again flowed within its banks, leaving behind drowned rats and sewer stench, dead fish and filth, a destroyed gas system and the most extensive total damage of any flood before or since.

Answer: The local "Celestials" organized rowing races along 2nd which were the object of considerable betting.

Portland disasters: The Vanport Flood

April 3, 1985

The 1948 flood affected downtown Portland as well as Vanport. Can you identify these two sites? (Answers below cartoon.)

World War II was raging and we were getting the worst of it. Federal Housing Project No. 35053 was to be a defense-worker residential facility, the largest of its kind in the country. And no time was wasted in getting it underway.

The contract between the Federal Public Housing Authority and Kaiser Company, Inc. was entered into on August 1, 1942. Work began three weeks later on 647 acres of farm and swamp land just south of the Columbia River.

Thirteen thousand people were employed during the course of constructing 720 apartment buildings and 45 community service buildings, including three yard stations, three fire stations, 10 ice houses, five recreation buildings,

Lucky flood victims who saved their cars and a few belongings

five schools, six day-care centers, a cafeteria, theater, post office and library, all connected by nine miles of roads and 50 miles of sidewalks.

Crews specializing in each stage of construction used assembly line techniques, keeping labor costs down and efficiency up. Prefabrication was employed wherever possible. Of 54 million board feet of lumber delivered, only 1.6 million was waste.

The first 934 apartments were released for occupancy on

Dec. 12, 1942. From then an average of 250 per week were completed with all 9,942 delivered by August 15, 1943. At its height, more than 30,000 workers and their families lived in the project that was dubbed Vanport City.

It was, however, a city in name only. Federally owned and operated, a rules and regulations booklet was issued to each resident along with a resident's handbook which began, "The apartment . . . is very simple in design. It is constructed of material that will not stand up unless you take care of it."

Vanport was meant to be temporary. By law, dwellings were to be demolished "within two years after hostilities cease." In March 1945, as the war wound down, Oregon's congressional representatives began to push for immediate redevelopment.

But low-cost housing was limited in the Portland area and thousands of workers chose to stay on after the war. By May 1948, the rapidly deteriorating development still had 18,700 inhabitants. Controversy surrounded Vanport's future. Then nature stepped in to settle matters summarily.

Late deep snows at low elevations were followed by a warming trend. As the Columbia rose, the first calls went out for Red Cross assistance. The Portland-Multnomah Chapter geared up and the National Guard stood by.

Everyone knew that Vanport was in imminent danger if one of the dikes gave way. Plans were laid for evacuation and temporary housing at schools but no action was taken. Sunday, May 30, at 4:12 p.m., the railroad landfill holding back Smith Lake disintegrated within minutes. First 50, then 300, then 600 feet were swept away.

The cause of the break at this unlikely point was never clearly determined. Within one hour, the water was 12 feet deep throughout Vanport City. Virtually every building was destroyed. Most floated off their thin cedar foundations. Many shattered into kindling. Miraculously, only 15 lives were confirmed lost with seven others unaccounted for. Vanport — five years, nine months and 10 days from start to finish.

Answers: The seawall (left photo) by the old Journal Building (now Waterfront Park), looking north to the old Morrison Bridge. S.E. Morrison & 1st looking west (right).

Columbus Day 1962: Holy hurricane

October 14, 1987

This crushed Caddy was just one of the thousands of vehicle storm victims. How many Oregon homes were damaged? What was the highest recorded wind velocity? (Answers below cartoon.)

Where were you and what were you doing on Friday, Oct. 12, 1962? If you were anywhere in Western Oregon or Southwestern Washington and at least grammar school age at the time, there's no way you'll ever forget. The events of that fateful day, 25 years ago, are indelibly ingrained on your memory.

That day was one for the record books — a once in a lifetime occurrence. It was Columbus Day, a day on which Oregonians discovered what a real windstorm was all about. This year marks its 25th anniversary.

Uprooted tree at City Hall. It survived.

There were early warning signs that something ominous was brewing off the Northern California coast that morning but they mostly went unheeded. Barometers began plummeting like a Mafia informer with concrete feet, yet meteorologists seemed confused. Hurricanes, after all, were unheard of in this part of the country. Until now.

Indeed, it was a freak. A rare combination of climatic circumstances created this natural calamity. All the more disastrous since populated areas in its path were totally unprepared.

The Columbus Day Storm was the unexpected offpsring of a dying typhoon dubbed Frieda. As Frieda blew herself out in the mid-Pacific, her own extreme low pressure continued eastward where it met clashing cold and warm fronts and gave birth to the new gale that promptly headed for land. Gaining momentum as it went, the storm struck the coast at Crescent City about noon. But the 70-mile-an-hour winds and torrential rains which caused widespread flooding in California's northwest corner were almost inconsequential compared to the devastation that descended upon Western Oregon.

Southern Oregon valley towns suffered extensive damage and the storm's effects were felt from the coast to Klamath Falls. Not until it reached the Willamette Valley, however, did this rampaging killer unleash its full force.

Hemmed in by two mountain ranges, the winds grew rapidly in both speed and intensity, attaining 125 miles per hour at Corvallis. By late afternoon, the storm had visited its violence throughout the valley and still it moved relentlessly northward, intent on adding Oregon's largest city to the victim list.

In the midst of the commuter rush hour, few Portlanders were aware of the swiftly approaching danger. One after another, each area had been hit by total surpirse, unable to spread the alarm before power and communications were cut off. Now, it was the big town's turn.

For those of us who experienced it, the unnerving, spooky stillness and the strange, orange-tinged, grey-white glow that preceeded the sudden onslaught, gave new meaning to the term "calm before the storm." Then it struck with the same ferocity that had already left two dozen dead and tens of millions of dollars in property damage. Only this time there was even more in the way.

Held helpless in the mindless monster's grasp for more than two hours, Portland suffered greater damage to public facilities than all other metropolitan areas combined. A half-dozen people lost their lives. The storm then swept into Southwestern Washington continuing to wreak havoc until it finally veered west just south of Seattle and moved out to sea again to end its brief but terrible existence.

During just 12 hours, the Columbus Day Storm had slashed a murderous swath 1,000 miles long and 125 miles wide across three states. Forty-eight people were dead, half of them in Oregon. Of the estimated 210 million dollars in damage, 170 million were in Oregon. More than 11 billion board feet of timber had been blown down. In some isolated areas, it took weeks before power could be restored.

Today, no evidence remains of the infamous "Big Blow" but its legacy lives on in the minds of all those who were there on Columbus Day 1962.

Answers: 52,013 including 84 totally destroyed. 170 mph at Hebo radar station on the Oregon coast.

The Portland Hotel:
Put up a parking lot
December 7, 1983

The Meier & Frank parking lot survived for 30 years. It was the site of one media event. What was it? (Answer below cartoon.)

The city block being transformed into Pioneer Courthouse Square has seen a lot of history. "From boots to bricks," as the publicity pundits have put it.

But what of the time in between those "boots," which, with $25, was reportedly the price paid by cobbler Elijah Hill to purchase the property in 1849, and today's monogrammed bricks again being offered to the public to help finance the new public showplace square?

Two views of the stately Portland Hotel from S.W. 6th.

Portland's school district bought the block in 1858 for $1,000 and erected the Central School, which remained until 1882 when Henry Villard's Northern Pacific Terminal Co. paid a princely $75,000 to acquire it.

By then, it was apparent that the site would soon be in the center of the rapidly growing downtown. But city population was still a modest 17,578.

As mentioned in earlier articles (Oct. 26, Nov. 2), Villard's railroad empire collapsed in 1883 and with it his ambitious plan to build the Portland Hotel. $150,000 had already been spent on the imposing English basalt foundation which stood unfinished for nearly four years and was referred to as "Villard's ruin."

In 1888 the project was resurrected by a young newcomer from Pennsylvania named George B. Markle, Jr., with the backing of the cream of Portland's power elite—Ladd, Corbett, Failing, et al—who raised $250,000, matched by other Portlanders.

The resulting Portland Hotel Company completed the Northwest's most elegant lodging establishment on April 7, 1890, at a cost of $750,000. Portland's population had multiplied to 46,855 during the seven intervening years.

For six decades, the six-story, 284-room hostelry was the

scene of Portland's most sumptuous and significant events. Eleven heads of state, from Harrison to FDR, slept in its Presidential Suite. Everyone who was anyone stayed at the Portland.

In its heyday the "structure of stature" was owned by the Corbetts, later falling to out-of-town interests. It was bought by Meier & Frank in 1944 and lived in the shadow of doom which finally came in 1951. On August 15 the hotel closed, following a Grand Auction and final dinner which served 500.

According to financial and attitudinal dictates of the day, a parking lot was practical. Refurbishing a distinguished, though declining, dowager was not. It's a shame the decision isn't being made today.

THE PORTLAND HOTEL IS JUST AHEAD MISTER PRESIDENT!

TEDDY R. IN TOWN TODAY MAY 21, 1903

BULLY, SENATOR SIMON. A GRAND EDIFICE, INDEED!

HOWEVER, MR. FORD MENTIONED THAT THEY MIGHT CONSIDER PROVIDING MORE PARKING!

Klooster '83

Answer: M&F ringed the lot with TV sets, just introduced to Portland, for the 1952 presidential conventions.

U.S.S. Oregon: Bulldog of the sea

December 3, 1986

The Oregon at the Battle of Santiago, 1898. Who saved her from destruction in 1920? Who tried to have her salvaged and rebuilt in 1956? (Answers below cartoon.)

By today's standards she would be a lumbering leviathan. In her day, she was the most devastating fortress afloat. The U.S.S. Oregon was the first modern-era battleship constructed for coastal defense at the Union Iron Works in San Francisco. When this 10,000-ton titan slid slowly out of the launching slip on Oct. 26, 1893, she was considered to be the new pride of the Navy, the future of the fleet. The Oregon would earn those accolades and much more.

Battleship Oregon Memorial Park, 1939.

Through the 1880s, the U.S. Navy was neglected by a Congress preoccupied with domestic development. But, when America finally turned its attention to world affairs and the need for national defense, its technological capabilities were formidable. Upon the completion of her outfitting in 1896, the Battleship Oregon was commissioned for duty — arguably the finest, fastest, most heavily armed and armored warship ever built at that time.

Two years later, when the sinking of the U.S.S. Maine in Havana harbor plunged America into war with Spain, all of the Oregon's capabilities were called upon. Sailing 'round the Horn in record breaking time, she participated in the month-long blockade of the Spanish fleet in Santiago de Cuba Harbor. Then, when the decisive day of battle came on July 3, 1898, she outran, outgunned and sank three of the enemy's finest vessels in 90 minutes.

After a rousing victory celebration in New York City, the Oregon was overhauled at the Brooklyn Navy Yard. Exchanging her gray war paint for peacetime white, she steamed around the southern tip of South America once again to reinforce Admiral Dewey's fleet in the Philippines. With the Oregon's presence in the Eastern Pacific, America's position was secured.

Her next tour of duty came in the summer of 1900 as China's Boxer Rebellion began to heat up. That assignment almost brought about the great ship's demise. Sailing out of Hong Kong into the South China Sea, she struck a submerged rock, sustaining severe hull damage. Only good weather and timely assistance from a Japanese cruiser saved the Oregon from sinking. She underwent emergency repairs in Japan and returned to the West Coast for refitting at Bremerton.

Called back into service, she played a prominent part in the gunboat diplomacy that ended the Chinese conflict in 1906. For the next 19 years, her fate swung back and forth between celebrity and the scrap heap. With the advent of WWI's dreadnaught battlewagons, she was obsolete militarily. In 1920, the State of Oregon petitioned the Navy Department to have her preserved as a war memorial on the Portland waterfront.

In 1925, the Oregon legislature created a permanent fund for the state's namesake ship and she was towed to Portland in time to open the Rose Festival that year. There she remained as a sighseeing attraction for 17 years moving only once, in 1938, from the northeast side of the Broadway Bridge to a memorial park at the southwest side of the Hawthorne Bridge.

Though the plan was to encase the hull in concrete, the grand naval relic was still afloat in 1942. As a result, she fell victim to misplaced patriotism. Although many argued for her historical importance over the need for scrap metal, President Roosevelt authorized the sale in October and the Oregon was towed from Portland, never to return.

Following removal of her superstructure, the armored hull was used for storage of explosives off Guam. In 1948 a fierce storm carried the hulk 500 miles out to sea. Found intact it languished another eight years at anchor until finally sold and reduced to scrap by a Japanese salvage firm. The mast, two smokestacks and some anchor chain are all that remain of the once mighty U.S. Battleship Oregon.

Answers: Then Assistant Secretary of the Navy Franklin D. Roosevelt. Oregon's prominent U.S. Senator Wayne Morse.

The Timber Temple: Log gone

October 7, 1987

The Forestry Building during the 1905 Lewis and Clark Fair. How tall was the building? How many people attended the fair? What was the admission? (Answers below cartoon.)

On the morning of Aug. 17, 1964, a structure unique on earth was lost forever, consumed by a raging conflagration that only an edifice constructed as this one was could create. It was the Forestry Building, the world's largest log cabin, showplace of Northwest forest products erected for the Lewis and Clark Centennial Exposition of 1905.

During its almost 60 years of existence, this shrine to the Douglas Fir hosted more than 10 million visitors. All who remember mourn its loss but none more so than Portlanders, including this writer, for whom it approached monument status.

Ion Lewis of Whidden and Lewis, Portland's most prominent architectural firm of the time, planned the commanding 206-by-102-foot structure. Design credits go to his associate, A.E. Doyle, who later became a noted architect in his own right. Construction was completed between November 1904 and March 1905.

The Central Hall under construction.

Putting together the "cabin," as some quaintly referred to it, would be no mean feat even for today's sophisticated equipment. With turn-of-the-century techniques, it was an amazing accomplishment. Hand-selected trees weighing up to 35 tons were painstakingly pulled from several nearby forests, floated to the fair's Guilds Lake site and slowly slid up a chute to preserve the bark. The largest logs were donated by Simon Benson off of his land on the Washington side of the Columbia across from Clatskanie. Others came from Clackamas and Columbia counties.

The finished product was breathtaking. Once through the massive portals of Oregon's wooden Parthenon, the sheer size of the central hall almost overwhelmed the observer. Fifty-two perfectly matched, Douglas fir giants, 54 feet high and 6 feet in diameter at the base, marched down the building's full length. These natural columns formed the uniform forest that prompted the official nickname "Gallery of Trees." In all, the herculean cabin's tall timbers contained something more than a million board feet of timber.

After a four-and-one-half month run as the feature attraction of the West's first ever world's fair, a syndicate representing Coney Island, with plans to dismantle, ship and reassemble the Forestry

Building at the world famous New York amusement park, offered $200,000 for it. Construction cost had been approximately $45,000. The new owners, the city of Portland, refused to sell and prepared plans for a permanent exhibit.

As originally designed, the 33,000-ton structure was not intended to hold up more than a couple of decades. In 1914, tycoon James J. Hill donated $6,000 for concrete foundations. Through the Depression, limited funds allowed only minimum maintenance while more important repairs went unattended. After World War II the need for major renovations to expand the life of the aging giant became pressing.

In 1949, the Park Bureau could still only afford patchwork repairs but public interest in the plight of the building was increasing. Three years later, in September 1952, the City Council authorized the Gallery of Trees Committee and *Oregon Journal* editor Marshall Dana was appointed as its chairman. Private funding allowed extensive refinishing and facelifting in addition to critical structural reinforcement. The lumber industry contributed $100,000 for new exhibits.

Over the next decade noteworthy installations included a working sawmill, "Peggy," a vintage locomotive used by Stimson Lumber Co., a donkey engine from Georgia-Pacific, and a huge grindstone used for papermaking in the late 1800s.

In March 1964, five months before its destruction, the Gallery of Trees was inspected and declared "sound and strong." The fire, a five-alarmer, was memorable. Flames leapt more than 100 feet into the sky. The only consolation is that the impetus for our handsome Western Forestry Center, completed in 1971, arose from the ashes.

THEY SHOULD **SPRUCE** THIS PLACE UP!

THAT **WOOD** BE NICE!

klooster '87

Answers: 72 feet at top of the Central Hall. 2.5 million attendance including complimentary. 50¢ for adults and 25¢ for children.

The Hoyt: Harvey's hotel at its height

November 9, 1983

Harvey Dick (left) and associate, Harold Harkins, view two of the dozens of oils that adorned the Hoyt. Why did these particular paintings hit the news? (Answers below cartoon.)

Opening in 1911, the 175-room Hoyt Hotel, right across the street from Union Station, was welcomed without reservation (pardon the pun). The hospitable hostelry enjoyed instant and continuing success.

In 1941, the Hoyt was purchased by local industrialist Harvey Dick, who played a significant part in bringing Henry Kaiser's wartime shipbuilding business to the Rose City, therefore using his hotel to full advantage.

500-capacity cabaret the equal of the most elaborate Las Vegas showroom.

Gregarious Gracie Hansen, a raucous rolypoly song belter, presided over Portland's premiere nightclub. With warmup comics and a classy chorus line, the Roaring '20s was the city's must attraction and scene of many an unforgettable event.

But the recession of the early 1970s brought tighter

The Hoyt from Union Station (left). The entry hall (ctr) and main showroom (rt) of the Roaring '20s.

Thousands of workers flocked to Portland and many availed themselves of the inexpensive lodging at the Hoyt. Dick selected the best of them for his Columbia Steel Casting plant.

As train travel waned in the late 1950s, so did the Hoyt. But Harvey Dick decided to bring business back by transforming his hotel into a splendid showcase.

Remodeling in stages during the early '60s, he first made over the old "515 Club" into an elegant 24-hour restaurant. Then came the fabulous gas-lighted Barbary Coast, followed by the paneled Men's Bar.

Dick filled his public palace with the largest collection of antique furnishings, lamps, paintings and memorabilia in the West. His crowning touch was the Roaring '20s, a

budgets and the hotel that thrived on extravagance was hard hit. Overnight, the "Boniface," as columnist Doug Baker called Dick, closed it down. August 2, 1972, was the date and despite disbelief, regret and lamentation, it was over.

In customary flamboyant fashion, Harvey held a huge auction that November, during which everything went. The tiffanies, the original oils, his pet parrots, even a vintage Rolls.

The county bought the hotel in 1975 and tore it down for a bus depot complex that has yet to materialize.

Maybe it was too good to last. But the place that was "not to be missed" surely is by all who knew Harvey Dick's Hoyt at its height.

HOYT HOTEL · A GOING CONCERN

GOING.. · GOING.. · GONE!

Klooster '83

Answer: Bought by Dick at auction, they turned out to be originals worth a fortune.

10. CITY OF ROSES: NOTES & ANECDOTES

Aug 4, 1987

Mr. Karl Klooster
This Week Magazine

April 26, 1984

Dear Sir:

Regarding your article in the April 25, 1984 issue of "This Week", commenting on Lotus Isl Did it pre-date The Oaks-1905?

Lotus Isle amusement park was developed aro 1929 or 1930 (this from memory) and was destroyed fire around 1931. It was pre-dated by Columbia Beach which could be reached by the Vancou Trolley Line, which operated down Union over a long trestle crossing Tomah the Interstate Bridge. Colum ily a bathing be

~ Mr. Klooster,
Kudos to all of you who pa reported in the recent Rockle C. Bridge revitalization. I, f would like to let you k the efforts to prese e sites do appreciated s in

2 January 1984

Mr. Karl Klooster
This Week Magazine
PO Box 23099
Tigard OR 97223

Re: Bridge article and possible correction

Dear Mr. Klooster,

Once before I took issue with your column on bridges and I do not want to discourage you from further informing the public on bridges, but I would like you to clarify a statement you made about there being no single leaf bascule bridges. — SEE CARTOON IN COLUMN OF 10 AUGUST 1983 — (attached)

Enclosed is a photocopy of a page from the 1957 Encyclopedia Britannica which comments on single leaf bascules.

Sincerely yours,
Alan Viewig
ALAN VIEWIG
AVmk

Karl Klooster
This Week
6960 S.W. Sandburg
Tigard, Or. 97223

I try to read all of your articles in my paper disappears before I have had tim really enjoy the articles and find them believe your article about Little Russia be at least partially wrong.

The Jewish settlement in Northwest been called Little Russia, in that are cause it was predominantly Jewish an did come over from Russia in Russian Germans, who ca called Albin and s were call opula

1520
Clac

Additions, corrections, comments and criticisms

Each and every season — winter, spring, summer, fall — four times a year for the past four and one-half years, Roses readers have had a forum in Notes & Anecdotes. Sometimes, they've been kind. Other times, cruel — but correct. Everything from typographical transposition to blatant blunders have been brought to my attention and admitted to in print.

Additions have been the headiest reward of this quarterly confessional. Valuable information from people who, often through personal, experience, knew the complete facts has augmented and enhanced certain stories.

The truth being out, Notes & Anecdotes has given me yet another opportunity to get in my two cents worth on past stories as well. I've also been able to plug events, give a little boost to organizations and bestow those bountiful *Round the Roses* bouquets on column contributors.

There's a bit of humor and a lot of good information here in Chapter 10. And, if you were wondering, yes, the concept will continue in all its unabashed openness each quarter as long as the *Roses* bloom in *This Week* magazine.

Notes & Anecdotes: Fall '83

September 28, 1983

What was Portland's greatest estimated population and in what year was it reached? (Answers below cartoon.)

Local history — events, people, places — is intriguing and, often, personally involving. I'd like to share with you some of the comments and contributions, observations and oddities that *Round the Roses* has elicited since its first appearance.

That first column (*Early Portland: The toss of a coin*—May 25) posed the question, "Who called what, when Pettygrove and Lovejoy flipped the fateful penny that named our fair city?" So far no one has come up with the answer. Let's hear it from you history students and Oregon buffs.

Some Portlanders take their roses very seriously. In response to the June 22 column (*City of Roses: A nickname takes root*), **Laurette Kenney** tells me she has been engaged in a campaign for almost 20 years to have the Madame Caroline Testout (pronounced Tehz-too) proclaimed Portland's official rose.

June 29), **Arthur McArthur** of Jantzen (*A plan for all seasons*—July 13) and **Steve Yaw** (*Hollywood: Heyday of the district*—Aug. 31), whose cooperation made those columns complete.

Josephine (Mrs. D.L.) O'Neal, who is 83, passes along her "first person" story of the original Steel Bridge (*Bridge River City*—Aug. 10). "The bridge would shake so (much) my mother had my sister and I go single file with one hand on the railing. She told us that if the bridge fails . . . hold on with both hands to the railing . . . it would float."

Nobody's perfect II. One of my ad agency compatriots and column critics, **Marla Jackson,** caught me on two more — the Conestoga, Cadillac of covered wagons (*Wagon wheels a rollin'*—Sept. 14) was never used on the Oregon Trail, only in the Ohio Valley — too heavy. She also tells me that I got the wrong side of the Holman family when

"TO ERR IS HUMAN; TO FORGIVE, DIVINE"

—ALEXANDER POPE not WILL SHAKESPEARE

ROUND THE ROSES City of Roses: Notes

BUT AN ERROR IN PRINT . . .

This Week Frank Talk

STEVE SINOVIC'S AROUND TOWN

IS. BETTER YOURS THAN MINE!

Klooster '83

BAKER SEZ!

Mrs. Kenney, who designed award-winning Rose Festival floats, first as a teenager in 1927 and again in 1961, makes a convincing case for the prolific pink beauty. No other rose has such historic credentials and there would undoubtedly be bickering about any Johnny-bloom-lately; so get with it, Portland Rose Society and Rose Festival Association.

Nobody's perfect. *This Week's* production staff, whose Herculean efforts produce Portland's largest circulation publication 52 times a year, are real pros but they got me in trouble by substituting the word "congressional" for "Congregational" in *Council Crest*—July 20. Now that's a real violation of the separation of church and state and the faithful turned out en masse to correct the error.

As to errors, my own errant diagonal line across the top half of the photo (*Meier & Frank: Meet me under the clock*—July 27) caused the lower half to be printed instead of the upper. So I got a crowd instead of the clock. Apologies to **Sandy Carpenter** of M&F, who helped me go through cartons of photos to find just the right one.

Speaking of assistance, *Round the Roses* bouquets to **Gene Clark** of Blitz-Weinhard (*From Henry to Heileman*—

referring to Frederick as a funeral director (June 22). He was an attorney and aide to Judge Matthew Deady. Just my luck to work with the wife of a descendant of this estimable pioneer family and a history buff to boot.

Happy to report that the Hawthorne Bridge (*The scandalous spans*—Aug. 17) is having its mossy planks replaced and is scheduled for repainting. I'd like to think this was the power of the pen but these projects were already in the works.

We leave these cogent comments and historical homilies with a bit of homespun humor from **Kevin Olsen,** descendant of the pioneer (1852) Willamette Valley Stevens clan (*Wagon wheels a rollin'*—Sept. 7).

What did the hapless covered-wagon driver lament when a shaky wheel flew off as he was descending a precarious mountain trail?

"You picked a fine time to leave me loose wheel."

Keep those additions, corrections, accolades and criticisms coming. You may very well see them, and your name, in a future installment of *Notes & Anecdotes.*

Answers: 412,100 in 1957. 1980 census showed city declined to 366,383 but metro area (1,242,638) continues to grow.

Notes & Anecdotes: Winter '83-'84

January 25, 1984

Mayor Terry D. Schrunk Plaza. What did Schrunk do that only one other Portland mayor has done? What prior office did he hold?

I am pleased to announce that the compelling question, "Who called what when Lovejoy and Pettygrove tossed the coin to name Portland?" has at last been answered by **Mrs. H.D. Taylor.**

When I first posed the query (*"Pettygrove's Portland"*—May 25), I didn't know the answer myself, honest. However, by the time I put forth the challenge again (*Notes & Anecdotes*—Sept. 28), I'd run across it on a poster promoting the 1905 Lewis and Clark Fair. Pettygrove called heads and won twice.

Unfortunately, Mrs. Taylor included neither her source of information nor her address, so I was unable to reply directly. Let's hope that she reads this article.

Down at the Oregon City Elks Club a while back, **Harold Lupke** drew me aside and said, "You know, Karl, that Interstate toll was 20 cents, not 25'" (*Over the Rivers*—Oct. 12). "Should've been, though. Making change was a pain."

Interstate Toll — 20 cents.

Fellow Lewis & Clark alum and fraternity brother **Roger Siegner** pointed out that I missed John Hambrick's Newsreel Theater and that the Fox was originally called the Mayfair (*Lights on Broadway*—Nov. 16).

I can be forgiven for these light oversights because the only time I ever came downtown in the '50s was to "drag Broadway." Whereas Roger, being from Beaverton (mostly farm country at the time), actually went to the movies — the *Newsreel?*

We Rose City Park residents could choose from a multitude of eastside emporiums, including the expansive Hollywood, the bountiful Bagdad and the opulent Oriental.

Small matters, these, in comparison with a major mistake (*Union Station*—Nov. 2). After painstakingly researching the chronology and cost of the depot itself, I didn't make a simple phone call to verify the number of daily arrivals and departures.

There are a dozen, not three, passenger trains daily, as Amtrak has continued to enlarge and improve its service since the information from which I quoted was published. Architect **Steven Fosler,** who took effusive exception to the statement, can be credited.

Train buff **Alan Viewig** should have been the one to call me on the Amtrak error but he's been too busy scrutinizing the bridge articles. Having already given me a "gottcha" on the Golden Gate-it was designed by Strauss, not Steinman-(*Scandalous Spans*-Aug. 17), attorney Alan also rapped my knuckles on the

bascule blunder (*Bridging River City*-Aug. 10) My cartoon comment "There's no such thing as" (see below) has been refuted by no less than the Encyclopedia Britannica-1957. Of course, the only place you ever see them is over castle moats.

THE DOUBLE-LEAF BASCULE
(there's no such thing as a single-leaf bascule)

Klooster '83

IN MODERN T.V. ACTION SERIES, CAR (a) JUMPS GAP-Knight Rider (b) PLUMMETS INTO RIVER-Chips (c) ROLLS BACK-Rockford

One leaf or two?

Louise Morgan protests that I've made pioneer wagoners look like auto drivers by placing them on the left side (*Wagon Wheels*—Sept. 7). It's a bit difficult to know, not having been on the trail personally, particularly when you see old illustrations such as that shown below.

HUTCHINGS' PANORAMIC SCENES. — CROSSING THE PLAINS.

Left-handed driver

Now from after-the-fact critique and correction to accolades for those who contributed to making some of these stories credible: *Round the Roses* bouquets to **Carolyn Zelle** of Pendleton (*The Wool to Succeed*—Oct. 19), retired Vice Chairman Rollin Killoran (*Fred Meyer*—Nove. 23 & 30) and **Mrs. M.F. Keyes,** who asked for the Peacock Lane article (Dec. 14).

And to all the lane residents who showed me such hospitality — **Betty Trueblood, Chalis Myers, Ruth** and **Bill Bonnett, Dorothy** and **Ed Hawes,** and **Barbara** and **Jon Christian** — a dozen long-stemmed *Round the Roses.*

Answers: Held the office longest (Nov. 1956-Nov. 1972 along with George L. Baker (1917-1933). He was Multnomah County Sheriff.

Notes & Anecdotes: Spring '84

April 25, 1984

Barbara Cady sent this rendering of Hefty's proposed City Hall: *The Municipal Mansion* (Mar. 7). Why is this illustration unique? (answer below)

If errors and omissions are the bane of a historical writer, additions and corrections are its rewards. With few exceptions the comments that come this columnist's way augment rather than criticize. Here are some of those received lately.

Although more than nine months have passed since the Jantzen beach story (July 6, 1983), more than one reader has mentioned a park that apparently preceded it called Lotus Isle. **Stephen Kenney, Jr.** first mentioned the place to me but further information is scant. Did it pre-date The Oaks — 1905?

Three articles (Jan. 4, 11, 18) were scarcely enough to do justice to Mt. Hood, so Battle Axe Inn went unmentioned. **Fred Jensen** and **Mrs. Hazel Hardwick** didn't let this pass unnoticed. Destroyed by fire in 1949, Battle Axe accommodated more guests than Timberline.

Fountain and lunch counter, Battle Axe Inn

Mark Karson, who succeeded his father as proprietor of the Hollywood Liquor Store, relates that it is one of only two in the entire state still at its original location — (*OLCC: The green front turns 50*—Feb. 1).

The Feb. 15 article, *Northwest Natural: A gas since 1859,* generated some unexpected heat. The cartoon was originally intended to show an older lady questioning a repairman as he worked on a pipe with these results . . .

Gas company contacts advised that this would be an insult to gasmen as they'd never confuse the two. Changing the cartoon dialogue at the last moment as shown below, I didn't consider the possibility that it ridiculed elderly and limited-income persons.

My apologies for this inadvertent oversight, in particular to **Betty Greer** who brought it to my attention.

Portland Airports: First were the fairways—Mar. 1, has drawn more supplemental information than any other *Round the Roses* article to date.

S.A. DeBonny, who has lived near Portland University for 68 years, writes that "around 1922 a strip was cleared on Mock's Bottom parallel to Swan Island. The SPADS (from the U.S. Army Flying Circus) roared overhead just clearing the bluff. Later, this landing strip was used by "Tex" Rankin's Flying Service."

Ken Coffman, founder of the North American Aviation Historical Society, also recalls John "Tex" Rankin, a World War I aviator who was Portland's pioneer pilot. "Tex" ran a flying school at another strip in the Delta Park area near Union Ave.

Walt Bohrer, a society charter member, was one of Rankin's instructors and an early-day barnstormer. His sister, **Ann,** was one of the very first airline stewardesses.

Swan Island's official name was The Port of Portland Airport. Our first landing field was at Westmoreland Park. This comes from Port librarian **Melody Livengood.**

For assistance with recent articles, *Round the Roses* bouquets go to **Geneive Cook**—(*OLCC*—Feb. 1); **Alice Cheatham**—(*Northwest Natural*—Feb. 15); **Austin Moller**—City hall series; **Mick Scott**—(*Ad Man Matlack*—Feb. 22); **Barbara Walker**—(*Pioneer Square*—April 11); and **Dick Montgomery**—(*Portland International*—April 18).

Answer: This picture, from an early Chamber of Commerce booklet, shows the "5th tower" missing from other illustrations.

Notes & Anecdotes: Summer '84

August 22, 1984

Mom at Columbia Beach ca. Summer, 1922. As we go to press, Portland's sunny streak is 49 days long. When and how long was the longest? (Answers below).

It appears that a lot of people remember Lotus Isle, closed in 1932, and adjacent Columbia Beach, a popular swimming spot since World War I. (*A bamboozle that backfired*—June 27). When my own mother produced a snapshot of herself at about age 8 wading in the river there, I discovered she was one of them.

Retired dentist **Collister Wheeler** spotted an error in (*When Old Town was new*—May 23). The venerable Ladd and Tilton Bank, a classic ironfront, was located at S.W. First and Stark, not Third and Washington. The U.S. National was there. Dr. Wheeler knows. He worked there.

Ladd & Tilton Bank, S.W. corner, 1st & Stark.

I'd have thought that the City Hall series (*Commission system*—May 2, *George Baker*—May 16 and *Carson to Riley*—June 20) would have elicited more response but apparently the political past is not the stuff of strong nostalgia. Despite this, plans still roll along for *Round the Roses* to tell the tales of all the mayors up to and including the incumbent.

Portland's consummate historian and author **E. Kimbark MacColl** did comment on the commission system, saying that there have always been four, never five, commissioners as my article states. During that first term under the new system, six persons held the posts, some short-lived. Thus my misinterpretation.

Consummate Portland P.R. man **Jack Matlack** remembers **Earl Riley** with fondness. Seems the mayor (1941-49) sent his chauffered limouisine to take Jack and his bride to and from their wedding in style.

Portland mayors don't have limos anymore. Is this image or budget or both? Perhaps **Bud Clark** could reinstate this tradition. He could park it next to the "Goose" and tow his rowboat behind. Would you believe, with a police escort?

Primary information source for *Rose Festival: The fleet makes it complete*—June 6 was retired Naval Captain **Bob Webb**. In conjunction with doing this article Elephant and Castle Manager **Chris Olsen** and I were among the invitees to a reception aboard the USS Willamette just prior to the festival. The mayor, mayor-designate and commissioners were all invited. Officers and men waited two hours. None showed. Bad Show!

(*The Juniors: Rose Festival favorites*—May 30) proved to be a popular article. Special thanks to old friend **Carol Heffler**, a 1950 princess, for her inside info on the old days and to **Rob** and **Judy Charlton**, parents of 1984 Princess **Cristen**, for their current insights.

However, there was controversy over the photo of the 1933 Junior Court. **Audrey Shibley** insists that this was not the '33 group. She was princess that year. **Jane DeNunzio Winike** wants a copy for her 90-year-old friend **Jeanette Bailey** who recognized her son, who was on that court, in the picture. The question of 1933 or not awaits further evidence.

JUNIOR COURT - PORTLAND ROSE FESTIVAL - 1933

1933 Junior Court or not?

William Kennel straightened me out on the early teams in the Pacific Coast League (*Vaughn St.*—July 25). My list included the clubs as they stood in the '50s. The Sacramento Bees and a Vernon (Calif.) club, whose nickname Kennell did not recall, played in earlier years.

In addition to those contributions already mentioned, long-stemmed *Round the Roses* go to **Stephen Kenney Jr.** (*Lotus Isle*), **Don Walker**, **Jon Richardson** and **Ron Tonkin** (*Vaughn St. and The Beavers*—Aug. 1) and the Multnomah Athletic Club's **Lorraine Miller** (*MAC: Parts I & II*—Aug. 8-15.)

Finally, big bouquets to TAG students, **Amy Moorman**, **Margaret Richen** and **Chris Soentpiet** of Beaumont Middle School; **Amelie Hastie**, **Joel Martin** and **Shanon Playford** of Grant High; **Julie Ducher**, **Melanie Morris** and **Michael Riley** of Lincoln High for an outstanding job on their articles appearing this month.

Answers: Longest on record is 71 days from June 23 to Sept. 1, 1967. The current dry spell began on June 29.

Notes & Anecdotes: Fall '84

November 21, 1984

On Jan. 31, 1926, this proposed stadium was featured in an *Oregonian* article. How many people would it seat? Who would like to have it in Portland today? (Answers below)

Heading the highlights of this quarterly recap is qualified good news. Coldwell Banker's **Jon Torgeson** advises that the investment group headed by attorney **Bob Stoll** has negotiated an exclusive option with the City of Portland for purchase of the Police Bureau block (*Old Town: The Police Bureau Bldg.*—Oct. 24, 31).

Based on Stoll's track record with the Yamhill Marketplace, the future for this important Old Town property could be bright if this option is exercised at the end of the year.

Special thanks go to retired **Sergeant Ralph O'Hara**, police historian and archivist, for his invaluable assistance in the development of the Police Bureau series (Oct. 3, 10, 17). Ralph, a consummate gentleman and classic Irish cop, was instrumental in establishing the Portland Police Historical Museum .

Proposed Chinatown Gate; W. Burnside & 4th.

Many readers remember Mayor Dorothy McCullough Lee with high regard (*Her Honor*—Aug. 29). In 1949, a year into her term of office, the Coon Chicken Inn closed its doors. (*It wasn't the Colonel*—Sept. 26).

Whether or not Mayor Lee's major move against prostitution and other vice crimes had an influence on its demise is problematical but old employees related that more than once during deliveries they were asked to trade Southern fried chicken for the favors of red-light ladies.

Apologies to any who were offended by the Coon Chicken column. Such episodes of history as it was, to my way of thinking, serve as valuable object lessons. I'd rather report on them than ignore them and I certainly wouldn't want to alter them to suit the sensitivities of the times as is done in some corners of the globe.

The story of Portland's Chinatown (Sept. 5 and 12) provided another piece of historical perspective. Of the more than 10,000 Chinese who once teemed along S.W. 1st and 2nd, little more than one fourth that number comprise today's community locally.

Thankfully, they continue to play an active, vital role in the city's society. So much that the Chinese Consolidated Benevolent Society, until recently presided over by **Dr. Sam Won,** is spearheading the new Chinatown Development Plan. In March of this year, a laudable proposal, based on a study funded by the U.S. Bancorp and the Oregon Historical Fund with staff assistance from the Portland Development Commission, was announced.

Along with Dr. Won, **Gene Chin** and **Mel Huie** of the Chinatown Development Committee propose to make Chinatown a dramatically distinctive district with Oriental style street lighting, banners, kiosks and a Chinese Gateway similar to the one over Grant Street at Bush in San Francisco.

Going all the way back to May 23 (*When Old Town was new*), **Dr. Collister Wheeler** won't let me get by with th is goof. So let's get it right. The classic Ladd & Tilton Bank was located at 1st and Stark. They moved to 3rd & Washington in 1911. The Stark St. building was torn down in 1958 to make way for the Morrison Bridge ramp. The U.S. National Bank was at 2nd & Stark until 1907 when they moved to 3rd & Oak and then to 6th & Stark in 1917. Dr. Wheeler worked at the second Ladd & Tilton location. Whew!

The new Portland Breakers football team (hope that name will be changed) would love to hear this one. In the columns on Multnomah Athletic Club (*The club and its stadium*—Aug. 8 and 15) I missed an interesting anecdote which **Carl Fox** has brought to my attention. Back in 1926, the original plan was to eventually expand the stadium's seating capacity from 35,000 to 100,000. The plan fell flat for lack of funds.

Perhaps acquistion of the USFL franchise will revitalize public energies to finance a first-class covered sports facility. And while we're on the subject, whose idea was it to drop the name Multnomah from that historic hippodrome? Along with the addition of a dome, maybe its rightful name can be restored.

Memories of the MAC come from **Barbara Pennington.** As a teenaged member of the club in the 1920s, she ran in the relay races during their annual picnics held at Crystal Lake Park in Milwaukie. Her folks were taken aback by such unladylike behavior. But the club had its positive side from another aspect of parental approval. Whereas her father frowned on Barbara's attending school dances, those at MAC were OK.

The Fall '84 long-stemmed *Round the Roses* go to the following for their column contributions. **Jim McCrory** (*Franz Bakery*—Sept. 19), **Mike Cramer** (*Coon Chicken Inn*—Sept. 26), **Pat Jordan, Bing Sheldon** and **Jon Torgeson** (*Police Bureau Bldg.*—Oct. 24 and 31) and **Rhonda Harris** (*Tik Tok*—Nov. 14).

Answers: Its approximately 100,000 capacity would have been music to the ears of the USFL Breakers, about to move to Portland.

Notes & Anecdotes: Winter '84-'85

February 13, 1985

The Jackson Tower across from Pioneer Square. When were its lovely lights installed? What was the building originally called? (Answers below).

History, it is said, repeats itself. It is also said that we can learn great lessons from history. I'd like to think that this column contributes to the latter. But it is obvious that the road to overcoming ignorance and intolerance is long and arduous.

My lament refers to the *Round the Roses* column of Jan. 30 (*Old Town: The new look is Naitoesque*). A caller, who shall remain anonymous, bitterly condemned my praise of the Naito family for their efforts in helping to preserve and upgrade Old Town. The only reason was that their heritage is Japanese.

Irma Case, who calls herself a "little old lady in tennis shoes," caught me on another building blunder. In the Police Sunshine Division pre-Christmas story (Dec. 12) I stated that the Hoot Owls, a group of local businessmen who entertained on KGW Radio in the 1920s, broadcast from the station's studios in Jackson Tower.

Chinatown tunnels had many uses

The studios were actually in the *Oregonian* building at Sixth and Alder. The paper owned the station at the time. The Jackson Tower, at Broadway and Yamhill, was the *Journal* building in those days, thus the mixup. It was later renamed for *Oregon Journal* founder C.S. Jackson. If Mrs. Case, a true Portlandophile, actually wears tennis shoes, they must be Nikes.

Mrs. John Piper didn't waste time putting pen to paper in taking me to task on the above blooper. She called. Thanks to both of you ladies for keeping me on my toes. Keep the corrections coming just so long as you tell me about them and not my editor.

A **Mrs. Bradley** writes to relate that her father had told her about the Chinese gambling in the tunnels under downtown streets (*Chinese connection*—Sept. 5 & 12). She didn't believe him until reading my articles. Well, Mrs. Bradley, I'm not certain that they actually gambled *in* the tunnels. It appears more likely that the games of chance took place in basement rooms adjacent to the tunnels

where they could provide convenient escape routes.

After reading the recent Old Town articles (Jan. 23 & 30), **Eric Eisemann,** director of the Oregon Preservation Research Center, would like to make readers aware of the award-winning documentary *Old Portland On Foot.* This 30-minute video presentation featuring **John Meynink** is available for public use without charge by the Center.

A challenge to the city and county

An even more delightful treat is to join the 85-year-old Meynink on his weekly walking tours of the Skidmore/Old Town Historic District. Call the Preservation Center at 243-1923 for more information.

And speaking of octogenarians who know what they're talking about, 88-year-old ex-Mayor **Fred Peterson** advises me that one of River City's first car washes was across the street from the Tik Tok (*An orphaned intersection*—Nov. 14), not on the same lot.

That would have put it where Scotty's Hamburgers stood for 20 years. And, speaking of Scotty's, I've been unable to find even a single snapshot of that once-burgeoning hamburger hangout. If anyone has one, hot dog impresario **Jim Roake** would love to get his hands on it.

More than one nostalgic Portlander reveled in the recollection of downtown on New Year's Eve in the late '40s and early '50s (*Headline highlights*—Jan. 2). Broadway was obviously our Times Square. And since we now have a real square, why not revive the tradition? Any takers for midnight, December 31, 1985?

In further hope of establishing new traditions, I'm prepared to persist in pursuing a crusade to light the central downtown bridges during the holidays. (*Symbols of the season*—Dec. 26). It would be an annual event which, in publicity value alone, would far outweigh the cost.

Long-stemmed *Round the Roses* to column contributors **Cindy McBurney** (*The Cinnamon Bear*—Dec. 12). **Ron Schmidt** and **Ken Manske** (*O Tannenbaum*—Dec. 19), **Buddy Meadows** (*Symbols of the season*—Dec. 26), **Fred "Pete" Peterson** for an incomparable interview (*Four years with Fred*—Jan. 16). **Bill Naito** (*Old Town*—Jan. 30) and **Jane Davies,** Hank Gaylord and Joe Littak (*View-Master*—Feb.6).

Answers: The light fixtures were part of the building from its completion in 1912. The *Oregon Journal* Building.

Notes & Anecdotes: Spring '85

May 8, 1985

This North Portland landmark was another victim of the 1948 (Vanport) flood. What facility lay behind the columned facade? (Answer below).

By now just about everyone in town knows that the Hawthorne Bridge is closed. What very few realize, however, is that it's the oldest of the downtown bridges and will celebrate its 75th birthday in December. So don't blame the Hawthorne for having a couple of cracks. Repair is preferable to replacement.

There's no one left around to recollect the city's early fires and floods. (*Portland Disasters: The Fire of '73*—Feb. 27 and *The Flood of '94*—Mar. 20) but a lot of Portlanders can recall the Vanport Flood of '48 (*Portland Disasters*—April 3), including yours truly.

My grandparents had a small farm on Schmeer Road just west of Portland Meadows at the time. The barn floated off its foundation and, even though the house (it's still there) sat on a knoll, the flood waters almost reached its eaves.

Black Hawthonre Br. (top), 1948 Flood. Old Morrison Br. swing span open (center).

I was a second-grader then but I remember well my dad and uncle complaining about the salvo of immunization shots they were required to undergo before launching a rowboat into the slowly receding waters to see what could be salvaged.

Retired fireman and sometime local office seeker **Bill Grenfell** has good reason to remember the fire department from the 1920s forward (*The Modern Era*—Mar. 27). His uncle, Edward Grenfell, was chief from 1928 to 1957. **Mrs. S.C. Spitzer** goes that one better. Her father was a good friend of turn-of-the-century Chief David Campbell (*Paid Protection*—Mar. 13).

To the many readers who have called *This Week* magazine and not heard back from me, my apologies. I assure you that I have tried to return your calls but was unable to reach you. If you have a question or comment, please drop me a note.

In reply to a number of *Roses* readers who, like **Sister Mary Mercy Taylor** and **Al Leichner,** want a complete set of *Round the Roses* columns, there are 102 as of this writing and my photocopying bills are beginning to look like the national debt. If you'll wait around one more year, I'll have enough for a book which is already in the planning.

The Portland Elks story (*Elkdom: A proud Brotherhood*—Mar. 6) elicited considerable response, not accolades (although the guys at Oregon City Lodge 1189 did have some much appreciated, complimentary comments) because of an error.

I'm afraid I brought this one on myself by writing that the Elks are "the largest and oldest" fraternal organization in these United States. Although the former statement is accurate, the latter is a blatant falsehood.

E.F. Brooks of Hillsboro points out that his Masonic Lodge was founded in 1853 and a legion of Masons made it quite clear to me that the order dates back to early 18th century colonial days in this country. Among its members

Fire Chief Grenfell and commissioner Earl with George Baker First Aid Car, 1953.

were some of America's greatest historical figures.,

As to the highly romanticized Chinatown tunnels, some of which were shown in a photo of the Elephant & Castle's basement (*Notes & Anecdotes*—Feb. 13), my good friend **Christine Olsen**, who was manager of that English-style pub for four years, reminds me that the tunnels weren't Chinese at all. These subterranean subways were built for the convenience of the merchants.

Christine may be able to enlighten us further on the Chinese connecton as she is about to depart for a year of study and work in Taiwan. I wish her the finest fortune and a speedy return.

Bouquets to column contributors: **Don Mayer** of the Portland Fire Bureau (Feb. 20, Mar. 13 & Mar. 27), **George Helzer** (*Elkdom*—Mar. 6), **Glen Gillespie** and **Al Matson** of PP&L (*The Lincoln Steam Plant*—April 10) and to **Bill** and **Sam Naito** for The Galleria (*Portland Merchants: Olds & Kings*—May 1).

To Oregon Historical Society photo library stalwarts, **Elizabeth Winroth** and **Diana Shenk**, for assistance above and beyond the call, etc., go a dozen long-stemmed *Round the Roses* (real ones).

Answer: It is the former front of the Pacific International Livestock Exposition Building (now the Expo Center).

Notes & Anecdotes: Summer '85

July 31, 1985

The Summer of '85 is a hot one. What was the hottest temperature ever recorded in Portland and when did it occur? (Answers below).

Almost two years ago I wrote about the migration to the Willamette Valley over the Old Oregon Trail (*Wagon Wheels a-Rollin'*—Sept. 17, 1983). That story, as with most that are condensed down to a quarter page, only skimmed the surface of the subject.

A retired Gresham couple, **Ruth** and **Orson Goodrich,** have lived the Oregon Trail, love it and tell folks about it in a two-hour slide/sychronized sound show. For more than 25 years the Goodriches have traced and retraced the trail as an obviously engrossing hobby.

Wagon wheels really rolled in the 1850s.

We're talking all 1,930 miles from Independence, Mo., to Oregon City via the Barlow Trail and rafting down the Columbia. If your group would like to see this fascinating presentation, they'll show it to you free within 15-20 miles of Gresham. For greater distances they'd appreciate having their auto expenses covered. Call them at 666-9070 or write Orson P. Goodrich, 579 N.E. Fleming, Gresham, OR 97030.

What would you do if the secretary to the principal of your grade school wrote to you and said she remembered you? If you still were in high school this wouldn't be so unnerving. However, for me high school is ancient history.

So when I received a delightful note from Mrs. Simpson, my first reaction was to feel flattered. But my second was to ask myself why **Ruth Simpson** remembers me. Thousands of kids went through Rose City Park Grade School during the years she worked there (1946-59). Paradoxically, she started the same year I did.

My memories of her are vague but quite positive. Her boss, and our head disciplinarian was another matter. **Mr. Childers** was old and stern. Not mean, mind you, but he ran the place like grade schools should be administered. You're there to learn and grow, not to play around and precipitate problems.

That's why a primary and secondary education was such a good one then. From all I can glean, they're still trying to make it that way. But, with parental apathy and lack of student respect and self-discipline, it's becoming more difficult.

So why do you remember me, Mrs. Simpson? Was it my outstanding learning abilities or my ability to stand in your office waiting to be talked to by Mr. Childers?

Answers: 107 degrees. August 8 and 10, 1981.

Laurette Kenney writes me about Lone Fir Cemetery (*Portland Memorials*—May 15) and the Sunday walks her family took through that serene setting in the early 1920s. She recalls the many Chinese graves at the west end, most of which were later removed for shipment back to China. I quote from Mrs. Kenney: "Small pieces of white paper with three holes in each were strewn throughout the grounds. I understand these papers were scattered by the funeral entourage along its route. The belief was that the Evil One had to go through each hole in each paper before he could accost the decedent. By doing this the deceased could be put safely away before he (the Evil One) arrived."

Like the Oregon Trail, the three-part series on Portland Trolleys (July 10, 17, 24) only touched the tip. This story fills a visually intriguing, thoroughly researched and painstakingly documented book *Fares Please!* by **John T. Labbe.** It and its author were my sources. Mr. Labbe also generously allowed me to use photographs from his extensive collection to illustrate these articles.

Ninety-three-year-old **Dora Martin Dunham** of Lake Oswego says that the Elks article (*A proud brotherhood in Portland*—March 6) evoked echoes of her past. She was part of the management team that ran the club's dining room and put on lavish dances and parties during the late 1920s and early '30s. "It was," proclaims Dora, "without exception, the most beautiful dining place in Portland."

The Elks Temple. Portland's finest dining room in the '20s.

Special bouquets to all the Commercial Club of Portland members who expressed such kind words for my May 29 story (*Portland Profiles: Isabel "The Hat" Hoyt*). I only wish I could have had one more "date" with that glorious gal.

And long-stemmed *Round the Roses* to quarterly column contributors **Harry Zimmerman** and **Norman Griffith** (*The two Riversides*—May 22), **Jim Rogers** (*Isabell Hoyt*—May 29), **Jerry Westin** (*The Portland Memorial*—June 5), **Stu LaGris** (*Grand Central Bowl*—June 19), and **Fred. L. "Pete" Peterson** (*Terry Schrunk*—June 26 & July 3).

Notes & Anecdotes: Fall '85

October 30, 1985

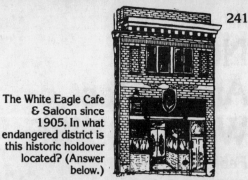

The White Eagle Cafe & Saloon since 1905. In what endangered district is this historic holdover located? (Answer below.)

"To err is human . . . "—Once again, I've proved to be all too human. Fortunately, those who called me to task for a couple of glaring errors have been "divinely forgiving."

Governing identities—It's one thing to succeed a man but quite another to be mistaken for him. And that's just what I did to Oregon Governor **Robert D. Holmes** who succeeded Paul Patterson in 1956. Patterson's name was mistakenly used with Holmes' picture in the Sept. 4 article (*OMSI: Scientifically funtasticational*). **Robert Sealy** of Seaside and **Frank Roberts** were quick to point it out. Sealy knew Holmes well, having worked for him in the radio business.

Gov. Holmes (not Patterson) with OMSI Man.

Mixed-up monkey business—Washington Zoo volunteer **Al Sulman** called to advise that Harry, the zoo's dominant male orangutan, was called "Charlie," which is the name of one of the chimpanzees in *A lot is new at the zoo* (Aug. 28). My apologies to Harry and Charlie, a couple of characters that really monkey around to show you a good time at the zoo.

Further zoo re-marks—The contributions of longtime zoo director Jack Marks (*High marks for the director*—Aug. 21) are remembered by **Vivian Goodrich Taylor.** She writes, "I understand Mr. Marks made daily rounds of food markets to get leftovers to feed the animals . . . his efforts to keep the Portland zoo alive and well have never been completely recognized."

Right day, wrong date—The foregoing faux pas give me an easy empathy with KPTV's news department which featured Portland's legendary Columbus Day Storm on its evening news segment to highlight this year's commemoration of the great explorer. Only trouble was something didn't quite ring true when the date October 14, 1962, appeared on the screen. Red faces were worn all around the station on S.W. 20th Place as phones rang off the hook the following day. Friendly reprimands from Portlanders who experienced the only hurricane in Oregon's recorded history let staffers know that **Columbus Day** fell on October 12th that year.

A tale of two citadels—A photo of U.S. National Bank's Corinthian colonnade at S.W., 6th and Stark was inadvertently switched with First National's (First Interstate) Greek revival edifice at S.W. 5th and Stark (*First was first*—Oct. 2). The eagle eye of **E. Dean Anderson,** among others, put me into the pillory on that one.

First National (not U.S.) Bank's Greek revival.

Earliest eatery—It's indusputable that Huber's since 1879 is Portland's oldest restaurant (*Early Eateries*—Sept. 11) but honors for oldest continuously operating in one place under the same name should apparently go to the White Eagle Cafe and Saloon, at N. Russell and Mississippi since 1905. That's two years earlier than Dan & Louis Oyster Bar founded at S.W. Ankeny and 2nd in 1907 (*Early eateries*—Sept. 18). The White Eagle has only had four owners in its 80-year history. **Chuck Hughes,** who took over in 1978, and his wife, **Sue,** are the current proud proprietors of this "Old Albina" establishment.

Mrs. C. M. Nelson has supplied me with the chronology of the volunteer support groups that ensured OMSI's survival during it early struggling years (*OMSI*—Sept. 4). In the 1949-'50 period the Pioneer Women's Committee made the difference, prying open pocketbooks around the state. The Junior League took over the task in the fifties with "OMSI Coffee Days" which led to the first auction in 1960.

A dozen long-stemmed *Round the Roses* to column contributors **Jessie Schuster** (*Alpenrose*—Aug.7) **Gene Leo** and **Jane Hartling** (*Washington Park Zoo*—Aug. 14, 21 & 28), **Barbara Curtis** and **Dean Ivey** (*OMSI*—Sept. 4), **James** and **David Louie** (*Huber's since 1879*—Sept. 11), **Louis** and **Doug Wachsmuth** (*Dan & Louis Oyster Bar*—Sept. 18), and **Bill McCormick** (*Jake's Famous Crawfish*—Sept.25). And more bouquets to Money Merchant series advisors **Floyd Smith** (*First was first*—Oct. 2), **Richard Griebel** (*Bank on U.S.*—Oct. 9) and **Mick Scott** (*Ben's equitable*—Oct. 16).

Answer: It is in a group of 1880s and '90s brick buildings at N. Russell and Mississippi, which are among the last "Old Albina" survivors.

Notes & Anecdotes: Winter '85-'86

February 5, 1985

Alameda Park brochure, 1910. What is the dazzling description of Alameda in Charles Larson's 1985 whodunnit novel, *The Portland Murders?* (answer below) .

The new year is over a month old. Resolutions have inevitably been broken — mine among them. One torn asunder for the second consecutive year, is "Thou shalt not make glaring errors in thy column." But, alas and alack, it happened again. Particularly "alack" as in a lack of 18 hours a day for research.

Lloyd Phillips writes to advise me that St. Patrick's Catholic Church at N.W. 19th and Savier, dedicated in 1891, is *not* the oldest Portland church in continuous use (*Enduring edifices*— Dec. 18). That singular distinction goes to First Immanuel Lutheran at N.W. 19th and Irving, built in 1882.

Here we have a classic case of yours truly being caught cribbing. You'd think all those sources I referred to, going at least 40 years back, would have gotten it right. Well, all I can say, Mr. Phillips, is "we try." And it's alert and knowledgeable readers like you who remind a writer like me that he must always check a number of sources just to be certain that the facts are correct.

St. Patrick's, oldest church?

When it comes to facts, however, you can only be absolutely certain if you've seen it with your own eyes. Although I don't think Mr. Phillips was around for the dedicaton of Immanuel Lutheran he does personally recall that the demise of the Swan Island Airport, a vintage (March 21, 1984) article, was due to more than dangerous winds and a short runway. In the 1920s and '30s much home heating was still wood, sawdust and coal. The "terrible pea soup atmosphere," as Phillips recalls it, severely limited visibility.

To an article suggestion from **Doris Bennett,** I'd like to respond that I too have been intrigued by the old buildings at the intersection of N. Russell and Mississippi. The White Eagle Cafe, mentioned in *Notes & Anecdotes*—Fall '85 (Oct. 30), is in the heart of this apparently doomed, two-block historic remnant of the City of Albina's original railyard area.

Historic Preservation League Director Eric Eisemann and his dedicated, primarily volunteer staff, have applied every legal means at their disposal to preserve this district. But it now seems apparent that the out-of-state banking interests, which own the key surviving 1890s buildings, are determined to have them demolished.

It may, regrettably, be too late for this district but the Historic Preservation League of Oregon would like to have interested citizens throughout the state as supporters of the ongoing battle to save Oregon's tangible history. Basic membership is $15 per year. Call 243-1923 for information.

As long as we're promoting for a good cause, you might be interested in tuning in KBOO Radio 90.7 FM this Friday night and for the next five weeks. Why? Because **Matthew Clark** and **Karl Klooster** will conducting a six-part series of one-hour dialogues entitled "River City Recollections." Catchy, don't you think?

Seriously, we've put a lot of research and rehearsal into this series. And Clark's delightful show, The *Starlight Express,* has been a popular Friday night feature on KBOO for 12 years. Did I say Friday night? Actually, it's Saturday morning at 1 a.m. You're all up then, right? So get in on this scintillating discussion — live. Don't wait for the recording to be aired later at a more convenient time.

One last commercial announcement. If you like your information first hand, my two-part Portland History series begins Feb. 6, 7-8:30 p.m. at the Sellwood Community Center. Call 236-4022 for reservations. At $10 I can guarantee it will be at least as entertaining and definitely more informative than two of your typical major motion pictures.

James Stephens's house, oldest residence?

Now that the pitches have been exhausted on to **Rick Reese,** a bus tour operator who pastes my columns in his windows. Although I, personally, am convinced that the oldest surviving residence in the City of Portland is **James B. Stephens'** house, circa 1862, your claim regarding the Scholls Ferry house will be fully investigated. A check of old and new city limits is first on the list. This could very well be a case of "close but no cigar." We'll be in touch.

A dozen long-stemmed *Round the Roses* to **Chuck Charnquist** (*Lewis & Clark*—Nov. 6), **Dr. James Covert** (*University of Portland*—Nov. 13), **Pres. Paul Bragdon, Prof. Dorothy Johansen** and **Harriet Watson** (*Reed College*—Nov. 20), **Clarence Hein** (*Portland State*—Nov. 27), **Julie Feinstein** and **Lora Meyer** of the Mittleman Jewish Community Center and the Jewish Historical Society (*Portland Church Series*—Dec. 4, 11, 18, 25).

Answer: "Alameda Drive dangles like a necklace along the hilltops of Northwest Portland."

Notes & Anecdotes: Spring '86

April 30, 1986

WE'VE RECEIVED SOME **INTRIGUING** OVER-THE-FREEWAY CONVENTION CENTER DESIGN PROPOSALS, BUD!

WE CERTAINLY **HAVE**, LLOYD!

Klooster '86

The proposed convention center. What are the projected How much will it add to the local economy? (Answers below).

Over the last three years a number of prominent Portland companies have been profiled in this column. Tektronix (*Long-time leader, technologically*—Feb. 12) was the most recent in the series.

As that article was about to go to press, **Howard Vollum,** Tektronix co-founder and chairman, passed away. He left behind a legacy of the largest ever Oregon corporation and the most generous bequests in the state's history. More than two dozen organizations and institutions were the beneficiaries of this unprecendented philanthropy.

Oswego's smelting furnace in George Rogers Park.

The primeval preserve we call Forest Park (*A natural evolution*—March 5) is recalled by **Jim Grande** who, as a boy scout in the early 1930s, went on weekend outings in the area. Grande remembers an abandoned mine that was apparently part of the regionwide search for iron ore deposits to supply the Oregon Iron Works at Oswego (*Irontown evolves*—April 9).

Mary Sauter has been a stalwart of Old Albina historic preservation (*Separate cities*—March 12) since 1968 when she and her husband purchased and began their magnificent restoration of the John Palmer House at N. Mississippi and Skidmore. Sauter would like readers to know that the North/Northeast Boosters are on the move.

Their second annual conference on February 8 focused on the original Albina City limits and promoted the area's history and tourism. Five potential historic districts lie within those early boundaries — Elliot, Piedmont, Irvington, Woodlawn and Kenton. Tours have been set up and a centennial celebration is planned for 1987. Call Mary for

more information at 284-5893.

Historic preservation will be an important part of Portland activities in May. From May 10 to 18, National Historic Preservation week will be celebrated with a full calendar of events. It begins with formal dedication of Ankeny Park and Arcade on May 10 conducted by the Historic Preservation League of Oregon. On May 15 the Portland Historic Landmarks Commission will present their 10th annual landmark awards honoring the best local restorations during the past year.

Central Eastside Industrial Council Executive Director **Peter Fry** presents the position of CEID members in discussing with me **Robert Mickelson's** over-the-freeway convention center concept (*A public proposal*—March 26). The council supports qualitative rather than quantitative development of the eastside core. They would like to retain the area's lowrise configuration and, in particular, the centrally located produce district which provides convenient service to Portland's major hotels and restaurants.

Mickelson's proposed convention center site would span Sullivan's Gulch, that imaginary boundary between the north and south sections of the eastside core. But, more than that, it would attract attention. Seattle is already in the process of building a similar facility in the heart of its downtown.

After almost a year of deliberations, the Regional (CTS) Committee has reduced its selection to four sites and does not seem inclined to conduct any additional feasibility studies. Although committee chairman **Robert Ridgely** and Mayor **Bud Clark** have both indicated interest to this writer in the freeway proposal, they cite the perceived high cost of construction as a primary impediment.

Ridgely also expressed concern over the possible public reaction to another prolonged period of Banfield congestion. To this Mickelson responds that it might get commuters onto Light Rail since it will be in operation well before convention center construction would commence.

One thing is certain. Unless voters in the tri-county area approve the general obligation bond measure this November, nothing will happen. Only with unanimity among all interests and support of the media can this occur.

Long-stemmed *Round the Roses* to column contributors **Susan Stone** (*Tektronix*—Feb. 12). **E. Kimbark MacColl** for his books "Shaping of a City" and "Growth of a City" which were invaluable in the Separate Cities series (March 12, 19 and April 2, 9, 16), **Margaret Pietsch** for material drawn from her book, "Riverwood: Yesterday and Today" and blossoming bouquets to **Robert Mickelson** for adding an exciting dimension to our quest for a convention center.

Answers: The four sites range fron $80 to $98 million. A minimum of $60 million annually not considering inflation.

Notes &
Anecdotes:
Summer '86

July 16 1986

Rocky Butte. How high is its flat-topped promontory? What is the highest point in Multnomah County? (Answers below).

It's never been too late for a *Round the Roses* column contribution. Two and a-half years ago, I asked attorney **Alan Viewig**, a member of the National Railway Historical Society, to verify how long it took the Empire Builder to travel between Portland and Minneapolis during the 1940s and '50s. My estimate was 46 hours (*Union Station*—Nov. 2, 1983). After obviously exhaustive research, Alan advised that the official timetable computed to 39½ hours — a real express run.

In addition to his activities in railroad antiquities, Alan is also attempting to establish a local chapter of the Society for Industrial Archaeology. The SIA is associated with the Smithsonian and is receiving increased attention for the role it plays in documenting society's technological advances. Anyone interested in supporting this important effort should contact Alan Viewig at 228-8655.

Four-time Rose Cup winner, Monte Shelton

Portland's celebration of Preservation Week (*Getting Historical*—May 7) was a resounding success and one of its highlights was the Portland Landmark Commission's recognition of one of its own. A one-of-a-kind award, "The Leo," was created to honor Portland Planning Bureau Chief Planner **Leo Williams** for his many contributions to local preservation, in particular the outstanding photographic documentation and presentations he developed over nearly two decades.

The *Round the Roses* column on Portland populist mayors (*Rose Buds: Past, present and future*—May 14) was based on the premise that history repeats itself. That old adage seems to be proving regrettably true as certain entrenched establishment interests (long-term Ivancie cronies stand up and show yourselves) continue to try and undermine **Mayor Bud Clark's** administration. It's sad testimony to the old boy *and* girl network in this city that has prevented Portland from realizing its potential in the past and appears to want to perpetuate that cozy, for a few, status quo.

Retired *Oregon Journal* reporter **Earl R. "Sarge" Goodwin,** who defined the Rose City Park district boundaries in a 1930 article (*A child's playground*—May 21), writes to say "I walked the entire area interviewing businessmen, neighbors and old-time residents and used my own judgement." He goes on to mention that the city engineer contacted him years later to try and determine what maps he used for his deductions since none could be found. Such is the stuff of historical precedent.

In regard to the same article, **Evelyn Henderson Lee** reflects on her years as a student at our mutual alma mater, Rose City Park Grade School; she was a first grader in 1912, the year the school opened. Mrs. Lee recalls the 1914 Rose Festival Electric Parade in which the entire school participated. "The school was given the theme 'The Japanese," she relates. "The majority of us walked the full distance dressed as Japanese girls and boys.

After reading the May 28 column (*Rocky Butte: An adolescent's adventure*), **Blaine Webster** asked me when I was going to write about the next stage in my Rocky Butte adventures. Well, Blaine, those mid-late teen years did include some educational experiences on the Butte, didn't they? But I think it best to demur on relating the details of those post-adolescent escapades.

Doug Sowles notes that local racing legend **Monte Shelton** was short-changed in my recap of his Rose Cup victories (*Racing for the roses*—June 11). Shelton won in 1972, '74, '76 and 1984, which was omitted. Just after the article appeared, he made it five by capturing this year's race in his newly-acquired Porsche.

I was steered to the 74-year history of the Portland stockyards (*Expo and environs*—June 18) by **Harold Harkins** who helped **Barry** and **Marian Brownell** revitalize the Red Steer Restaurant in 1984. That eating and entertainment establishment has been part of the area since 1917 and is worth visiting today for the Brownells' butterfly collection alone.

Burnside Community Council Executive Director **Michael Stoops** conveys his thanks for being edified about the U.S. Customs House (*Hail to the port*—July 2). Thank you for your kind words, Michael. There's no way this city can thank you for your good works.

Long-stemmed *Round the Roses* to the column contributors **Eric Eisemann, Pam Johnson** and **Judith Rees** (*Preservation Week*—May 17), **Bob Ames and Bill Hildick** (*Racing for the roses*—June 11) and **Elizabeth Winroth** (*the Willamette Stone*—June 25). To **Dave Kiel, Chuck Heffler, Mike McManigal** and **Jerry Strand** go special bouquets for the reminisces (*A child's playground*—May 21) and (*An adolescent's adventures*—May 28) resulting from the real life growing pains we shared.

Answers: Rocky Butte is 612 feet high at the highest point in J.W. Hill Park. Larch Mountain at 4058 feet, is the county's highest.

Notes & Anecdotes: Fall '86

October 22, 1986

The Northwest's premier tourism promotor, Frank Branch Riley (*Oregon's Ambassador* — Sept. 17) on Mt. Hood, 1920s. To which prominent Portland club did he belong? (Answer below.)

How high is up (elevation wise) in Multnomah County? In *Notes & Anecdotes Summer 1986*—July 16, I quoted the summit of Larch Mountain, at 4058 feet, as the county's highest point. Several Rose readers challenged that statement saying the mountain is in Hood River County. To settle the disagreement, **Alan Young** of Multnomah County's Surveys and Records Office checked their detailed topographic map. Larch Mountain is entirely in Multnomah but Hood River needn't feel inferior since Mount Hood's summit is within its boundaries.

Speaking of higher-up, many of the local higher-ups belong to the city's prestigious private clubs which were chronicled over the past several weeks in this column. Social clubs have come and gone in Portland. Some of them were important elements of their era, which makes the survivors all the more significant.

One, The Lang Syne Society, consisted of powerful business and political figures who met for annual dinners each January. This men-only organization lasted from the 1890s until the late 1930s when many of its members were well past retirement age. The Turn Verein, an all-German social society, thrived from the 1870s through the 1920s when national identity was no longer a cohesive force for the group.

The Turn Verein (German Club) on S.W. 13th near Jefferson, ca. 1920

Tradition rooted in pioneer power mark the 19th century clubs that have carried forward to the present. Bouquets of Madame Testout roses for those column contributors who made these stories complete. **Bob Hedges** (*Arlington Club*—July 30), **Jan Richter** and **Genevieve Smith** (*University Club*—Aug. 6), **Ed Francis** and **Calvin Buswell** (*Waverley Country Club*—Aug. 13), **Emery Neale** and **Sam Lee** (*Irvington Club*—Sept. 3).

Bringing the background of Portland's most exclusive women's social club, founded in 1928, into focus (*The Town Club*—Aug. 27) were **Mrs. Walter H. "Sally" Evans** and **Michael Roberts.** The youngest of the elite organizations originated in the 1930s and its history was provided by the people who made it. The Menefee Cup filled with Round the Roses is shared by **Joan Metz, Robert Warren Sr., Bob Noyes Jr., Mrs. Theodore "Marie" Miller, Sam Lee** (a double contributor) and **Betsy Stark** for their team effort on *The Racquet Club*—Sept. 10.

Giving out accolades is a lot easier than admitting to errors. Fessin' up, **Dagmar Zoubek** caught me and my usually eagle-eyed editor with our dictionaries down. Going back to the July 2 article (*The Customs House: Hail to the Port*) there was not one but two incorrect words. Fortunately, this seldumb happens. We do try.

In that story, *populous* (the adjective) was used instead of *populace* (the noun). Worse, *balustrades* (the architectural term for low parapets topped by a rail) was butchered by yours truly, coming out *ballistrades*, in print.

Young attorney C.E.S. Wood, mid-1880s.

However, Dagmar, your insistence that the possessive "its" should have an apostrophe is not correct. It's confusing, but the "it" rule is an exception. "Its", as in "its place in history" has no apostrophe, whereas the contraction "it's" as in "it's (it is) correct" does.

Enough of the English lesson. We can always learn more about the proper construction of our vexingly complex and marvelously rich language. We can also learn something from the *Round the Roses* column (*Bud Clark: Burned by Brokaw*—Oct. 1). As much as I was down on TV **Tom Brokaw** for his inexcusable public reiteration of the mayor's inappropriate private remark, the NBC news anchor does seem to have more on-air charisma than either of his competitive network counterparts — **Dan Rather** and **Peter Jennings.**

Emerging fron the forest of political faux pas to the Woods of Portland prominence, Charles Erskine Scott Wood (*Renaissance radical*—Sept. 24) and his offspring (*A Portland family*—Oct. 8) broke the mold when it comes to local eclecticism. A blooming bevy of five-petaled centerpieces to a number of Wood descendants for their invaluable input.

With a surplus of high society stories surfacing in this quarterly recap, a bit of the regular guy is a welcome relief. Let's hear it for G.I. Joe's (*A surplus of success*—July 23). To **David Orkney,** for his anecdotes about his father, company founder Ed Orkney, goes a *Round the Roses* ribbon of merit.

Lastly, but not leastly, is the story of Matthew Deady (*Justice for all*—Oct. 15). If you'd like to learn a lot more about Portland and this pivotal figure in Oregon law, seek out the personal perspectives of the 33-year, U.S. District Court judge. "Pharisee Among Philistines" is the private, almost daily diary of the dynamic Deady covering the last 21 years (1871-1892) of his career.

Answer: Riley was a member of the exclusive University Club at S.W. Sixth and Jefferson for more than 60 years.

Notes & Anecdotes: Winter '86-'87

January 21, 1987

Deco statue in Battleship Oregon Memorial Park, late 1930s. What happened to it? (Answer below)

One benefit to egg on the face is that it hides the reddened cheeks of chagrin. Attempting to dislodge foot from mouth, this writer reeled as a deluge of indignant letters assailed him during October. Members of the Lang Syne Society were in arms about the mistaken statement in (*Notes & Anecdotes: Fall '86*—Oct. 22) that their organization was no longer in existence.

"It's 73rd meeting was held April 29, 1986, with 250 attending. Not quite rigor mortis," chided 93-year-old retired dentist **Collister Wheeler.** "We may be old — but we're not dead," chimed in the society's current secretary/treasurer, **J. Elliot Busey,** a well-known local lawyer. **C.H. Campbell** commented, "originally formed in 1913 to cement the bonds of friendship among early businessmen . . . the society remains alive and well."

Lang Syne Society reunion, Jan. 26, 1916

A list of Lang Syne's past presidents reads like a who's who of Portland. Present membership is equally impressive. It consists of men who "have held positions of responsibility and trust in the metropolitan district for a period of 25 years or more." The society holds only one event each year — its annual reunion dinner.

Concluding the corrections for this quarter, **Bernard Lowenthal** was "incited" to send me a missive concerning a spelling error. In the C.E.S. Wood story (*Renaissance radical*—Sept. 24), "insightful" appeared as "inciteful." The fact that the latter word doesn't exist is shortsighted enough to arouse any grammatical additct to action.

A query comes from **Mrs. Robert F. "Mary" Budrow** of Silverton in regard to early Oregon jurist Mathew P. Deady (*Justice for all*—Oct. 15) and his descendants. In answer to your first question, Mrs. Budrow, the information for my story came from a combination of sources — a biography, "History of the Life of Matthew P. Deady" by Hubert Howe Bancroft published in 1890, Deady's own diary, "Pharisee Among Philistines," edited by Malcolm Clark Jr. in 1975 and the Oregon Historical Society's scrapbook collection.

In regard to your hope of contacting a current Deady family member. I'll let the following excerpt from you letter speak for itself. Perhaps it will elicit a response from some Roses' reader. "Judge Deady had a grandson named Hanover Deady who was employed by the gas company for many years. I have been trying to locate him for some time as I have an item which should belong to his family."

After reading (*Iron Firemen: Stoking the home fires*—Nov. 19), **Haskell Carter** sent me a copy of his personal memoirs. Thirty-four of its 145 pages are devoted to Carter's firsthand account of his quarter-of-a-century career with the company as production manager and chief engineer.

Just turned 89 on Jan. 15, Mr. Carter still heads Carter Manufacturing Company which he founded in 1951, the year he left Iron Fireman.

The Battleship Oregon article (*Bulldog of the sea*—Dec. 3) pushed the personal nostalgia button for a number of native Portlanders who remember the grand old warrior from her museum days on the waterfront. Both **Laurette Kenney** and **Al Leichner** relate the role played by local youngsters in the drive to preserve the ship as a permanent memorial.

"We were told that if every schoolchild contributed a 10-cent piece it would create a fund that would endow the Oregon in perpetuity," recalls Kenney from her experience in the early 1920s. According to Leichner, the effort extended into the 1930s. "Children donated pennies, nickels and dimes to help preserve the Battleship Oregon . . . the teacher came to each desk with a tin can. We were later to learn that it was a lost cause." Mrs. Kenney provides further perspective. "Our country was submerged into World War II. The people of Portland were asked to sacrifice our precious ship. The story proferred was that the nation needed the metal."

A silver punchbowl and silverware settings were presented to the ship by the people of Oregon. The punchbowl is still "somewhere in the state," according to the Oregon Maritime Museum. That "somewhere" is at The Oregon Historical Society. Most Portlanders knwo that the main military mast, the smokestacks and anchors survive. But few are aware that the Oregon's anchor chain languishes in a huge heap at the lowest level of PP&L's Lincoln steam plant just south of RiverPlace.

Lending a touch of mystery to the tale, **Lloyd Phillips** has sent a snapshot of a splendid statue that stood briefly in the Battleship's Memorial Park. "it lasted about six months and then disappeared," he states.

Long-stemmed *Round the Roses* go to this quarter's column contributors; **Barbara Hutchison, Mildred Schwab** and **Gregg Kantor** (*The Goldschmidt Legacy*—Oct. 29), **Alan Miller** (*Miller's for Men*—Nov. 12), **Sarah Russell, Carl Kato** and **Frank Womack** (*The Portland Chamber*—Nov. 26), **Emery Neale** (*Christmas Northwest*—Dec. 17, **Wayne Strohecker** (*The heights of service*—Dec. 24) and **Oscar Larsen** (*Hazelwood Creamery*—Jan. 7)

Answer: Basic research sources, admittedly not exhaustive, turned up no references to this Depression-era monument.

Notes & Anecdotes: Spring '87

April 29, 1987

The Marshall House (post commander's residence) on Officer's Row (left) Upon completion, 1886, and (right) in 1938 when Gen. Marshall occupied it. What is it used for now? (Answer below).

Bright ideas revisited. Currently before the City Council is a proposal to install twinkling lights on the Morrison Bridge, which celebrates its 100th anniversary this month. Two and one-half years ago, in the *Round the Roses* column of Dec. 26, 1984 (*Portland Christmas Symbols of the Season*), I proposed lighting all of the Willamette's core bridges (Steel, Burnside, Morrison and Hawthorne) during each holiday season. That suggestion still stands. But it's an expensive undertaking and one bridge is better than none.

So, let's not let this idea fizzle out with only a brief flicker. Write our mayor and commissioners or anyone else who has some clout. Let's light up the Morrison and bring a new dimension to downtown at night.

The record-setting, 100-foot wing span, Soviet ANT-25 at Vancouver's Pearson Field, June 1937

On to events that enlighten. The evening of April 9, I attended a gala celebration at the Marshall House on Officers' Row in Vancouver. The occasion was the opening of an exhibit honoring the 50th anniversary of the historic Soviet transpolar flight (*Vancouver Barracks*—April 8).

At the party, **Mayor Wayne Stuart** of San Jacinto, Calif., reminded me that only three weeks after the Chkalov-Baidukov-Belyakov triumph, another trio of Russians duplicated the feat and did it better.

M.M. Gromov, S.A. Danilin and A.B. Yumashov landed in San Jacinto on July 14, 1937, breaking both the time and distance records set by their countrymen. Coming so close on the heels of that "first ever" flight, the second accomplishment received far less press.

Though the Soviets established aviation hallmarks with these flights, they have had a tendency to change history to suit ideology. *This Week* magazine intended no such hubris by placing the Spanish-American War in 1889 rather than 1898. To all you readers who wrote in, please be assured that this was only transposition (as in oops), not time warp (as in H.G. Wells).

Northwest battle buff **Alvin R. Leichner** knows more about the hostilities between white and red men hereabouts than a platoon of history professors. He's traced the day-by-day details, searched battle sites for artifacts and chronicled his findings in publications such as *True West*. Leichner also knows that the First Artillery, not the Fourth Infantry, was the earliest Army outfits to occupy Columbia (later Vancouver) Barracks (*General development*—March 25).

The three-part series on Bull Run (*Portland Water*—Feb. 4, 11, and 18), opened a pipeline of commentary from several sources. **Ward Svart** would like to make it crystal clear that the Bull Run watershed is not fed by Mount Hood run-off. Readers may have inferred this from my context in the initial segment (*Bull Run's beginning*—Jan. 28).

I said " . . . the snow-laden peak on the eastern horizon and the deep, blue lake on its western slope." Though, when viewed from Portland, the reserve would appear to be adjacent to Mt. Hood. Bull Run Lake and the reservoirs later created below it are fed by a foothill watershed that rises separately just west of the mountain's lower slopes.

As a Bull-Run water quality engineer from 1972 to 1979, **Earl Paulson** would like to mention the closure of Reservoir No. 2 at southeast 60th and Division in 1976 due to pesticides, fertilizers and lead from automobile exhaust that had accumulated in minute, but detectable quantities.

This demonstrates the vital importance of the water quality control teams both at the headworks and in the city who perform tests daily to ensure that the highest standards are met.

The Water Bureau cannot, however, ensure the quality from the watershed, itself. Management of the reserve determines that factor and a public interest group, Citizens Interested in Bull Run Inc., feels that the U.S. Forest Service could be doing a better job.

One very active member of this organization, **Frank Gearhart,** points out that logging is even now underway at Falcon Creek in the northeastern section of the watershed. "It is our belief," says Gearhart, "that the Bull Run ecosystem is too fragile and its purpose too important for any activity of such intensity to take place."

To the Sons and Daughters of the Oregon Pioneers, I'd like to extend my thanks for the pleasure of being the featured speaker at your annual banquet on February 15. It's probably the only time I'll ever be able to fill in for the governor.

As thanks for this quarter's column contributions, the spring's first crop of *Round the Roses* bouquets go to **Jeanne McCormick** and **Liz Ozmond** (*Bull Run series*—Jan. 28, Feb. 4, 11), **Linda Giltin** (*Oregon Symphony*—Feb. 18, 25), **Irv Williams** (*Buckmans' consummate cleaner*—March 4), **Janice Rutherford** and **Mary Kline** (*Fort Vancouver and Barracks series*—March 18, 25, April 1) and **Shannon Stroud** and **Chris Tyle** (*OHSU: 100th Anniversary*—April 15 and 22).

Answer: Now owned by the city of Vancouver, its main floor is for public events. The Chkalov Transpolar flight 50th Anniversary Exhibition is on display there from April 9 to June 30. The upstairs and basement are offices.

Notes & Anecdotes: Summer '87

July 29, 1987

Portland television personality Bob Amsberry with Mickey Mouse puppet at Hollywood Lions Club, June 1956. How long was Walt Disney's Mickey Mouse Club on the air.? (Answer below).

Acknowledging the need for historic preservation and appreciating its results as was pointed out in recent *Roses* columns (May 6, 13 and 27), is one thing. Hands on preservation and restoration work is quite another. To find out first hand, **Christine Olsen** and I joined a half dozen other Historic Preservation League volunteers last June 13 in a personal, decidedly physical preservation act.

The Ruckle Creek Bridge, on an abandoned section of the historic Columbia River Highway just east of Eagle Creek Park, lay under years of accumulated growth and debris. Our cleanup crew tackled the chore with picks and shovels, wire brushes and brooms. Despite a few blisters and sore backs, the result proved rewarding for all.

The hillside bridge and its still smoothly surfaced, immediate approaches were spruced up and each of us felt at least a small sense of accomplishment. Our only regret was that a portion of the bridge's handhewn stone wall has obviously been vandalized over the years. Thanks to **Mike Graves** and **Kathryn Elsesser** for coordinating a worthwhile project.

Multnomah Lodge on Scenic Highway, 1917.

This intimate encounter with the Northwest's first scenic highway helped me in developing the two-part series on the Columbia Gorge (*Viewpoints revisited*—June 17, and *It's highway and hotel*—June 24). Although they produced a handsome result, techniques of the Teens were pretty primitive when compared with the advanced engineering of the 1950s that allowed road-builders to span long ravines, build up roadbeds and carve out a much straighter course for the new route.

Eighty-year-old **Myron McCamley** of Beaverton added some personal anecdotes of his own to the Columbia Gorge Hotel story (June 24). McCamley grew up on a farm about a mile from the hotel and worked there during the summers of 1922 and 1923 as a busboy. "I remember Henry Thiele (then general manager) very well," Myron relates. "And his temper tantrums, too. He was a perfectionist. I assisted in the kitchen and the early electric dishwasher had a tumbler filled with BBs and phonograph needles that kept the silverware brightly polished."

Isabel Smith of Portland recalls the old scenic highway and its hostelries, too. But the location of one old roadside inn has escaped her. Isabel and her husband, **Robert**, visited a place called the Maxwell House in April 1945. She has a snapshot that says "On Mt. Hood Highway or Columbia River Highway." It was white with clapboard siding. The owner was Elsie Maxwell. If any *Roses* reader has further information about this elusive establishment, please write to me c/o *This Week* magazine.

Goodwill Industries' good works have been going on for three-score years in Portland (*Goodwill*—May 20) and their need for donations never ends. Help **Michael Miller** and his staff keep their 300 workers fully employed by making an extra effort to bring your no-longer-needed clothing and household items to one of Goodwill's 34 donation stations. For furniture pickup call 238-6100.

Special thanks to **Nick Taylor** for his input on early Portland radio and television (*The early ether*—July 1, *Air for all ages*—July 8 and *Getting channeled*—July 15). Nick was an engineer with KOIN Radio from 1942 to 1953 when he moved over to the brand new KOIN-TV Channel 6. He remained at the CBS affiliate as an engineer and cameraman until his retirement in 1983. Nick's recollections of the times contributed measurably to these stories.

Harkening back to an earlier episode, the *Roses* column on Col. Charles Erskine Scott Wood (*Renaissance radical*—Sept. 24, 1986) prompted **Ransome Rader** to inquire into my art appraisal expertise. Rader has a Wood watercolor and would like to know its value. **Marian Wood Kolisch**, herself an artist of some accomplishment with a camera, indicates that her grandfather's paintings can range in price fron the mid-hundreds to the low thousands. They will continue to appreciate as collectibles, particularly in the Northwest where awareness of attorney, soldier, poet, painter C.E.S. Wood and his accomplishments has had the greatest public exposure.

Having made my midnight raid on the Rose Gardens, I can give bevies of bouquets to those *Round the Roses* contributors who helped enliven last quarter's columns. So here go dozens of the long-stemmed, multi-petaled beauties to **Eric Eisemann, Sue Jensen** and **Kathryn Elsesser** (*Preservation Week*—May 6), **Karen Zisman** and **Barbara Grimala** (*Eastside emphasis*—May 13), **Karen deVoll** (*Goodwill*—May 20), **Bill McDonald** and **Jim Nielson** (*The Rosarians 75th*—May 3), **Jan Markstaller Donnelly** (*Royal reflections*—June 10), **Nick Taylor** and **Byron Swanson** (*Portland radio and TV*—July 1, 8 and 15), and **Gene Brendler** (*Mr. KPTV*—July 22).

Answer: Mickey Mouse Club ran on ABC from 1955 to 1959.

Notes & Anecdotes: Fall '87 - Part I

October 28, 1987

Mt. Zion Baptist Church at Northeast 9th and Fremont, a survivor of Albina's "Little Russian" era. When was it built and for which denomination? (Answers below).

Mein Gott in Himmel, have I ever incurred the wrath of the American Historical Society of Germans from Russia. Dedicated descendants of these "Volga" Germans have descended upon me from as far away as Arizona to advise that the "Little Russia" I described in the Roses article of Aug. 19 (*A lost community*) was but one of two Russian immigrant enclaves that thrived in Portland during the late 19th and early 20th centuries.

South Portland's Little Russia (the one discussed in that article) was a community composed principally of Russian Jews that maintained its ethnic identity to the end. In 1926, the western approaches to the newly completed Ross Island Bridge cut through the heart of its commercial district.

Philadelphia Community Mission Brethern Church, N.W. Mason at Garfield. Erected 1927. Originally Congregational Evangelical German Brethren Church.

Meanwhile, a group of Russia Germans had begun to establish an equally close-knit community across the river in Albina beginning around 1888-89. Thanks to numerous interested parties, I now have a comprehensive picture of that Little Russia, where Roses reader **Karen Gilbert's** great-grandparents, who had come from Norka in the Volga region, lived during the early part of this century.

As a result of the veritable plethora of interesting information I have received, this entire *Notes and Anecdotes* article is devoted to Portland's Russia Germans. Next week an unprecedented *Notes and Anecdotes—Part II* will appear to complete the coverage of responses to last quarter's articles including the Oregon Historical Society, East Portland's founder James B. Stephens, the local postal service, Blue Lake Park and the Columbus Day Storm.

As preface to the tale of the little Albina community, let's find out how German colonies came to be situated well within the borders of Mother Russia in the first place. In the mid-18th century, it seems

that Catherine the Great needed more farmers to cultivate the fertile Volga River Valley. In order to encourage capable immigrants, she dangled a tantalizing enticement — free land.

Thousands of Germans took the Czarina up on her offer. In 1767 several hundred of them founded the town of Norka in the upper Volga region — where they grew grain, intermarried and retained their own language and customs for 125 years.

But, with the tides of time came changes in the political climate, and, just as many Russian Jews departed during the 1880s and 90s, so did many of the transplanted Germans who, although living on the Volga for generations, had never really embraced Russia as their homeland. Word of the wide-open opportunities in Western America had reached into every corner of Europe. Although they were a few decades on the downside of the big land grab, hundreds of thousands of hopeful immigrants poured into the country. The Northwest appeared particularly attractive to the Russia Germans and, in addition to Portland, they developed sizable districts in Toppenish and Walla Walla, Wash.

Emigres from a number of Volga towns settled in Portland's eastside "Little Russia." The villages of Balzar and Frank were well represented. With Norka, however, some say it was almost as if the place had picked itself up and moved halfway around the world. Dozens of former neighbors once again lived and worked side by side.

This Old World microcosm stretched along Northeast Union and Seventh avenues from Fremont to Shaver. Retail businesses run by Volga Germans abounded along these blocks. Hildermann's, Repp Bros., Hergert's, Krombein's, Greenfell's and Bihn's all supplied groceries. Repp's, Krombein's and Hergert's specialized in meats. Geist's sold shoes. Trupp repaired them. Weimer's was the hardware and furniture dealer.

World War I produced a strange paradox for the former Volga villagers. Anti-German sentiment ran deep in Portland but these folks were hybrids. Better, they undoubtedly reasoned, to be a "damned Rooshun" than a "hated Hun." Still they clung to their roots and it wasn't until the beginning of the next great war that the well-entrenched community began to break down.

Financial pressures during the Depression forced widespread splits in the old family cohesion. A society centered around church life suffered as the size of congregations dwindled. Then, the war which took the young men for military service and brought a huge new wave of shipyard workers to the area, dealt the final blow.

The offspring of the Volga immigrants disseminated throughout Portland and elsewhere as another group of newcomers began to take their place. Like the Russia Germans, who had been a distinct minority, the blacks that concentrated in Albina, did so not only because of available housing at affordable rent. They, too, had a need for belonging — a sense of community in the midst of the larger, often unfriendly, world.

Special thanks to **George Brill, Cliff Haberman, Ruth Huber, Marie Krieger** and **Nicholas Schnell** (the Arizona connection) whose contributions made this story possible.

Answers: "Erbaut (constructed) 1914,' its dedication plaque proudly states. It was originally Zion Congregational. Many German reform Lutherans became Congregationalists.

Notes & Anecdotes: Fall '87 - Part II

November 4, 1987

The missing Avington Building entry arch is the Historic Preservation League of Oregon's symbol. When was the league founded? What was their most recent major event? (Answers below).

As regular Roses readers know, *Notes & Anecdotes* appears quarterly primarily to address responses to previously published articles. In the four and one-half-year history of this column, these comments to the columnist have been confined to four installments per year. Not that there hasn't often been enough material to fill this space several times over, but then some of the stories, themselves, would have been sacrificed.

Last week was the first-ever exception. It was a special story that merited the unprecedented departure from normal practice. Two vital and active Russian immigrant communities existed separately and simultaneously in the Rose City during the late 19th and early 20th centuries. One was in South Portland, the other in Albina. I had chronicled the former (Aug. 19) but not the latter and descendants of the Russia Germans who settled in that northeast enclave made resoundingly certain it did not go unnoticed.

Speaking of descendants, as a shirttail relative of James B. Stephens (*East Portland's founder*—Aug. 26), I got into a discussion of our noted mutual ancestor (my great-great grandfather was his half-brother) at the Stephens' annual reunion this past August. **Craig Keyes**, one of the crowd of cousins on hand, mentioned that he'd come across an interesting aside about James. B.

It seems that not only did the 1844 pioneer found East Portland and establish the Stark Street Ferry, he also made the first applejack in Oregon and planted the immediate area's first orchards and berry patches. So prized were Stephens' fruits and berries that brazen Westside boys made summertime sport of swimming across the river to raid "Uncle Jimmie's bountiful larder. There were no reports, however, of them pilfering a jug of jack fron his cellar to wash down the purloined produce.

Having introduced a relative tone to this column, another comment fron a relative (considerably closer kin than a cousin) is relevant. My father, **Leslie Klooster**, notes that, in the story on the evolution of local postal service (*Tales of the mails*—Sept. 9), I neglected to mention the Portland airport's role as one of the earliest experimental post offices to expedite all First Class Mail by air. Since Dad was superintendent of the facility and I worked there during the 1961 Christmas rush period while on vacation from college, that oversight may portend early Alzheimer's.

INTERIOR FORESTRY

The story of Portland's incomparable log cabin (*The Timber Temple*—Oct. 7) prompted **Don Miller, Bob Mickelson** and **Billy Hults** to add personal recollections. The first plywood ever produced was presented at the Forestry Center during the Lewis and Clark Exposition. A 9-foot-wide plank, hewn from a single tree, was also on display. And, hung all along the towering walls were 300 photos of American Indians by renowned photographer Edward S. Curtis who made a lifelong work of documenting North America's aborigines before their ancient way of life was gone forever.

A Roses reader inquiry has struck paydirt. **Isabel Smith** asked for information about the Maxwell House on the Columbia River Highway (*Notes & Anecdotes: Summer '87*—July 29). Not only was I able to locate the still extant structure in an inventory book with the help of **Elizabeth Winroth** at the Historical Society, but also the current owner/occupants of the house have written in and provided detailed background information.

The home, located one mile west of Bridal Veil on the old Scenic Highway, opened originally in 1916 as a chicken restaurant called Forest Hall. Over the years it has gone fron a private residence back to a restaurant (the Maxwell House that Mrs. Smith recalls from the late 1940s), to a rest home and back to a private residence again. Thanks to **Pat** and **Ellen Brothers** for their enlightening response.

Another query in need of an answer comes from a man who, along with his recently deceased partner, has become a legend in local preservation circles. First, a little background. **Benny Milligan** and **Jerry Bosco**, long-time co-owners of Victorian Facades, earned a well-deserved reputation over more than two decades as the premier Portland experts in Victorian-era residential restoration.

Glass making, plaster casting and wood graining were among the demanding skills they mastered resurrecting old relics and winning awards for the owners in the process. Just prior to Jerry's death in October fron a terminal illness, he and Benny decided to make a unique bequest to the Historic Preservation League of Oregon.

The Bosco-Milligan Bequest consists of three residential buildings, a historic commerical building on Southeast Grand Avenue, and thousands of Victorian house parts. The funds generated from the bequest may lead to a major grant for establishment of a regional preservation center in the 11,500 foot Grand Avenue facility.

Not to the question or, more properly, the quest. The logo/symbol of the Historic Preservation League is a Palladian arch. That particular arch once graced the entry of the Avington (later the Davis) Building on Southwest Third between Washington and Stark. **Benny Milligan** recalls that, when the building was razed, the arch was sold to "an insurance man from Washington County." Short of acquiring it, many historically inclined localites would like to see that the arch is still "alive and well."

Lovely, late blooming roses of this unusual season to column contributors **Marguerite Wright** (*Oregon Historical Society*—Aug. 5 and 12), **Mary Lou** and **Lee Johnson** (*Blue Lake Park*—Sept. 2) and to **Bob Swanson** at KEX Radio for his complimentary on-air comments about the Sept. 16 column (*City Streets: By the name and numbers*).

Answers: Founded in 1977. The 11th Annual Governor's Conference on Historic Preservation (Oct. 22-24) at Timberline Lodge.

ROSY REFERENCES

THE ROSE CITY CHAPTER 3.
Notes & Anecdote.
Fall '84
November
City Hall:
The Goldschmidt legacy
technologically
February 12, 1986
Forest Park
Tektronix:
Longtime leader,
Rose City Radio: Air for all ages
July 8, 1987
Frank Branch Riley:
Oregon's Ambassador
September 17, 1986
Fred Meyer:
A My-Te-Fine Merchant
Portland water:
Bullish on Bull Run
February 11, 1987
Portland Churches:
Notes & Anecdote
Washington Park Zoo:
The Timber Temple: Log gone
Portland's Fire Dept.: Paid protection
March 13, 1984
Rose City Park: A child's playground
May 21, 1986
OHSU: A century of medical education
April 15, 1987
Oregon Historical Society
The Vaughan Era
August 12, 1987
Waverley Country Club

RUNNING
ESTABLISHED IN STUMPTOWN
WILLAMETTE CLASS DISASTER STRIKES
RIVER CITY RECOLLECTIONS

Portland Mayors (1851-1987)

One-Year Term

Hugh D. O'Bryant	1851-1852
A. C. Bonnell	1852, *resigned*
Simon B. Marye	*chosen at special election* 1852-1853
Josiah Failing	1853-1854
William Sargent Ladd	1854-1855
George W. Vaughn	1855-1856
James A. O'Neil	1856-1857
James A. O'Neil	1857-1858
A. M. Starr	1858-1859
S. J. McCormick	1859-1860
George C. Robbins	1860-1861
John M. Breck	1861-1862
William H. Farrar	1862-1863
David Logan	1863-1864
Henry Failing	1864-1865
Henry Failing	1865, *resigned*
Thomas J. Holmes	*appointed,* 1865-1866
Thomas J. Holmes	1866-1867
Thomas J. Holmes	1867, *died June 18*
Aaron E. Wait	*appointed pro tem* 1867-
Dr. J.A. Chapman	*chosen at special election* 1867-1868
Hamilton Boyd	1868-1869

Two-Year Term

Bernard Goldsmith	1869-1871
Philip Wasserman	1871-1873
Henry Failing	1873-1875
Dr. J. A. Chapman	1875-1877
W. S. Newbury	1877-1879
David P. Thompson	1879-1881
David P. Thompson	*change in city charter* 1881-1882
	fixed 1882 for election

Three-Year Term

Dr. J. A. Chapman	1882-1885
John Gates	1885-1888, *died April 27*
C. M. Forbes, *acting mayor*	April 27-May 2, 1888
Van B. de Lashmutt	*appointed* May 2-July 1, 1888
Van B. de Lashmutt	1888-1891
William S. Mason	1891-1894

Two-Year Term

George P. Frank	1894-1896
Sylvester Pennoyer	1896-1898
William S. Mason	1898-1899, *died March 27*
W. A. Storey, *appointed*	1899-1900
Henry S. Rowe	1900-1902
George H. Williams	*change in city charter* 1902-1905
	fixed 1905 for election
Harry Lane	1905-1907
Harry Lane	1907-1909
Joseph Simon	1909-1911
Allen G. Rushlight	1911-1913

Four-Year Term

H. R. Albee	1913-1917
George L. Baker	1917-1921
George L. Baker	1921-1925
George L. Baker	1925-1929
George L. Baker	1929-1933
Joseph K. Carson, Jr.	1933-1937
Joseph K. Carson, Jr.	1937-1941
Earl Riley	1941-1945
Earl Riley	1945-1949
Dorothy McCullough Lee	1949-1953
Fred Peterson	1953-1957
Terry D. Schrunk	1957-1961
Terry D. Schrunk	1961-1965
Terry D. Schrunk	1965-1969
Terry D. Schrunk	1969-1973
Neil E. Goldschmidt	1973-1977
Neil E. Goldschmidt	1977-1979 *resigned to*
	become U.S. Secretary of Transportation
Connie McCready, *appointed*	1979-1981
Frank Ivancie	1981-1985
John E. "Bud" Clark	1985-

Milestones in Portland History

1844 - Asa Lovejoy and William Overton file donation land claim on "The Clearing".

1845 - Lovejoy and Francis W. Pettygrove "snap up a copper" to determine townsite name. Pettygrove, from Portland, Maine, wins. First 16 blocks platted.

1851 - January 14; City of Portland incorporated, Hugh D. O'Bryant, a carpenter, elected first mayor.

1854 - Multnomah County created to bring about autonomy from Washington County.

1859 - February 14; Oregon admitted to the Union as the 33rd state. Gas service available.

1860 - Henry Corbett's stagecoach line offers daily service between Portland and Sacramento. Contracts to carry U.S. Mail.

1864 - Portland hooked up to transcontinental telegraph system. Electorate chooses Salem as state capital.

1870 - East Portland incorporated.

1872 - December 7; First horsecar trolley begins operation.

1873 - August 2; The Great Fire destroys 22 central blocks.

1875 - U.S. Post Office, Court and Customs House opens.

1883 - September 11; First transcontinental train arrives in East Portland.

1887 - First bridge across Willamette River, a wooden toll bridge, the Morrison, opens.

1889 - Electricity available from first long-distance hydroelectric power line in the country - from The Falls at Oregon City.

1894 - May-June, a spring "freshet" causes longest lasting, highest flood waters in Portland history.

1895 - Bull Run Water System begins operation.

1896 - Union Station completed.

1898 - First automobile arrives in Portland - Henry Wemme's Locomobile.

1905 - Lewis & Clark Centennial Expostiion held from June 1st to October 15th. Largest single event in city's history.

1907 - Rose Show and Fiesta held - immediate predecessor to Portland Rose Festival.

1913 - Commission System (the Galveston Plan) adopted as new form of city government. H.R. Albee elected first four-year mayor.

1922 - KGW Radio goes on the air as the area's first commercial broadcasting facility.

1927 - Swan Island (Port of Portland) Airport opens.

1928 - Docks removed from waterfront. Seawall built. Public Auditorium completed.

1937 - Bonneville Dam and Timberline Lodge both begin operating and are dedicated by President Franklin D. Roosevelt.

1941 - The Portland-Columbia "Super" Airport opens.

1942 - Henry Kaiser converts Portland area into America's wartime shipbuilding center.

1948 - May 30; Vanport Flood destroys nation's largest federal housing project. Dorothy McCullough Lee elected first woman mayor.

1952 - KPTV Channel 27 begins broadcasting as first Portland television station and first UHF in the world.

1960 - Lloyd Center opens - world's largest mall.

1962 - Memorial Coliseum completed, October 12, first recorded hurricane in local history devastates Western Oregon with worst damage in Portland.

1972 - First National (Interstate) Tower completed - tallest building in Oregon at 546 feet.

1975 - Transit Mall opens on S.W. 5th and 6th Aves.

1977 - Portland Trailblazers win NBA World Championship.

1984 - Pioneer Courthouse Square completed.

1985 - Portlandia, 2nd largest pounded copper statue in the country, is put into place on the Portland Building.

1986 - Light Rail commuter line (MAX-Metropolitan Area Express) begins service between downtown Portland and Gresham.

1987 - Portland Center for the Performing Arts opens.

INDEX

(Cont'd.)

PHOTOGRAPHS and ILLUSTRATIONS
Credits and References

NOTES: (OHS) indicates Oregon Historical Society. All credits and OHS photo negative numbers are indicated in order of appearance on the page from top to bottom and left to right.
2. (OHS) Orhi 21604 11. (OHS) 13. Orhi 4289, Ft. Vancouver Historical Society, (OHS) Orhi 38777 14. (OHS) 245, 21591 16. (OHS) 17. Karl Klooster, (OHS) 1858 18. (OHS) 939 19. Orhi 31534, Orhi 24707 20. (OHS) 740 22. (OHS) 77105, 67021 23. (OHS) Orhi 44083, Orhi 56566, Orhi 73493 24. (OHS) Karl Klooster (OHS) Orhi 77075 25. (OHS) 60495 26. (OHS) 68582, 4146, 73222 27. (OHS) 4601 28. (OHS) 50306, 11729 29. (OHS) Orhi 39350, Orhi 4777 30. (OHS) 50310, 77056, 77053, 77055 31. (OHS) Orhi 67523, Orhi 44331 32. (OHS) 16140, 54309, 55573 33. Arlington Club 34. University Club 35. Ed Francis, (OHS) 49135 36. Karl Klooster 37. Town Club and Michael Roberts 38. Multnomah Athletic Club 39. Multnomah Athletic Club 40. Sam Lee and Emery Neale 41. (OHS) 2. Max Pelletier, Karl Klooster 43. Royal Rosarians 44. Royal Rosarians 45. (OHS) Orhi 76879, Orhi 5700, Orhi 76877 46. Rose Festival Association, (OHS) 67132 47. Rose Festival Association, (OHS) 48. (OHS) 72070, 67087, 67113, 67082 49. Jan Markstaller Donnelly 50. Robert Ames 51. Karl Klooster, courtesy of Max Pelletier 52. Royal Rosarians 53. (OHS) 54. Portland Archives and Records (OHS) 55. Karl Klooster, (OHS) 54772, 39434, 70850 56. Karl Klooster, courtesy of Portland City Archives 57. Portland Police Museum 58. John T. Labbe 60. John T. Labbe 61. Portland Water Bureau 62. (OHS) 35128, 28102, 4556, 5079 63. (OHS) Orhi 55108 64. Portland Police Museum 65. (OHS) 25173, 35161, 67681 66. (OHS) John Labbe 67. (OHS) Orhi 78004, Orhi 35386 68. (OHS) 41762, 41767 69. (OHS) 5659, 62093, 71372 70. (OHS) 72076, 72072, 72073, 72069 71. Portland Police Museum 72. (OHS) 51921, 46103 73. Portland Police Museum 75. courtesy of USPS, (OHS) Orhi 13122 77. (OHS) 72642, 72643, 72646 78. Karl Klooster, Police Sunshine Division, (OHS) 72068 79. (OHS) Orhi 48493, Orhi 74591 80. (OHS) 74590, 74588 81. courtesy of The Boeing Co., (OHS) 82. Neil Goldschmidt 83. Karl Klooster, Photo-Art Commercial Studios 84. **Portland Chamber of Commerce,** (OHS) Orhi 68996 85. (OHS) 86. (OHS) 47183, Orhi 759 87. (OHS) Orhi 11962, Orhi 73268 88. (OHS) 3515, 49960 89. (OHS) 39917, 13314 90. (OHS) 59078 91. (OHS) 51025, 14011 93. Karl Klooster, (OHS) Orhi 48011, Karl Klooster 94. (OHS) 95. (OHS) Orhi 5506 96. (OHS) Orhi 53569, Orhi 46763 97. (OHS) cop 02609, Orhi 45949, Orhi 39213 98. (OHS) Orhi 74524, Orhi 21593 99. (OHS) Orhi 36363, Orhi 47144 100. Lewis and Clark College 101. University of Portland, (OHS) Orhi 24307 102. (OHS) 75391, 68569 103. Portland State University 104. (OHS) 7100, 22084 105. (OHS) Orhi 28114, Orhi 95794, Orhi 75795 106. (OHS) Orhi 75877, Orhi 35034, Orhi 59478, Orhi 75878 107. (OHS) 75881, 37801, Karl Klooster 108. Karl Klooster .109. Karl Klooster 110. Karl Klooster, Portland Memorial 111. (OHS) 112. Blitz Weinhard, (OHS), Blitz Weinhard 113. (OHS) Orhi 72536, 28286, Orhi 76842 114. Northwest Natural Gas 115. First Interstate Bank, (OHS) Orhi 24994, Orhi 3521 116. (OHS) Orhi 74386, Orhi 57233, 4371 117. (OHS) 74294 118. Huber's 119. MAC, Kim McColl 120. (OHS) Orhi 74767, Orhi 78357 121. Oregon Symphony Association 122. (OHS) Orhi 26021, Orhi 20003 123. (OHS) Orhi 12922, Orhi 79922 124. (OHS) Oreg 4238, Orhi 69017 125. (OHS) Orhi 11390, Orhi 39262 126. (OHS) 127. Alan Miller 128. Franz Bakery 129. (OHS) 1721, 66173, 66918, 66917 130. Dan and Louis Oyster Bar 131. Jake's Famous Crawfish 132. Pendleton Woolen Mills 133. Jantzen, Inc. 134. (OHS) GI 9696, GI 10281-A 135. Richard Larrowe 136. (OHS) Orhi 65104 137. (OHS) 69019, Fred Meyer Inc. 138. Alpenrose Dairy 139. (OHS) Orhi 77099, Orhi 77098, Orhi 62389 140. The Benj. Franklin 141. Goodwill Industries of Oregon 142. Grand Central Bowl 143. Michael Cramer 144. OLCC 145. Tektronix, Inc. 146. View-Master International 147. G.I. Joe's 148. Karl Klooster 150. Karl Klooster 151. Karl Klooster 152. Jon and Barbara Christian 153. Frederick & Nelson 154. (OHS) 60714, 53567 155. Portland Public Library 156 Portland Public Library 157. (OHS) Orhi 74384 158. Karl Klooster 159. (OHS) 67620, 5699 160. (OHS) 63060, 67512 161. Stephen Kenney Jr. 162. (OHS) orhi 64027, Mary Lou (Welsh) Johnson 163. (OHS) 73265, 73264 164. (OHS) Orhi 26903 165. (OHS) 166. (OHS) Orhi 63777, Orhi 63757 168. Portland Beavers 169. (OHS) 66893, Karl Klooster 170. (OHS) 58943, 41226 171. The Harris family 172. Karl Klooster, (OHS) 174. (OHS) Orhi 7713, Orhi 3714 175. (OHS) Orhi 4235, Orhi 20762 176. Burlington Northern R.R., (OHS) COP297 177. (OHS) 1503, 9098, 42580 178. Portland Public Library, (OHS) 72812, 72811 179. (OHS) 38408, 35267 180. (OHS) 47942, 47952, 17623 181. Mazamas, (OHS) 11610, 11641 182. (OHS) 183. Mt. Hood Meadows, RLK Corp, Timberline Lodge 184. Portland Parks Bureau 185. (OHS) 49109, 17538, 17629 186. (OHS) 67039, 73021, 73054 187. Courtesy of OMSI 188. Karl Klooster 189. (OHS) 4054, 28080, 28137 190. (OHS) Orhi 35767, Orhi 67636, GI 6566 191. (OHS) Orhi 67517, Orhi 14614 192. Courtesy of Barry Brownell 193. (OHS) 73899, 54823, 54817, 54824 194. Pacific Power and Light 195. Karl Klooster, (OHS) Orhi 50199 196. (OHS) Orhi 71152, 56140 197. (OHS) Orhi 29193, Orhi 42458, Orhi 49965 198. Karl Klooster, (OHS) 199. Oregon Maritime Center and Museum 201. White Stag 202. (OHS) 203. Greg Kozawa, (OHS) 204. (OHS) 205. (OHS) 206. HPLO, Karl Klooster, Courtesy of HPLO, (OHS) 207. (OHS), HPLO 208. (OHS), PGE-130-84 209 (OHS), Ritchie-McFarland Corp. 210 (OHS) 211. Karl Klooster 212. Portland Police Museum 213. Karl Klooster 214. (OHS) 12176, 47303-A, 11317, 8356-A 215 Christine Olsen, (OHS) 216 (OHS) Orhi 59053, Orhi 57934 217. Karl Klooster 218. Karl Klooster 219. **Portland Public Library, Karl Klooster** 220. Karl Klooster 221 (OHS), Rae Carey 222. Rae Carey, KGW-TV 223. (OHS) 224. (OHS) 7097, 7120, 36952 225. (OHS) 47104, 57959, 1437 226. (OHS) 23894, 73892, 3622 227. (OHS) Orhi 65299, Orhi 76579 228. (OHS) R-285, 21170, 1027 229. (OHS) Orhi 1459, orhi 4689 230. (OHS) Orhi 39201, Orhi 47071 231. (OHS) 68435, 68436, 68438, 53058, 53055 232. (OHS) 233. (OHS) Orhi 75327 234. Karl Klooster, (OHS) 45697 235. Barbara Cady, (OHS) 236. (OHS) 237. Oregon Journal 238. (OHS), Christine Olsen 239. (OHS) 73896, 12707, 73757 240. (OHS) Orhi 6552, 54817 241. (OHS) 242. (OHS) 54817 243. (OHS) Orhi 39488 244. (OHS) 58943, Robert Ames 246. (OHS) Orhi 77063 247. (OHS), Clark County Museum 248. (OHS) 249. (OHS) 250. (OHS) Orhi 47513